THE CERVANTEAN HERITAGE
RECEPTION AND INFLUENCE OF CERVANTES IN BRITAIN

LEGENDA

LEGENDA, founded in 1995 by the European Humanities Research Centre of the University of Oxford, is now a joint imprint of the Modern Humanities Research Association and Maney Publishing. Titles range from medieval texts to contemporary cinema and form a widely comparative view of the modern humanities, including works on Arabic, Catalan, English, French, German, Greek, Italian, Portuguese, Russian, Spanish, and Yiddish literature. An Editorial Board of distinguished academic specialists works in collaboration with leading scholarly bodies such as the Society for French Studies and the British Comparative Literature Association.

MHRA

The Modern Humanities Research Association (MHRA) encourages and promotes advanced study and research in the field of the modern humanities, especially modern European languages and literature, including English, and also cinema. It also aims to break down the barriers between scholars working in different disciplines and to maintain the unity of humanistic scholarship in the face of increasing specialization. The Association fulfils this purpose primarily through the publication of journals, bibliographies, monographs and other aids to research.

MANEY
publishing

Maney Publishing is one of the few remaining independent British academic publishers. Founded in 1900 the company has offices both in the UK, in Leeds and London, and in North America, in Boston. Since 1945 Maney Publishing has worked closely with learned societies, their editors, authors, and members, in publishing academic books and journals to the highest traditional standards of materials and production.

The Cervantean Heritage

Reception and Influence of Cervantes in Britain

EDITED BY J. A. G. ARDILA

LEGENDA

Modern Humanities Research Association and Maney Publishing
2009

Published by the
Modern Humanities Research Association and Maney Publishing
1 Carlton House Terrace
London SW1Y 5AF
United Kingdom

LEGENDA is an imprint of the
Modern Humanities Research Association and Maney Publishing

Maney Publishing is the trading name of W. S. Maney & Son Ltd,
whose registered office is at Suite 1C, Joseph's Well, Hanover Walk, Leeds LS3 1AB

ISBN 978-1-906540-03-6

First published 2009

Printed in Great Britain

Cover: 875 Design

Copy-Editor: Richard Correll

CONTENTS

TO JOHN, EDWARD, ANTHONY AND JANE ARDILA–NEVILLE

PREFACE

Since 2005 — the 400th anniversary of the publication of *Don Quixote* Part I, in 1605 — several book-length studies of Cervantes's influence upon English-speaking writers have been published in Spain, Germany, Britain and the US. Of these, only four are by single authors: Sarah Wood's *Quixotic Fictions of the USA* (2005), Scott Gordon's *The Practice of Quixotism* (2006), my *Cervantes en Inglaterra* (2006), and Dale Randall and Jackson Boswell's *Cervantes in Seventeenth-Century England* (2009). The others are the multiple-author volumes *Cervantes in the English-Speaking World* (2005) edited by Darío Fernández-Morera and Michael Hanke, *Cervantes y el ámbito anglosajón* (2005) edited by Diego Martínez Torrón and Bernd Dietz, *Between Shakespeare and Cervantes: Trails Along the Renaissance* (2006), conference proceedings edited by Zenón Luis-Martínez and Luis Gómez Canseco, and *La huella de Cervantes y del Quijote en la cultura anglosajona* (2007) edited by José Manuel Barrio Marco and María José Crespo Allué.

This sudden and extraordinary proliferation in the number of books stems from a sort of Cervantesmania that blossomed in and after 2005, but it is mostly the fruit of the works of many scholars who had published articles before that year. Generally speaking, the multiple-author volumes published since 2005 leave many *lacunae* — they include chapters on authors from different countries and different times, ignoring many important names; and they surprisingly neglect or omit former research, causing their arguments to be, at times, somewhat deficient and uninformed. Furthermore, the analytical method followed by many researchers very often proves to be controversial and inadequate. To claim simply that a particular text was endowed with the same literary methods or the same topics as *Don Quixote* may be pointless and irrelevant — those who search for metafictional levels, unreliable narrators, and good-natured, monomaniac characters after 1615 are bound to find them in many works that do not owe anything to Cervantes. *The Cervantean Heritage*, then, has been written by those pre-2005 scholars who have done most to reveal Cervantes's actual influence on British literature. Regrettably, it has not been possible to find any suitable contributors to write in detail about some authors, who are nonetheless discussed in the chapter 'The Influence and Reception of Cervantes in Britain, 1607–2005'. Yet *The Cervantean Heritage* does consider the main literary figures who are indebted to Cervantes — Fielding, Sterne, Smollett, Lennox, Dickens, Mary Shelley, Eliot, Chapman, Fletcher, Rowley, and also Shakespeare and Defoe, all of whom are here examined by those scholars who have successfully analysed the influence of Cervantes on British Literature.

I am grateful to the University of Edinburgh Moray Endowment Fund and School of Literatures, Languages and Cultures, for their financial aid towards the preparation of this volume. The image on the book cover was made available by José Manuel Lucía Megías.   J. A. G. ARDILA

ABOUT THE CONTRIBUTORS

J. A. G. Ardila is Reader in Hispanic Studies at the University of Edinburgh. He is the author of *Cervantes en Inglaterra: el Quijote en los albores de la novela británica* (2006), 'Sancho Panza en Inglaterra' (2005) and 'Thomas D'Urfey y la recepción del *Quijote* en el siglo XVII inglés' (2009). His publications also include the books *El género picaresco en la crítica literaria* (2008), *Etnografía y politología del 98* (2007), *Sociopragmática y retórica interpersonal* (2005), and *Charlotte Temple* (2002).

Clark Colahan is Professor of Spanish at Whitman College, Washington state. He co-authored the University of California English translation of *Persiles and Sigismunda* (1989) and 'Cervantine Imagery and Sex-Role Reversal in Fletcher and Massinger's *The Custom of the Country*' (1985). His books include *The Visions of Sor María de Agreda* (1994), and *Defying the Inquisition in Colonial New Mexico* (2006).

Stelio Cro is Hugh and Georgia Hagan Chair of Languages and Literatures at King College, Bristol, Tennessee. He has published 'Structure and Symbol in Cervantes, Shakespeare and Pirandello' (1994) and 'The Play within the Play in Pirandello, Cervantes and Shakespeare' (1994). He is the author of *Realidad y utopía en el descubrimiento y conquista de la América Hispana (1492–1682)* (1983), and *The Noble Savage* (1990).

Trudi L. Darby is Honorary Research Fellow at King's College London (University of London). She is the author of 'Resistance to Rape in *Persiles and Sigismunda* and *The Custom of the Country*' (1995) and 'Cervantes in England: The Influence of Golden-Age Prose Fiction on Jacobean Drama, c.1615–1625' (1997). She has edited *A Critical, Old-Spelling Edition of William Rowley's A New Wonder, A Woman Never Vexed* (1988) and *A Shoemaker, A Gentleman* (2002).

Frans De Bruyn is Professor of English at the University of Ottawa. He is the author of 'Edmund Burke the Political Quixote: Romance, Chivalry, and the Political Imagination' (2004). His publications include *The Literary Genres of Edmund Burke: The Political Uses of Literary Form* (1996) and numerous articles on eighteenth-century studies.

Darcy Donahue is Associate Professor of Spanish and Women's Studies at Miami University of Ohio. She has published a translation and critical edition of the works of Ana de San Bartolomé for University of Chicago Press (2008), as well as articles on Cervantes.

Edward H. Friedman is Chancellor's Professor of Spanish and Professor of Comparative Literature at Vanderbilt University. He is the author of 'Voices Within: Robin Chapman's *The Duchess' Diary* and the Intertextual Conundrum of Don Quixote'

(1990). His books include *The Unifying Concept* (1981), *The Antiheroine's Voice* (1987), and *Cervantes in the Middle* (2006). He is the author of *Wit's End* (2000) an adaptation of Lope de Vega's *La dama boba*. Further to his edition of Lope's *El caballero de Olmedo* (2004), he has edited and co-edited several scholarly books, including *Magical Parts: Approaches to Don Quixote*, (1994) and *Brave New Words: Studies in Spanish Golden Age Literature* (1996). He is editor of the *Bulletin of the Comediantes* and past president of the Cervantes Society of America.

BREAN HAMMOND is Professor of Modern English Literature at the University of Nottingham. He is the author of 'Mid-Century Quixotism and the Defence of the Novel' (1998), and has published the books *Pope and Bolingbroke* (1984), *Pope* (1986), *Professional Imaginative Writing in England 1670–1740* (1997), and *Alexander Pope Amongst the Satirists 1660–1750* (2005). He has also co-authored *Making the Novel: Fiction and Society in Britain, 1660–1789* (2006) and edited John Vanbrugh's *The Relapse and Other Plays* (2004) for Oxford University Press.

JULIE CANDLER HAYES is Professor of French at the University of Massachusetts Amherst. She has published 'Tobias Smollett and the Translations of the *Quijote*' (2004). The author of *Translation, Subjectivity, and Culture in France and England, 1600–1800* (2008), *Reading the French Enlightenment* (1999), *Identity and Ideology* (1991), she has co-edited *Using the Encyclopédie* (2002), and *Emilie Du Châtelet* (2006).

PAMELA H. LONG is Assistant Professor of International Studies at Auburn University Montgomery. She is the author of 'Fagin and Monipodio: The Source of *Oliver Twist* in Cervantes's *Rinconete and Cortadillo*' (1994).

FRANCES LUTTIKHUIZEN was Profesora Asociada at the Universidad de Barcelona. She is the author of 'Traducciones inglesas de las *Novelas ejemplares*' (1987) and 'Don Diego Puede-Ser (James Mabbe)'s Rendering of Cervantes' (2005). She has edited the *Exemplary Novels* (1994) for Editorial Planeta.

MICHAEL J. MCGRATH is Associate Professor of Spanish Literature at Georgia Southern University. Among his publications are: 'Tilting at Windmills: *Don Quijote* in English' (2006) and 'Looking at Flemish Tapestries from the Front: A "Perfect" English Translation of *Don Quijote*' (2002); editions of *El mágico prodigioso* (2003), *La traición en la amistad* (2007), and *Novelas ejemplares* (2008). He is the editor of Juan de la Cuesta Hispanic Monographs.

HOWARD MANCING is Professor of Spanish at Purdue University. He is the author of 'The Quixotic Novel in British and American Literature' (2005, 2006), *The Chivalric World of Don Quijote: Style, Structure, and Narrative Technique* (1982), *The Cervantes Encyclopedia* (2004), and *Miguel de Cervantes' Don Quixote: A Reference Guide* (2006). He has co-edited *Text, Theory, and Performance: Golden Age Comedia Studies* (1994). He is currently the Vice President of the Cervantes Society of America.

ARANTZA MAYO is University Lecturer at the University of Cambridge and Fellow at Corpus Christi College. She is the author of *La lírica sacra de Lope de Vega y José de Valdivielso* (2007), and of a number of articles on early modern Spanish literature and twentieth-century Bolivian poetry.

CHESTER ST. H. MILLS is Associate Professor of English and Foreign Languages at Southern University at New Orleans. He has been co-contributor to the Caribbean section in *The Year's Work in English Studies* (2000–03). His publications include the Preface in *Emerging Perspectives on Flora Nwapa* (1998), and 'Eliot's Spanish Connection: Casaubon, the Avatar of Quixote' (1994).

CHRIS NAROZNY is a doctoral candidate at the University of Denver. He has published fiction in the *American Literary Review*, the *Denver Quarterly*, *Elimae*, and *Marginalia*.

AMY PAWL is a senior lecturer in English at Washington University in St. Louis, where she teaches courses on eighteenth-century British literature, epistolary fiction, and gender in the early novel. She is the author of 'Feminine Transformations of the Quixote in Eighteenth-Century England: Lennox's *Female Quixote* and Her Sisters'. She has also published articles on eighteenth-century women authors, including Charlotte Lennox, Frances Burney, and Jane Austen.

ALEXANDER SAMSON is Lecturer in Spanish Golden-Age Literature at University College London (University of London). He is the author of *Mary Tudor and the Habsburg Marriage: England and Spain, 1553–1557* (2008). He has edited *The Spanish Match* (2006), and co-edited *A Companion to Lope de Vega* (2008).

DIANA DE ARMAS WILSON is Professor Emerita of English and Renaissance Studies at the University of Denver. She is the author of 'Contesting the Custom of the Country: Cervantes and Fletcher' (1987), 'Of Piracy and Plackets: Cervantes' *La señora Cornelia* and Fletcher's *The Chances*' (2000). Her books include *Allegories of Love: Cervantes's Persiles and Sigismunda* (1991) and *Cervantes, the Novel, and the New World* (2000). She has co-edited *Quixotic Desire: Psychoanalytic Perspectives on Cervantes* (1993), and edited the Norton critical edition of *Don Quixote* (1999).

PART I

CERVANTES IN
BRITISH LITERATURE AND CRITICISM

CHAPTER 1

The Influence and Reception
of Cervantes in Britain, 1607–2005

J. A. G. Ardila

Many English literature scholars continue to believe that the novel *rose* in eighteenth-century England.[1] Today, however, there is emerging a much fuller and clearer picture which presents in a more objective light the fact that, more than a century before Defoe, Richardson, Fielding and Smollett, a number of Spanish writers had produced several works which should be classed as novels. The anonymous *Lazarillo de Tormes* (first extant editions 1554), Mateo Alemán's *Guzmán de Alfarache* (Part I 1599, Part II 1604) and Miguel de Cervantes's *Don Quixote* (Part I 1605, Part II 1615) have all been the object of detailed studies which categorize them as novels.[2] Their influence upon English letters has been much more constructive, more pervasive and deeper than they are generally given credit for. When, in the first half of the eighteenth century, some English writers were trying new narrative nomenclatures, they were aware of a corpus of Spanish novels published during the Golden Age of Spanish Literature and translated into English in the seventeenth century. Cervantes's *Don Quixote, Exemplary Novels, Persiles*, and also the picaresque novels *Lazarillo de Tormes, Guzmán de Alfarache, El Buscón, La pícara Justina*, and *Estebanillo González* were known and read in Britain during the seventeenth century. *Lazarillo* was one of Shakespeare's favourite books;[3] the so-called *gusmanry*,[4] or Guzmán-mania, prompted imitations of *Guzmán* such as *The Dutch Rogue; or, Guzman of Amsterdam* (1683), *Teague O'Divelly; or, the Irish Rogue* (1690) and *The French Rogue* (1672), and also the plays *The Spanish Rogue* (1672, 1673) by Thomas Duffet and *Guzman* (1669) by Roger Boyle. Not only were these Spanish picaresque novels influential upon authors unknown today, they were also read and enjoyed by the literary masters of the seventeen and eighteenth centuries — John Bunyan's *The Life and Death of Mr Badman* has often been related to the picaresque genre; several novels by Tobias Smollett have been regarded as picaresque; even Defoe, who has been credited with the *rise* the novel, by turning the puritan conduct-book into the novel, wrote under the influence of the Spanish picaresque, and in *Moll Flanders, Captain Jack* and *Roxana* he emulated the contents and form of the Spanish novels.[5] Nonetheless, the literary category *picaresque*, as it is understood in English,[6] has very little in common with the picaresque novel conceived in sixteenth-century Spain. In English, *picaresque* is, in Anthony Burgess's words, a 'term originally applicable only to novels in which the leading character is a rogue [...] It is a term which lends itself to description of all the novels in which the bulk of the action takes place on the road, on a journey, and in which eccentric and low-life characters appear'.[7] This definition, however, fails to describe what the picaresque genre actually is.[8] Under such spurious terminology, *Don Quixote* has been considered a picaresque novel.

The adulteration of the term *picaresque novel* is tantamount to the misunderstanding of *quixotic fiction* and, ultimately, with the reception of Cervantes in Britain. Most readers in English-speaking countries think of *Don Quixote* as a picaresque novel, as the source of several eighteenth-century imitations of insignificant literary quality, amongst which only Charlotte Lennox's *The Female Quixote* (1752) and Tobias Smollett's *Sir Launcelot Greaves* (1762) deserve a place in literary history. By comparison, *Don Quixote* was read, mentioned, imitated and emulated in Britain from as early as 1607, scarcely two years after its publication in Madrid. As Walter Reed has argued, 'The novel first emerged as a significant literary phenomenon in Spain. *Don Quixote* and the Golden Age picaresque novels constituted a popular and self-conscious innovation within Spanish literary culture that rapidly passed beyond that national literature to the rest of Western Europe'.[9] Those who have conducted research into Cervantes in Britain[10] agree unanimously that *Don Quixote* has been the most influential foreign book in English intellectual life, as a literary source for emulations and adaptations, as a subject for literary criticism, and as a lexical source, e.g. by transfusing the words 'Quixote', 'quixotic', 'Dulcinea', 'duenna', and the expression 'to tilt at windmills' into the English language.[11] Although most critics are inclined to believe that nowhere did *Don Quixote* have a bigger impact than in eighteenth-century England,[12] in reality this novel exerted a continuous and regular influence which spans from as early as 1607 to the twenty-first century.

More than a thousand allusions to characters and passages from Cervantes's works have been found in seventeenth-century English literature.[13] The first written mention of *Don Quixote* dates from 1607 (possibly 1606), from George Wilkins's play *The Miseries of Inforst Marriage*, where one of the characters, named William Scarborow, exclaims: 'now I am armed to fight with a windmill', alluding to the windmill adventure in Cervantes's novel.[14] Wilkins was the first of the many authors who mentioned a character or an adventure in *Don Quixote*; there is an allusion to the windmills in Middleton's *Your Five Gallants* (1607), allusions to Don Quixote in Ben Jonson's *The Epicoene* (c.1610) and *The Alchemist* (1611), to the knight and his squire in Michael Drayton's *Nimphidia* (1627), and to Maritornes in Robert Anton's *Mariomachia* (1613).[15] In *The Young Gallants Whirligigg* (1619), Francis Lenton exposes the 'absurd actions, and profuse expenses of unbridled and affectated youth', whom he accuses of reading 'Don Quix-Zot'. Other allusions can be found in Thomas Overbury's *A Roaring Boy* (1614), in Thomas May's *The Heire* (1620), in Philip Massinger's *The Virgin Martyr* (1622), in John Ford's *The Witch of Edmonton* (1623), in Thomas Randolph's *The Conceited Peddler* (1630) and *Hey for Honesty* (1651), in James Shirley's *The Ball* (1632), in Henry Glapthorne's *The Lady Mother* (1635) and *Wit in a Constable* (1639), in the anonymous *The London Chanticleers* (1636), in John Cleveland's *The Character of a London Diurnal* (1644), *Smectymmuus, the Club-Diuines* (1647) and *The Character of a Country-Commiteeman* (1649), in John Taylor's *Crop-

Eare Curried (1644), in Edmund Waller's *To the Mutable Fair* (1645), in Marchmond Needham's *Mercurius* (1648), in James Shirley's *Honoria and Mammon* (1652), and in Aston Cokain's *The Obstinate Lady* (1657).

This widespread familiarity with Cervantes's novel among the playwrights of the time — and, therefore, among theatre audiences — is particularly astounding because the first translation of *Don Quixote* to any language was Thomas Shelton's English version published in 1612.[16] How the English could develop such a continuing fascination with the adventures of the Spanish knight, even before they were rendered into English, is still open to speculation. After the death of Elizabeth I, James I endeavoured to make peace with Spain. Likewise, Spain's failures to land her armies on English soil, caused the Spanish king, Philip III, to conclude that diplomacy was the only means to put a stop to the disputes with England. In 1605 the English king sent an envoy, Lord Howard, to attend the baptism of the crown prince of Spain. Modern Cervantes biographers[17] have speculated about Shakespeare being a member of Lord Howard's entourage and about the possibility that the two authors met. However, the baptism may hold the explanation of Don Quixote's popularity in England before the first translation was published in 1612. In the interlude of a bullfight attended by the king's guests, a one-act farce recreating the adventures of Don Quixote and Sancho was staged. In all likelihood, the Englishmen who were present at the bullfight passed the adventures of Don Quixote by word of mouth in the English court.[18] In addition to this, it is worth noting that for several decades before the publication of *Don Quixote* there had been in Britain a deep appreciation of Spanish literature. From 1530 to 1603, approximately 170 Spanish books by 110 Spanish authors were translated into English and published in Britain.[19] Furthermore, Spanish was at the time the lingua franca,[20] and every literate Englishman was expected to be acquainted with Spanish books such as *Amadís*, *Cárcel de Amor*, and *Celestina*.[21] The first Spanish grammar book for English-speaking students, William Stepney's *The Spanish Schoole-Master*, and the first English–Spanish dictionary, the *Biblioteca Hispanica*, were published in 1591. Moreover, Spanish books used to reach England soon after their publication. Indeed, a copy of *Don Quixote*, donated by the Earl of Southampton, was catalogued at Oxford University library on 30 August 1605.[22]

Lord Howard and his entourage could have enjoyed the quixotic farce as much as Spaniards enjoyed the novel, for the trace of Cervantes in England is not only found in the form of sporadic allusions; many London playwrights soon began to borrow Cervantine plots. The first of these borrowers were John Fletcher, in a story included in his *Coxcomb* (1609), and Nathaniel Field, in *Amends for Ladies* (1611); both stories are based on *El curioso impertinente* [the curious impertinent],[23] an interpolated *novella* in *Don Quixote*. English writers and readers soon became extraordinarily fond of this short story, in which newlywed Anselmo, eager to ascertain his wife's faithfulness, asks his friend Lotario to court her. The lady succumbs to the seducer's charms, leaving the readers to reflect on the inappropriateness of Anselmo's curiosity. It is very unlikely that the one-act play performed in the bullring contained a second play in *mise en abîme*, and Fletcher's and Field's knowledge of *The Curious Impertinent* indicates that writers did actually read *Don Quixote* in either Spanish or English.

Sancho soon became extremely popular. He was the model for a number of theatre characters: Castruccio in John Fletcher's *The Double Marriage* (1619), where the Barataria episodes in *Don Quixote* are recreated, Geta in Fletcher and Massinger's *The Prophetess* (1622), which is also based on Sancho's adventures as governor of Barataria, Boraccio in William D'Avenant's *The Cruel Brother* (1627), and a servant in Massinger's *The Picture* (1629). Given that Thomas Shelton wrote his translation in 1607,[24] and that he declared that it was intended to allow a friend to read the Spanish novel, it has been suggested[25] that his friend could have been Beaumont,[26] who collaborated and even shared his quarters with Fletcher. After a number of years, and owing to the soaring popularity of *Don Quixote* amongst the London playwrights, Shelton allowed his translation to be put into print.

The first English imitation of *Don Quixote*, Beaumont's *The Knight of the Burning Pestle*, appeared in 1612. It opens with a grocer, George, along with his wife, Nell, and their apprentice, Rafe, watching a play entitled *The London Merchant*. Dissatisfied with what they see performed in front of them, the grocer and his wife repeatedly insist on their apprentice taking a part in the play. He is a Quixote, who carries a pestle as a weapon, is faithful to his platonic love Susan, and behaves according to chivalric protocol, which inexorably clashes with reality. Many passages are borrowed from *Don Quixote*, e.g. Rafe's mistaking an inn for a castle and refusing to pay the innkeeper; the liberation of Barbaroso's prisoners; and Princess Pompiona's declarations of love. In 1614 Ben Jonson's *Bartholomew Fair* was staged; its main characters, Master Bartholomew Cokes and his servant Mr Waspe have been identified as a Quixote–Sancho pair.[27]

Within London literary circles between approximately 1610 and 1625, playwrights extended their interest in Cervantes beyond *Don Quixote*. The *Exemplary Novels* were printed in Spain in 1613. The first English translation, by James Mabbe, appeared in 1640, but it included only six of the twelve stories in the Spanish original. (Mabbe also translated Fernando de Rojas's *Celestina* [1499], which he renamed *The Spanish Bawd*, and Mateo Aleman's *Guzmán de Alfarache*, which he entitled *The Rogue*.) Yet the first French translation of the *Exemplary Novels*, by François Rosset and Vital D'Audignier, appeared in 1615, overshadowing the fame of *Don Quixote* in France. For the French who could read Spanish, Cervantes's *novellas* became household reading.[28] It was almost certainly in French that the English playwrights read the *Exemplary Novels*. In terms of intertextuality, these short stories had, from 1610 to 1625, a much deeper impact on English literature than *Don Quixote*. The first ones to borrow from the *Exemplary Novels* were Fletcher and Beaumont in their play *Love's Pilgrimage*, based on *Las dos doncellas*. Fletcher and Massinger's *A Very Woman*, staged in 1621, takes its plot from *El amante liberal*. Middleton and Rowley's *The Spanish Gipsy*, staged in 1623, combines the plots of *La gitanilla* and *La fuerza de la sangre*. Fletcher's *Rule a Wife and Have a Wife*, of 1624, is based on *El casamiento engañoso*. One year later, in 1625, Fletcher borrowed the plot of *La señora Cornelia* for *The Chances*, and the plot of *La ilustre fregona* for *The Fair Maid of the Inn*.[29] To all these, literary history has added the lost play *Cardenio*, attributed to Shakespeare (who perhaps co-wrote it with Fletcher).

The influence of Cervantes on Shakespeare is a fascinating subject on which one can only speculate. The only proven fact is that Shakespeare wrote *Cardenio* (1613), supposedly based on the Cardenio story in *Don Quixote* Part I. It is also known that Shakespeare had many friends who relished things Spanish. The Earl of Southampton, who in 1605 donated a copy of *Don Quixote* to Oxford University, was a friend of Shakespeare's, and so was James Mabbe, translator of Cervantes's *Exemplary Novels*. Not less important seems the popularity of the Earl of Godomar, a Spanish diplomat in London who became well known to the aristocracy and within literary circles. Godomar was a confidant of James I and a friend of Ben Jonson. It is very likely that his connections in the court and among the playwrights of the day enabled him to meet Shakespeare. And Godomar was indeed a cultivated gentleman who loved theatre and literature.[30] It is therefore certain that Shakespeare knew about Cervantes, *Don Quixote* and very possibly the *Exemplary Novels*, which reinforces belief in the Cervantine nature of *Cardenio*. Other theories are mere speculation: Charles Hamilton's hypothesis that Cardenio is actually *The Second Maiden's Tragedy* cannot be proved,[31] and neither can Astrana Marín's suggestion that Shakespeare was part of Lord Howard's entourage in Valladolid and met Cervantes there.[32]

The fast-developing theatre business in the early seventeenth century, as a cultural phenomenon but also as a very profitable industry, pushed the playwrights to write in haste. They soon began to collaborate with each other and also to look at classical texts and national history for inspiration. Authors such as Fletcher, Middleton and Massinger found in the *Exemplary Novels* a plentiful source of plots unknown to the bulk of the English playgoers. Indeed playwrights were not coy in taking as much as they could from Cervantes; Fletcher and Massinger produced in 1620 *The Custom of the Country*, a play based on Cervantes's romance *Persiles y Sigismunda* (published posthumously in Spanish in 1616), rendered into French in 1618 and anonymously into English in 1619. Massinger also found a good source in Cervantes's *Entremeses*,[33] not available in English translation until the eighteenth century. Massinger's *The Renegado*, written in 1624, is based on *Los baños de Argel* and *The Fatal Dowry* of 1619 (commonly attributed to Massinger) on *El viejo celoso*. Fitzmaurice-Kelly conjectured that Massinger could have purchased a copy of the Spanish 1613 *editio princeps* of the *Exemplary Novels*.[34] Never before and never again would English literature witness such an exploitation of a foreign author in such a short period of time.[35] This intertextual flux was suddenly interrupted when all London theatres closed in 1625 because of the plague (which caused the death of Fletcher) and also, perhaps, the end of the Pax Hispanica and the death of James I.

After the dwindling of Jacobean drama and for the rest of the seventeenth century, *Don Quixote* continued to be a favourite source for imitations and adaptations. So famous did it become that there was even a popular dance called the Sancho Panza. *The Triumph of Peace* (1634) by Shirley includes a quixotic character. There is also in William Chamberlayne's poem *Pharonnida* (1659) a quixotic couple who accept chivalry as true. However, the story of Anselmo's curiosity remained the most revisited Cervantine theme. Aphra Behn, one of the most notorious woman writers in English literature, included a secondary plot based on Cervantes's story in her *Amorous Prince; or, The Curious Husband* (1684). Thomas Sotherne's *The*

Disappointment (1694) includes another secondary plot also drawn from *The Curious Impertinent*. So well liked and well known did *The Curious Impertinent* become that in 1694 John Crowne referred to it in the subtitle of his play *The Married Beau; or, The Curious Impertinent*. Crowne made a very superficial use of Cervantes's tale, but his choice of subtitle suggests that the theatre audiences were much acquainted with *The Curious Impertinent*, which Crowne took to lure them.

Most interesting is *The Pilgrim's Progress* (1678) by John Bunyan, possibly the first specimen of Cervantean emulation. This classic text of puritanical literature narrates the adventures of Christian, a religious man obsessed with and turned insane from reading the Bible, who sets on a journey in search of a heavenly city. The parallels with *Don Quixote* are obvious; both characters suffer from a monomania resulting from their excessive reading, and both characters undergo a journey. In addition to Don Quixote's behavioural attitudes and perhaps some passages which may have taken from the Spanish novel, *The Pilgrim's Progress*, a prose fiction, uses a number of Cervantine narrative features: the plot takes place in a very realistic setting, there is a mix of drama and humour, and dialogue becomes an essential element in the development of the characters. In *The Life and Death of Mr Badman* (1680), Bunyan had borrowed some of the narrative features of the Spanish picaresque novels. In The *Pilgrim's Progress* he used the popular Quixote figure, but also wrote, for the first time in Britain, a prose fiction which borrowed from the most obvious narrative features in *Don Quixote*, namely, realism, humour, and dialogue.

Further to *The Pilgrim's Progress*, the stage adaptations of *The Curious Impertinent*, the *Exemplary Novels* and *Persiles*, Cervantes's presence in Britain during the seventeenth century is best known through the works of Samuel Butler, Edmund Gayton and Thomas D'Urfey. After Beaumont's imitation of *Don Quixote* in *The Knight of the Burning Pestle*, Butler used the quixotic theme in his poem *Hudibras*, published in three parts in 1663, 1664 and 1678. Butler's poem occupies a pre-eminent place in English literature for giving birth to the whole genre of hudibrastic verse. Like the story of the Manchegan knight, *Hudibras* is a satire in which a set of archaic values clash dramatically with social reality. In *Don Quixote*, early seventeenth-century Spanish society is criticized for having waived the noble values upheld in chivalric romances. Conversely, Butler endowed *Hudibras* with the values of the extinct Puritan Republic in order to ridicule them. The satirical method is conspicuously quixotic, although it resulted in a farcical and unsophisticated specimen of Cervantean satire.[36]

Gayton's *Pleasant Notes upon Don Quixot*, published in 1654, have been condemned by many critics,[37] and taken as exemplary of the seventeenth-century's superficial reception of *Don Quixote*. Gayton portrays Don Quixote and Sancho as a pair of buffoons at whom everyone jeers. However, a close reading of the *Pleasant Notes* shows that Gayton, and probably his contemporaries, were not completely at ease with reading the novel as merely a coarse comedy of uncouth humour.[38] In one of the poems included in the preliminaries of the *Pleasant Notes*, William Taylor claims that after Don Quixote had been translated into English 'then 'twas fit, there should be next, / A Comment to so darke a Text'.[39] In another preliminary poem it is affirmed that, 'Nor is our Author [Gayton] a Translator / But a Criticall

Comentator'.[40] Indeed, although his superfluous views have demoted him, Gayton must be credited with being the author of the first critical analysis of *Don Quixote*, where he managed to envisage the ontological qualities of Cervantes's hero. Yet John Bowle has been singled out as the first *serious* Cervantes scholar and his *Letter to Reverend Dr Percy* the first critical analysis of Cervantes's novel.[41]

A comedy entitled *History of Donquixot; or, the Knight of the Illfavoured Face* was advertised three times, once in 1658 and twice in 1661, by the bookseller Nathaniel Brook. But given that this comedy was never published or staged, Thomas D'Urfey's *Comical History of Don Quixot* remains the first theatrical adaptation of Cervantes's novel in Britain. Part I and II of *The Comical History* were published in 1694, and Part III in 1694. Today, D'Urfey's staging is remembered for its music, composed by Henry Purcell. *The Comical History* has been condemned for being much too comical and for exemplifying the shallow perception of *Don Quixote* in the second half of the seventeenth century.[42] However, a closer reading of D'Urfey's work shows the dignity and uprightness of his Don Quixote.[43] In the preliminaries, the author describes him as the 'Truly Noble, and most Dearly Lov'd Heroe abroad'[44] (pp. 2–3), and after he dies Quitteria regrets, ''Tis pity he's condemn'd such Extravagance, the man has Excellent parts' (p. 290), and Carrasco adds, 'And on all Theams, excepting his Knight Errantry, most read and acute' (p. 290). He is also praised by Perez (p. 66), Pedro (p. 87), and Basilio (p. 210). Conversely, Sancho is persistently mocked, insulted and vilified by secondary characters. In order to emphasize the squire's ludicrousness, D'Urfey furnished him with a daughter, Mary the Buxom, who — alongside Sancho's wife Teresa — adds to Sancho's comical behaviour. From the role of Sancho Panza in D'Urfey's play one realizes that the squire was as popular a character as Don Quixote.

Gayton and D'Urfey attest to the comical perception of *Don Quixote* in the seventeenth century, but they also show that there was an awareness, however slight, of Cervantes's novel being something other than a farce. It has been suggested that the reception of Cervantes in England progressed through three stages: the comical reading in the seventeenth century, the satirical understanding in the first half of the eighteenth century, and the Romanticized reading from the middle of the eighteenth century onwards.[45] The edition of Gayton's *Notes* as late as 1771 proves that later interpretations did not completely supersede the comical reading — and so does the fact that *The Comical History* was staged in the late 1730s. Even before the publication of D'Urfey's play, John Locke in 1690 had praised *Don Quixote* for its 'usefulness, pleasantry and [...] constant decorum'.[46]

Prior to Butler, English philosophers had found in *Don Quixote* a thought-provoking source of inspiration. The first of these was Francis Bacon,[47] whose *Redargutio Philosophiarum* (1608), Rodríguez García argues, takes three ideas from *Don Quixote* Part I: '(1) the consideration of the book as an offspring of the author's mind; (2) the difficulty encountered by the author in granting legitimacy to an enterprise that consists precisely in refuting extant modes of scholarly and patrilinear authority; and (3) the sudden arrival of a male friend in the author's studio with a timely solution to this predicament'.[48] Robert Burton analysed Don Quixote's insanity in *Anatomy of Melancholy* (1621). Thomas Hobbes condemned romances in *Human Nature* (1650). In *Leviathan* (1651) Hobbes wrote, 'when a man compoundeth the image of his own person with the actions of another man, as when a man imagines himself a Hercules or an Alexander (which happeneth often to them that are much taken with reading of romances), it is a compound imagination and properly but a fiction of the mind'.[49] Hobbes inferred from Cervantes's novel that romances could have a potentially pernicious effect on the mind that leads to a compound imagination.[50] For Hobbes, imagination is related to *enthusiasm*, a state of mind which 'takes away both Reason and Revelation'.[51] In the second half of the seventeenth century, enthusiasm had become the stigma commonly attached to Puritans. Hudibras suffers from that very enthusiasm which Don Quixote embodied, and from Hudibras to the quixotic fictions of the late eighteenth century, quixotism was regarded as the prototype for enthusiasm. Other seventeenth-century philosophers who wrote under the influence of Cervantes include John Locke and Francis Bacon. Locke kept three different translations of Don Quixote in his library: Shelton's, Motteux's and the French version by Filleau de Saint Martin.[52] In *Essay Concerning Human Understanding* (1690), Locke extolled *Don Quixote* and argued that all gentlemen should read it.

During the Puritan Republic, *Guzmán de Alfarache* became the favourite reading in Loyalist circles, where the rogue's anti-Puritanical licentiousness was enjoyed and interpreted as the opposite of Puritan ethics. During the Restoration, *Don Quixote* began to be read as a satire, and the two main political parties utilized it to attack each other. In a time of impassioned philosophical and political debate, the Manchegan knight was fostered by the two main schools of philosophical thought, the Ancients and the Moderns, and was portrayed by their political counterparts — the Tories and the Whigs respectively — as a champion of their causes. The first political use of the knight of La Mancha is in John Milton's *Paradise Lost* (1667), where Satan, like the Spanish hidalgo, serves as a literary means to scrutinize realism within the framework of a Cervantean heteroglossia of literary traditions. The political perception of Cervantes's novel continued in the first two decades of the eighteenth century. In 1704, Tory writer Jonathan Swift included in his *Tale of a Tub* the chapter 'A Digression concerning Madness', where a quixotic character turns insane from reading Whig literature, specifically romances. Further, *A Tale of a Tub* is Cervantean in its use of an unreliable narrator, who, like the main narrator of *Don Quixote* (i.e. the Spanish narrator, not Cide Hamete or the Arab translator), acknowledges the unreliability of literature. Swift's *The Battle of the Books* (1704) has also been taken as inspired by Cervantes's *A Trip to Parnassus*, because it presents a critique of contemporaneous writers.[53] In 1712, Joseph Addison critiqued *Don Quixote* in his literary essays for *The Spectator*. For Addison, *Don Quixote* is the quintessential comedy, a work superior to Lucian's *Dialogues of the Gods* — Lucian being for Addison the prototypical burlesque. Comedy derides people as they actually are; the burlesque scorns an absurd version of people. Reading the adventures of the Manchegan madman, Addison identified the Tories' incapacity to understand society with the knight's incapacity to comprehend the world. From this understanding of *Don Quixote*, Addison managed to theorize a whole conception of literary comedy which, he thought, the Spanish author had constructed upon the principle of grave irony.[54] Later in the century, David Hume found in *Don Quixote* the optimal illustration of the concept *delicacy*, which he developed in his essay 'Of the Standard of Taste' (1757).[55]

During the eighteenth century, Cervantes's influence on English literature was pre-eminent, to an extent that remains beyond compare;[56] from being the source of theatrical imitations, *Don Quixote* was soon held, by some of the most accomplished writers of the century, as the gold standard of the novel. Yet imitations and adaptations continued to be written. Nicholas Rowe's *The Fair Penitent* (1703) recreated *The Curious Impertinent*, although Rowe's source might have been Massinger's *The Fatal Dowry*.[57] *El celoso extremeño*, one of the *Exemplary Novels*, was the source of Charles Johnson's *The Generous Husband* (1713) and of Isaac Bickerstaff's *The Padlock* (1768). Sancho's fame is attested by two stage adaptations of his adventures as governor of Barataria[58] — James Ayres's *Sancho at Court; or, the Mock Governor. An Opera-Comedy, as it Was Designed to be Acted at the Theatre-Royal in Drury Lane* (1742), which was published but not staged, and Frederick Pilon's *Barataria; or, Sancho Turn'd Governor* (1785), 'taken from the Second Part of D'Urfey's *Don Quixote*'.[59] Henry Fielding wrote (in 1728, although it was not published until 1734) the play *Don Quixote in England*, the story of Don Quixote and Sancho in search of adventures on English soil. The 'Introduction' bears proof of Don Quixote's popularity at the time. In the 'Introduction', to be acted as part of the play, a 'Man' asks the 'Author', 'But don't you think a Play, with so odd a Title as yours, requires to be a little explain'd? May they [the audience] not be too much surpris'd at some things'; and the Author responds, 'Not at all. The Audience, I believe, are all acquainted with the Character[s] of Don Quixote and Sancho'.[60] Indeed, during the eighteenth century there were in England forty-five editions of *Don Quixote* (whereas in Spain there were only thirty-three), and it acquired an unrivalled fame.[61] So much did the English appreciate *Don Quixote* that statesman Lord Carteret commissioned the first critical edition in Spanish (and in any other language), published in 1738. Allegedly, when in 1735 Carteret visited Queen Caroline's new palace in Richmond, he realized the library lacked a copy of *Don Quixote*, and determined to furnish it with a swish edition of the Spanish text. And lavish it was: it contained the first ever biography of Cervantes, by Gregorio Mayans, and splendid illustrations by John Vanderbank (others by Hogarth were rejected by the editors).[62] The 1781 edition by John Bowle is considered the founding stone of Cervantes studies. Daniel Eisenberg has listed twenty-one critical innovations in Bowle's edition: he numbers the lines in the novel; he provides a comprehensive annotation; he adds indexes of words and proper names; he includes a map of Spain; he called attention to the importance of the paratext; he restores the dedications; he discusses previous editions; he notes that Sancho's linguistic errors are intentional; he uses English and Italian translations to understand the text; he claims that it cannot be translated successfully; he argues that Part II is superior to Avellaneda's sequel; he lists Don Quixote's adventures; he acknowledges that Rocinante and Sancho's donkey must be regarded as characters; he analyses the poems; he lists the sayings in the texts; he suggests the need to re-read *Don Quixote*; he recognizes the irony of the text; he presents Cervantes as the best Spanish author and compares him to Shakespeare; he notices that Shakespeare and Cervantes died on the same day; he claims that Cervantes should be considered a classic author; and he regards Cervantes as an international author.[63]

During the first half of the century, Cervantes was systematically praised as one of the greatest authors of all times by many writers, including Shaftesbury, Dr. Johnson, Steele, Addison, Temple, Wharton, Hume, Locke, Arbuthnot and Lady Montagu.[64] At a time when authors had become obsessed with defining the nature of prose fiction, *Don Quixote* became a peremptory reference. In *The Progress of Romance* (1785), Clara Reeve struggled to understand the qualities of Cervantes's work, although she praises the knight's righteousness. Those who strove to transcend the romance and to write novels found an inspirational model in *Don Quixote*. Most scholars of English literature, though, have failed to realize Cervantes's impact on the eighteenth-century English novel. Although some of the best studies of *Don Quixote* have been written in English — by British scholars such as Riley, and Americans such as Mancing, Friedman, Parr, Allen, and others — the vast majority of scholars of the English novel continue to ignore them. As suggested above, the terminology used within English literary studies has hindered the proper understanding of the eighteenth-century novel. *Quixotic* has come to encompass anything related to *Don Quixote* the novel and Don Quixote the character, and the term *quixotic fiction* has been associated with the second and third-rate novels whose titles bear the name *Quixote* and which narrate the adventures of characters who resemble the Spanish knight.

There are, however, four key terms to refer to Cervantes's work and to *Don Quixote* in particular: *quixotic*, *Cervantean*, *Cervantic*, and *Cervantine*. In her recent book *Cervantic Fictions of the USA*, Sarah Wood refuses to employ any other term but *Quixotic* (with capital Q), and describes Quixotic fiction as a category of literary texts which 'incorporate or encounter literary genres such as Menippean satire, sentimental fiction, Moorish captivities, the burlesque, the pastoral and the picaresque'.[65] She thus discards all adjectives but *quixotic* in an attempt to make her 'definition of Quixotic fiction [...] intentionally simple, inclusive, and comfortable with the co-existence of other literary genres'.[66] As a matter of fact, however, the influence of Cervantes in English literature (be it British or American) is not at all a 'simple' issue and cannot be analysed in an 'inclusive' manner. Critics before Wood put forward a number of proposals for a more accurate use of the terminology, one that would help to understand the actual dimension of Cervantes's impact on English prose fiction.[67] There exists a category which we should term the *Cervantic novel*, comprising novels written and conceived under the influence of Cervantes. Within this category there are *quixotic fictions* and also *Cervantean novels*.

A *quixotic fiction* is a narrative which relates the adventures of a Quixote — and a Quixote is an individual who, through excessive reading of a certain literary genre, has become a psychotic monomaniac and hence espouses the obsolete values which that genre proclaims. The trade mark of most (but not all) quixotic fictions is their bearing the name Quixote in the title. Unlike Don Quixote, in some of these novels the main characters do not suffer a psychotic disorder; they are neurotic monomaniacs instead. (Such differences require a precise use of the terminology:

Quixote should refer to the psychotic monomaniac but also to the neurotic characters who are inspired by the crazy Spaniard. In order to be as precise as possible, I will henceforth use the terms *neurotic Quixote* and *Quixote* to differentiate the neurotic from the psychotic.) The label *quixotic* should refer to content, not to form. Quixotic fictions are generally satirical and they use the quixotic figure with the same satirical ends as in *Don Quixote* — the first quixotic fiction is Cervantes's own *Licenciado Vidriera*, one of his exemplary novels published in 1613. Although Lennox's *The Female Quixote* (1752) has traditionally been regarded as the first quixotic fiction, William Winstanly's *The Essex Champion; or, The Famous History of Sir Billy of Billerecay and his Squire Ricardo* (1690) has been named as the earliest example.[68] In Sarah Fielding's *The Adventures of David Simple* (1744) and *Volume the Last* (1753) there is one character that may be regarded as a female Quixote. In 1678 there appeared the English translation of Adrien Thomas Perdou de Subligny's *La Fausse Clélie*, under the title *Mock-Clelia; or, Madame Quixote*, a parody of sentimental romances such as Madelaine de Scudéry's *Clélie* (1660). Lennox's novel was one of the greatest literary sensations of the mid-eighteenth century. Sentimental romances, mostly translated from the French, appealed to many English female readers, a vogue which Lennox turned into a cliché with her Cervantean parody *The Female Quixote*. From Lennox stemmed this trend of quixotic parodies and satires. So successful was *The Female Quixote* that some scholars have even maintained that the many subsequent quixotic fictions were not imitations of *Don Quixote* but of Lennox's novel.[69] This claim, however, was not acknowledged by Susan Staves in one of the most lucid essays written on this topic;[70] and it was later proved, using textual evidence, that *Northanger Abbey* was directly influenced by Cervantes.[71]

There are two *waves* of quixotic fiction — the first in the eighteenth century and the early nineteenth century, and the second thereafter. The first wave comprises a group of texts published between 1752 and 1813 — with the antecedent of Winstanly's *The Essex Champion* (1690) and the belated *Donna Quixote* by Justin McCarthy, serialized in the magazine *Belgravia* in 1878 and 1879. The quixotic fictions whose titles bear the name Quixote are: *Tarrataria; or, Don Quixote the Second* (1761) by (as the subtitle reads) 'a Traveller of Distinction', *Fizigigg; or, the Modern Quixote* (1763), Richard Graves's *The Spiritual Quixote; or, the Summer Rumbles of Mr. Geoffrey Wildgoose* (1773; in 1827 appeared a version in verse entitled *The Spiritual Quixote, Geoffrey Wildgoose, in Cheltenham; or, A Discourse on a Race-Course*), *The Philosophical Quixote; or, Memories of David Wilkins* (1782), *The Country Quixote* (1785), *The City Quixote* (1785), *The Amicable Quixote; or, The Enthusiasm of Friendship* (1788), Jane Purbeck's *William Thornborough, the Benevolent Quixote* (1791), *The History of Sir George Warrington; or, The Political Quixote* (1797),[72] Charles Lucas's *The Infernal Quixote* (1801), and George Buxton's *The Political Quixote; or, the Adventures of the Renowned Don Blackibo, Dwarfino, and his Trusty Squire Seditiono* (1820).[73] In 1754 the *Monthly Review* announced the book *The Spiritual Quixote; or, the Entertaining History of Don Ignatius Loyola, founder of the Order of Jesuits*, which is only quixotic in its title. *A Bristol Oddity* (1772) is another quixotic fiction. Smollett's *Sir Launcelot Greaves* (1762), is, alongside Lennox's novel, the best known of quixotic fictions. Charlotte Smith also used a quixotic main character in both

The Old Manor House (1793) and *The Young Philosopher* (1798). So did Mary Hays in *Memoirs of Emma Courtney* (1796) and Elizabeth Hamilton in *Memoirs of Modern Philosophers* (1800). Outside prose fiction are *Angelica; or, Quixote in Petticoats. A Comedy in Two Acts* (1758), and the farce *Polly Honeycomb* (1760) by George Colman. Around the same time, the adventures of a number of Quixotes were published in the United States: Tabitha Gilman Tenney's *Female Quixotism* (1801), Hugh Henry Brackenbridge's *Modern Chivalry, Containing the Adventures of Captain John Farrago, and Teague O'Regan, His Servant* (1792–1815), Royall Tyler's *The Algerine Captive; or, The Life and Adventures of Doctor Updike Underhill* (1797), Charles Brockden Brown's *Arthur Mervyn* (1799–1800), and possibly Washington Irving's *A History of New York, from the Beginning of the World to the End of the Dutch Dynasty* (1809).[74]

The English quixotic fictions are first and foremost satires which borrow the Quixote figure as a straightforward and popular means to pass judgement on English society. In the second half of the century, politically committed authors of quite varied viewpoints used the Spanish knight in order to attack their opponents — conservatives to deride utopian entelechies, and radicals to expose the inadequacies of the old aristocratic order. Geoffrey Wildgoose, the central character in Graves's *The Spiritual Quixote*, is a steadfast Methodist of unswerving ideals who venerates George Whitfield, an influential Methodist preacher. Like Hudibras in the seventeenth century, Wildgoose champions the obsolete puritanical values which Graves intends to satirize. Unlike in the Spanish novel, the English spiritual Quixote is usually reprimanded by the narrator. George Bruce in *The Amicable Quixote* places friendship above any other human qualities. His quixotism is mild, almost insipid, for although Bruce's monomania jeopardizes his relationship with Emily Bryant and delays their wedding, only on very few occasions does he go into quixotic rages. *The Political Quixote* reflects on the French Revolution from a disapproving viewpoint. Sir George Warrington, the political Quixote, has acquired a favourable opinion of the revolution through Thomas Paine's *Rights of Man*. Warrington is a Quixote for he obdurately upholds his political monomania and seeks to propagate his beliefs. In reading about the French Revolution in the English newspapers, the political Quixote gradually realizes the callousness of the revolutionary ideals. Satire is thus achieved, and the English notions of liberty and democracy prevail over the French Revolution. The title of *The Infernal Quixote* alludes to John Milton's infernal spirits in *Satan*, whose infamous motto was 'Better to reign in Hell than to serve in Heaven'. Captain James Marauder, Lucas's infernal Quixote, takes on the role of an anti-Christ, who ravishes women and takes part in the horrors perpetrated by the radicals of the French revolution. Marauder is another political Quixote, who has read Thomas Paine's *Age of Reason* and Godwin's *Political Justice*, which Lucas seems to hold to account for his Quixote's moral maladies. He is completely devoid of the essential features of the Quixote; he is simply a nefarious antihero who perpetrates unspeakable felonies. Marauder lacks the noble qualities of Don Quixote, which in this text are embodied by Wilson Wilson, the hero who rises as the antihero falls. The quixotism in Lucas's novel lies in its satirical portrayal of the French revolution.

A novel is Cervantean when its form has been influenced, in one way or another, by Cervantes's novelistic techniques as employed in *Don Quixote*. Although this is seldom the case, Cervantean novels may recount the adventures of a Quixote or of a neurotic Quixote, e.g. in *The Female Quixote*, *Northanger Abbey*, *Joseph Andrews* and *Tristram Shandy*. Eighteenth-century English writers found inspiration in *Don Quixote* as a source of parody and as a model for narrative technique. Research has demonstrated the Cervantean nature of the following novels: Fielding's *Joseph Andrews* and *Tom Jones*, Lennox's *The Female Quixote*, Sterne's *Tristram Shandy*, Smollett's *Roderick Random* and *Humphry Clinker*, and Austen's *Northanger Abbey*. Whether or not this is the tip of a gigantic iceberg is, perhaps, a matter of secondary consequence; the real consequence lies in the fact that these Cervantean novels are some of the best novels ever written in English. Not only was Cervantes the favourite author of many eighteenth-century writers, he was furthermore the heaviest influence upon their works. *Don Quixote* was, as some critics have proved without a shadow of a doubt,[75] the canon out of which Fielding and Smollett modelled the English novel.

Fielding and Smollett shared a common love for Cervantes and for *Don Quixote*, as they explicitly acknowledged — Fielding used the characters of the knight and his squire in *Don Quixote in England* and pointed out the influence of Cervantes in the subtitle of *Joseph Andrews*; Smollett translated *Don Quixote*, wrote a biography of Cervantes, made several allusions to Don Quixote, and used Cervantine vocabulary such as 'Dulcinea' and 'duenna'. These two authors renovated English prose fiction by defining a new genre which left behind the sentimental romance whose hyperbolic elements they abhorred. Although Richardson had succeeded in turning the sentimental tradition into a form of didacticism free from the excesses of the romance, both Fielding and Smollett craved something radically different. And they held *Don Quixote* as their canon. Fielding first attempted the renovation of prose fiction with a parody in the Cervantean fashion — Joseph Andrews behaves according to the social conventions of the sentimental romance, which is proved ridiculous in 1748 England. *Joseph Andrews* is therefore a Cervantean novel because it is a Cervantean parody of the sentimental romance, and it is also a quixotic novel because its main character is a neurotic Quixote. The Cervantean qualities of *Tom Jones* are much more complex. Fielding intended *Tom Jones* to be an epic poem in prose in the fashion of *Don Quixote*, and created its narrative structure in *Don Quixote*'s own structure — using an episodic plot, parallel strands, analepsis, prolepsis, interpolated stories, metafiction, the same focalization techniques, and a *deus ex machina*.[76] Following Cervantes, who had referred to *Don Quixote* as a 'historia', Fielding refers to *Tom Jones* as a 'history' and to novel writers as 'historians'. Smollett's chief objective was also to transcend the romance, and to do so he recurred to Cervantean techniques. As in *Don Quixote*, the story told in *Roderick Random* conforms to realism and includes a number of romance stories which become realistic and therefore novelistic when they merge with the main plot. *Humphry Clinker* recreates the dialogism in *Don Quixote*.

Sterne's *Tristram Shandy* contains quixotic characters, utilizes Cervantean narrative methods, and bears numerous allusions to Cervantes, Don Quixote and Sancho, to such an extent that Müllenbrock has called Sterne 'the most congenial of Cervantes's followers'.[77] Some of the characters in this novel are neurotic Quixotes because their obsessions — or *hobby-horses*, as they are called in the novel — mislead their perception of reality; Walter's hobby-horse is scholasticism,[78] Toby's is military engineering, and Tristram's is writing. In all instances, the hobby-horse distorts reality. Yorick is also a Quixote; the narrator writes of him, 'I have the highest idea of the spiritual and refined sentiments of this reverend gentleman, from this single stroke in his character, which I think comes up to any of the honest refinements of the peerless knight of La Mancha, whom, by the bye, with all his follies, I love more, and would actually have gone further to have paid a visit to, than the greatest hero in antiquity'.[79] Both Toby and Yorick reflect the same honourable qualities that Sterne's contemporaries perceived in the Spanish knight.[80] Sterne's characters are, in Reed's words, 'a partial, domesticated, and largely immobilized version of Cervantes's hero. They are Don Quixote in retirement, a pastoral scale mode of the "Cervantick" original'.[81] Like quixotic fictions, *Tristram Shandy* is a satire. But unlike other quixotic imitations, Sterne went much further than the simple imitation of Cervantes. Sterne's narrator is Cervantean in as much as he self-consciously rises from the intratextual dimension in order to critique his own text from a metafictional level.[82] Also Cervantean in *Tristram Shandy* is affectation, the same sort of comic affectation as in Fielding's novel. Sterne, however, did acknowledge that in *Tristram Shandy* 'the events [...] are of so singular a nature, and so Cervantick a cast' (p. 277) and its comic style follows 'Cervantic gravity' (p. 139), which Sterne defined elsewhere as 'Cervantic humour [which] arises from [...] describing silly and trifling Events, with the Circumstantial Pomp of great Ones'.[83] The references to Cervantes, the quixotism of the main characters, the narrative method and the Cervantic humour, all make *Tristram Shandy* a Cervantean novel, and demonstrate that Sterne found in *Don Quixote* his literary model, which, like Fielding and Smollett, he emulated in order to create a literary masterpiece.[84]

The Female Quixote and *Northanger Abbey* are quixotic in their usage of a Quixote and a neurotic Quixote respectively. From the Spanish novel Lennox borrowed characters and incidents with the same objective as Cervantes, to parody a declining genre. The main character, Arabella, is a Quixote who reads French sentimental romances, becomes insane and thinks that sentimentality prevails in mid-eighteenth-century society. Austen's novel is Cervantean because it is a parody of the mainstream literary tradition of its day; after reading Gothic romances, Catherine believes that they tell real stories, and when she stays at Northanger Abbey she constantly believes that she is at the point of living a Gothic adventure. Unlike the Spanish knight, Catherine is a neurotic Quixote;[85] nonetheless, she perceives a distorted reality.

A very close imitation of *Don Quixote*, but also a parody of the sentimental romance, *The Female Quixote* is a Cervantean novel. The sentimental romance was largely eradicated from the English literary panorama by *The Female Quixote*. In the last decade of the century, however, following the publication of Horace Walpole's *Castle of Otranto* (1765), a new form of romance monopolized the literary taste of English readers: the Gothic romance. The romance came back into fashion and grew extremely popular in the 1790s with the works by Ann Radcliffe, *The Romance of the Forest* (1791), *The Mysteries of Udolpho* (1794), and *The Italian* (1797). After the turn of the century, some authors revisited the quixotic formula in order to parody the Gothic romance, which had been taken to extremes with the scandalous novel *The Monk* (1796) by Matthew Lewis. The best known of the parodies of these is Jane Austen's *Northanger Abbey* (finished in 1799 although not published until 1818, as the title page of the *editio princeps* reads). Catherine, the main character, is a neurotic monomaniac, but *Northanger Abbey* is a Cervantean novel because it is a parody. Other parodies of the Gothic romance include *Susanna; or, Traits of a Modern Miss* (1795), Maria Edgeworth's 'Angelina' (1801), and Sarah Greene's *Romance Readers and Romance Writers* (1810), all of which bring in quixotic figures. Published in 1813, *The Heroine; or, Adventures of a fair Romance Reader* by Eaton Stannard Barrett is perhaps the closest imitation of *Don Quixote* after Lennox's novel — Barrett acknowledges Cervantes's influence and borrows the main psychological features of Don Quixote to conceive his Cherry Wilkinson, who turns insane from reading Gothic romances and styles herself Cherubina. Both *Romance Readers and Romance Writers* and *The Heroine* are quixotic fictions because of their quixotic heroines, but they are also Cervantean novels in as much as they parody the predominant literary genre. After these parodies two other authors utilized quixotic characters in their works. William Combe's Dr Syntax is the quixotic protagonist of *The Tour of Dr Syntax in Search of the Picturesque* (1809–11), *The Second Tour of Dr Syntax in Search of Consolation* (1820), and *The Third Tour of Dr Syntax in Search of a Wife* (1821). The second is John Cunningham, author of *Sancho; or, the Proverbialist* (1816). However, the most intriguing of all these authors of Cervantean parodies is Austen, not only because she is the best-known English female author, but also because her works are interspersed with Cervantic features.

Cervantes's influence on Austen was not restricted to *Northanger Abbey*. The Cervantic mode of parody — the employment of a quixotic character obsessed with the adventures and stereotypes they have read in romances — recurs through-out Austen's works. The father of the heroine in *Love and Freindship* [*sic*] is a quixotic character. *Juvenalia* can also be classed as a quixotic parody.[86] Marianne Dashwood, a secondary character in *Sense and Sensibility* (1811), believes in the love code depicted in the works of Walter Scott and others. She contemplates the world through the lenses of Romantic fiction, which proves unrealistic when her sentimental relationship with Willoughby fails and Marianne recognizes his egotism and her own. Marianne is a neurotic monomaniac who bases her existence on Romantic fiction before she becomes conscious of the differences between real life and literary fiction. Elizabeth Bennet is the main character of *Pride and Prejudice* (1813) and a very unlikely Quixote. Although the family library has become a sanctuary for her father and sister, Elizabeth is not the victim of excessive reading. She does, however, exaggerate reality when she believes that her suitor is a nefarious character, but in the end realizes that she was wrong. The scheme is very similar to Marianne's story. Neither has the eponymous heroine in *Emma* (1816) read excessively.[87] Her own ignorance leads Emma to misread reality: she interprets the actions of others according to her fantasies, leading to a number of misunderstandings. From the Cervantean parody in *Northanger Abbey*, employed against the Gothic novel, Austen's subsequent heroines retain the psychological progression from misinterpreting reality to realizing their mistake at the end of an educational journey. The Cervantean parody thus gave way to the feminine *Bildungsroman*.

During the eighteenth century, the satirical nature of *Don Quixote* eclipsed its perception as a comical book. However, the Romantic perception of Cervantes's novel, enunciated by German writers, was forestalled by the English. Although Smollett was not the first British voice to eulogize Cervantes and *Don Quixote*, his 'Life of Cervantes', published in the preliminaries of his own translation of *Don Quixote* (1755), reached many more readers than any other commentary. In Smollett's view, *Don Quixote* is not a lampoon of chivalry, because Cervantes himself held chivalry very dearly in his heart:

> Not that Cervantes had any intention to combat the spirit of knight errantry, so prevalent among the Spaniards; on the contrary, I am persuaded he would have been the first man in the nation, to stand up for the honour and defence of chivalry, which, when restrained within the due bounds, was an excellent institution, that inspired the most heroic sentiments of courage and patriotism, and in many occasions conduced to the peace and safety of the commonwealth.[88]

In the last paragraph of 'The Life of Cervantes', the Spanish author is famously acclaimed, in a eulogistic tone previously unheard:

> Cervantes, whether considered as a writer or a man, will be found worthy of universal approbation and esteem; as we cannot help applauding that fortitude and courage which no difficulty could disturb, and no danger dismay; while we admire that delightful stream of humour and invention, which flowed so plenteous and so pure, surmounting ludicrous all the mounds of malice and adversity.[89]

Before Smollett, however, others had already evoked this legendary image of the Spanish knight. Fielding must be credited with realizing Don Quixote's being the honest and honourable champion of gentility, when in *Rape Upon Rape* (1730) he declared that 'Good-nature is Quixotism'.[90] In his *Essay Towards Fixing the True Standards of Wit, Humour, Raillery, Satire, and Ridicule* (1744), Corbyn Morris presents Don Quixote as the paradigm of bravery and honour, retaining the comical and satirical perception of the novel, but clearly enlightening the positive qualities of the knight. In the second volume of *The Rambler* (1750), Dr Johnson had proclaimed that all men have something of Don Quixote in them, anticipating his mythical status.[91] The most ardent of the post-Smollett encomiums came from Henry Brooke who, in his classic sentimental novel *Fool of Quality* (1766), wrote:

> How greatly, how gloriously, how divinely superior was our hero of the Mancha! Who went about righting of wrongs, and redressing of injuries, lifting up the fallen, and pulling down those whom iniquity had exalted. In this his marvellous undertaking, what buffetings, what bruisings, what tramplings of ribs, what pounding of pack staves did his bones not endure? [...] But, toil was his bed of down, and the house of pain was, to him, a bower of delight, while he consider'd himself as engaged in giving ease, advantage, and happiness to others.[92]

This same mystification of the quixotic hero is further emphasized in Henry Mackenzie's *Man of Feeling* (1771). After the publication of Smollett's translation, similar panegyrics can be read in Edward Clarke's *Letters Concerning the Spanish Nation* (1763), and in Sterne's *Tristram Shandy*.

In sum, while the German Romanticists disseminated the Romantic perception of *Don Quixote*, which prevails today, Cervantes's and Don Quixote's Romantic qualities of good-nature, honour, freedom, generosity and wit had been succinctly posited by Fielding, Smollett and others in eighteenth-century England. Certainly, the Germans grew fascinated by Spanish literature, especially by Calderón's plays, because of their portrayal of the concept of honour. In Germany, Don Quixote became a myth that conveyed all those noble principles. The English Romantic poets also extolled Don Quixote. Wordsworth mentioned Cervantes's novel in *The Prelude*. In *Modern Painters* (1843), John Ruskin reflected on the satirical nature of Cervantes's novel, and praised its wit, elegance and moral beauty. Coleridge discussed it in his lectures on literature, providing a new reading of the book, not as a parody, but as a fine piece of irony.[93] But it was Byron who wrote the more memorable and enduring lines on the hidalgo, expressing the satirical perception of the novel when, in *Don Juan*, he claims that Cervantes 'smiled Spain's chivalry away'. In this poem, Byron presented Don Quixote as 'the saddest' of all books, and therefore the quintessential Romantic story and character. The poet praises Don Quixote's goodness and blames the world for his insanity:

> Of all tales 'tis the saddest — and more sad,
> Because he makes us smile: the hero's right,
> And still pursues the right; — to curb the bad
> His only object, and 'gainst odds to fight
> His guerdon: 'tis his virtue makes him mad!
> But his adventures form a sorry sight; —
> A sorrier still is the great moral taught
> By the real epic unto all who have thought.

The same exalted tone is found in Charles Lamb's 'The Barrenness of the Imaginative Faculty in the Productions of Modern Art'. And in the footsteps of Byron followed other commentators who also praised Cervantes and *Don Quixote* in one way of another.

By the end of the eighteenth century the admiration for Cervantes seems to have surpassed the interest in his novel. From Smollett, readers saw the knight as a champion of honour and generosity, but also assigned these values to Cervantes, in the conviction that his purpose in writing *Don Quixote* was to glorify them. In the later years of the eighteenth century English readers began to read other works by Cervantes. Although not translated into English until 1780 (by Gordon W. J. Gyll), the *Viaje del Parnaso* was the source for Susanna Haswell Rowson's *A Trip to Parnassus; or, the Judgement of Apollo on Dramatic Authors and Performers. A Poem* (1788). *Viaje del Parnaso* is a long poem in which Cervantes critiques the poets of his time. Rowson's *Trip to Parnassus* is a long poem in which she critiques playwrights and actors. Cervantes longed to be a poet and in this poem he acknowledged his limitations; startlingly, Rowson had been an unsuccessful actress and she too admitted to his professional failure.[94] In the prologue to her play *Slaves in Algiers* (1794), Rowson

— whose novel *Charlotte Temple*, partly inspired by *Celestina*, is unanimously regarded as the most popular literary text in the United States until World War I — extolled Cervantes for having written the best ever comic and moralistic satire, and acknowledged that 'the plot [of *Slaves in Algiers*] is taken from the Story of the Captive, related by Cervantes, in his inimitable Romance Don Quixote'.[95]

In 1791 the first English translation of *La Galatea* — as *Galatea. A Pastoral Romance* — by an anonymous translator, was published in Dublin. Very soon after, in 1798, a second anonymous translation was printed in the Massachusetts city of Boston. The third rendering was by a Miss Highly, published in London in 1804. The fourth and fifth are also by English translators: W. M. Craig (London, 1813) and Gordon Willoughby (London, 1867). In addition to emulations and translations, Cervantes's works were themselves widely read. The most enchanting example of Britain's love for Cervantes is told by John G. Lockhart, a relative of Walter Scott and editor of Motteux's *Don Quixote*, who recalled that, when Walter Scott was on his death-bed, days away from death, Wordsworth visited and read them Cervantes's prologue to *Persiles*.

Don Quixote continued to be the most read of Cervantes's works. During the nineteenth century, three theatrical adaptations of the novel were staged and published: Mrs Matthew Stuart's *Don Quixote; or, The Knight of la Mancha* (1834), George Almar's *Don Quixote; or, The Knight of the Woeful Countenance* (1833), and George Morrison's *Alonzo Quixano, Otherwise Don Quixote* (1895).[96] Stuart's play demonstrates that, even after the Romanticists' perception was established and propagated, the novel was still read and enjoyed as a comic book: the subtitle presents it as 'a comic opera'. The great majority of readers, however, did read *Don Quixote* as a sad book. Morrison's play focuses on Alonso and considers his insanity, as Byron had suggested, to be an accident caused by society, and introduces Don Quixote as 'the Christ of fiction'.[97]

Many nineteenth-century English novelists have been counted amongst Cervantes's literary progeny. Nonetheless, after the Cervantean parodies of the Gothic romance published in the 1810s, the Cervantean novel vanishes, giving way to the second wave of quixotic fictions. The novel had risen in the previous century, with the works of Defoe, Richardson and others, first, and later with the Cervantean novels by Fielding, Sterne and Smollett. Withal, English readers continued to read and enjoy Cervantes's works, and Cervantic elements are found in many novels. After the pioneering critical attempts by Bowle in the eighteenth century, a scholarly interest in Cervantes soared during the nineteenth century.

Mancing's list of novelists who are likely to have been influenced by Cervantes includes Lewis Carroll, Walter Scott, Mary Shelley, Charles Dickens, William Thackeray, and George Eliot.[98] In the novels written by these authors, however, the Cervantean elements do not impregnate the whole of the text, but are introduced as dispensable elements. They bear Cervantes's influence mostly in their usage of quixotic characters. The lasting love for Cervantes is perhaps most noticeable in Walter Scott, who might have read the original Spanish text and considered the possibility of translating it. The eponymous hero in *Waverley* is an avid reader of romances, and a wholly neurotic Quixote.

Mary Shelley mentioned *Don Quixote* in her journals and letters, and also wrote a *Life of Cervantes* (1837). There are similarities between Don Quixote and Victor Frankenstein — the Spanish knight seeks to impose his chivalric ideas upon others (e.g. forcing everyone to vow that Dulcinea is the most beautiful lady), and Frankenstein tries to impose his science upon nature; Don Quixote has read chivalry romances, and the Creature has tried to educate himself by reading Milton, Plutarch and Goethe. *Frankenstein* may be regarded as a parody of the Gothic romance, as *Don Quixote* is a parody of the chivalric romance. And in her novel *Lodore*, Shelley compared the main characters to Don Quixote and Dulcinea.

There are allusions to *Don Quixote* in several works by Dickens. *The Posthumous Papers of the Pickwick Club* (1836) was immediately associated with Cervantes: the *Edinburgh Review* referred to Dickens's characters, Mr Pickwick and his friend Sam Weller, as 'Modern Quixote and Sancho of Cocaigne' and a friend of Dickens pointed out that 'Sam Weller and Mr Pickwick are Sancho and Quixote of Londoners'.[99] Indeed Pickwick lives his life according to the particular conceptions which he has formed in his mind. Like the Spanish knight, Pickwick sets out in search of adventures. Like Sancho, his companion Sam behaves in a most comical way, and draws an earthy contrast with Pickwick's lofty ideals. Further, there are passages which resemble Cervantes's novel — the morning when the main character makes his first sally, and the rescue of damsels in distress. Like eighteenth-century novelists, Dickens borrows plot and characters. Yet it would be problematic to consider *The Posthumous Papers* a quixotic fiction since Pickwick's quixotism is somewhat flimsy — he is certainly a monomaniac, but he is neither psychotic nor neurotic. In *Oliver Twist* one can also perceive the mark of *Rinconete and Cortadillo*, one of Cervantes's experimental uses of the picaresque genre, the tale of its eponymous protagonists' entrance into a society of rogues.

William Thackeray's *Vanity Fair* (1847–48) shows very subtle traces of Cervantes's influence, in its usage of parody, heteroglossia, and metafiction. Walter Reed has regarded Colonel Thomas Newcome, the main character in Thackeray's *The Newcomers* (1853), a Quixote, in the vogue of the eighteenth-century British Quixotes,[100] since he is a self-made gentleman of ordinary origins. Newcome is furthermore the product of the Romanticists' perception of the Manchegan knight, a character that exemplifies the aspirations and values of Victorian England. Not only is he compared to Don Quixote by the narrator and by other characters, but he declares his admiration for Cervantes's hero and proclaims that he always carries a copy of the Spanish novel.

George Eliot's *The Mill on the Floss* (1860) and *Middlemarch* (1871–72) retain some of the Cervantean features developed by Austen. In *The Mill on the Floss*, Maggie expects situations and people to conform to idyllic literature, only to realize later that she was mistaken. Throughout the novel, Maggie, like Don Quixote, imagines she lives in a world dominated by generosity and honour. The prologue to *Middlemarch* exalts the sixteenth-century Spanish Saint Theresa for her bravery as a girl in embarking with her brother on a mission that would take them to Northern Africa to fight the Moors; Saint Theresa's valour stemmed from her reading chivalric novels. In Eliot's novel, Dorothea Brooke espouses the philanthropic ideas embodied by Don Quixote. She marries Casaubon hoping that he will help her to improve her intellect, but her idolized husband fails to measure up to her expectations. Despite the references to Saint Theresa and to *Don Quixote* in *Middlemarch*, the influence of Cervantes on this novel is very subtle. As in Austen's novels, from conceiving a neurotic quixotic character in *The Mill on the Floss*, Eliot develops in *Middlemarch* a topic that had been largely treated by the Romanticists — disillusionment in love. Eliot's *The Spanish Gypsy* (1868) borrows title, plot and characters from Cervantes's *La gitanilla*. In the Spanish *novella*, Juan falls in love with Preciosa, a beautiful gypsy girl who, the reader learns subsequently, is the daughter of a nobleman. In Eliot's text, Don Silva falls in love with Fedalma, a member of the nobility who turns out to be a gypsy girl. In both texts, the heroes defy social conventions to marry women from a different social class.

The twentieth century marks a renaissance in quixotic fictions and the development of a celebrated line of Cervantes scholars. The twentieth-century novels which bear the name 'Quixote' in their titles are Douglas Blackburn's *Burgher Quixote* (1903), G. K. Chesterton's *The Return of D. Quixote* (1926–27), and Graham Greene's *Monsignor Quixote* (1981). Blackburn's novel features Sarel Erasmus, who claims: 'The mistakes I have made, and I admit they are many, will help the world to know the real character of many of my countrymen, among whom I have been as a Don Quixote, fighting on behalf of Great Britain against the folly and ignorance that have caused such loss and suffering'.[101]

The influence of Cervantes is noticeable in Chesterton's works: *The Return of D. Quixote* was preceded by his essay 'The Divine Parody of D. Quixote' (1901), where Cervantes's novel is interpreted as a study of idealism against reality; later, in 1911, in 'The True Romance', he also referred to Cervantes to illustrate that modern society had turned away from chivalric values, a hypothesis reinforced in his poem 'Lepanto'. Chesterton's first novel, *Napoleon in Notting Hill* (1904), tells of Quinn and Wayne, a Quijote–Sancho pair who represent the opposition of idealism and realism in the uchronic England of 1984 — whilst Quinn seeks to live a life without restraints, Wayne proclaims the need for the law. *The Return of D. Quixote* was serialized in *G.K.'s Weekly* in 1926 and 1927, and translated into Spanish in 1927. It tells of a company of actors who, after playing the story of King Arthur's troubadour — named Blondel — resolve to restore chivalry in England. The actors set out on their mission wearing mediaeval costumes, led by Mr Herne, a librarian, who had played the role of King Arthur. Chesterton's novel conveys a strong political message; for him, chivalry encompasses a new political vision which rejects both capitalism and socialism, a sort of liberalism which conveys the ideology of Christian socialists such as John Ruskin, Maurice Reckitt, Vincent Morrison, and of *G.K.'s Weekly*.[102] For Chesterton, Don Quixote symbolized Christian ideals.

Graham Greene's *Monsignor Quixote* tells of Father Quijote, a humble priest from La Mancha who is unexpectedly and somewhat comically promoted to monsignor, before setting out on a journey with his Sanchoesque companion, Enrique Zancas. The most obvious borrowing from Cervantes is, perhaps, the Quixote–Sancho dialogues; other Cervantic images include a herd of sheep and some inns. There are also implicit allusions to Cervantes's novel: when the main characters come across two police officers, Zancas compares them to the windmills in *Don Quixote*. Greene's Quijote is quixotic in as much as he sometimes perceives a distorted reality, for example in the Salamanca brothel and in the Valladolid cinema. Yet he is not always and constantly affected by his monomania. When Sancho compares the policemen to the windmills, Monsignor Quijote sees them as officers. It is difficult to assess the Cervantic qualities in Greene's novel. His interest in Spanish politics emerges at different times in *Monsignor Quixote* — Zancas, a former mayor of Toboso, is a Marxist who was imprisoned during the Francoist years, and both Franco and Lenin are mentioned in the novel. In matching a Catholic Quixote with a Marxist Sancho, Greene, a Catholic convert himself, puts the two fighting sides of the Spanish Civil War face to face — the intrinsically Catholic Nationalists of Franco, who rebelled against the undemocratic and anti-Catholic Marxist government which, having reached power after a legitimate election, was threatening their democratic rights.[103] In Greene's novel, Don Quixote represents Spain's Christianity; Greene's quixotism is intrinsically Christian. Canavaggio has suggested that Greene's *Monsignor Quixote* is more Unamunesque than Cervantic.[104] Greene's knowledge of and admiration for Unamuno leaves no doubt — Zancas proudly declares himself to have been a pupil of Unamuno, professor of Greek and Comparative Linguistics and vice-chancellor of the University of Salamanca. Unamuno had published in 1905 *Vida de Don Quijote y Sancho* [the life of Don Quixote and Sancho] a hermeneutical rewriting of Cervantes's novel, in which he presented the knight as the quintessential symbol of the Spanish people.[105]

No other twentieth-century works bear such an obvious Cervantic mark as Douglas's *Burgher Quixote*, Chesterton's *The Return*, Greene's *Monsignor Quijote* and Chapman's *The Duchess's Diary*.[106] Yet, in addition to Chesterton and Greene, critics have highlighted the influence of Cervantes on Max Beerbohm, Anthony Burgess, Joseph Conrad, John Fowles, Wyndham Lewis, Salman Rushdie, Muriel Spark, Malcolm Lowry, J. B. Priestly, and Virginia Woolf.[107] Albeit the pristine novelistic mould of *Don Quixote* became less and less innovatory, *Don Quixote*'s enormous popularity remained intact in the twentieth century. Theatrical adaptations continued to be written and staged, namely *Don Quixote: A Dramatization of Cervantes' Novel* (1938) by Paul Kester, and *Don Quixote: A Romantic Drama* (1941) by Mabel Dearmer. At the end of the century, popular artists have acknowledged their admiration for Sancho Panza. The song 'No more heroes' (1977), by pop band The Stranglers, mentions him: 'Whatever happened to dear old Lenny? / The great Elmyra and Sancho Panza? / Whatever happened to the heroes?' The squire's name was surprisingly adopted in the 1990s by London indie band Sancho Panza.[108]

The twentieth century was also a time of thriving scholarly interest in Cervantes and *Don Quixote*. England had been the land of the first Cervantes scholars, from Gayton and Bowle to Coleridge.[109] For centuries, most critical analyses appeared in the preliminaries to the translations. The critical opinions expressed by translators such as Motteux (1700) and Smollett (1755) determined to a great extent the perception of *Don Quixote* in England.[110] Yet it was in the last two decades of the nineteenth century that Cervantes scholarship launched and established Spanish studies in Britain. Three new translations were issued in the 1880s, by Alexander

James Duffield (1881), John Ormsby (1885), and Henry Edward Watts (1888), all of which were annotated and included preliminary studies. Of these, Ormsby (an Irishman of English descent who settled in Britain) stands out because of his acute and elegant translation (regarded as one of the best) and also due to his insightful introduction — where he argues that *Don Quixote* must be considered the most influential book in world literature after the Bible.[111] In subsequent years, Cervantes's novel was also discussed in many scholarly works by some of the leading intellectuals of the time. In *An Essay on Comedy* (1897), George Meredith praises the combination of humour and tragedy in *Don Quixote*. In the lecture 'The continuity of Letters', given at the University of Oxford in 1916, Meredith placed *Don Quixote* amongst the finest classic works of world literature. The Romantic perception expressed by Meredith is shared by Arthur Machen in *Hieroglyphics* (1923), where ontological qualities are observed in Don Quixote. In the same period, several essays on Cervantes appeared in England: James Fitzmaurice-Kelly's *Life of Miguel de Cervantes Saavedra* (1892), W. P. Ker's *Don Quixote* (1908), Sir Walter Raleigh's *Don Quixote* (1916), and Sir Herbert Grierson's *Don Quixote, Some Wartime Reflections on Its Character and Influence* (1921). Ker reinforces the Romantic reading of *Don Quixote* by complementing Schelling's scrutiny of its philosophical depth. Ker was also the first to explore the intertextual links between Cervantes and Shakespeare.

Notwithstanding the value of the essays by Ker, Raleigh and Grierson, the impact of Fitzmaurice-Kelly's critical works was considerable in Britain and abroad. His *Life of Miguel de Cervantes Saavedra* was the most accomplished biography of Cervantes at the time of its publication, and remained so until the second half of the twentieth century. He edited Cervantes's works and published studies such as a *History of Spanish Literature*, translated into German, French and Spanish (the latter running to eight editions). A corresponding Member of the Spanish Royal Academy, in 1908 Fitzmaurice-Kelly won the first British chair of Spanish studies, the Gilmour Chair at the University of Liverpool. His intellectual work inspired many, and with him began the modern British school of Cervantes scholarship.

During the twentieth century, research on the Golden Age was the main area of research for British Hispanists. British scholars produced some of the most authoritative studies into that period, e.g. Dorothy Sherman Severin on *Celestina*, Peter Dunn on the picaresque novel, John Elliott and John Lynch on Spanish history, or Alexander Parker and Barry Ife on various literary topics. Yet Cervantes was the centre of academic activity. An exegetical trend was initiated by Peter Russell, for whom *Don Quixote* is essentially a comic book.[112] This line of thought was pursued by Anthony Close in his works *The Romantic Approach to Don Quixote* (1978) and *Cervantes and the Comic Mind of his Age* (2000).[113] However, the Romantic approach, as Close termed it, has been seconded by the great bulk of scholars,[114] and it is so inherently rooted in *Don Quixote* that very few readers interpret it solely as a comic book. The examples are countless: since Edmund Gayton, who envisaged a meaning much more profound than the clumsy and humorous misadventures of Don Quixote, to Fielding's 'good-natured' quixotism, to Dickens's philanthropic Pickwick,[115] to readers outside Britain, in the most remote regions of Europe, e.g. Stein Steinarr, Iceland's best-known poet of the twentieth century.[116] Maurice

Bataillon has presented Mateo Alemán as the precursor of Hobbes's *homo homini lupus*;[117] likewise, *Don Quixote* is the precursor of Romantic sensibility. British scholars have also produced some general studies of *Don Quixote*, namely Riley's *Don Quixote* (1986), Russell's *Cervantes*, and Close's *Cervantes: Don Quixote* (1990).[118] Yet there is one book which stands out within Cervantes scholarship: Riley's *Cervantes's Theory of the Novel* (1962), where the author achieves to systematize Cervantes's ideas of the novel as a genre and to prove cogently that Cervantes 'was one of the first European writers — perhaps the very first — to have had a theory of the novel of any considerable scope at all'.[119]

Riley's books were translated into Spanish,[120] and his impact on Cervantes studies has remained paramount. Although Cervantes studies are no longer the chief topic for research within British Hispanism, and *Don Quixote* is no longer regarded as a canon by novelists and playwrights — perhaps because they are not in need of one — , Cervantes and his knight still maintain their status as Spain's best-known author and character. In the twentieth century, Chapman has continued his series of *Don Quixote* sequels with the publication of *Sancho's Golden Age* (2004) and *Pasamonte's Life* (2005). In *Sancho's Golden Age*, Sancho travels to the mountains, where he attempts to recreate the pastoral adventures which in Cervantes's novel he encouraged Alonso Quijano to live. *Pasamonte's Life* is Pasamonte's autobiography, about which this character tells Don Quixote in the 1605 novel. In 2003, Julian Branston published his debut novel *The Eternal Quest* (published in the United States under the title *Tilting at Windmills: A Novel of Cervantes and the Errant Knight*) a fiction that tells of Cervantes's life and writing of *Don Quixote* which shows the fascination that Cervantes still holds in the twenty-first century.

In sum, after four centuries of inspiring imitations, emulations, and adaptations, *Don Quixote* has deservedly earned its status as the most influential foreign book in British literary history.

Notes to Chapter 1

1. This thesis was posited by Ian Watt in his *Rise of the Novel. Studies in Defoe, Richardson and Fielding* (London: Chatto and Windus, 1957), and is today contended by many. In Howard Mancing's words, 'The thesis known as "the rise of the novel" in eighteenth-century England is patently false'. In Howard Mancing, 'The Quixotic Novel in British and American Literature', *CIEFL Bulletin*, 15–16 (2005–06), 1–18 (p. 1). For a monographic criticism of Watt's theory see Jenny Mander (ed.), *Remapping the Novel. The Rise of the Novel in Europe* (Oxford: Diderot Society, 2007).
2. Of these three texts, *Don Quixote* is the best known internationally. Discussions on the novelistic nature of *Don Quixote* are countless, and range from those who refuse to term it a novel to those who consider it the first novel. For a recent discussion of this topic see James A. Parr, *Don Quixote: A Touchstone for Literary Criticism* (Kassel: Edition Reichenberger, 2005), which is a reworking of his *Don Quixote: An Anatomy of Subversive Discourse* (Newark, DE: Juan de la Cuesta, 1988), and Antonio Garrido Domínguez, *Aspectos de la novela en Cervantes* (Alcalá de Henares: Centro de Estudios Cervantinos, 2007). Whilst Parr considers *Don Quixote* a pre-novel, Garrido Domínguez argues cogently that Cervantes's text is a novel. For a summary of the critical stances in the last twenty-five years, with a complete bibliography, see Michel Moner, 'Cervantes y la invención de la novela: estado de la cuestión', in *La invención de la novela*, ed. by Jean Canavaggio (Madrid: Casa de Velázquez, 1999), pp. 233–68. The most recent studies that vindicate the novelistic nature of *Guzmán de Alfarache* are Pedro M. Piñero Ramírez, 'La

publicación del *Guzmán de Alfarache* (Madrid, 1599) y la invención de la novela moderna', in *Atalayas del Guzmán de Alfarache*, ed. by Pedro M. Piñero Ramírez (Seville: Universidad de Sevilla and Diputación de Sevilla, 2002), pp. 11–28, and Edmond Cros, '*Guzmán de Alfarache* y los orígenes de la novela moderna', in *Atalayas del Guzmán de Alfarache*, pp. 167–76. Fernando Lázaro Carreter, the best-reputed Spanish literary scholar of the second half of the twentieth century, proved that *Lazarillo de Tormes* is a novel, in *Lazarillo de Tormes en la picaresca* (Barcelona: Ariel, 1972). Lázaro Carreter's views have been seconded by many, e.g. Antonio Rey Hazas, *La novela picaresca* (Madrid: Anaya, 1990) and J. A. G. Ardila, *El género picaresco en la crítica literaria* (Madrid: Biblioteca Nueva, 2008).

3. Cf. J. A. G. Ardila, 'La tradición picaresca española en Inglaterra', *Bulletin of Hispanic Studies*, 76 (1999), 453–69.

4. See Gustav Ungerer, 'English Criminal Biography and Guzmán de Alfarache's Fall from Rogue to Highwayman, Pander and Astrologer', *Bulletin of Hispanic Studies*, 76 (1999), 189–97.

5. Research conducted into the English picaresque is copious. For a detailed bibliographical review see J. A. G. Ardila, *El género picaresco en la crítica literaria*. For Defoe see, *inter alia*, J. A. G. Ardila, 'La tradición picaresca española en Inglaterra', and Edward H. Friedman, *The Antiheroine's Voice: Narrative Discourse and Transformations of the Picaresque* (Columbia: University of Missouri Press, 1987). For Smollett see Robert Giddins, *The Tradition of Smollett* (London: Methuen, 1967). For Fielding see Rosa Pastalosky, *Henry Fielding y la tradición picaresca* (Buenos Aires: Solar, 1970), although Fielding's novels cannot be considered *picaresque*. Many general works on the picaresque in Europe have been published in the past decades. The most influential of these is Alexander A. Parker, *Literature and the Delinquent: The Picaresque Novel in Spain and Europe, 1599–1753* (Edinburgh: Edinburgh University Press, 1967), translated into Spanish as *Los pícaros en la literatura. La novela picaresca en España y Europa (1599–1753)* (Madrid: Gredos, 1971). A very clear account is given in Harry Sieber's *The Picaresque* (London: Methuen, 1977).

6. In English and in other languages. The most recent example of the excessively inclusive interpretation of the picaresque in Europe is provided in *Das Paradigma des Pikaresken / The Paradigm of the Picaresque*, ed. by Christoph Ehland and Robert Fajen (Heidelberg: Winter, 2007), where even the film maker Michael Moore is credited with belonging to the picaresque category.

7. Anthony Burgess, *English Literature* (Harlow: Longman, 1996), p. 159.

8. For a review of the many studies of the picaresque see J. A. G. Ardila, *El género picaresco en la crítica literaria*. The most recent definitions of the picaresque novel as a genre are in Florencio Sevilla, 'Presentación', in *La novela picaresca española*, ed. by Florencio Sevilla (Madrid: Castalia, 2001) and J. A. G. Ardila, *El género picaresco en la crítica literaria*. For Florencio Sevilla (p. xii), a picaresque novel is characterized for (1) being (generally but not always) the work of an amateur writer who (2) holds strong political bias, (3) a text which relates the story of an antihero, (4) is written in the form of an autobiography, and (5) is dialogic. In *El género picaresco en la crítica literaria* I describe the picaresque as (1) a text whose narrator's aims lie in presenting and justifying his final situation (e.g. the rumours about the narrator's adulterous wife in *Lazarillo*; the main character's religious conversion in *Guzmán*), (2) of a satirical nature, which results from the author's political bias, given in an ironic style that conforms with the maxim *nulla esthetica sine ethica*, and (3) with a rogue as a protagonist, a rogue being an individual who becomes a rogue by necessity, never by inclination, who is a social outsider, who survives by using his wit, and who stubbornly seeks social ascent.

9. Walter L. Reed, *An Exemplary History of the Novel: The Quixotic versus the Picaresque* (Chicago and London: University of Chicago Press, 1981), p. 93.

10. For a list of these see J. A. G. Ardila, *Cervantes en Inglaterra: el Quijote en los albores de la novela británica* (Liverpool: Liverpool University Press, 2006), pp. 7–11.

11. The Cervantine words included in the *OED* are: quixote (1648), quixotism (1688), quixotery (1718), quixotic (1815), quixotish (1810), quixotical (1850), quixotically (1862), quixoticism (1882), quixotize (1831), Don Quixote (1870), Don Quixotism (1719), Dulcinea (1748), and Sancho (1870). Likewise the *Trésor de la langue française* and *Base historique du vocabulaire fraçaise* include: Don Quichotte (1631), donquichottisme (1738), donquichottesque (1887), donquichotterie (1792), quichottesque (1943), dulcinée (1718), maritorne (1798). For the Cervantine vocabulary in the

Spanish language, with a list of English and French words, see Pedro Álvarez de Miranda, 'La estela lingüística del *Quijote*', in *El Quijote en el Siglo de las Luces*, ed. by Enrique Jiménez (Alicante: Universidad de Alicante, 2006), pp. 43–78.

12. The only study of Cervantic influence in Europe is Jean Canavaggio, *Don Quichotte du livre au mythe. Quatre siècles d'errance* (Paris: Fayard, 2005), translated into Spanish as *Don Quijote, del mito al libro* (Madrid: Espasa-Calpe, 2006).

13. Apud Dale B. J. Randall and Jackson C. Boswell, *Cervantes in Seventeenth-Century England: The Tapestry Turned* (Oxford: Oxford University Press, 2009), this book is in print at the time of writing. Edwin B. Knowles, 'Allusions to *Don Quixote* before 1660', *Philological Quarterly*, 20 (1941), 573–86, found eighty allusions to characters and passages from *Don Quixote* before 1660.

14. Cf. Juan Bautista Avalle Arce, 'Quijotes y quijotismos del inglés', *Ojáncano*, 2 (1989), 58–66 (p. 59); James Fitzmaurice-Kelly, 'Cervantes in England', *Proceedings of the British Academy*, 3 (1905–06), 11–30 (p. 17).

15. See J. A. G. Ardila, *Cervantes en Inglaterra*, pp. 18–19.

16. A. Lo Ré, in *Essays on the Periphery of the Quijote* (Newark, DE: Juan de la Cuesta, 1991) suggests that the translation of Part II, generally attributed to Shelton, was actually carried out by a Leonard Digges.

17. Luis Astrana Marín, *Vida ejemplar y heroica de Miguel de Cervantes Saavedra*, 7 vols (Madrid: Instituto Editorial Reus, 1948–58); Jean Canavaggio, *Cervantès* (Paris: Fayard, 1986), translated into Spanish as *Cervantes* (Madrid: Espasa-Calpe, 2003).

18. Cf. Canavaggio, *Cervantes*, p. 308.

19. Cf. Julio César Santoyo, 'El libro español en la Inglaterra isabelina', *Estudios Literarios Ingleses: Renacimiento y Barroco*, ed. by S. Onega (Madrid: Cátedra, 1986), pp. 77–98 (p. 89); José María Ruiz Ruiz, 'Diólogo entre Espana e Inglaterra en la época del Renacimiento', *ES: Revista de Filología Inglesa*, 14 (1990), 61–80 (p. 67).

20. Cf. J. A. G. Ardila, *Cervantes en Inglaterra*, p. 135.

21. Cf. José Manuel Barrio Marco, 'La proyección artística y literaria de Cervantes y Don Quijote en la Inglaterra del siglo XVII: los cauces de recepción en el contexto político y cultural de la época', in *La huella de Cervantes y del Quijote en la cultura anglosajona*, ed. by José Manuel Barrio Marco and María José Crespo Allué (Valladolid: Universidad de Valladolid, 2007), pp. 19–72 (pp. 19–20).

22. Cf. Gustav Ungerer, 'Recovering Unrecorded Quixote Allusions in Ephemeral Publications of the Late 1650s', *Bodleian Library Record*, 17 (2000), 65–69 (p. 65).

23. The title of this story has usually been translated into English as 'The Curious Impertinent'. Yet this rendering is incorrect. In the Spanish title, *curioso* is a noun and *impertinente* is an adjective. Conversely, in the English translation *curious* is an adjective and *impertinent* a noun. The *Gran Diccionario Oxford Español–Inglés, Inglés–Español* gives the following translations of *curioso*: 'onlooker' and 'busybody'. Since a straightforward translation without paraphrasing seems problematic, I shall here prefer the established rendering 'The Curious Impertinent', although I am fully aware of its unsuitability.

24. Cf. Edgar Allison Peers, 'Cervantes in England', *Bulletin of Spanish Studies*, 25 (1947), 226–38; Trudi L. Darby, 'Cervantes in England: the Influence of Golden-Age Prose Fiction on Jacobean Drama, c.1615–1625', *Bulletin of Hispanic Studies*, 74 (1997), 425–41.

25. Apud J. A. G. Ardila, 'Fletcher, John', in *Gran Enciclopedia Cervantina*, ed. by Carlos Alvar (Madrid: Castalia, 2005–07).

26. Thomas Lodge, like Shelton an exiled Catholic in Flanders, has been proposed as Shelton's famous friend by A. G. Lo Ré in *Essays on the Periphery of the Quixote*. Lo Ré also suggests that the English translation of Part II was not by Shelton, but by Leonard Digges. Sandra Gerhard has proposed Richard Verstegan, an English Catholic who like Shelton lived in Holland. See Sandra Gerhard, *Don Quixote and the Shelton Translation* (Madrid and Potomac: José Porrúa, 1982).

27. P. Reyher, *Les Masques Anglais: Etudes sur les ballets et la vie de cour en Anglaterre (1512–1640)* (Paris: Libraire Hachette, 1909), pp. 327–28.

28. Cf. Canavaggio, *Cervantes*, p. 356.

29. More controversial is the case of *The Queen of Corinth* and *The Beggar's Bush*, and also the

borrowing of the pyramid in John Webster's *The Duchess of Malfi* (possibly written before 1605). See F. M. Todd, 'Webster and Cervantes', *Modern Language Review*, 51 (1956), 321–23; and N. W. Bawcutt, '*Don Quixote*, Part I, and *The Duchess of Malfi*', *Modern Language Review*, 66 (1971), 488–91.

30. On Godomar see Alfonso Par, *Shakespeare y la literatura española* (Madrid: Victoriano Suárez, 1935); and Patricia Shaw, 'Testimonios ingleses contemporáneos sobre la figura de Godomar', *ES: Revista de Filología Inglesa*, 9 (1979), 109–48.

31. Apud Charles Hamilton (ed.), *Cardenio; or, The Second Maiden's Tragedy* (Lakewood, CO: Glenbridge, 1994).

32. Luis Astrana Marín, 'Estudio preliminary', in *William Shakespeare. Obras completas* (Madrid: Aguilar, 1932), pp. 13–130 (p. 20). In disagreement with Astrana is Pedro Duque, *España en Shakespeare* (Bilbao: Universidad de Deusto, 1991), p. 25.

33. 'Entremés' in Spanish is a dramatic interlude.

34. Fitzmaurice-Kelly, 'Cervantes in England'.

35. For a more detailed account of the 1610–1625 period see the most recent studies: Trudi L. Darby, 'Cervantes in England: The Influence of Golden-Age Prose Fiction on Jacobean Drama, *c.*1615–1625', and J. A. G. Ardila and Pedro Javier Pardo García, 'Reino Unido', in *Gran Enciclopedia Cervantina*. See also: Edwin B. Knowles, *Four Articles on Don Quixote in England* (New York: New York University Press, 1941), Francisco Ayala, 'Los dos amigos', *Revista de Occidente*, 10 (1965), 287–306; William Peery, '*The Curious Impertinent* in *Amend for Ladies*', *Hispanic Review*, 14 (1946), 344–53; Abraham Rosenbach, '*The Curious Impertinent* in English Dramatic Literature before Shelton's Translation of *Don Quixote*', *Modern Language Notes*, 17 (1902), 357–67; John, Freehafer, '*Cardenio*, by Shakespeare and Fletcher', *PMLA*, 84 (1969), 501–13; Patricia Grant, 'Cervantes' *El casamiento engañoso* and Fletcher's *Rule a Wife and Have a Wife*', *Hispanic Review*, 12 (1944) 330–38; Alejandro Ramírez, 'Cervantes y Fletcher: El *Persiles* y *The Custom of the Country*', in *Homenaje a Sherman H. Eoff* (Madrid: Castalia, 1970), pp. 203–20; C. E. Weller and C. A. Colahan, 'Cervantine Imagery and Sex-Role Reversal in Fletcher and Massinger's *The Custom of the Country*', *Cervantes*, 5. 1 (1985), 27–43; A. Argelli, 'Una "Novela ejemplar" al teatro: hacia un estudio de las adaptaciones teatrales inglesas de Cervantes', *Hispanófila*, 133 (2001), 53–68.

36. Cf. Canavaggio, *Don Quichotte du livre au mythe*, p. 70.

37. The most recent of critics are Ardila, *Cervantes en Inglaterra*, pp. 35–36, and Annalisa Argelli, 'De Cervantes a Butler: análisis de una transposición', *Estudios Ingleses de la Universidad Complutense*, 7 (1999), 265–78 (pp. 266–67).

38. Vide J. A. G. Ardila, 'Thomas D'Urfey y la recepción del *Quijote* en el siglo XVII inglés', *Hispanic Research Journal*, 10. 2 (forthcoming 2009).

39. Edmund Gayton, *Pleasant Notes upon Don Quixote* (London: W. Hunt, 1654), p. 9.

40. Gayton, *Pleasant Notes*, p. 5.

41. On Bowle see R. Merritt Cox, *An English Ilustrado: The Reverend John Bowle* (Bern: Peter Lang, 1977). The most recent study is Daniel Eisenberg, 'The Man who Made *Don Quijote* a Classic: The Rev. John Bowle', in *Between Shakespeare and Cervantes: Trails Along the Renaissance*, ed. by Zenón Luis-Martínez and Luis Gómez Canseco (Newark, DE: Juan de la Cuesta, 2006), pp. 39–71.

42. See Canavaggio, *Don Quichotte du livre au mythe*, and J. A. G. Ardila, 'D'Urfey, Thomas', in *Gran Enciclopedia Cervantina*.

43. Which I have done in 'Thomas D'Urfey y la recepción del *Quijote* en el siglo XVII inglés'.

44. References to *The Comical History* are taken from Thomas D'Urfey, *The Comical History of Don Quixote* (London: J. Darby, 1729).

45. Namely Stuart M. Tave, *The Amiable Humorist: A Study of the Comic Theory and Criticism of the Eighteenth and Early Nineteenth Centuries* (Chicago and London: Chicago University Press, 1960); A. P. Barton, 'Cervantes the Man Seen through English Eyes in the Seventeenth and Eighteenth Centuries', *Bulletin of Hispanic Studies*, 45 (1968), 1–15; Susan Staves, 'Don Quijote in Eighteenth-Century England', *Comparative Literature*, 24. 3 (1972), 193–215; J. A. G. Ardila, 'Traducción y recepción del *Quijote* en Gran Bretaña (1612–1774)', *Anales Cervantinos*, 37 (2005), 253–65; José Manuel Lucía Megías, *Leer el Quijote en imágenes. Hacia una teoría de los modelos iconográficos* (Madrid: Calambur, 2006).

46. Quoted in P. Cherchi, *Capitoli di critica cervantina (1605–1789)* (Rome: Bulzoni, 1977), p. 71.

47. Francis Carr has gone as far as to claim that Bacon is the actual author of *Don Quixote*. Carr argues that the lack of documents regarding Cervantes and the immediate success of *Don Quixote* in Britain prove, alongside certain textual evidences, that Bacon (and not Cervantes) was the author. Among these textual evidences, Carr argues the times Cide Hamete Benengeli is mentioned, that this name may mean Sir Hamlet of England (i.e. Cid Hamete Ben-Engeli). This hypothesis is, of course, implausible. See Francis Carr, *Who Wrote Don Quixote* (London: Xlibris Corporation, 2004).

48. José María Rodríguez García, 'Solitude and Procreation in Francis Bacon's Scientific Writings: The Spanish Connection', *Comparative Literature Studies*, 35. 3 (1998), 278–300 (pp. 278–79).

49. Thomas Hobbes, *Leviathan* (Oxford: Oxford University Press, 1960), p. 10, cited in Roland Paulson, *Don Quixote in England: The Aesthetics of Laughter* (Baltimore: Johns Hopkins University Press, 1998), p. 8.

50. Roland Paulson, *Don Quixote in England*, p. 9.

51. Also cited in Paulson, *Don Quixote in England*, p. 9.

52. Cf. John Harrison and Peter Lasnett, *The Library of John Locke* (Oxford: Oxford University Press, 1965), p. 104.

53. See Juana Bando Domínguez, 'La huella cervantina en *The Battle of the Books* de Jonathan Swift', in *La huella de Cervantes y del Quixote en la cultura anglosajona*, pp. 105–12; Juan de Dios Torralbo Caballero and Cristina María Gómez Fernández, 'La influencia de *Viaje del Parnaso* en *The Battle of the Books*', in *La huella de Cervantes y del Quixote en la cultura anglosajona*, pp. 113–20.

54. Addison's reading of *Don Quixote* is the object of Paulson's book *Don Quixote in England*, a study of the Cervantean aesthetics of laughter as Addison understood it.

55. See Patricia Tabarés Pérez and Leonor Pérez Ruiz, 'The Praise of Quixotic Delicacy in David Hume's "Of the Standard of Taste"', in *La huella de Cervantes y del Quixote en la cultura anglosajona*, pp. 122–31.

56. That *Don Quixote* became the most influential book on eighteenth-century English writers was suggested unreservedly by Frederick R. Karl, *A Reader's Guide to the Development of the English Novel in the Eighteenth Century* (London: Thames and Hudson, 1975), pp. 55–67.

57. Howard Mancing, *The Cervantes Encyclopedia* (Westport and London: Greenwood Press, 2004), has noted that *The Fatal Dowry* 'retained great popularity into the nineteenth century, and Lotario became so well-known a character that his name entered English by antonomasia (alongside Don Juan and Casanova) as that of a seducer' (p. 629).

58. Cf. J. A. G. Ardila, 'Sancho Panza en Inglaterra: *Sancho at Court* de Ayres y *Barataria* de Pilon', *Bulletin of Hispanic Studies*, 82 (2005), 551–69.

59. Frederick Pilon, *Barataria; or, Sancho Turn'd Governor* (London: W. Lowndes, 1793), p. 7.

60. Henry Fielding, *Don Quixote in England. A Comedy. As it is Acted in the New Theatre in the Hay-Market* (London: J. Watts, 1734), this page, as all others in the preliminaries, is not numbered.

61. It has been suggested by Knowles, 'Cervantes and English Literature', in *Cervantes Across the Centuries*, ed. by Á. Flores and M. J. Benardete (New York: Gordian Press, 1969), pp. 277–303: 'Along with the Bible, Bunyan, and Shakespeare it [*Don Quixote*] has been a book that almost every literate English-man for the past two hundred years has read, at least in part' (p. 302).

62. For the latest study of the illustrations of *Don Quixote* editions in Europe see Lucía Megías, *Leer el Quijote en imágenes*.

63. Eisenberg, 'The Man who Made *Don Quijote* a Classic: The Rev. John Bowle', pp. 61–64.

64. For a repertoire of quotations see Knowles, 'Cervantes and English Literature', pp. 289–92.

65. Sarah F. Wood, *Quixotic Fictions of the USA, 1792–1815* (Oxford: Oxford University Press, 2005), p. vii.

66. Wood, *Quixotic Fictions of the USA, 1792–1815*, p. vii.

67. Namely Ronald Paulson, *Don Quixote in England*, Brean S. Hammond, 'Mid-Century Quixotism and the Defence of the Novel', *Eighteenth-Century Fiction*, 10. 3 (1998), 247–68, and J. A. G. Ardila, 'La influencia de la narrativa del Siglo de Oro en la novela británica del XVIII', *Revista de Literatura*, 63. 126 (2001), 401–23, and 'Recepción de la narrativa áurea en la Gran Bretaña setecentina', in *Cervantes en Inglaterra*, pp. 7–31. Harry Levin, 'The Quixotic Principle: Cervantes and Other Novelists', *Harvard English Studies*, 1 (1970), 45–66, uses the terms 'imitators' and 'emulators'. Writers of quixotic fiction imitate, whereas writers of Cervantean

novels emulate. This is a distinction formulated by Spanish thinker Ortega y Gasset. Wood does refer to Paulson and also to Diana de Armas Wilson, *Cervantes, the Novel, and the New World* (Oxford: Oxford University Press, 2000), p. 11.

68. Apud J. A. G. Ardila, 'Recepción de la narrativa áurea en la Gran Bretaña setecentina', pp. 27–28.

69. The first of these critics was Miriam Rossiter Small, 'The Female Quixote and Other Quixotic Imitations of the Eighteenth Century', in *Charlotte Ramsey Lennox: An Eighteenth-Century Lady of Letters* (New Haven: Yale University Press, 1935), pp. 64–117. Small is undecided about which work, Cervantes's or Lennox's is to be credited with being the inspiration for female fictions. Acknowledging that *The Female Quixote* was the first of many other imitations of *Don Quixote*, Small first notes that 'these famous quixotic characters from well-known novels [by Fielding and Smollett] are not the only influences of Cervantes' masterpiece in this century. There grew up a school of imitations in title and general plan, of which Mrs. Lennox's was the most successful' (p. 93). However, she subsequently suggests that 'The first literary influence from *The Female Quixote* is to be seen in an obscure play never acted but published in 1758', referring to *Angelica*, and presenting Lennox's novel as the model for the quixotic fictions that followed her. Elaine M. Kauvar, 'Jane Austen and *The Female Quixote*', *Studies in the Novel*, 2 (1970), 211–21, presented a letter from Jane Austen to her sister Cassandra in which the author of *Northanger Abbey* praised *The Female Quixote*. Jane Austen, *Letters*, ed. by R. W. Chapman, 2 vols (Oxford: Clarendon Press, 1932), I, 173: 'We changed it [reading *Alphonsine*] for "The Female Quixote", which now makes our evening amusement; to me a very high one, as I find the work quite equal to what I remembered it'. Staves takes this letter as the telltale evidence that Austen found inspiration in Lennox rather than in Cervantes and that 'Jane Austen might have been attracted to *The Female Quixote* for something more significant than simply its stylistic techniques' (p. 212). In the opinion of this scholar, Austen was influenced by Lennox alone, and both their works are feminist examples of the *Bildungsroman*. Kauvar's ideas were later taken by Pedro Javier Pardo García, 'El Quijote femenino como variante del mito quijotesco', in *Actas del V Congreso Internacional de la Asociación de Cervantistas*, ed. by Alicia Villar Lecumberri (Lisbon: Asociación de Cervantistas, 2004), pp. 1627–44. Pardo, however, does not refer to Kauvar.

70. Staves, 'Don Quijote in Eighteenth-Century England': 'In the last few decades of the eighteenth century certain novelists realized that the satirical possibilities of the Quixote idea were not limited to attacks on various kinds of fiction' (p. 199).

71. Apud J. A. G. Ardila, 'Cervantes y la *quixotic fiction*: la parodia de géneros', *Anales Cervantinos*, 34 (1998), 145–68, and J. A. G. Ardila, 'La parodia de géneros: *The Female Quixote* de Charlotte Lennox and *Northanger Abbey* de Jane Austen'.

72. The title page attributed the work to Charlotte Lennox. However, Jerry Beasley has argued that *The Political Quixote* is one of several works wrongly attributed to Lennox. See Jerry C. Beasley, 'Charlotte Lennox', *DLB*, 39 (1985), 306–12.

73. The most detailed survey of quixotic fiction is in Small, 'The Female Quixote and Other Quixotic Imitations of the Eighteenth Century'. See also Staves, 'Don Quijote in Eighteenth-Century England'; Judith Sloman, 'The Female Quixote as an Eighteenth-Century Character Type', *Transactions of the Samuel Johnson Society of the Northwest*, 4 (1976), 86–101; Sally C. Hoople, 'The Spanish, English and American Quixotes', *Anales Cervantinos*, 22 (1984), 119–42; and Sarah F. Wood, *Quixotic Fictions of the USA, 1792–1815*, pp. 8–28.

74. These works have been extensively discussed in Wood, *Quixotic Fictions of the USA, 1792–1812*. For a general view on the influence of Cervantes upon American literature see M. F. Heiser, 'Cervantes in the United States', *Hispanic Review*, 15 (1947), 409–35. On specific authors see George Santana, 'Tom Sawyer and Don Quixote', *Mark Twain Quarterly*, 9. 2 (1952), 1–3; Joseph Harry Karkey, 'Don Quixote and American Fiction through Mark Twain' (unpublished doctoral thesis, University of Tennessee, 1967); Joseph Harry Karkey, 'The *Don Quixote* of the Frontier: Brackenridge's *Modern Chivalry*', *EAL*, 7 (1973), 193–203; Harry Levin, 'Don Quixote and *Moby Dick*', in Flores & Bernadete (eds.), *Cervantes Across the Centuries*, pp. 227–36; Henry B. Wonham, 'Mark Twain: The American Cervantes', in *Cervantes in the English-Speaking World*, pp. 159–61.

75. See Paulson, *Don Quixote in England*; Hammond 'Mid-Century Quixotism and the Defence of the Novel'; Ardila, *Cervantes en Inglaterra*.

76. See J. A. G. Ardila, 'La horma narratológica: *Tom Jones* de Henry Fielding', in *Cervantes en Inglaterra*, pp. 49–79.

77. Heinz-Joachim Müllenbrock, 'Don Quijote and Eighteenth-Century English Literature', in *Intercultural Encounters: Studies in English Literature*, ed. by Heinz Antor and Kevin L. Cope (Heidelberg: Winter, 1999), pp. 197–209 (p. 207).

78. Staves, 'Don Quijote in Eighteenth-Century England', has called Shandy an 'ideological quixote' (p. 202).

79. Laurence Sterne, *The Life and Opinions of Tristram Shandy, Gentleman* (Harmondsworth: Penguin, 1997), p. 51. Further references to *Tristram Shandy* are taken from this edition.

80. They are as 'goodhearted [and] innocent' as Don Quixote, writes Edward Niehus in 'Quixotic Figures in the Novels of Sterne', *Essays in Literature*, 22 (1985), 41–60 (p. 43).

81. Reed, *An Exemplary History of the Novel*, p. 144.

82. See Wayne C. Booth, 'The Self-Conscious Narrator in Comic Fiction before *Tristram Shandy*', *PMLA*, 67 (1952), 163–85.

83. Laurence Sterne, *Letters of Laurence Sterne*, ed. by Lewis Perry Curtis (Oxford: Clarendon Press, 1965), p. 77.

84. This is, roughly, the conclusion given by Felicitas Kleber, 'Laurence Sterne's *Tristram Shandy* and *Don Quixote*', in *Cervantes in the English-Speaking World: New Essays*, ed. by Darío Fernández-Morera and Michael Hanke (Barcelona and Kassel: Edition Reichenberger, 2005), pp. 65–80 (p. 80).

85. Cf. J. A. G. Ardila, 'La parodia de géneros: *The Female Quixote* de Charlotte Lennox y *Northanger Abbey* de Jane Austen', pp. 102–32 (pp. 126–27).

86. On *Love and Freindship* and *Juvenalia* see A. Walton Litz, *Jane Austen: A Study of her Artistic Development* (London: Chatto and Windus, 1965).

87. Cf. Mary Lascelles, *Jane Austen and Her Work* (Oxford: Clarendon Press, 1939); Henrietta Ten Harmsel, *Jane Austen: A Study in Fictional Conventions* (London and The Hague: Mouton, 1964).

88. Tobias Smollett, 'The Life of Cervantes', in Miguel de Cervantes, *The History and Adventures of the Renowned Don Quixote*, trans. by Tobias Smollett (New York: Random House, 2001), p. 17.

89. Tobias Smollett, 'The Life of Cervantes', p. 19. For a more detailed discussion of this biography see J. A. G. Ardila, 'El ideal caballeresco y sentimental a partir de Smollett (1755)', in *Cervantes en Inglaterra*, pp. 40–45.

90. Henry Fielding, *Rape Upon Rape; or, The Justice Caught in his Own Trap* (London: Watts, 1930), p. 31.

91. The best study to date of *Don Quixote* as myth is Alexander Welsh, *Reflections on the Hero as a Quixote* (Princeton, NJ: Princeton University Press, 1981). See also Ian Watt, *Myths of Modern Idealism: Faust, Don Quixote, Don Juan, Robinson Crusoe* (Cambridge: Cambridge University Press, 1996).

92. Henry Brooke, *Man of Quality*, 2 vols (London: W. Johnston, 1766), I, 153–54.

93. See Samuel Taylor Coleridge, *Lectures, 1808–19: On Literature*, ed. by R. A. Foakes (Princeton, NJ: Princeton University Press, 1987).

94. For a discussion of Rowson's *Trip to Parnassus* see J. A. G. Ardila, *Charlotte Temple. Estudio de tradiciones, géneros y fuentes* (Cáceres: Universidad de Extremadura, 2002), pp. 227–28.

95. Susana Haswell Rowson, *Slaves in Algiers; or, A Struggle for Freedom* (Philadelphia: Wrigley and Berriman, 1794), p. ii.

96. No research has been published on any of these plays except for one paragraph in Edwin B. Knowles 'Cervantes and English Literature', pp. 297–98, and the article J. A. G. Ardila, 'Morrison, George', in *Gran Enciclopedia Cervantina*.

97. G. E. Morrison, *Alonzo Quixano, otherwise Don Quixote: A Dramatization of the Novel of Cervantes, and especially of those parts which he left unwritten* (London: Elkin Mathews, n.d.), p. iv. On the title page of the copy in Cambridge University Library there is the year 1895, hand-written. The handwriting is the same as in the dedication signed by Morrison.

98. The list is provided in Mancing, *The Cervantes Encyclopedia*, p. 127. See also Mancing's chapter in this volume.

99. John Forster, *The Life of Charles Dickens* (London: Dent, 1948), p. 11.

100. Reed, *An Exemplary History of the Novel*, p. 182.

101. Douglas Blackburn, *A Burgher Quixote* (Cape Town and Johannesburg: David Philip, 1984), p. 15.

102. Cf. Pilar Vega Rodríguez, 'El regreso de D. Quijote de Chesterton. Tradición y utopía', *Anales Cervantinos*, 37 (2005), 239–52 (pp. 244–45).

103. For Catholicism and *Monsignor Quixote* see John F. Desmond, 'The Heart of (the) Matter: The Mystery of the Real in *Monsignor Quixote*', *Religion and Literature*, 22. 1 (1990), 59–77; G. Holderness, '"Knight-Errant or Faith"?: *Monsignor Quixote* as "Catholic Fiction"', *Journal of Literature and Theology*, 7 (1993), 259–83; Eric J. Ziolkowski, *Santification of Don Quixote: From Hidalgo to Priest* (University Park: Pennsylvania State University Press, 1991).

104. Apud Jean Canavaggio, '*Monseñor Don Quijote*, de Graham Greene, o el penúltimo avatar del quijotismo', in *Actas del coloquio cervantino, Würzburg 1983*, ed. by Theodor Berchem and Hugo Laintenberger (Münster: Aschendorffsche Verlagsbuchhandlung, 1987), pp. 1–10.

105. Cf. Stephen G. H. Roberts, *Miguel de Unamuno o la creación del intelectual moderno español* (Salamanca: Ediciones Universidad de Salamanca, 2007), pp. 73–107.

106. On Chapman's *The Duchess's Diary*, see Edward Friedman's chapter in this volume.

107. See Mancing, *The Cervantes Encyclopedia*, p. 127; Alberto Lázaro Lafuente, 'Estampas del *Quijote* en la novela británica contemporánea', in *La huella de Cervantes en la cultura anglosajona*, pp. 253–77.

108. See <www.sanchopanza.org> [accessed 6 February 2008].

109. See Frans De Bruyn's chapter in this volume.

110. See J. A. G. Ardila, 'Traducción y recepción del *Quijote* en Gran Bretaña, 1612–1774'.

111. For a discussion of Ormsby's translation and introduction see J. A. G. Ardila, 'Ormsby, John', in *Gran Enciclopedia Cervantina*.

112. Peter Russell, '*Don Quijote* y la risa a carcajadas', in *Temas de 'La Celestina'* (Barcelona: Ariel, 1978), pp. 406–39.

113. *The Romantic Approach to Don Quixote* (Cambridge: Cambridge University Press, 1978), and *Cervantes and the Comic Mind of his Age* (Oxford: Oxford University Press, 2000).

114. The strongest arguments have been put forward in J. G. Weiger, *The Substance of Cervantes* (Cambridge: Cambridge University Press, 1985); G. Lo Ré, 'The Three Deaths of Don Quixote: Comments in Favour of the Romantic Approach', *Cervantes*, 4 (1989), 21–41; A. Sicroff, 'En torno al *Quijote* como obra cómica', *Actas del II Coloquio Internacional de la Asociación de Cervantistas* (Barcelona: Anthropos, 1991), pp. 353–66; and Anthony Cascardi, '"Comi-tragedia" in Cervantes: *Don Quixote* and the Genealogy of the "Funny Book"', *CIEFL Bulletin*, 15–16 (2005–06), 19–38.

115. It was pointed out in J. A. G. Ardila, *Cervantes en Inglaterra* (p. 3, note 8) that the adjective *pickwickian* in English means 'good-natured'.

116. Stein Steinarr (1908–58) is the author of the poem 'Don Quijóte Ávarpar Vindmyllurnar' [Don Quixote conquers the windmills], where the knight is presented as 'hinn aumkunnarverdi riddari réttlætisins' [the aching knight of justice], 'verjandi sakleysisins' [defender of innocence], to whom God gave 'fulltingi sannleikans, hins hreina, djúpa, eilífa sannaleika' [the support of truth, of pure, deep and eternal truth]. Steinarr finishes his poem: 'Med hálfum sanneleika besrt ég gegn algerri lygi' [With my half truth I fight against full lies]. The poem was reprinted in José Antonio Fernández Romero, 'Otro poema islandés sobre don Quijote', *Anales Cervantinos*, 37 (2005), 323–25.

117. Joseph Ricapito, 'En la mente de Mateo Alemán', in *Atalayas del Guzmán de Alfarache*, pp. 113–39.

118. Edward C. Riley, *Don Quixote* (London: Allen & Unwin, 1986); Peter Russell, *Cervantes* (Oxford and New York: Oxford University Press, 1985); Anthony J. Close, *Cervantes: Don Quixote* (Cambridge: Cambridge University Press, 1990).

119. Edward C. Riley, *Cervantes's Theory of the Novel* (Oxford: Clarendon Press, 1962), p. 221.

120. *Cervantes's Theory of the Novel* appeared as *Teoría de la novela en Cervantes*, trans. by Carlos Sahagún (Madrid: Taurus, 1971) and *Don Quixote* as *Introducción al Quijote*, trans. by Enrique Torner Montoya (Barcelona: Crítica, 1990).

CHAPTER 2

The Critical Reception of
Don Quixote in England, 1605–1900

Frans De Bruyn

The history of the critical reception of *Don Quixote* in the English-speaking world is rich, complex, and problematic. In a critical monograph whose title — *Don Quixote: Hero or Fool?* — neatly encapsulates that complexity, John J. Allen goes so far as to suggest that 'the problem of the reader's attitude toward Don Quixote is perhaps unparalleled in the history of literature, both in duration and extent'.[1] 'Unparalleled' may be an overstatement, but Allen is certainly right in pointing to the durability and scope of the problem. In the twentieth century, conflicting readings of the novel have been summed up, as Oscar Mandel puts it in a well-known essay, as an opposition between hard and soft interpretations, between those that tend to regard Don Quixote as deluded, as an object of satire, however comical, and those that stress the nobility and heroism of his quest.[2] The critical reception of *Don Quixote* in the three centuries following its initial publication in 1605 and 1615 has been said to play out this opposition chronologically, with initial views of the novel as farcical and burlesque giving way over time to more exalted conceptions of the book's generic affiliations, even to claims that it is tragic in mode. How could it ever happen, inquired A. J. Duffield in 1880, 'that a book so pure in spirit and so chaste in words, so lofty in style and yet so full of human sympathy and love as *Don Quijote* came to be regarded by English men of letters as a book of lowly buffoonery?'[3]

John Ruskin saw the diversity of responses to *Don Quixote* as indicative of an unequal endowment of aesthetic and moral feeling in readers of the novel:

> The lowest mind would find in it perpetual and brutal amusement in the misfortunes of the knight, and perpetual pleasure in sympathy with the squire. A mind of average feeling would perceive the satirical meaning and force of the book, would appreciate its wit, its elegance, and its truth. But only elevated and peculiar minds discover, in addition to all this, the full moral beauty of the love and truth which are the constant associates of all that is even most weak and erring in the character of its hero.[4]

Redeployed chronologically, this hierarchy of sensibility outlines in broad terms the way in which Romantic writers and critics of the nineteenth century understood the reception history of *Don Quixote*.

   This historical narrative is emphatically progressive or Whiggish in tendency, a circumstance that places the novel's early readers in an unflattering light, their assessments of Cervantes's achievement to be written off as obtuse, at best, or captious and mean-spirited, at worst. It is certainly true that seventeenth-century readers tended to view *Don Quixote* as a comic or burlesque performance, and passing remarks in the period sometimes dismissed it as another specimen of chivalric romance, as an instance of the very genre Cervantes had set out to parody. But critical opinions formed in an era of great literature and humanist scholarship are not casually to be discarded as reflections of a barbarous and uncouth age (a standard rhetorical ploy of eighteenth-century critics commenting on the writings of their forebears). A more productive reception history should seek to understand how and why readers contemporary to Cervantes perceived his fictional narrative as they did, and why this perception changed so radically over time.

   My assumption in this essay, which surveys the English critical reception of Cervantes before the twentieth century, is that the pronouncements of early readers, however odd, puzzling, or opaque they may now appear, are the products of a discernible critical rationale and epistemological norm. It follows that a history of critical reception should aim to reconstruct a historical sense of readerly expectations. Hans Robert Jauss argues in *Toward an Aesthetic of Reception* that the historical consciousness of readers exists as a horizon of expectations that each generation brings to its reading, based on its familiarity with pre-existing and con-temporaneous literary genres and texts. He proposes a history of reception based on a reconstruction of successive readerly horizons over time: 'The reconstruction of the horizon of expectations, in the face of which a work was created and received in the past, enables one [...] to pose questions that the text gave an answer to, and thereby to discover how the contemporary reader could have viewed and understood the work. This approach corrects the mostly unrecognized norms of a classicist or modernizing understanding of art, and avoids the circular recourse to a general spirit of the age'.[5]

   Such a methodology would recognize, for example, that Renaissance readers experienced a very different relationship to the genre of romance than did their eighteenth- and nineteenth-century descendants. Modes of reading and inter-pretation in the early seventeenth century also differed significantly from those of subsequent generations, tending in character to the emblematic, analogical, and allegorical, nor did there exist as yet a critical tradition or analytical vocabulary to account for new vernacular forms of writing, especially forms of prose fiction. Unlike the twenty-first-century reader, for whom the novel is a pervasive and dominant literary form underpinned by an extensive critical discourse, seventeenth-century readers of *Don Quixote* had few precedents to guide them in their encounters with Cervantes's novel experiment.

   The initial English response to Cervantes must be seen, therefore, against the background of humanist conceptions of reading, which were didactic, pedagogical, and rhetorical in focus; and in the context of critical and scholarly practices concerned almost exclusively with classical Greek and Roman texts. An individual imbued with humanist assumptions about reading, an activity whose primary purpose was understood to be preceptive (furnishing models of public heroism, prudence, and piety for gentlemen to emulate), would be unlikely to find in Don Quixote a promising exemplar of courtly, diplomatic, or military conduct. Richard Brathwaite's dismissal of 'fabulous Histories' in his survey, *The Schollers Medley; or, an Intermixt Discourse vpon Historicall and Poeticall Relations* (1614), is motivated by precisely such assumptions. The worst of these narratives, he writes, are the 'phantasticke writings of some supposed Knights, (*Don Quixotte* transformed into a Knight with the *Golden Pestle*) with many other fruitlesse inuentions, moulded onely for delight without profit. These Histories I altogether exclude my *Oeconomy*, or priuate family'.[6]

An instructive point of contrast, however, and an early indicator of changing perceptions regarding the novel is John Locke's favourable judgment in 'Some Thoughts Concerning Reading and Study for a Gentleman', an appendix to *An Essay Concerning Human Understanding* (written 1703). Though Locke shares Brathwaite's humanist model of reading, he is more open to the possibility that 'diversion and delight' are legitimate uses of reading. Accordingly, he affirms that, 'Of all the books of fiction, I know none that equals Cervantes's *History of Don Quixot* in usefulness, pleasantry, and a constant *decorum*. And indeed no writings can be pleasant, which have not Nature at the bottom, and are not drawn after her copy'.[7] High praise indeed from a distinguished quarter, and an assessment that, grounded as it is in Locke's empiricism, anticipates the direction of critical assumptions in the eighteenth century.

In the early seventeenth century, however, theories of literature designed to account for vernacular texts were as yet barely conceived of, and critical assessments as penetrating and admiring as Locke's at the end of the century were exceptional. Neoclassicism, as a critical discourse, was in fact in its infancy, emerging initially, as the example of Ben Jonson attests, in the context of dramatic writing and staging practices. It is noteworthy, in this connection, that the first sustained literary responses to *Don Quixote* appeared in the form of allusions to the novel in seventeenth-century dramatic comedies.[8] These allusions signal how early readers of the novel grasped at familiar generic contexts (the comic and the burlesque) as a means of naturalizing the unfamiliar, distinguishing it in the process from the formality and seriousness of romance. At its most reductive extreme, exemplified in Edmund Gayton's *Pleasant Notes upon Don Quixot* (1654), the comic response (diminished to nothing more than laughter) trivializes the novel, treating it as little more than a jest-book.[9] The comic and burlesque view persisted into the Restoration and beyond, as is attested by the productions of John Phillips (his burlesque translation of *Don Quixote* in the spirit of Gayton's jest-book), Thomas D'Urfey (his comic dramatization set to music by Henry Purcell), and Ned Ward (his rendering of the novel in Hudibrastic verse).[10]

Most of the early reactions to the novel are difficult to assess because the evidence is so meagre, amounting in many instances to no more than fragmentary allusions.[11] Yet these fragments hint, from time to time, at more sophisticated views on the part of seventeenth-century readers than they have been credited with by modern critics. Yumiko Yamada argues, for example, that Ben Jonson held a considerably more nuanced view of *Don Quixote* than has been generally acknowledged, not least by his twentieth-century editors, who claim Jonson was 'hostile to this great romance'.[12] Jonson's editors base their judgment on internal evidence drawn from his writings, citing, for example, a passage in the poem 'An Execration upon Vulcan' that refers disparagingly to 'The learned Librarie of *Don Quixote*'. Yet the context of this verse makes clear that Jonson is remarking on the worthlessness of the Don's books rather than on the quality of Cervantes's novel.[13] Another commentator is William Vaughan, who remarks approvingly in the opening pages of his treatise *The Golden Fleece* on the facility with which Spanish writers combine light and serious matter in their books, luring their readers with promises of entertainment and then edifying them with solid wisdom: 'Excellent in this Art of Cookerie were those *Spaniards,* which wrot the life of *Guzman the Rogue,* and the Aduentures of *Don Quixot de la Mancha,* the former seruing to withdraw a licentious young man from Prodigalitie, Whoredome, and Deceit; and the latter to reclaime a riotous running wit from taking delight in those prodigious, idle, and time-wasting *Bookes,* called the *Mirrour of Knighthood, the Knights of the Round Table, Palmerin de Oliua,* and the like rabblement'.[14] In *The Anatomy of Melancholy* (1621), Robert Burton likewise shows himself a perceptive reader who understands the central narrative premise of Don Quixote's madness and recognizes the need to distinguish between the stories that drive Don Quixote mad and the story of that madness and its consequences.

Vaughan's remarks suggest that comedy, laughter, and parody can be deployed for serious moral purposes: they are not to be dismissed as modes of mere frivolity. Ben Jonson himself claimed that comedy, rightly understood, serves to 'shew an Image of the times, / And sport with humane follies, not with crimes'.[15] As neoclassical literary theory in England came into wider acceptance and grew in sophistication, analogous arguments were mounted in justification of burlesque, especially high burlesque (what we today term 'mock-heroic'). In the case of *Don Quixote*, critical vindication of the novel as a high burlesque performance appeared initially in the context of critical discussions prompted by Samuel Butler's *Hudibras*, a satirical poem patterned in important ways after the model imparted by Cervantes.

Imitation of pre-existing literary texts was a central literary procedure during the Restoration and the early eighteenth century, and if, as proverbial wisdom has it, imitation is the sincerest form of flattery, then the publication of *Hudibras* (1663–78) represents a turning point in the critical reception of *Don Quixote* in the English-speaking world. For *Hudibras*, despite its rough, doggerel manner, was a work of serious intellectual ambition and commanded great respect as a poetic achievement. Butler's debt to Cervantes has been downplayed in recent decades, but Werner von Koppenfels argues persuasively that the structural influence of *Don Quixote* is pervasive. Not only is the 'Cervantine intertextuality' of *Hudibras* 'well-marked' — of a different order of consequence, indeed, than Butler's many other learned allusions — but the poem's imitative debt pervades its very structure, albeit in an idiosyncratic manner. The Quixotism of Sir Hudibras is metaphoric, 'the mock image and the ironic instrument of that ironclad and hard-hitting agent of poetic justice, satire; whom Butler defines in a much-quoted passage from his Notebooks as "a kinde of Knight-Errant that goe's upon Adventures, to Relieve the Distressed Damsel Virtue, and Redeeme Honor out of Inchanted Castles, And opprest Truth, and Reason out of the Captivity of Gyants and Magitians" '.[16] Koppenfels might have gone on to cite Butler's words immediately following, which are equally to the point: 'though his [satire's] meaning be very honest, yet some believe he is no wiser then those wandring Heros used to be'.[17] In allegorizing or emblematizing satire as a knight errant, Butler places the author at the centre of the Quixotic quest and elevates it in literary and generic dignity.

An author's decision to imitate a predecessor, which bespeaks at some level an attitude of homage, is clearly an important datum for a reception history, but as the focus of this essay is on the critical, rather than the broader literary reception of Cervantes, the question to be pursued is not the 'how' or 'what' of imitation (the enumeration and analysis of parallels in structural features or episodes) but rather the 'why'. The fact that *Hudibras* was hailed as a distinguished poetic performance reflects new modes of critical thinking that were simultaneously to transform the critical reputation of *Don Quixote*. For a time, indeed, the critical reception of the two works was intimately intertwined.

In his annotated scholarly edition of *Hudibras*, published in 1744, Zachary Grey declares that the critical notes to the poem are designed 'to prove that it is at least equal to the most celebrated Poems in the *English* Language: and it's conformity in some respects to *Epic* Poetry, will be evinc'd, and comparisons here and there drawn from *Homer*, *Virgil*, and *Milton*'.[18] Grey's comment exhibits several key procedures of eighteenth-century neoclassical criticism. Belying its reputation for rigidity and prescriptiveness, criticism in the period showed great ingenuity in its justifications for new literary experiments. One such justification, invoked by Grey, was to assimilate new forms to established ones, in this instance by arguing that *Hudibras*, despite its parodic form, aspires to the completeness and perfection of epic, the acme of the literary hierarchy. Grey's claim is grounded in an understanding of generic systems as flexible, inclusive, and interrelated, with lesser forms in the literary hierarchy being understood as structurally integral to higher ones. If anything, eighteenth-century criticism lagged behind authorial practice: writers exploited literary forms, like the social relations they reflected, in ways that highlight variety, heterogeneity, and novelty. Such views on literary form were readily capable of explaining and esteeming works that deviated from classical generic patterns, including, as will appear, *Don Quixote*.

An important circumstance that fostered this critical flexibility was the need to account for the example of Shakespeare, whose plays transgress the prescriptive generic boundaries of a rigid neoclassicism. *Don Quixote* posed a similar challenge to critical preconceptions, one that eighteenth-century readers actively embraced, for Cervantes's novel appeared to supply a glaring lack in the literary models bequeathed by antiquity. Illustrious examples of serious narrative form (the Homeric and Virgilian epic) lay readily to hand, but no archetypal instance of the comic had survived the ravages of time. Aristotle, as Henry Fielding reminds the reader in his Preface to *Joseph Andrews* (1742), refers in the *Poetics* to Homer's comic performance, the *Margites*, which bears 'the same relation to Comedy which his *Iliad* does to Tragedy', but this work had long since perished.[19] Miraculously, Cervantes, a modern, had made up the deficiency. Like Shakespeare, he exerted a powerful leavening influence on eighteenth-century critical thought, countering dogmatic tendencies by his illustrious example. A kind of virtuous hermeneutic circle was established, in which Cervantes's writings shaped critical assumptions and readerly expectations that in turn enriched the period's understanding of his artistic achievement.

Ronald Paulson argues that as a work that eluded conventional critical categories, *Don Quixote* ultimately called into question classical authority itself: 'Don Quixote made it possible to read the *Aeneid* as another Quixotic fiction that says classical epic is as inappropriate to our "modern" times as chivalric romance was to Cervantes'.[20] In this manner, burlesque and travesty are rehabilitated as tools of critical evaluation. A further reclamation of burlesque was effected by Addison, who distinguishes high burlesque or mock-heroic from low burlesque or travesty, and identifies *Don Quixote* with the former (an identification that elides the novel's scenes of low jests and physical indignities). Finally, the laughter excited by the novel is itself rehabilitated, as Addison plays down the classical understanding of laughter as a sign of contempt to emphasize its therapeutic powers. Laughter 'breaks the Gloom which is apt to depress the Mind [...] with transient unexpected gleams of joy', an effect, Addison notes, associated by Saint-Evremond with Cervantes: 'Don *Quixote* can give more relief to an heavy Heart than *Plutarch* or *Seneca*, as it is much easier to divert Grief than to conquer it'.[21] Redefining laughter as cure dignified the unseemliness from which it was seen to arise (Don Quixote's broken teeth or Sancho's blanket-tossing), an argument Grey uses to vindicate *Hudibras*, which he prescribes 'as an infallible Cure not only of the *Spleen* and *Vapours*, but of *Enthusiasm* and *Hypocrisy*'.[22] In support of his argument, Grey again cites Saint-Evremond (via *The Spectator*), designating *Don Quixote* 'a Potion to give Relief to an Heavy Heart'.[23]

The apotheosis of these critical and theoretical revaluations is Samuel Johnson's admiring assessment of both *Don Quixote* and *Hudibras* in his 'Life of Butler' (1779), where he lauds Butler's poem as an ornament of English literature and emphasizes its formal and thematic originality. That originality is not entirely Butler's, however. As Johnson notes, Butler does imitate a literary model, albeit not an ancient one: 'The poem of Hudibras is not wholly English; the original idea is to be found in the History of Don Quixote; a book to which a mind of the greatest powers may be indebted without disgrace'.[24] Johnson's remarks exhibit that flexible neoclassicism fostered by the example of Cervantes: Butler's poem is praised as formally innovative, even as it is seen to participate in the neoclassical practice of imitation. Just as Johnson had declared in the case of Shakespeare, that he had begun 'to assume the dignity of an ancient', so too Cervantes is here accorded the prestige of a classic.[25] The charmed circle of classical authors was not, for eighteenth-century criticism, a closed one.

While it has been widely claimed that the Romantic exaltation of Don Quixote as a saintly hero is the great divide in the reception history of Cervantes's novel, it can equally be argued that the gentrification of the laughter evoked by the novel, along with the revaluation of the generic sources of that laughter, is the decisive moment, for this renovation is what makes possible the respectful views of *Don Quixote* that follow. Thus, in 1751 Richard Owen Cambridge argued, rather implausibly, that the true mock-heroic is a consistently serious mode that should eschew parody throughout: 'the author should never be seen to laugh, but constantly wear that grave irony which *Cervantes* only has inviolably preserv'd'.[26] The great triumph of *Don Quixote*, one that classes it as 'a work which would give as much satisfaction in a critical examination as most of the compositions of the ancients',[27] is the deadpan propriety with which its ridicule is deployed. By thus redefining Cervantes's narrative method as one of sustained irony, eighteenth-century critics succeed in explaining away the novel's buffoonery and in vindicating its seriousness. An exemplary instance is John Bowle, a pioneer in Cervantine scholarship, who castigated his contemporary Charles Henry Wilmot for publishing a translation of *Don Quixote* with a title-page that 'ascribes to the Divine Original *Ludicrous Dialogues &c & Drollery*, instead of what every where occurs Grave & Serious Irony, which by an Art peculiar to himself The Author has made the Vehicle of Morality & useful Instruction for the Conduct of Life'.[28]

Purifying the laughter and parody of *Don Quixote* had a second and more far-reaching consequence, which was to authorize it as a model of narrative realism. If, as Cambridge insists, the true mock-heroic rejects the impropriety of 'Beaux and Belles, or Booksellers' addressing themselves to heathen gods, offering sacrifices, and consulting oracles (he alludes here to Alexander Pope's *The Rape of the Lock* and *The Dunciad*), then the consequence, in the case of *Don Quixote*, is that the 'marvellous' in the narrative is made 'reconcileable to probability, as the author led his Hero into that species of absurdity only, which it was natural for an imagination, heated with the continual reading of books of Chivalry, to fall into'.[29] The marvellous in Cervantes is domesticated as nothing more than the projection of a man's intermittent madness, opening up a large space for readings of the novel as a realistic reflection of the manners and social mores of late Renaissance Spain. Here, the changing horizon of readerly expectations begins to distinguish *Don Quixote* as a prototype of a more realistic mode of prose fiction. Cervantes's text has come to be understood, in retrospect, as marking a transformation in epistemological and historical consciousness towards an empirical and historicist outlook crucial to the shaping of the English novel. Michael McKeon argues 'that the two parts of *Don Quixote* enact, albeit over a decade, that schematic movement (from naïve empiricism to extreme scepticism, from progressive ideology to conservative ideology) which in the English context is spread over a much greater period and range of works'.[30] As these changes struck root in the English-speaking world, Cervantes's novel underwent a corresponding critical revaluation, gaining in cultural prestige.

It must be acknowledged, however, that the classical conception of laughter as an expression of ridicule and contempt does not simply vanish in the face of these critical revisions: the two perspectives continue in some measure to co-exist. The sense that the ridicule deployed in *Don Quixote* could be damaging was perhaps most famously captured in Sir William Temple's anecdote of a Spaniard he met in Brussels, who claimed that *Don Quixote* had undermined the Spanish polity, for 'before that time Love and Valour were all Romance among them'. After the appearance of Cervantes's novel, however, whose 'inimitable Wit and Humour turned all this Romantick Honour and Love into Ridicule, the *Spaniards*, he said, began to grow ashamed of both [...] and the consequences of this, both upon their Bodies and their Minds, this *Spaniard* would needs have pass for a great Cause of the Ruin of *Spain*, or of its Greatness and Power'.[31] Temple does not appear to take this anecdote altogether seriously, but it voices a reading of the novel that persisted into the nineteenth century (passed on by such writers as Richard Steele, Daniel Defoe, William Warburton, and Richard Hurd). This reading understands the novel as satirical in its thrust, with the object of that satire being the institution and practices of chivalry themselves rather than the extravagant romances written to celebrate them. Wit, in this view, is a sharp-edged knife that can injure the innocent along with the guilty.

This ambivalent attitude towards wit forms part of a much larger debate in the eighteenth century about the dangers posed by ridicule, however well it might be intended. Warburton remarked in 1742 that even when ridicule is directed at 'false Virtue, which surely deserves no Quarter', it can be 'attended with very mischievous Effects', and he illustrates his point with reference to both *Don Quixote* and *Hudibras*. 'The *Spaniards*', he writes, 'have lamented, and I believe truly, that *Cervantes's* just and inimitable Ridicule of *Knight-Errantry* rooted up, with that Folly, a great deal of their *true Honour*. And it appears very evident, that *Butler's* fine satire on *Fanaticism* contributed not a little to bring *sober Piety* into Discredit during the licentious Times of *Charles* II'.[32] Some eighty years later Lord Byron famously attributed the collapse of Spain as a major power to a single author's smile:

> Cervantes smiled Spain's chivalry away;
> A single laugh demolish'd the right arm
> Of his own country; — seldom since that day
> Has Spain had heroes.
> [...]
> And therefore have his volumes done such harm,
> That all their glory, as a composition,
> Was dearly purchased by his land's perdition.[33]

Byron's critique brings the eighteenth-century's uneasiness about the effects of ridicule to an apocalyptic climax, branding Cervantes, in the words of Anthony Close, as 'an irresponsible or cynical iconoclast' whose relentlessness in highlighting the absurdities of chivalry destroys Romantic idealism altogether.[34] Must the 'noblest views', Byron asks, must ideals of 'Redressing injury, revenging wrong, / To aid the damsel and destroy the caitiff', become 'for mere fancy's sport a theme creative, / A jest, a riddle'? Some years earlier, Edmund Burke had expressed the same view in the context of the French Revolution with his lament in *Reflections on the Revolution in France* (1790) for the destruction of chivalric idealism at the hands of modern enlightenment rationalism. His declaration that 'the age of chivalry is gone' was inspired in no small part by his familiarity with *Don Quixote* and the romance tradition on which it draws.[35]

In the meantime, however (for Byron's elegy of the defeat of Romantic idealism belongs properly to the nineteenth-century reception of *Don Quixote*), the prevailing trend was towards an attenuation and generalizing of Cervantes's satire. Don Quixote's obsession with chivalric romance came to be seen as arising from an impulse well-nigh universal in the human soul. As early as 1700, Peter Motteux remarked in the Preface to a new translation of the novel that, 'Every Man has something of *Don Quixote* in his Humour, some darling *Dulcinea* of his Thoughts, that sets him very often upon mad Adventures. What *Quixotes* does not every Age produce in Politicks and Religion, who fancying themselves to be in the Right of something, which all the World tells 'em is wrong, make very good sport to the Publick'.[36] Besides political and religious zealots, Motteux identifies 'Modern Philosophers', virtuosi, and projectors as quintessential Quixotes. The hobby-horses may vary from individual to individual, but the underlying condition in each case is the same. Motteux's classification of enthusiasts reads in fact like a key to eighteenth-century Scriblerian satire, encompassing such Quixotic figures as Martinus Scriblerus himself and the fanatical Jack in Jonathan Swift's *A Tale of a Tub* (1704).

For Swift, as for Butler, such 'enthusiasms' are not only quixotic but dangerous, the products of a private imagination run wild, rapt with fantasies of direct access to divine truth. These strains of delusion were thought to imperil civil and religious peace. The very term 'enthusiasm' was at the time almost universally used disparagingly, and it is telling that the most vivid instances of quixotism to be found in late-seventeenth- and early-eighteenth-century English literature portray what Samuel Johnson would later designate as the 'dangerous prevalence of imagination'. In Johnson's moral fable *Rasselas* (1759), Imlac diagnoses this malady in terms that call Don Quixote to mind: 'To indulge the power of fiction, and send the imagination out upon the wing, is often the sport of those who delight too much in silent speculation [...] He who has nothing external that can divert him, must find pleasure in his own thoughts, and must conceive himself what he is not; for who is pleased with what he is?'[37] In Johnson's view we all have something of the quixotic in us: 'very few readers [...] can deny that they have admitted visions of the same kind' as the knight of La Mancha. 'When we pity him, we reflect on our own disappointments, and when we laugh, our hearts inform us that he is not more ridiculous than ourselves, except that he tells what we only thought'.[38]

Johnson identifies, to borrow Harry Levin's phrase, a 'Quixotic principle' that governs human behaviour generally. We all cherish illusions, Johnson suggests, and yet we need to be disabused of them, to mature, to become self-aware. This dialectical dynamic, as Levin points out, comes to define the tradition of the realistic novel.[39] An index of this rehabilitation of the Quixotic hero as an Everyman, as someone we laugh *with* rather than *at*, is the figure of Geoffrey Wildgoose in Richard Graves's novel *The Spiritual Quixote* (1773). Like Sir Hudibras, Wildgoose is a religious enthusiast (of the Methodist persuasion), but while his enthusiasm is deplored by the author, it is portrayed as a humorous distemper, and Wildgoose himself proves at bottom to be a benign soul. Eighteenth-century fiction is populated by such 'amiable humorists', as Stuart Tave terms them, from Addison's Sir Roger de Coverley and Fielding's Parson Adams to Charlotte Lennox's Arabella and Laurence Sterne's Uncle Toby.

The vogue for these humorous characters, deemed in their eccentricity to embody a defining English national trait, belongs to the history of the *literary* response to *Don Quixote*. In terms of critical reception, the readerly fondness for protagonists of marked eccentricity coincided with the emergence of an innovative critical methodology of character analysis that critics began to apply to such writers as Shakespeare and Cervantes. This new character analysis moved away from a Theophrastan conception of the 'character' as an moral or social type (the hypocrite, the penny-pincher) to a psychologically grounded, individualized, and subjectivized conception of character: individuals moulded by a particular time, place, and situation. Building on the ancient psychology of humours, character analysis, as defined by Corbyn Morris in the mid-eighteenth century, focuses on a defining trait that both individualizes a person and accounts for his or her motivation. 'If a *Person* in real Life, discovers any odd and remarkable *Features* of Temper or Conduct, I call such a Person in the *Book* of *Mankind*, a *Character*. So that the chief Subjects of Humour are Persons in real Life, who are *Characters*'.[40] In Don Quixote's case, the 'strange Absurdity' of his chivalric obsession gives direction to his 'character' and motivation, but this is offset by his 'excellent Sense, Learning, and Judgment, upon any Subjects which are not ally'd to his Errantry' and by his 'perfect *good Breeding* and *Civility*'. In consequence, Morris assures the reader, 'you yourself, if he existed in real Life, would be fond of his company at your own Table' (pp. 39–40).

Numerous commentators from the mid-eighteenth century onwards responded in this way to Don Quixote as a simulacrum of a flesh-and-blood individual. Such responses served to validate *Don Quixote* ever more substantially as a realistic performance. The increasingly sentimental actualization of Don Quixote in the later eighteenth century — as a 'benevolent eccentric, thwarted melancholic, yet a man of exquisite feeling withal', in John Skinner's summation[41] — alters the reader's orientation toward him. This quixotic sentimental traveller is not to be confused with the subsequent Romantic conception of Don Quixote as a hero of self-transcending imagination, but the redirection of readerly attitudes in the later eighteenth century undoubtedly engendered a receptiveness to his apotheosis in the following century. The affection and esteem repeatedly voiced in eighteenth-century discussions of Don Quixote's character fostered an atmosphere of growing critical seriousness that intensified greatly in the following century.

A reliable gauge of the rising esteem for *Don Quixote* in the eighteenth century is the fact that the book (like the works of other newly canonical vernacular writers, such as Chaucer, Shakespeare, Spenser, Milton, and Butler) began to receive the kind of scholarly attention previously reserved for classical authors. Perhaps the most dramatic indicator of Cervantes's growing reputation in England was the Spanish-language edition of *Don Quixote* sponsored by the Whig opposition statesman John Carteret, Earl of Grenville. Carteret's edition, published in 1738, was the first anywhere to present the novel in sumptuous dress, with a biography of the author (the first ever written) by Gregorio Mayans y Siscar, some literary commentary, two portraits of the author (one by William Kent), and a series of illustrations by John Vanderbank. Mayans's biography was translated into English by John Ozell,[42] and it was followed in 1755 by Smollett's biography, which relies heavily on Ozell's translation. Smollett did, however, consult a new source for his biography, Joseph Morgan's *Complete History of Algiers* (1728–29), which he used to detail Cervantes's period of captivity in Algiers.[43] Carteret's elegant literary monument was followed later in the century by another English first: a collated text of the novel, fully annotated and indexed, edited by the Reverend John Bowle. In this Spanish-language edition, *Don Quixote* received, for the first time anywhere, the full scholarly treatment that earlier humanist scholars had reserved for ancient Greek and Roman texts. As he states in a published letter to Thomas Percy, Bowle was induced 'from the commencement of my intimacy with the text of Don Quixote […] to consider the great author as a Classic, and to treat him as such'.[44]

Treating Cervantes 'as such' meant, for Bowle, to establish a reliable text, based on the earliest editions (rather than on Lord Carteret's edition of 1738), and to provide detailed notes and indices, the latter gathered separately in volumes five and six of the edition. In his *Letter to the Reverend Dr. Percy* (1777), Bowle claims to have collated 'minutely' the first editions of 1605 and 1615 with the edition of 1738, but Ralph Merritt Cox states that the evidence points to his having used the Madrid edition of 1608, which, Cox conjectures, Bowle must have consulted after publishing his *Letter to Percy*.[45] In matters of collation and textual scholarship generally, eighteenth-century editors often claimed more than they actually delivered, but by the standards of his time Bowle produced a well-edited edition with a scholarly apparatus that reflected the latest methodology, in sharp contrast, as he emphasizes, to the 1750 Spanish edition of Pedro Alonso y Padilla, which Bowle also consulted but found woefully deficient. As he himself describes his labours, 'I have all along insisted on a correct text; this naturally requires an explanation of difficult passages, which makes a principal part of the Notes: and these, besides pointing out the Historical and other References, will in various places shew a propriety in the Original absolutely un-transferrable into any other Language' (p. 54).

Two critical insights advanced by Bowle in the *Letter to Percy* indicate the course that Cervantine scholarship was to take in the decades following the appearance of his edition. The first is his recognition of the extraordinary range and virtuosity of Cervantes's style, which, Bowle declares, 'merits every encomium'. It sounds every register of the Spanish language, from the lofty and formal, to the homely, domestic, and colloquial, flowing like 'the noblest river, that now rapid runs with proper velocity, now gently glides along, and suffers its cristal current to be tinged with hues, which it receives from the lesser streams that mingle with its waters' (p. 34). The second is his insistence that the chivalric romances of Renaissance Spain are not to be dismissed by the serious reader with scorn, but are to be treated as sources that Cervantes himself knew intimately and as literary documents of historical value. The '*Libros de Cavallerias*', Bowle contends, furnish 'faithful and exact descriptions of the manners and customs of the times in which they were wrote […] In this respect, they deserve some esteem as histories' (p. 3). He acknowledges that the characters and adventures encountered in the romances are often fanciful, but the narratives nonetheless convey an accurate picture of social codes and military practices then in use.

Bowle's edition aroused the ire of Joseph Baretti, who attacked it in a polemic of extraordinary violence, even by the combative standards of eighteenth-century controversy. Baretti impugned Bowle's qualifications as an editor of Cervantes and called into question his editorial principles. He regarded Bowle's scholarly project as pedantically misconceived: *Don Quixote*, he insists, stands in as little need of commentary as does *Robinson Crusoe*. Nowhere is Bowle's ponderous scholarship more woefully misapplied, in Baretti's view, than in his annotations, which elucidate all manner of irrelevancies, including the chivalric literature that addled Don Quixote's brain: 'Far from [...] hinting, that, to understand his Don Quixote, we were to read the chivalry and other silly books he had read himself, Cervantes condemned them all to be burnt by means of the Curate [...] How could a thick-bearded man like you lose his time in treasuring up all that farrago of silly pieces, as if they had all been Greek fragments of the remotest antiquity?[46] Baretti's reaction suggests that the idea of deploying the panoply of humanist textual scholarship on a work of comic prose fiction, however illustrious, remained for many late-eighteenth-century readers a misconceived critical ambition. Not everyone was ready to accept, in this instance, the precedent of Shakespeare cited by Bowle in his *Letter to Percy*: 'I shall apply to my own intentions what your friend Mr. Warton has said of Shakespeare: If Cervantes is worth reading, he is worth explaining'.[47]

Posterity has been considerably kinder to Bowle, however; his annotations are now recognized as the foundation of all subsequent editorial work on *Don Quixote*. Baretti's dismissal of Bowle's painstaking efforts to reconstruct the Spanish literary context of chivalric romance ran counter, in fact, to a nascent historicizing consciousness in the late eighteenth century that was redefining Europe's medieval past. No longer were the social institutions of the Middle Ages (chivalry, feudalism) and its literary productions (romance) to be dismissed as gothic barbarism; increasingly, they were being re-evaluated as significant and enduring cultural developments. It was widely held that modern European civilization — its learning, commerce, and social mores — had flourished on account of the ameliorative influence imparted, in Burke's words, by 'the spirit of a gentleman and the spirit of religion'.[48] Because of chivalry, Europe had made decisive advances beyond ancient Greece and Rome toward a culture of 'politeness', as enlightenment thinkers termed it, particularly with regard to modern rules of warfare and gender relations. Bowle's friend and collaborator Thomas Percy echoes this view in his essay, 'On the Ancient Metrical Romances' where he writes of 'that respectful complaisance shewn' by the votaries of chivalry 'to the fair sex, (so different from the manners of the Greeks and Romans)'.[49]

The significance of this historicized (and newly favourable) view of chivalry and romance is that it mandated a corresponding revaluation of *Don Quixote*, which gained in stature as the genre of romance was rehabilitated. Rich new interpretive possibilities opened up: Cervantes's novel was observed to conceal hitherto unsuspected depths. This changing horizon of expectations can be discerned in the literary history of the Swiss writer J. C. L. Simonde de Sismondi, whose *De la littérature du midi de l'europe* (1813) saw numerous editions in English translation. Sismondi's reading of *Don Quixote* begins by accepting the revised historical view of chivalry: 'This chivalric mythology probably contributed more than any other to impress the imagination with notions of morality and honour, and thus to produce a beneficial effect on the character of modern nations'.[50] From this premise he goes on to argue that the novel can be read in a far more exalted mode than had hitherto been the norm: 'The imagination, the feelings, and all the generous qualities, tend to raise Don Quixote in our esteem. Men of elevated minds make it the object of their lives to defend the weak, to aid the oppressed, to be the champions of justice and innocence. Like Don Quixote, they everywhere discover the image of those virtues which they worship' (III, 328).

The experience of an imagination thus endued, however, as it encounters Cervantes's novel, is one of ironic dissonance: 'A character [...] which excites our admiration, when viewed from an elevated situation, is often ridiculous when seen from the level of the earth [...] nothing can be more powerfully contrasted than poetry and prose; the romance of the imagination, and the petty details of social life; the valour and the great appetite of the hero; the palace of Armida and an inn; the enchanted princesses and Maritorna' (III, 329). The outcome, Sismondi ruefully concludes, is that *Don Quixote* can appear to the reader as 'the most melancholy book that was ever written'; the clash between the novel's poetry and prose exposes 'the vanity of noble feelings and the illusions of heroism' (III, 328). Perhaps the most pessimistic of such readings, certainly the most memorably expressed, is Byron's lament that the Quixotic desire to make the world right is doomed perpetually to failure: 'Of all such tales 'tis the saddest, and the more sad, / Because it makes us smile' (V, 528).

Conceptually, Sismondi's analysis of *Don Quixote* is heavily indebted to the German theorists of Romanticism: the Schlegel brothers (Friedrich and August Wilhelm), Johann Ludwig Tieck, Friedrich von Schelling, and Jean Paul Richter. Sismondi, together with Friedrich Bouterwek, whose volumes on Spanish and Portuguese literature were translated into English in 1823, played a prominent role in transmitting German Romantic views of *Don Quixote* to the rest of Europe and to the English speaking world, where they had a lasting impact.[51] Bouterwek's and Sismondi's critical opinions were critiqued by Henry Hallam (who cites and paraphrases Bouterwek freely) in his *Introduction to the Literature of Europe in the 15th, 16th, and 17th Centuries* (1837), a work reprinted frequently in the nineteenth century. The culmination of these literary histories — and by far the most accurate and definitive of them all — was the work of the distinguished American Hispanist George Ticknor, the three-volume *History of Spanish Literature* published in 1849.

Bouterwek and Sismondi both evince in their criticism the influence of key ideas promulgated by the Germans. Their literary histories present Cervantes at the centre of a national literary tradition: his *Don Quixote* is the embodiment of the history, religion, customs, and traditions of the Spanish nation. It is, in Lienhard Bergel's phrase, 'an expression of the national genius, a *Nationalwerk*'.[52] The novel is not only the organic outgrowth of a specific historical evolution; it is also, in its valorization of the poetic (identified with chivalry and romance) over the prosaic, a leading instance of progressive universal poetry, a poetry that embraces the infinite, represents life in all its variety, and reunites all literary genres. This sort of grand theorizing about the ontological status of the work of art spawned numerous abstract philosophical and allegorical interpretations of *Don Quixote*. The novel is understood variously as playing out an opposition between poetry and prose, mind and body, the ideal and the real, spirit and matter, subject and object, freedom and necessity. In the words of John Gibson Lockhart, prefaced to a reissue of the Motteux translation in 1822, Don Quixote exhibits not a Spanish but 'a more universal madness — he is the symbol of Imagination, continually struggling and contrasted with Reality — he represents the eternal warfare between Enthusiasm and Necessity — the eternal discrepancy between the aspirations and the occupations of man — the omnipotence and the vanity of human dreams'.[53]

Cervantes is seen also as an originator of what came to be known as romantic irony, a complex idea that addresses the relation between the artist and the work of art, but that is also applied to the condition of human existence itself. The artist who creates an illusion of being, of reality, in a work of art only to shatter that illusion by revealing the conventionality of the artistic creation — lifting the curtain to show the artist at work — is a practitioner of romantic irony in the first sense. Irony in the larger, existential sense presents itself whenever the artist confronts in the work of art, as Don Quixote was thought to do in his life, the ironic disparity between the absolute and the finite, between imagination and the recalcitrance of material reality, between language and existence.

The new Romantic aesthetic undoubtedly transformed critical discussion of *Don Quixote*, but the polemical zeal of Romantic theorists also misrepresented and denigrated the critical understanding of their predecessors. Though the theoretical premises of critical debate shifted decisively at the outset of the nineteenth century, many of the features in the artistry of Cervantes that the Romantics found so distinctive had already been identified by their predecessors — in practice, certainly, if not in theory. Eighteenth-century writers were acknowledged masters of irony, for instance, and they recognized in Cervantes a fellow proficient in this mode. If romantic irony is understood in terms of the artist's self-reflexive awareness, then the meta-fictional narrative practices of Fielding and Sterne display a profound appreciation of this dimension of Cervantine art. Still, when eighteenth-century critics laud the 'sustained irony' of *Don Quixote*, they are thinking primarily of irony as a rhetorical trope, though not without a recognition that its systematic deployment by such writers as Cervantes or Swift bespeaks a sceptical, demystifying epistemological mindset. Similarly, eighteenth-century British critics acknowledged the multiplicity of Cervantes's narrative — its tonal virtuosity, its interpolated stories, its structure of episodes peopled with characters from all walks of life and social ranks — but their praise of this virtuosity is couched in terms of an aesthetic of variety that is grounded in an empirical epistemology and a psychology of audience response. For Romantic critics like Friedrich Schlegel, by contrast, the same multiplicity is a manifestation of an organic conception of form that embraces fully the prodigal variety of the real. In short, Romantic critics shift the theoretical grounds of debate and thereby gain new insight into the text, but they deploy their new perspective on textual features already recognized by their predecessors.

The consequence for a history of the critical reception of *Don Quixote*, in the

English speaking world at least, is that it is better understood as a palimpsest, as a document superimposed and overwritten by new ideas, rather than as one destroyed in a moment of revolutionary rupture. The great Victorian translator John Ormsby rejected trenchantly those critical efforts that sought to imbue the novel with lofty purpose at the expense of its humour and ridicule. Interestingly, Ormsby attributes the retreat of laughter in the face of Romantic critical earnestness to the 'zeal of publishers, editors, and annotators', whose success in canonizing *Don Quixote* required a concomitant high seriousness on the part of its readers. 'A vast number of its admirers began to grow ashamed of laughing over it. It became almost a crime to treat it as a humorous book'.[54]

Ormsby's scepticism echoes that of Hallam, who argues that abstract allegorical readings of *Don Quixote* are historically 'presentist' in their critical assumptions: 'the generalisation which the hypothesis of Bouterwek and Sismondi requires for the leading conception of Don Quixote, besides its being a little inconsistent with the valorous and romantic character of its author, belongs to a more advanced period of philosophy than his own'.[55] Hallam sides with Cervantes's earlier readers, yet he acknowledges that more recent critics also have a point. Hallam's pragmatic refusal to jettison the comic dimension of the novel voices a persistent view of *Don Quixote* in the English-speaking world, a view reiterated influentially in the twentieth-century discussions of P. E. Russell and Anthony Close.[56] In sum, the lively spectrum of critical debate in evidence throughout the nineteenth century resists reductive categorization or historical schematization.

English Romanticism produced some richly insightful readings of *Don Quixote*. Samuel Taylor Coleridge combines the theorist's powers of abstraction and synthesis with the poet's ear for telling detail and nuance of language to arrive at a critique of the novel that is at once conceptual and vividly concrete. He argues that the character of Don Quixote is symbolic, in the deepest sense of that term, by which he means a conception that 'is always itself a part of that, of the whole of which it is representative'.[57] Unlike allegory, which is a trope of conscious substitution, the symbolic coalesces naturally around a 'general truth' that may well 'be working unconsciously in the writer's mind' (p. 99). Thus, a detail as seemingly trivial as Cervantes's play on the Don's name (is it '*Quixada* or *Quesada*'?), by 'insinuating the association of *lantern-jaws* into the reader's mind, yet not retaining it obtrusively like the names in old farces and in the Pilgrim's Progress', contributes to a rich sense of Quixote's physical presence that embodies, rather than stands for, the novel's 'general truth': 'Don Quixote's leanness and featureliness are happy exponents of the excess of formativeness or imaginative in him, contrasted with Sancho's plump rotundity, and recipiency of external impression' (p. 100).

Coleridge recognizes that the rich interplay between Don Quixote and Sancho Panza — their unending conversation — is the chief source of the novel's pleasure and the core of its meaning. That meaning, symbolically realized as it is, cannot be abstracted from its representation. In this sense, *Don Quixote* is a perfect instance of what Coleridge understands as organic form. Put Sancho and his master together,

> and they form a perfect intellect; but they are separated and without cement;
> and hence each having a need of the other for its own completeness, each has

at times a mastery over the other [...] These two characters possess the world, alternately and interchangeably the cheater and the cheated. To impersonate them, and to combine the permanent with the individual, is one of the highest creations of genius, and has been achieved by Cervantes and Shakespeare, almost alone' (p. 102).

Those who simply abstract from the traffic between the novel's two central characters an opposition between 'imagination' and 'common sense' fail to appreciate how perfectly Cervantes incarnates his characters and grounds their behaviour. For Coleridge, 'Don Quixote grows at length to be a man out of his wits; his understanding is deranged; and hence without the least deviation from the truth of nature, without losing the least trait of personal individuality, he becomes a substantial living allegory, or personification of the reason and the moral sense, divested of the judgment and the understanding' (p. 102). In effect, Coleridge anticipates such would-be objectors as Hallam and Ormsby by arguing that much of what he posits to be the true meaning of the text is the product of the author's unconscious mind and that to credit Cervantes on this basis with achieving more as a writer than he explicitly aims at is not to argue anachronistically but simply to recognize what was latent in the work from the outset.

The other indispensable critical statement bequeathed by the English Romantics appears in William Hazlitt's *Lectures on the English Comic Writers* (1819). Hazlitt begins by claiming Cervantes as an English author by naturalization, an assertion that complicates the Romantic nationalist claim that Cervantes is the soul of the Spanish nation. He is, it would appear, a writer of dual nationality. What Hazlitt means most explicitly is that Cervantes is as widely read in England as most, if not all, English novelists and that he is a universally acknowledged progenitor of English fiction. But Hazlitt also sees in Don Quixote (and in this respect he is the heir of a late-eighteenth-century sentimental readership) a model of the quintessentially English 'amiable humorist' or loveable eccentric: 'The character of Don Quixote himself is one of the most perfect disinterestedness. He is an enthusiast of the most amiable kind; of a nature equally open, gentle, and generous; a lover of truth and justice'.[58] It is significant that Hazlitt here uses the word 'enthusiasm' in a wholly positive sense — a reversal of the disapproval and contempt its use had previously conveyed.

Perhaps because he discusses Cervantes in the context of a lecture on eighteenth-century English fiction, Hazlitt exhibits a greater continuity with the critical views of the preceding century than Coleridge, though these views acquire under his hand a characteristically Romantic inflection. He recognizes that the novel is often ludicrous. Yet, 'there cannot be a greater mistake than to consider Don Quixote as a merely satirical work, or as a vulgar attempt to explode "the long forgotten order of chivalry"' (p. 108). Hazlitt gives the latter (persistent) critical crux a characteristically radical political inflection by declaring that what 'the mouldering flame of Spanish liberty' needs is more, rather than less, of the quixotic spirit of 'generous sentiment and generous enterprise' (p. 108). As these remarks indicate, the longstanding debate over the historical impact of chivalry and the attitude of Cervantes towards it did not play out along predictable political and intellectual lines: the idiom of chivalry engrossed radical and conservative alike.[59] Hazlitt agrees with Coleridge on two key points: the centrality of the relationship between Don Quixote and Sancho Panza (a point of growing critical interest), and the pre-eminence of Cervantes as a writer singularly blessed with the 'instinct of the imagination', which is 'what stamps the character of genius on the productions of art more than any other circumstance' (p. 109).

One of the most influential critical legacies of the Romantic perspective on *Don Quixote* is the defining pattern it bequeathed to realistic fiction in the nineteenth century. The classic realistic novel came to be understood as a conflict between individual aspiration and desire, on the one hand, and the limitations imposed by social codes and conventions, on the other. The paradigmatic plot pattern of the realistic novel depicts the protagonist as either rebelling against those constraints, or achieving an accommodation with them, or being defeated and destroyed by them. All three of these outcomes find some measure of precedent or validation in the story of Don Quixote. From Jane Austen, Walter Scott, and Charles Dickens to George Eliot, Henry James, and Mark Twain, nineteenth-century novelists explore in myriad ways these realistic plot archetypes.

By the mid-nineteenth century, the broad lines of Cervantine criticism in the English speaking world were well entrenched, and they have shaped critical debate to this day. The commentary produced by Victorian critics tended to elaborate on, rather than depart radically from, the critical themes promulgated by their eighteenth-century and Romantic predecessors.[60] The late Victorian period produced one of the great English translations of *Don Quixote*, by Ormsby, who also furnished it with a splendid introduction that makes a significant contribution to Cervantine criticism. In the introduction, which amounts almost to a short monograph, Ormsby surveys incisively the history and challenges of translating *Don Quixote* into English, evaluating the strengths and weaknesses of previous translations; he revises the biographical record with a view to distinguishing fact from accumulated conjecture (for lack of information, he observes, biographers of Cervantes have been 'forced to make bricks without straw'); and he provides a lively, insightful critical overview that dismisses as nonsense the idealizing tendencies of Romantic criticism.

Ormsby is especially acute in his analysis of the novel's evolution, arguing that Cervantes had no extended plan for *Don Quixote* when he began to write. Sancho Panza did not even figure in the original conception, which amounted to little more than a short story, but his arrival on the scene changed everything, as Ormsby notes with characteristic animation: 'To try to think of a Don Quixote without Sancho Panza is like trying to think of a one-bladed pair of scissors'.[61] Evidence for the novel's fitful, yet extraordinary, evolution, is to be found in the author's conception of Don Quixote himself. Picking up on Hallam's perceptive observation that Don Quixote has, in an important sense, 'no character at all' because in his ideals (of honour, bravery, and so forth) he is nothing more than 'the echo of romance',[62] Ormsby shows how comprehensively Cervantes surpassed these narrow beginnings in the novel's second part, where Don Quixote's discernment on any subject other than chivalry shines through. Cervantes's recasting of Don Quixote allows him advantageously 'to make use of Don Quixote as a mouthpiece for his own reflections, and so, without seeming to digress, allow himself the relief of digression when he requires it, as freely as in a commonplace book' (p. 66). Even more extraordinary is the new-found prominence and complexity in the author's rendering of Sancho, who becomes the driving force of the plot, for 'it is his matchless mendacity about Dulcinea that to a great extent supplies the action of the story'. The parodic character of the novel also deepens; it is now 'the spirit rather than the incidents of the chivalry romances that is the subject of the burlesque' (p. 67).

The appearance of Ormsby's edition of *Don Quixote* marks a kind of watershed in the Anglo-American critical reception of Cervantes, signalling an escalation of Cervantine commentary and scholarship at the end of the nineteenth century. The 1880s in fact saw two creditable translations of *Don Quixote* besides Ormsby's, those of Alexander J. Duffield and Henry Edward Watts. New subjects of inquiry were broached, including claims that *Don Quixote* is a case study of insanity and its symptoms, and speculations that the novel conceals esoteric historical, political, and religious meanings. Such suppositions are rejected with characteristic vigour by Ormsby, who writes of the religious satire allegedly concealed in the novel, that only 'nineteenth-century self-conceit' could suppose 'those poor blind stupid officers of the Inquisition' incapable of detecting what 'our superior intelligence' so glibly perceives (p. 57). In 1892 James Fitzmaurice-Kelly published a new and extensive *Life of Miguel de Cervantes Saavedra* (updated in 1913, in light of new documentation uncovered by Cristóbal Pérez Pastor), followed by a *History of Spanish Literature* in 1898 that cemented his international reputation as a Hispanist. From the turn of the twentieth century, critical study of Cervantes became increasingly specialized and academic in character.

The range of critical responses to *Don Quixote* in the three centuries following its initial publication is, finally, as much a tribute to the rich complexity of Cervantes's narrative as a reflection of changing critical, cultural, and philosophical assumptions. There was undeniably a sea-change in the critical perception of Don Quixote and his quest at the beginning of the nineteenth century, yet the critical insights of the eighteenth century survived and were kept in dialectical play with the newer perspectives imparted by Romanticism. Rather than one critical orthodoxy being displaced by another, the trend, in the Anglo-American context at least, was towards a greater diversity and complexity of opinion.

Perhaps the most influential historical factor shaping the Cervantine critical record from the Renaissance onwards was the evolution of literary criticism itself as a cultural practice. The shift in critical focus from classical genres and norms to vernacular texts, and from philological annotation to more discursive forms of commentary, contributed to a growing sophistication of critical insight into *Don Quixote*. Meanwhile, a burgeoning print culture and reading public spurred the production of critical editions and new avenues of critical discussion (in periodicals and miscellanies), thereby contributing to an extraordinary growth in the volume and variety of critical commentary. Throughout these changes, however, the great constant of Cervantine criticism has been the ever-growing esteem accorded his critical masterpiece. Whether it is Ormsby, with his brisk, no-nonsense approach to

Don Quixote, or G. E. Morrison, who declared in 1895 that Cervantes did not rise from his authorial labours until 'he had created the Christ of fiction', critics from the eighteenth century onwards have been unanimous in recognizing Cervantes as *primus inter pares*.[63] As the epigraph to Morrison's book puts it, summarizing three centuries of criticism, *Don Quixote* represents 'A comedy to him who thinks, / A tragedy to him who feels'.

Notes to Chapter 2

1. John J. Allen, *Don Quixote: Hero or Fool?* (Gainesville: University of Florida Press, 1969), p. 3.
2. Oscar Mandel, 'The Function of the Norm in *Don Quixote*', *Modern Philology*, 55 (1958), 154–63 (p. 154).
3. Alexander J. Duffield, '*Don Quijote*', *Notes and Queries*, 6th series, 1 (3 January 1880), 22 (p. 22).
4. John Ruskin, *Modern Painters*, first American edn, 3 vols (New York: Wiley, 1860), I, 3.
5. Hans Robert Jauss, *Toward an Aesthetic of Reception*, trans. by Timothy Bahti (Brighton: Harvester Press, 1982), p. 28.
6. Richard Brathwaite, *The Schollers Medley; or, an Intermixt Discourse vpon Historicall and Poeticall Relations* (London: Printed by N[icholas] O[kes], 1614), p. 99.
7. John Locke, *A Collection of Several Pieces of Mr. John Locke* (London: Printed by J. Bettenham for R. Francklin, 1720), p. 244.
8. For a list of some thirty allusions in seventeenth-century English plays, see Edwin B. Knowles, 'Allusions to *Don Quixote* before 1660', *Philological Quarterly*, 20 (1941), 573–86 (p. 574, note 1). Knowles's publications on the early reception are collected in *Four Articles on Don Quixote in England* (New York: New York University Press, 1941). Knowles extends his survey of the literary reception down to the nineteenth century in 'Cervantes and English Literature', in *Cervantes across the Centuries*, ed. by Ángel Flores and M. J. Benardete (New York: Gordian Press, 1969), pp. 277–303. Gustav Becker surveys an extensive body of seventeenth- and eighteenth-century English texts that imitate, remark on, or allude to *Don Quixote*, in *Die Aufnahme des Don Quijote in die englische Literatur (1605–c.1770)* (Berlin: Mayer & Müller, 1906). See also Edward M. Wilson, 'Cervantes and English Literature of the Seventeenth Century', *Bulletin Hispanique*, 50 (1948), 27–52; and Johannes Hartau, 'Don Quixote in Broadsheets of the Seventeenth and Early Eighteenth Centuries', *Journal of the Warburg and Courtauld Institutes*, 48 (1985), 234–38.
9. Edmund Gayton, *Pleasant Notes upon Don Quixot* (London: Printed by William Hunt, 1654). For discussions of Gayton's commentary, see Becker, *Die Aufnahme des Don Quijote in die englische Literatur (1605–c.1770)*, pp. 77–82; Edward M. Wilson, 'Edmund Gayton on Don Quixote, Andrés, and Juan Haldudo', *Comparative Literature*, 2 (1950), 64–72; Wilson, 'Cervantes and English Literature', pp. 29–34; and J. A. G. Ardila, 'Gayton, Edmund', in *Gran enciclopedia cervantina*, ed. by Carlos Alvar, 7 vols (Madrid: Castalia, 2005–07).
10. *The History of the Most Renowned Don Quixote*, trans. by John Philips (London: Printed by Tho. Hodgkin, 1687); Thomas D'Urfey, *The Comical History of Don Quixote* (London: Printed for Samuel Briscoe, 1694); Edward Ward, *The Life and Notable Adventures of That Renown'd Knight, Don Quixote de la Mancha. Merrily Translated into Hudibrastick Verse* (London: Printed for T. Norris, and A. Bettesworth, 1711–12).
11. Knowles details forty-eight allusions in non-dramatic texts published before 1660 (see 'Allusions', pp. 574–83). This list does not include Gayton's *Pleasant Notes*.
12. Ben Jonson, *Ben Jonson*, ed. by C. H. Herford Percy and Evelyn Simpson, 11 vols (Oxford: Clarendon Press, 1950), x, 30. See Yumiko Yamada, *Ben Jonson and Cervantes: Tilting against Chivalric Romances* (Tokyo: Maruzen, 2000); and Yamada, 'Ben Jonson: A Neoclassical Response to Cervantes', in *Cervantes in the English-Speaking World: New Essays*, ed. by Darío Fernández-Morera and Michael Hanke (Kassel: Reichenberger, 2005), pp. 3–23.
13. Jonson, *Ben Jonson*, VIII, 203–04.
14. William Vaughan, *The Golden Fleece Diuided into Three Parts, Vnder Which Are Discouered the Errours of Religion, the Vices and Decayes of The Kingdome, and Lastly the Wayes to Get Wealth, and*

to Restore Trading So Much Complayned of (London: Printed for Francis Williams, 1626), p. 11.

15. Jonson, *Ben Jonson*, iii, 303.

16. Werner von Koppenfels, 'Samuel Butler's *Hudibras*', in *Cervantes in the English-Speaking World*, pp. 25–42 (pp. 28–29). For further discussion of Butler's debt to Cervantes, see Wilson, 'Cervantes and English Literature', pp. 45–52.

17. Samuel Butler, *Prose Observations*, ed. by Hugh de Quehen (Oxford: Clarendon Press, 1979), p. 215.

18. Samuel Butler, *Hudibras, in Three Parts, Written in the Time of the Late Wars: Corrected and Amended. With Large Annotations and a Preface*, ed. by Zachary Grey, 2 vols (Cambridge: Printed by J. Bentham, Printer to the University, 1744), i, p. i.

19. Henry Fielding, *Joseph Andrews*, ed. by Martin C. Battestin (Oxford: Clarendon Press, 1967), p. 3.

20. Ronald Paulson, *Don Quixote in England: The Aesthetics of Laughter* (Baltimore and London: Johns Hopkins University Press, 1998), p. ix.

21. Joseph Addison, *Spectator*, 249 (15 December 1711) and 163 (6 September 1711), in *The Spectator*, ed. by Donald F. Bond, 5 vols (Oxford: Clarendon Press, 1965), ii, 466; ii, 141–42. See Saint-Evremond, 'A Letter to Count d'Olonne', in *The Works of Monsieur de St. Evremond, Made English from the French Original*, 3 vols (London: Printed for J. Churchill, J. Darby, J. Round, E. Curll and R. Gosling, and T. Baker, 1714), ii, 3: 'I recommend to you *Don Quixot* above all; let your Affliction be what it will, the Delicacy of his Ridicule will insensibly make you relish Mirth'.

22. Grey, 'Preface', in *Hudibras*, i, p. xxiv.

23. Grey, 'Preface', i, p. xxiv.

24. Samuel Johnson, *The Lives of the Most Eminent English Poets; with Critical Observations on Their Works*, ed. by Roger Lonsdale, 4 vols (Oxford: Clarendon Press, 2006), ii, 5.

25. Samuel Johnson, *The Yale Edition of the Works of Johnson*, 18 vols (New Haven and London: Yale University Press, 1958), vii, 61.

26. Richard Owen Cambridge, 'Preface', in *The Scribleriad: An Heroic Poem* (London: Printed for R. Dodsley, 1751), p. v.

27. Cambridge, 'Preface', p. vi.

28. Letter to Thomas Percy, 31 March 1774, in John Bowle and Thomas Percy, *Cervantine Correspondence*, ed. by Daniel Eisenberg (Exeter: University of Exeter Press, 1987), p. 34. The offending title page of Wilmot's translation, which appears to have been published in 1769, describes the *Don Quixote* as 'Interspersed with Ludicrous Dialogues, Rhapsodies, Madrigals, and Serenades. The Whole Replete with Infinite Humour and Drollery'.

29. Cambridge, 'Preface', p. vi.

30. Michael McKeon, *The Origins of the English Novel, 1660–1740* (Baltimore: Johns Hopkins University Press, 1987), p. 292.

31. Sir William Temple, *An Essay upon the Ancient and Modern Learning* (1690), in *Critical Essays of the Seventeenth Century*, ed. by J. E. Spingarn, 3 vols (Oxford: Oxford University Press, 1908), iii, 32–72 (pp. 71–72).

32. William Warburton, *The Divine Legation of Moses Demonstrated* (London: Printed for the Executor of the late Mr. Fletcher Gyles, 1742), p. xviii.

33. George Gordon, Lord Byron, *The Complete Poetical Works*, ed. by Jerome J. McGann, 7 vols (Oxford: Clarendon Press, 1980–93), v, 528.

34. Anthony Close, *The Romantic Approach to 'Don Quixote': A Critical History of the Romantic Tradition in 'Quixote' Criticism* (Cambridge: Cambridge University Press, 1977), p. 56.

35. See Frans De Bruyn, 'Edmund Burke the Political Quixote: Romance, Chivalry, and the Political Imagination', *Eighteenth-Century Fiction*, 16 (2004), 695–733.

36. Miguel de Cervantes Saavedra, *The History of the Renowned Don Quixote de la Mancha*, trans. by Peter Motteux, 4 vols (London: Printed for Sam. Buckley, 1700).

37. Johnson, *The Yale Edition of the Works of Johnson*, xvi, 151–52.

38. Johnson, *The Yale Edition of the Works of Johnson*, iii, 11.

39. Harry Levin, 'The Quixotic Principle', in *The Interpretation of Narrative: Theory and Practice*, ed. by Morton W. Bloomfield (Cambridge, MA: Harvard University Press, 1970), pp. 45–66.

40. Corby Morris, *An Essay towards Fixing the True Standards of Wit, Humour, Raillery, Satire, and Ridicule, to Which Is Added, an Analysis of the Characters of an Humourist* (London: Printed for J. Roberts; and W. Bickerton, 1744), p. 12.

41. John Skinner, '*Don Quixote* in 18th-Century England: A Study in Reader Response', *Cervantes: Bulletin of the Cervantes Society of America*, 7 (1987), 45–57 (p. 55).

42. Gregorio Mayans y Siscar, *The Life of Michael de Cervantes Saavedra. Written by Don Gregorio Mayáns & Siscár*, trans. by John Ozell (London: Printed for J. and R. Tonson, 1738).

43. Early biographical views of Cervantes are discussed in A. P. Burton, 'Cervantes the Man Seen through English Eyes in the Seventeenth and Eighteenth Centuries', *Bulletin of Hispanic Studies*, 45 (1968), 1–15.

44. John Bowle, *A Letter to the Reverend Dr. Percy, Concerning a New and Classical Edition of Historia del valeroso cavallero Don Quixote de la Mancha* (London: Printed for B. White, 1777), p. 1. Subsequent references are to this edition.

45. Ralph Merritt Cox, *The Rev. John Bowle: The Genesis of Cervantean Criticism* (Chapel Hill: University of North Carolina Press, 1971), pp. 59–60.

46. Giuseppe Marco Antonio Baretti, *Tolondron. Speeches to John Bowle about His Edition of Don Quixote* (London: Printed for R. Faulder, 1786), pp. 309–11.

47. Baretti, *Tolondron*, p. 47.

48. Edmund Burke, *Reflections on the Revolution in France*, in *The Writings and Speeches of Edmund Burke*, ed. by Paul Langford and others, 9 vols (Oxford: Clarendon Press, 1981–), VIII, 130.

49. Thomas Percy, *Reliques of Ancient English Poetry*, 2nd edn, 3 vols (London: Printed for J. Dodsley, 1767), II, p. iv.

50. J. C. L. Sismonde de Sismondi, *Historical View of the Literature of the South of Europe*, trans. by Thomas Roscoe, 4 vols (London: Printed for Henry Colburn and Co., 1823), III, 332. Subsequent references are from this edition.

51. Friedrich Bouterwek, *Geschichte der Poesie und Beredsamkeit seit dem Ende des dreizehnten Jahrhunderts*, 12 vols (Göttingen: J.F. Röwer, 1801); volumes 3 and 4 were translated into English by Thomasina Ross as *History of Spanish and Portuguese Literature*, 2 vols (London: Boosey and Sons, 1823).

52. Lienhard Bergel, 'Cervantes in Germany', in *Cervantes across the Centuries*, pp. 315–52 (p. 333).

53. Miguel de Cervantes Saavedra, *The Achievements of the Ingenious Gentleman Don Quixote de la Mancha*, A Translation Based on That of Peter Anthony Motteux, with the Memoir and Notes of John Gibson Lockhart, 2 vols (London: George Bell and Sons, 1891), I, pp. xliii–xliv.

54. Miguel de Cervantes Saavedra, *The Ingenious Gentleman Don Quixote of la Mancha*, trans. by John Ormsby, 4 vols (London: Smith, Elder, and Co., 1885), I, 54–55.

55. Henry Hallam, *Introduction to the Literature of Europe, in the Fifteenth, Sixteenth, and Seventeenth Centuries*, 3 vols (London: John Murray, 1839), III, 669.

56. See P. E. Russell, '*Don Quixote* as a Funny Book', *Modern Language Review*, 64 (1969), 312–26; and Close, *The Romantic Approach*.

57. Samuel Taylor Coleridge, *Coleridge's Miscellaneous Criticism*, ed. by Thomas Middleton Raysor (Cambridge, MA: Harvard University Press, 1936), p. 99. Subsequent references are to this edition.

58. William Hazlitt, *Lectures on the English Comic Writers*, in *The Complete Works of William Hazlitt*, ed. by P. P. Howe, 21 vols (London and Toronto: Dent, 1931), VI, 108. Subsequent references are to this edition.

59. See David Duff, *Romance and Revolution: Shelley and the Politics of a Genre* (Cambridge: Cambridge University Press, 1994), p. 30.

60. For an informative guide to nineteenth-century criticism of *Don Quixote*, see Dana B. Drake and Dominick L. Finello, *An Analytical and Bibliographical Guide to Criticism on Don Quixote (1790–1893)* (Newark, DE: Juan de la Cuesta, 1987), pp. 32–37, 174–211.

61. John Ormsby, 'Introduction', in Miguel de Cervantes, *The Ingenious Gentleman Don Quixote of la Mancha*, trans. by John Ormsby, 4 vols (London: Smith, Elder, and Co., 1885), I, 62–63. Subsequent references are to this edition.

62. Hallam, *Introduction to the Literature of Europe, in the Fifteenth, Sixteenth, and Seventeenth Centuries*, III, 670.

63. G. E. Morrison, *Alonzo Quixano, Otherwise Don Quixote. A Dramatization of the Novel of Cervantes, and Especially of Those Parts Which He Left Unwritten* (London: Elkin Mathews, 1895), p. 15.

PART II

Cervantes and His Translators

CHAPTER 3

The English Translations of Cervantes's Works across the Centuries

Arantza Mayo and J. A. G. Ardila

The history of English translations of works by Cervantes in the course of the seventeenth and eighteenth centuries is, almost exclusively, the history of the translations of *Don Quixote* and their influence upon its reception in Britain. This is not to say that all other works have been wholly disregarded, although their popularity has certainly been limited in comparison to that of Cervantes's novel. Best known of all, particularly in the seventeenth century, were the *Exemplary Novels*, which enjoyed a degree of popularity through their dramatic adaptations by playwrights such as Fletcher and Middleton. There were however no published English versions available until the middle years of the seventeenth century when the first and most relevant collection of translated novellas was undertaken by James Mabbe. Mabbe's approach to translation is hermeneutic and while his texts are peppered by diegetic additions as well as by frequent adjectival and rhetorical flourishes, they reveal a shared sense of style with the originals which sets his work apart from that of most later versionists. This is partly helped by the short chronological distance which separates their publication from that of Cervantes's original *Novels*, but it seems obvious that the translator's own first-hand experience of Spanish Golden Age language and literature, as well as of Spain itself, proved a determining factor in his preserving of their stylistic flair. Despite the relative success of the *Novels*, other works by Cervantes did not fuel the interest of English translators to a comparable extent.

Over this period Cervantes's reputation in Britain rested on the fame achieved by *Don Quixote*, the first part of which appeared in English as early as 1612 under the title *The History of the Valerous and Wittie Knight-Errant, Don Quijote of the Mancha*. The translator, now identified as Thomas Shelton, also prepared a version of the second part which was published in 1620.[1] Shelton, by his own account, was moved to translate the first part to make the work available to a friend who could not read Spanish, a job he claims to have undertaken in the unlikely span of forty days. Regardless of the precise length of the enterprise, his translation betrays a degree of haste and a lexical carelessness made worse by a faltering command of Cervantes's language. More significantly, Shelton's lack of familiarity with the peninsular chivalric literary tradition that so crucially underpins *Don Quixote* led him to ignore the constant references that endow the original with its parodic texture. As a result, in seventeenth-century Britain the character of Don Quixote acquired the reductive profile of a buffoonesque madman and the novel that of a merely comic book, which nonetheless was warmly received. Notwithstanding the fact that a number of contemporary literary works draw on the characters of the Spanish novel, giving a strong indication of their popularity amongst their audience, the way in which Don Quixote is portrayed is directly derived from Shelton's influential translation.

John Phillips, second English translator of *Don Quixote*, published his version in 1687. Rather than attempting to produce an entirely new edition, Phillips set out to revise and polish Shelton's work with the additional insights provided by the French version of Filleau de Saint-Martin (1677–78), but also incorporating elements from the distorted vision of the knight which had crystallized through the influence of Gayton and others. Phillips's *Don Quixote* and the occasionally lewd language of his version have more than a touch of Guzmán de Alfarache's roguishness, removing the novel further from its original version. These features are not reversed in John Stevens's 1700 translation, which is essentially a modestly amended version of Shelton's own and does not offer any more faithful a view of the original novel at the hermeneutic level.

By contrast, Peter Anthony Motteux's four-part version (1700–03) marks a slight departure from the one-dimensional *Don Quixote* offered by Shelton and further reduced by other seventeenth-century translators and writers such as Gayton and D'Urfey. Although he consulted the editions of Shelton and Filleau de Saint-Martin, his work is most closely related to that of Phillips, particularly at a grammatical level. His 'Account of the Author' presents the novel as a fierce attack on the Spanish aristocracy, a view that had been earlier posed by René Rapin, though the Frenchman's reading only acquired currency in the British Isles from this point. As a result, and by extension of this anti-aristocratic interpretation, the parodic character of Cervantes's work finally began to emerge.

Alongside the appreciative recognition of Motteux's attention to detail as evidenced in his many footnotes, and of his determination to offer a dynamic equivalent of the original text, his work has been subject to criticism for often turning the original's subtle irony into explicit jest, for being excessively liberal with the addition and removal of adjectives, and for misinterpreting many idioms and puns. Owing to its strengths — and in spite of its flaws — Motteux's work has found favour with publishers and readers over the centuries: the eighteenth century saw ten editions, followed by an additional twelve issues of John Gibson Lockhart's own edition of the translator's version in the course of the nineteenth century. More recently, Wordsworth Classics opted for Motteux's translation in their 1993 edition of Cervantes's novel.

Some forty years after Motteux's version was first published, Charles Jarvis (also known as Jervas) produced what can be regarded as the most literal translation of Cervantes's novel to that date and one of the most relevant in general terms, *The Life and Exploits of the Ingenious Gentleman Don Quixote de la Mancha* whose first 1742 edition would be followed by another five before the end of the century. The author's emphasis on literalness offers unsatisfactory results particularly as regards idioms but the preliminaries of the work — an essay by William Warburton on chivalric fiction, a biography of Cervantes by Gregorio Mayans, and a critical prologue by Jarvis himself— were to be of significant importance in the reassessment of the novel as a work of literary parody, superseding the established notion that Cervantes had been solely concerned with social satire. In 1992, Oxford University Press published Jarvis's translation, edited by E. C. Riley, in the Oxford's World's Classics Series.

The interest in the original novel's literary parody was soon to be shifted by the publication of Tobias Smollett's *The History and Adventures of the Renowned Don Quixote* in 1755. This version, which took the novelist four years to finish and which would become the most widespread edition of the work in the eighteenth century, also included important preliminaries. Amongst them, Smollett's influential analytical account of Cervantes's life and his understanding of the relationship between the novelist's biography and work contributes the author's reading of the novel as a critical parody of 'absurd' chivalric romances alongside that of its main character as a truly heroic defender of worthy chivalric principles and ideals. The Spanish writer thus emerges as a courageous and wronged individual, bravely patriotic but deeply misunderstood by his own people. Smollett does not concern himself only with *Don Quixote* in his biographical essay but includes some insights on Cervantes's drama and his other prose works, revealing the extent of the Scottish novelist's admiration for the Spaniard. Also in the preliminaries, in a separate note as translator, Smollett sets out the differences between his work and that of previous versionists. He affirms that his own translation presents Don Quixote and Sancho in the precise light intended in the original novel, in direct contrast with the degrading fashion in which they had been represented by other versions. He insists that his work offers a hermeneutic approach which is careful to respect the particular character and tone of the original Spanish language and that it is simultaneously faithful and meticulous in its representation of satire and allusion, not least through the addition of numerous footnotes. Smollett's perception of Cervantes, *Don Quixote* and its main characters would transform the British understanding of the work and, in particular, of Don Quixote and Sancho as characters who went on to be regarded respectively as a martyr hero and a dignified peasant in a range of works which drew on their adventures and ideals for inspiration.

Smollett's highly influential version was followed by George Kelly's translation, published in 1769. The work is merely a superficial revision of Motteux's version and offers no contribution of its own, going as far as to include the former translator's prologue, with its anti-aristocratic interpretation, at a time when such a view had been wholly superseded. Just as Kelly simply revises Motteux, Charles Henry Wilmot's work (1774), the last translation of the novel undertaken in the eighteenth century, is deeply indebted to Smollett's, although his perception of Don Quixote as an ideal and idealistic hero is more exalted, signalling even more clearly the inexorable move towards Romanticism in British letters.

The early-nineteenth-century Romanticists read *Don Quixote* as a purely Romantic, i.e. a sad and idealistic novel, instead of a comedy. The adventures of the Spanish knight, however, were not the object of any new English translations during and after the period known in the history of literature as Romanticism. For most of the nineteenth century, readers relied on the many good translations produced in the seventeenth and eighteenth centuries — mostly Shelton's, Motteux's, Jarvis's, and Smollett's. The biography of Cervantes included in the preliminaries of Smollett's *Don Quixote* already emphasized the noble qualities of Cervantes and Don Quixote that the Romanticists extolled.

Three new English translations of *Don Quixote* were published in the nineteenth century — Alexander James Duffield's (1881), John Ormsby's (1885), and Henry Edward Watts's (1888). Ormsby's *Don Quixote* has been regarded as the best translation in English. After publishing an English version of the Spanish medieval poem the *Cid*, Ormsby decided to edit Shelton's text. However, he soon realized that for the contemporary reader a new translation, avoiding Shelton's errors, would be a better option. In addition to his translation, Ormsby wrote a critical introduction which may be regarded as the best analysis of *Don Quixote* published before the twentieth century. In the second chapter of this introduction, Ormsby explains the conditions in which Cervantes conceived and wrote *Don Quixote*. His exaggerated praise of the Spanish author is particularly interesting — Ormsby pays tribute to the author's courage during his imprisonment in Africa, and highlights Cervantes's loyalty to his Christian fellow prisoners, who failed to escape and whose names he never revealed to the Arab authorities, despite the tortures he endured. Although previous commentators of Cervantes's life, such as Lockhart and Duffield, had presented him as a helpless victim, Ormsby sees him as a brave and strong man who survived the most adverse difficulties. Overall, Ormsby's critical assessment of *Don Quixote* is extremely positive — in the introduction, Cervantes's novel is glorified as the second best-known book in the world after the Bible. For Ormsby, *Don Quixote* can still, in the late nineteenth century, be read as a modern book concerned with modern issues. Although the 1885 translation agrees with the Romanticists' view of Cervantes, Ormsby was innovatory in as much as he strove to reveal the extent to which *Don Quixote* is a classic work that will always appeal to readers everywhere. In the introduction, Ormsby disagrees with Byron's thesis that 'Cervantes smiled Spain's chivalry away', because, Ormsby argues, in Spain chivalry became obsolete after the Reconquest, completed in 1492 with the liberation of Granada. Ormsby also suggests that Cervantes's superb style and humour causes readers from all cultures and of all times to enjoy *Don Quixote*.

It may have been the popularity and quality of Ormsby's translation that prevented the appearance of any other English versions of *Don Quixote* in Britain until 1950, when John Michael Cohen's was published by Penguin. In the twentieth century, publishers and academic editors still preferred to reprint the works of Shelton, Motteux, Smollett and Ormsby. In 2000 Penguin issued a new translation, by John Rutherford, who pledged to modernize Cervantes's Golden-Age prose. Today, British and other English-speaking readers have access to *Don Quixote* in many different English versions — Shelton's retains the early seventeenth-century tone that is contemporary to Cervantes's times, Smollett's is endowed with his beautiful prose, and Ormsby's is free from the flaws of his predecessors. Further to these three, contemporary readers and reviewers have become very fond of Edith Grossman's *Don Quixote*, first published in 2003.[2]

In addition to *Don Quixote*, other works by Cervantes were also translated into English. The *Exemplary Novels* were published regularly along the centuries; the volumes seldom contained all the stories, but the translations of Cervantes's novellas outnumber those of *Don Quixote*. The *Exemplary Novels* were first published in Spain in 1613, and the first English translation, including just six novellas, was made by James Mabbe and appeared in 1640. Mabbe also produced the first English versions of the Spanish classic works *Celestina* by Fernando de Rojas and *Guzmán de Alfarache* by Mateo Alemán. For three centuries, English translators published versions of Cervantes's *Novels* that failed to incorporate all twelve stories — not until 1846 did they appear in a single volume by a single translator, namely Walter Kelly.

Date	Translator	Inclusions
1640	J. Mabbe	*Las dos doncellas, La señora Cornelia, El amante liberal, La fuerza de la sangre, La española inglesa, El celoso extremeño*
1681	anonymous	*El celoso extremeño*
1687	R. L'Estrange	*Las dos doncellas, La señora Cornelia, El amante liberal, La fuerza de la sangre, La española inglesa*
1694	W. Pope	*Las dos doncellas, La señora Cornelia, El amante liberal, La fuerza de la sangre, La española inglesa, El licenciado Vidriera*
1709	J. Ozell	*El celoso extremeño, La gitanilla, El casamiento engañoso, El coloquio de los perros*
1720	R. Croxall	*Las dos doncellas, La señora Cornelia, El amante liberal, La fuerza de la sangre, La española inglesa, El celoso extremeño, La gitanilla, La ilustre fregona*
1728	H. Bridges	*El celoso extremeño, La gitanilla, El casamiento engañoso, El coloquio de los perros, La ilustre fregona, Rinconete y Cortadillo*
1741	R. Goadby	*El coloquio de los perros, Rinconete y Cortadillo*
1800	anonymous	*La fuerza de la sangre*
1811	W. Hewetson	*El coloquio de los perros*
1822	S. Moore	*Las dos doncellas, El amante liberal, La fuerza de la sangre, La española inglesa, El celoso extremeño, La gitanilla, El casamiento engañoso, El coloquio de los perros, La ilustre fregona*
1832	T. Roscoe	*El amante liberal, Rinconete y Cortadillo*
1846	W. Kelly	all twelve novellas
1889	C. Vanderbilt	*La gitanilla*
1902	MacColl	all twelve novellas
1908	anonymous	*La gitanilla*
1917	M. Lorente	*Rinconete y Cortadillo*
1926	anonymous	*La fuerza de la sangre, La española inglesa, El licenciado Vidriera*
1928	J. Trend	*La fuerza de la sangre*, and *La española inglesa*
1950	S. Putnam	*El licenciado Vidriera, El coloquio de los perros, Rinconete y Cortadillo*
1960	Á. Flores	*La fuerza de la sangre*
1961	H. Onís	*La fuerza de la sangre, El celoso extremeño, El licenciado Vidriera, La gitanilla, El coloquio de los perros, La ilustre fregona, Rinconete y Cortadillo*
1962	J. Cohen	*El casamiento engañoso, El coloquio de los perros, Rinconete y Cortadillo*
1963	W. Starkie	*El licenciado Vidriera, La gitanilla, El casamiento engañoso, El coloquio de los perros, La ilustre fregona, Rinconete y Cortadillo*
1972	C. Jones	*El celoso extremeño, El licenciado Vidriera, La gitanilla, El casamiento engañoso, El coloquio de los perros, Rinconete y Cortadillo*

1992	B. Ife et al.	all twelve novellas
1998	L. Lipson	*La gitanilla, El celoso extremeño, El licenciado Vidriera, Rinconete y Cortadillo, El casamiento engañoso, El coloquio de los perros, La ilustre fregona, La fuerza de la sangre*
2006	S Applebaum	*La gitanilla, El coloquio de los perros, Rinconete y Cortadillo*

Despite the great number of versions available today, Mabbe's translation retains a strong appeal. In addition to being contemporary to Cervantes's prose, Mabbe's style is elegant and virtually flawless. As with *Celestina* and *Guzmán de Alfarache*, Mabbe did a superior job translating the *Exemplary Novels*, and one can only regret that he did not undertake a translation of *Don Quixote*. Alongside Mabbe, the versions by Putnam and Cohen — both American, and both translators of *Don Quixote* — are particularly commendable, as are those of Kelly and McColl, and Ife's new version, that appeared in the 1990s. Also of interest to the curious reader are Moore's and L'Estrange's versions. Moore, who belonged with the Blue Stockings, followed a French translation, which she altered freely, adding many sermons. L'Estrange published *The Spanish Decameron*, which comprises five stories taken from *La garduña de Sevilla* and five of Cervantes's novellas, which he vaguely attributed to a 'famous' Spanish author. L'Estrange took Mabbe's translations (with the exception of *El celoso extremeño*) and changed the names of places and characters.

Cervantes's last work, the novel *Persiles y Sigismunda*, was published posthumously in Spain in 1616. It was first translated into English in 1619, by an anonymous translator, as *The Travels of Persiles and Sigismunda. A Northern History*. The second rendering appeared only 150 years later, in 1854. The second translator, Louisa Dorothea Stanley, entitled her work *The Wanderings of Persiles and Sigismunda*. A second edition of Stanley's translation appeared in 1856. It is possible that the extraordinary popularity of both *Don Quixote* and the *Exemplary Novels* overshadowed *Persiles and Sigismunda* in the seventeenth and eighteenth centuries. This novel was also translated in the twentieth century by the American scholars Clark Colahan and Celia Weller.

Nearly two centuries passed until the publication of the first English version of Cervantes's pastoral romance *La Galatea*. It finally appeared in Dublin in 1791 as *Galatea. A Pastoral Romance*. Another translation was printed in Boston in 1798. Both translations were anonymous. An English version of *Galatea* was not published in Britain until 1804, by a Miss Highly. Another two versions, by two different translators, followed shortly after — W. M. Craig's in 1813, and Gordon Willoughby's in 1867.

Cervantes's *Viaje del Parnaso* was not translated until 1870, when *The Voyage to Parnassus* by Gordon W. J. Gyll appeared in London. James Young Gibson's *Journey to Parnassus* was then published in 1883.

On the whole, seventeenth- and eighteenth-century English translations of *Don Quijote* preserved the original narrative structure of the novel; yet this general faithfulness did not extend to the finer linguistic aspects of the work, its wide range of registers, its irony and its key parodic aspects. Despite the limited dynamic equivalence between these versions and Cervantes's original, the influence of *Don Quixote* on British letters in the two centuries following its publication in Spanish was significant, if wholly shaped by these translators and their more or less explicit interpretations of the novel. For all their shortcomings, these versions allowed the British public access to the adventures of the *hidalgo*. By contrast, in the nineteenth and twentieth centuries, most translators endeavoured to modernize Cervantes's language. The English translations help to understand the popularity of Cervantes's works in Britain and how he and his works were perceived differently along the centuries. The English translation of Part I of *Don Quixote*, finished in 1607 and published in 1612, gives an idea of the immediate success of Cervantes in Britain. The many English translations of *Don Quixote* illustrate how immensely popular this novel was among readers, authors and academics. With their critical remarks, given generally in the form of introductions, the translators determined the perception *Don Quixote* not only in Britain, but in the rest of Europe. Similarly, the English versions of the *Exemplary Novels* highlight the unremitting interest in this work. In sum, Cervantes's texts have been known to British readers, who have been able to enjoy each of his works in more than one translation.[3]

Notes to Chapter 3

1. Lo Ré has suggested that Part II was actually translated by a Leonard Digges. See A. Lo Ré, *Essays on the Periphery of the Quijote* (Newark, DE: Juan de la Cuesta, 1991), pp. 29–43.
2. Outside Britain, *Don Quixote* has been translated into English by the Americans Robinson Smith (*c.*1910), Samuel Putnam (1949) and Burton Raffel (1995), and by the Irish Walter Starkie (1964).
3. The latest studies of the translations are J. A. G. Ardila, 'Traducción y recepción del *Quijote* en Gran Bretaña, 1612–1774', *Anales Cervantinos*, 37 (2005), 253–65; John Rutherford, 'Brevísima historia de las traducciones inglesas de *Don Quijote*', in *La huella de Cervantes y del Quijote en la cultural anglosajona*, ed. By José Manuel Barrio Marco and María José Crespo Allué (Valladolid: Universidad de Valladolid, 2007), pp. 481–98; Frances Luttikhuizen, 'Don Diego Puede-Ser (James Mabbe)'s English Rendering of Cervantes' Novelas ejemplares', in *Cervantes y el ámbito anglosajón*, ed. by Diego Martínez Torrón and Bernd Dietz (Madrid: Sial, 2005), 200–10.

CHAPTER 4

Shelton and the
Farcical Perception of *Don Quixote* in
Seventeenth-Century Britain

Clark Colahan

Thomas Shelton hurriedly translated Part I of *Don Quixote* in 1607, which was printed in 1612 as *The History of the Valorous and Wittie Knight Errant, Don Quixote of the Mancha*. With a few corrections made in 1620, the same year that Shelton's version of Part II appeared, and further revisions in 1652, his translation remained well known and one of only two available throughout the century. The other was a biting travesty by John Phillips produced in 1687, much more a testimony to the work's popularity as Englished by Shelton than a serious attempt to transmit the sense of the original Spanish. It appears to have reached only a small readership and had little influence on eighteenth-century translators, except as a stimulus to greater faithfulness to Cervantes's text.

Read for most of the century as yet another of the romances it parodies, and seen as a mixture of farce and the more sentimental elements of its plot — the stories of Cardenio and Luscinda, Dorotea and Fernando, and *The Curious Impertinent* — *Don Quixote* only gradually entered popular culture, but references to Don Quixote and Sancho, as well as a number of abridgements, appeared more and more. By the 1690s, when Thomas D'Urfey wrote the first English musical comedy (*The Comical History of Don Quixote*, a successful trilogy), the protagonist was easily recognizable and clearly liked as a comic figure,[1] and this in spite of having been lampooned and saddled with an abundance of bad qualities in portrayals similar to Phillips's. D'Urfey was able to draw on this character recognition and emotional capital to proclaim the pseudo-knight's finer qualities in contrast to defects common in members of English society. In so doing, he added a striking new dignity to a figure that for almost a century had been considered aesthetically ridiculous and morally either pathetic or contemptible. But to what extent Shelton's translation had been responsible for such a simplistic reception — of a literary figure that later came to be considered emblematic of a worldview famously ironic and open-ended — is hard to say with certainty.

Shelton worked from the 1607 edition of the novel printed in Brussels, and his marginal notes are addressed to someone living outside Great Britain. Not much is known about the translator, although he has been identified with a homonymous Irish political exile whose name is on a list of students living in the Irish residence at the University of Salamanca. It appears that he later sojourned in Flanders, and then Paris. In his prologue Shelton says that he did the entire job at the request of a close friend, and in only forty days.[2]

Shelton's style closely follows the Spanish, to such an extent that it has provoked both praise and censure (*v. infra*). A twenty-first-century reader is particularly struck by his practice, in part doubtless motivated by haste, of choosing English words simply because they sound like the Spanish word in question and/or are cognates of it. In the 1620 corrections to Part I some of the more egregious examples of this *modus festinandi* were cleaned up. Shelton also transferred the complex sentence structure typical of the Spanish Baroque into English with little simplification, and many readers have found the results confusing and clumsy.

On the other hand, Shelton's most fervent defender, Sandra Gerhard, has argued that the English of the time was much closer to Spanish in both its lexis and syntax. Shelton's truly archaic terms, i.e. those out of date even for the early seventeenth-century, are used primarily to flavour Don Quixote's actions and speeches that are especially old-fashioned. Shelton also distinguishes clearly between a high and low register, unlike the many subsequent versions that reflect a horror of violating decorum or otherwise undermining the place that the work — originally parodic and at times even carnivalistic — has been accorded within high culture. Gerhard also points to the effective preservation of the rhythm and energy of the Cervantine text in the retention of features such as pronounced antithesis, enumerations and accumulations, and forceful sentence openings. She illustrates his nuanced command of English vocabulary in the use of verbs that she calls 'vigorous, concrete, and dynamic'.[3]

But within the last twenty years critics have not been as enthusiastic. As Pym has pointed out, twentieth- and twenty-first-century translators have made a concerted effort to place the novel within its own culture and time, while Shelton, like the eighteenth-century translators, often sought to domesticate it.[4] It should be remembered that the preference for a Spanish or an English flavour has varied from one period to another. Whereas once the creation of a reader-friendly, 'rambunctious' rendering of *Don Quixote* — to fit the comic subject matter — was by many considered paramount, in the last two centuries the work's entrance into the canon of high literature has produced a different result — a felt need for historical and cultural authenticity.

An even stronger case against Shelton's version has been made in the observation that British readers developed a distorted, burlesque mental image of the protagonist. From our perspective today as heirs of the Romantic and existentialist interpretations of the mad *hidalgo*, in which he is essentially heroic, it seems particularly offensive that he was taken for a crazy braggart, a sort of deranged *miles gloriosus*. The focus on the demeaning within the quixotic was particularly pronounced, as Ardila notes,[5] among the British, who did not know the romances centred around *Amadís de Gaula*, the first best-seller in Spain. As a result they were unable to respond to the simultaneous parody and residual awe implied by Don Quixote's choice of role model. Most readers who know well, in Spanish, the richness of Cervantes's style, may find it hard to believe that a more supple translation would not have transmitted more clearly the echoes of the subject's noble dimension, albeit mixed with ridicule.

However, in Shelton's defence, it may not be entirely realistic to think that character distortion could have been avoided, short of a thoroughly annotated critical edition, with readings on and taken from the literary milieu of Cervantes's Spain, British caricature of Spanish culture had other roots in the period. Most influential was probably the Puritan work ethic.[6] In its middle-class valuing of practical business and commercial success, it challenged and derided the older, aristocratic, impractical pride of rank that the hidalgo class was thought to represent. More concretely, Cervantes's novel did not catch on in Britain, at least as a serious work of literature, as fast as in France, and due to clearly identifiable social circumstances. Its publication came at a time when the Spanish monarchy and church, having impinged on British society in the form of the Armada and Catholic persecution of Protestants as the result of royal marriage, were ongoing anxieties.[7]

Similar socio-political conditions should mediate Allen's[8] well-documented finding that Shelton, like other early translators, failed to reproduce Cervantes's multi-tiered linguistic register, which varies not only from one character to another but from one moment to another in the plot, as well as the frequent ambiguities that contribute so much to the work's pervading irony. But seventeenth-century writing on social topics in Britain was predominately anything but subtle and self-questioning. Coming in the aftermath of the country's bitter years of religious conflict, in an intellectual environment more tolerant of controversy than was permitted in Spain, the age was one of partisan pamphleteers intent on vitriolic attack.

In the first half of the sixteenth century, the literary cultures of both countries had shared the humanists' use of irony to protect authors' radical views, as is demonstrated by the highly inconsistent history of the interpretation of the young Thomas More's *Utopia*. The same can be said of the anonymous Spanish classic *Lazarillo de Tormes*. But in the thick of the explosive and openly fought political and religious issues of More's later years, his writings become increasingly one-sided and aggressive. In contrast, the fear of official reprisals that underlies both the anonymity and the ambiguity of the *Lazarillo* seems to be present, even more markedly, in the second picaresque novel, *Guzmán de Alfarache*, published in 1599 and 1604, shortly before *Don Quixote*. In Britain, conditions would have to settle, the time for irony would have to wait until eighteenth-century writers could return to a lighter touch — and a better appreciation of the polyvalent nature of Cervantes's text. In Swift, where that historical moment and his anger at English mistreatment of the Irish came together, an ironic treatment of society could at times flourish, as in *Gulliver's Travels*, but at others it boiled over into sarcasm, as in *A Modest Proposal*.

The aggressively jocular tone of Phillips's 1687 version of *Don Quixote* owed much to the first commentary ever written on it, Edmund Gayton's *Pleasant notes upon Don Quixote* (1654).[9] John Phillips, author of the 1587 travesty *The Life and Achievements of the most Renown'd Don Quixote of Mancha*,[10] was the nephew of Milton, who provided him with an excellent classical education and made him his assistant. But he shook off his uncle's protection and moral shackles to become a satiric, bawdy writer in the fashion of the Restoration. Without consulting the Spanish original and drawing instead on Shelton and the French translation of Filleau de Saint-Martin, he modified and amplified their serious efforts with enthusiastic licence in the service of a superficial reading of the novel and a vulgar sense of humour. In this undertaking he was in the fashionable line of Paul Scarron, whose *Le Virgile travesty en vers burlesques* was published in Paris in 1648 and Charles Cotton's *Scarronides; or, Virgile Travestie, A Mock-Poem. Being the First Book of Virgils Aeneis in English, Burlesque*, which appeared in London in 1664. Nearly every critic who has written about Phillips's book has been scathing, and Putnam's comment is typical: 'A disgraceful performance [...] The less said about Phillips the better.'[11]

But all this righteous indignation notwithstanding, Hayes points out that Phillips was in all likelihood not aiming his barbs at first-time readers of the novel wanting to get to know it, and their numbers in Great Britain by the latter part of the century must have been relatively small. His attraction, instead, was the collusion he made available to second- and third-time readers, the sense of intellectual superiority produced by being in on the joke.[12] In addition, Phillips is a fascinating example of the tendency for travesty, both in seventeenth-century England and perennially, to go hand in hand with energetic domestication of any text.[13]

Phillips's rendering of Don Quixote's conversion to knight errantry recalls Gayton's hard-headed reading, and on top of it heaps up — rather in the style of Sancho — proverbial sayings associated with foolish activities:

> Nothing else in the World would serve him, but he must needs Dub himself and turn *Knight Errant*; with a design to roam about the World in quest of Adventures, and to put in practice whatever he had Read; in imitation of those wand'ring Champions in former times, that trotted from Post to Pillar, Pot valiant and Fool hardy, seeking all occasions to pick Quarrels for the Relief of injur'd Virgins; abus'd Marry'd Women, and oppress'd Widows, in defiance of all Danger' (p. 3).

Similarly, there are no tenderly understanding reflections on Alonso Quijano's faint-hearted crush on Aldonza, or on Dulcinea's real character, even though Sancho's description of her when he learns her identity in real life allows readers to infer most of what Phillips proclaims: 'You cannot imagine how the Knight was transported with Joy [...] having withal bethought himself where to find a *Trugmallion* fit for his turn. [...] There liv'd, it seems, in a Village adjoining to his own Lordship, a young fresh-colour'd smerking Country-Wench that went for a Maid, but in truth, was a crackt piece of Ware' (p. 5).

And finally, for vividness and energy of description — albeit achieved by jettisoning nearly every pretence of linguistic and cultural accuracy, along with a certain amount of loyalty usually expected to the author's vision — there is Phillips's rendering of Cervantes' s opening description of his typical, bored hidalgo, now transformed into an English 'Country Squire'. We are told, in part, that:

> Beef-steaks stew'd in a Nasty Pipkin, with a Red-Herring to taste his Liquor a Nights; Fasting and Prayer a Fridays, parch'd Pease a Saturdays, with a Lark now and then a Sundays to mend his Commons, consum'd three parts of his

Estate. The rest he as prodigally wasted in an extravagant Wardrobe: In which
was an ancient Plush-Jacket, purchas'd from a Mountebanks Widow; a Pair
of Black Bays Breeches for Holiday, purchas'd of the Hangman; and a Pair of
Boots, first Exchang'd for Heath-Brooms, and then new Vamp't by the Cobler
[...]. And you may add to these his Extravagances, one Sute more of *Irish* Frize
for Workydays. He kept in his House a grave Matron of Fifty for Service, a
Niece of Twenty for private Recreation, and a Skip-kennel to Saddle his Horse,
and Rob Orchards for Second Course (p. 1).

One assumes that such a novelistic hero, though different from Cervantes's, would
have been instantly recognizable as a stereotype, more or less related to the one
conjured up in the original for Spain, existing in seventeenth-century Britain.
Thanks to Shelton's widely distributed translation, readers would have been aware
of the exaggeration involved in the crossing over of the protagonist from Spain to
England. Ironically, aside from some sly smiles and belly laughs, the primary result
of Phillips's excessively snide view of the subject was probably the reaction it helped
to produce, the eighteenth-century redefinition of Don Quixote as someone not
bereft of many good qualities in a world deservedly whipped by Cervantes's satire.

Notes to Chapter 4

1. Thomas D'Urfey, *Comical History of Don Quixote as it is Acted at the Queen's Theatre in Dorset Garden By Their Majesties Servants*, 3 parts (London: Samuel Briscoe, 1694–96).
2. On Shelton's life see Sandra Forbes Gerhard, *Don Quixote and the Shelton Translation: A Stylistic Analysis* (Potomac, MD: Studia Humanitatis, 1982), pp. 4–7.
3. Gerhard, p. 42.
4. Anthony Pym, 'The Translator as Author: Two Quixotes', *Translation and Literature*, 14. 1 (2005), 71–81 (p. 80).
5. J. A. G. Ardila, 'Traducción y recepción del 'Quijote' en Gran Bretaña (1612–1774)', *Anales Cervantinos*, 37 (2005), 253–65 (p. 256).
6. See Ardila, op. cit., p. 256.
7. See Ronald Paulson, *Don Quixote in England: The Aesthetics of Laughter* (Baltimore and London: Johns Hopkins University Press, 1998), p. 34.
8. John J. Allen, 'Traduttori Traditori: Don Quixote in English', *Crítica Hispánica*, 1 (1979), 1–13 (pp. 7–8).
9. See Edmund Gayton, *Festivous notes on the History and adventures of the renowned Don Quixote* (London: Newbery, 1768).
10. See Miguel de Cervantes Saavedra, *The history of the most renowned Don Quixote of Mancha and his trusty squire Sancho Pancha now made English according to the humour of our modern language and adorned with copper plates by J. P.*, trans. by John Phillips (London: Thomas Hodgkin, 1687). References to Phillips translation are to this edition.
11. For more derogation of Phillips's adaptation, see Samuel Putnam, 'Translator's Introduction', in Miguel de Cervantes Saavedra, *The Ingenious Gentleman Don Quixote de la Mancha* (New York: Viking Press, 1949), pp. vii–xxiv (p. xii).
12. See Julie Candler Hayes, 'Tobias Smollett and the Translators of the *Quixote*', *Huntington Library Quarterly*, 67 (2004), 651–68 (pp. 654–55).
13. Paulson, *Don Quixote in England*, p. x.

CHAPTER 5

Eighteenth-Century English Translations of *Don Quixote*

Julie Candler Hayes

The evolution of extended prose fiction in Europe is inextricably linked to translation and intercultural communication in general, and to what Franco Moretti has called the Anglo-French 'core' of novelistic production, in particular.[1] Within this core, translations play a major role. Perhaps more than any single work written in England, *Don Quixote*'s successive translations chart not only changing views of translation and authorship, but also the consolidation of a new notion, the vernacular literary 'classic'. My purpose in this essay is to examine the ways in which the eighteenth-century English translations presented themselves to their readers. Moretti's quantitative analysis of the 'translation waves' of *Don Quixote* — the 'first international bestseller', as he puts it — sheds light on the role of variously configured reading publics in the constitution of European identity.[2] Like Moretti, I am interested in the ways in which the successive versions of the work reflect other shifts in the literary field. Unlike Moretti, I will be looking at what the translators themselves have to say about the work — and about each other — in their critical prefaces and notes, for what they can tell us about changing attitudes towards language, literature, authorship, and translation.[3] One of the most thoroughly 'naturalized' texts of all time, *Don Quixote*'s many versions show us why translations do not entirely fade into their surroundings.

Despite the significance of the earliest translations, Shelton's in England and the Oudin-Rosset version in France, most critics agree that French and English reception during the seventeenth century remained largely superficial, treating the novel only in its most farcical sense, giving rise to parodies and light theatrical adaptations of various episodes.[4] English appreciation for the novel's social and epistemological complexity deepened with the dawning of the eighteenth century, which saw a series of new translations: in 1700, John Stevens's revised and corrected edition of Shelton, as well as a new translation by Huguenot émigré Peter Motteux and 'several hands', as stated in the subtitle. Motteux's translation proved quite successful; following his death in 1718, the fourth edition (1719) appeared with revisions and corrections by the prolific translator John Ozell. In 1743 — the year of his own death — Ozell published an expanded seventh edition, 'revis'd a-new' and with copious 'Explanatory Notes'. Ozell's notes and revisions took advantage of the publication in 1742 of a completely new translation by Charles Jervas (or 'Jarvis' as the name appears in print), portrait painter and friend of Alexander Pope. As Tobias Smollett set about his translation in the late 1740s, he was thus able to draw on the work of these numerous predecessors, as well as references such as Stevens's Spanish–English *Dictionary* of 1706.

When John Stevens published his revised edition of Shelton in 1700, he had his predecessors clearly in mind: 'This I think (to Speak in his own Language) may very well be call'd *Don Quixote's* third Sally amongst us, since he has twice before appear'd in English, and now comes abroad again to seek Adventures, somewhat more refin'd in Language than the first time, and much more like himself than the second'.[5] The 'second' was of course John Phillips's 1687 version, one which has been generally dismissed by modern commentators, but as Stevens's reference indicates was considered a translation, if a loose one, in its own day.[6] Stevens borrows Phillips's image of *Don Quixote* as a 'Book-Errant' in his account of the noble book under attack in a cruel world: 'Thus the Adventurer in Print is in all respects equally expos'd, and finds much the same Entertainment as does the Knight in Armour: the base and meaner sort Persecute, but the wise and generous support him' (A4^r). Unlike his predecessors' short introductory remarks, Stevens offers a full-scale critical preface, a form of writing that had been current in France and Italy since the Renaissance but less prevalent in England until the late seventeenth century.

Stevens's preface takes up first the question of his relationship to Shelton, explaining that the text is 'partly Corrected and partly Translated anew' (A4^r), then outlines the principles underlying his own approach to translation. Stevens is at some pains to emphasize the depth of his revisions and the extent of an entirely new translation. Shelton's version, he tells us, was frequently incorrect: 'the English was so antiquated or corrupt, and the Meaning of the Spanish so entirely lost, that I have been forced to Translate sometimes half and sometimes whole Pages' (A4^{r-v}). He also defends himself against any charge of second-hand translation. Stevens further underscores the fidelity of his version: 'choosing rather to be blam'd for adhering too servilly to my Author, as it is generally term'd, than to alter any thing of his Sense' (A4^v).

Stevens's insistence on literality, while consistent with Shelton's approach, is at odds to a certain extent with much of his contemporaries' discussions of translation, which since mid-century had emphasized the translator's relative freedom and creativity: 'the middle way', as Dryden and many others put it, between the extravagant licence of adaptations such as Phillips's Cervantes and the 'servile' approach here explicitly endorsed by Stevens. It may well be that the literalness of the Shelton translation was precisely what attracted Stevens, serving him as an anchor — a literal pre-text — to ground his own version in response to the flurry of imitations and adaptations.[7] At the same time, Stevens's emphasis on his own contribution to the project and his shunning of second-hand translation from the French bespeak the need for self-authorization that also underpins much of the discourse of free translation.

In 1700, the same year as Stevens's revision of Shelton, there appeared a new translation by Peter Anthony Motteux. A French Huguenot whose family had settled in England following the revocation of the Edict of Nantes, this journalist and translator is probably best remembered for his revision and completion of Thomas Urquhart's translation of Rabelais (1694), a version still much appreciated for its colloquial energy and verve. Motteux brought the same talents to his translation of Cervantes; his version quickly dominated the market and it continues to be reprinted today in the Modern Library edition. Like Stevens, Motteux sets his translation in the context of the international and multilingual circulation of *Don Quixote*, observing in his dedication to Henry Thyne, 'This Piece, Sir, has had the Fortune to be very happily patroniz'd in other Languages'.[8]

Motteux's preface has been cited as representing something of a sea change in the English appreciation of *Don Quixote*, the shift from seeing the main character as a purely extravagant, ridiculous figure to considering him in universal terms:[9] 'Every man has something of *Don Quixote* in his Humor, some darling *Dulcinea* of his thoughts, that sets him very often upon mad Adventures. What *Quixotes* does not every Age produce in Politics and Religion, who fancying themselves to be in the right of something, which all the World tells 'em is wrong, make very good sport to the Public, and shew that they themselves need the chiefest Amendment' (p. A5ʳ). Motteux is unsparing in his judgments of his predecessors, criticizing Shelton's literal approach and dismissing Stevens's version as 'hastily furbish'd up' and Phillips's as 'a Burlesque Imitation of the *French* Translation'. Motteux claims that a literal translation 'wou'd be to make the Book unintelligible, and not English' (p. A6ʳ), but still prides himself on maintaining the authenticity of the original: 'Tho our Spaniard speaks English, he is still in his own Country, and preserves his native Gravity and Port' (p. A6ʳ).

It is often averred that translators' statements do not always coincide with their actual practice, and Motteux may well fall into that category; his version would eventually be denounced as 'a kind of loose paraphrase [...] taken wholly from the French' by Jervas and as 'distinctly Franco-cockney [...] an absolute falsification of the spirit of the book' by Ormsby.[10] Prefaces such as Motteux's may provide imperfect road maps to the translations themselves, but they tell us much about the world of discourse that sustains them, about the norms and expectations of the reading public, and about the translators' ideals, if not their reality — their 'Dulcinea' as Motteux might have put it. Whether or not Motteux, a native speaker of French, based his version as much or more on a French translation than on a Spanish text, as Jervas claimed, it was necessary for him, as it was for Stevens, emphatically to state that he had not translated from an intermediate translation — even though we know that such 'second-hand' translation continued to be a frequent practice among translators throughout the period. It is also significant to see Motteux drawing such a clear distinction between his version and that of John Phillips, a distinction that is largely lost on modern ears. One could frame two responses to his claim: on the one hand, for him to claim to be quite different from Phillips, he must have had some expectation of finding agreement among his readers, which suggests that we need to tune our twenty-first-century responses to these older translations more keenly. On the other hand, Motteux's critique of Phillips may point to their very resemblance and the 'narcissism of minor differences'. In either case, what is more telling than Motteux's actual practice is his need to distance himself from the burlesque tradition as well as from second-hand translation, neither of which corresponded to the norms and expectations of 'translation' among his audience.[11]

The opprobrium attached to second-hand translation is writ large in Charles Jervas's preface to his translation, published in 1742, a few years after his death. Whereas earlier translators had criticized Shelton's version as simply outdated, Jervas levied another accusation, claiming that although it 'has hitherto passed as translated from the original, though many passages in it manifestly shew it to have been taken from the *Italian* of *Lorenzo Franciosini*', and going on to cite faulty emendations in Franciosini that are replicated in Shelton.[12] Given, however, that the Shelton translation of Part I appeared in print fully twelve years before Franciosini's, the borrowing apparently took place in the other direction. Jervas entirely discounts Stevens's edition and, as we have seen, judges the Motteux version to be based on the French. Given the inaccuracy of Jervas's account of the origins of Shelton's translation, one is entitled to some doubts about his casual dismissal of the French translation, particularly inasmuch as it is not clear which one was meant.[13] Jervas's own translation — termed 'wooden' by Ormsby and 'lifeless' by Martin Battestin[14] — is considered to be reasonably close to the text, but lacking in literary value.

In 1719, the year following Motteux's death, a fourth edition of his translation appeared, '*Carefully* Revised' by John Ozell. Ozell was one of the most prolific translators of the period, specializing in the work of recent and contemporary French writers (he translated works by Corneille, Molière, Fénelon, Boileau, Montesquieu, Jean Le Clerc, and others); he contributed revisions to the Motteux/ Urquhart Rabelais and produced a blank-verse rendition of Anne Dacier's *Iliad*, along with a translation of her preface. His brief 'Avertisement' to the Motteux fourth edition simply notes that he has complied with the booksellers' request to bring Motteux's translation in line with the more recent Madrid edition of the novel: 'I may safely affirm many *Mis-interpretations* have been rectify'd, and not a few *Omissions* supply'd'.[15] A cursory examination of the 1719 edition suggests nothing more: emendations and corrections here and there, a few explanatory footnotes, some carried over from Motteux. In 1743, the year following the publication of Jervas's translation, Ozell came out with a seventh edition of the Motteux/Ozell version, 'Revis'd a-new' and with copious annotations based on Jervas and others.[16] In this edition, something new happens on the very first page.

> In a certain Village in *La Mancha*,★ which I shall not name, there liv'd not long ago one of those old-fashion'd Gentlemen who are never without a Lance upon a Rack, an old Target, a lean Horse, and a Greyhound. His Diet consisted more of Beef† than Mutton; and with minc'd Meat on most Nights, Lentils on *Fridays*, Eggs and Bacon‡ on *Saturdays*, and a Pigion extraordinary on *Sundays*, he consumed three Quarters of his revenue: The rest was laid out in a Plush-Coat, Velvet-Breeches, with Slippers of the same, for Holidays; and a Suit of the very best home-spun Cloth, which he bestowed on himself for Working-days.

While Ozell's first two footnotes are of the ordinary explicative variety, noting the location of La Mancha and observing that beef is 'cheaper in Spain than Mutton' —

both notes appearing in earlier editions — his third note overwhelms the reader:

> Strictly, *Sorrow for his Sops*, on *Saturdays. Duelos y Quebrantos*; in *English, Gruntings and Groanings*. He that can tell us what Sort of Edible the Author means by those Words, *Erit mihi magnus Apollo. Caesar Oudin*, the famous *French* Traveller, Negotiator, Translator and Dictionary-maker, will have it to be *Eggs and Bacon*, as above. Our Translator and Dictionary-maker, *Stevens*, has it, *Eggs and Collops*, (I suppose he means *Scotch-Collops*) but that's too good a Dish to mortify withal. Signor Sobrino's *Spanish* Dictionary says, *Duelos y Quebrantos* is Pease-Soup. Mr. *Jarvis* translates it as an *Amlet* (*Aumulette* in *French*) which *Boyer* says is a Pancake made of Eggs, tho' I always understood *Aumulette* to be a *Bacon-froise* (or rather *Bacon-fryze*, from its being *fry'd*, from *frit* in *French*). Some will have it to mean *Brains fry'd with Eggs*, which, we are told by Mr. *Jarvis*, the Church allows in poor Countries in defect of Fish. Others have guest it to mean some windy kind of Diet, as Peas, Herbs, &c. which are apt to occasion Cholicks, as if one should say, *Greens and Gripes on Saturdays*. To conclude, the 'forecited Author of the new Translation (if a Translator may be call'd an Author) absolutely says, *Duelos y Quebrantos* is a Cant-Phrase for some Fasting-Day-Dish in use in *la Mancha*. After all these learned Disquisitions, who knows but the Author means a Dish of Nichils![17]

The meaning of the phrase *duelos y quebrantos* has caused much ink to spill, and not only among translators. Contemporary editors concur that the term refers to a meal of semi-abstinence, but point to a long tradition of vexed commentary among Cervantists;[18] for some, the 'gripes and grumblings' inspired by the ham-and-egg dish suggest a 'New Christian' subtext.[19]

Smollett's comic spirit is clearly inspired by Ozell's lead:

> In a certain corner of la Mancha, the name of which I do not choose to remember, there lately lived one of those country gentlemen, who adorn their halls with a rusty lance and worm-eaten target, and ride forth on the skeleton of a horse, to course with a sort of a starved greyhound.
>
> Three fourths of his income were scarce sufficient to afford a dish of hodge-podge, in which the mutton bore★ no proportion to the beef, for dinner; a plate of salmagundy, commonly at supper†; gripes and grumblings‡ on Saturdays, lentils on Fridays, and the addition of a pigeon or somesuch thing on the Lord's-day (p. 27).

In his first two notes, Smollett also observes that 'Mutton in Spain is counted greatly preferable to beef' and justifies his translation of *salpicón* by 'salmagundy'. He then launches his third note:

> Gripes and grumblings, in Spanish *Duelos y Quebrantos*: the true meaning of which, the former translators have been at great pains to investigate, as the importance of the subject (no doubt) required. But their labours have, unhappily, ended in nothing else but conjectures, which, for the entertainment and instruction of our readers, we beg leave to repeat. One interprets the phrase into collops and eggs, 'being', saith he, 'a very sorry dish'. In this decision, however, he is contradicted by another commentator, who affirms, 'it is a mess too good to mortify withal'; neither can this virtuoso agree with a late editor, who translates the passage in question, into an amlet, but takes occasion to fall out with Boyer for his description of that dish, which he most sagaciously

understands to be a 'bacon froize', or 'rather fryze, from its being fried, from *frit* in French'; and concludes with this judicious query, 'after all these learned disquisitions, who knows but the author means a dish of nichils?' If this was his meaning indeed, surely we may venture to conclude, that fasting was very expensive in la Mancha; for the author mentions the *Duelos y Quebrantos*, among those articles that consumed three fourths of the knight's income.

Having considered this momentous affair with all the deliberation it deserves, we in our turn present the reader, with cucumbers, greens, or pease porridge, as the fruit of our industrious researches; being thereunto determined by the literal signification of the text, which is not 'grumblings and groanings', as the last mentioned ingenious annotator seems to think; but rather pains and breakings; and evidently points at such eatables as generate and expel wind; qualities (as every body knows) eminently inherent in those vegetables we have mentioned as our hero's saturday's repast (p. 27).

Smollett's send-up of 'the former translators' is a fine satire on translators' notes — many more of which he will produce, both from his own reflections as well as from earlier translators, especially Jervas. Smollett's careful reading of his predecessors produces a wonderful palimpsest of versions and revisions that foreground Smollett's writerly verve and allow us insights into his reading process.

Smollett's translation went through nineteen editions and reprints before the end of the century, while Jervas's and Motteux/Ozell's were reprinted four times each. The critical tide began to turn against Smollett, however, with the assessment of Alexander Tytler, Lord Woodhouselee, whose 1791 *Essay on the Principles of Translation* included an entire chapter comparing Smollett and Motteux, to the disadvantage of the former.

Tytler sums up the relative strengths of his two translators thus:

> *Smollet* inherited from nature a strong sense of ridicule, a great fund of original humour, and a happy versatility of talent, by which he could accommodate his style to almost every species of writing. He could adopt alternately the solemn, the lively, the sarcastic, the burlesque, and the vulgar. To these qualifications he joined an inventive genius, and a vigorous imagination. As he possessed talents equal to the composition of original works of the same species with the novel of Cervantes; so it is not perhaps possible to conceive a writer more completely qualified to give a perfect translation of that novel.
>
> *Motteux*, with no great abilities as an original writer, appears to me to have been endowed with a strong perception of the ridiculous in human character; a just discernment of the weaknesses and follies of mankind. He seems likewise to have had a great command of the various styles which are accommodated to the expression both of grave burlesque, and of low humour.[20]

Despite his admiration for Smollett's talent as a writer, Tytler ultimately finds Motteux's translation superior, arguing that Smollett relied too heavily on 'the armour of Jarvis',[21] whose literality and 'studied rejection' of Motteux's version led him, and through him Smollett, to make poor choices in the use of colloquial speech and idiomatic expressions. Tytler's position throughout the *Essay* is to be sympathetic toward adaptative translations and critical of close or literal translations; in his scheme, the freer Motteux version has every advantage over the literal Jervas version to begin with and the chapter on *Don Quixote*, as an object lesson on idioms, the prime pitfall of literality, is set up to make that point.[22] By thus yoking Smollett to Jervas, Tytler set the stage for later critics to dismiss Smollett's version as entirely derivative — indeed, as no translation at all. By the 1880s, John Ormsby, while showing a renewed appreciation of Jervas's literalism (which he termed 'ascetic abstinence'), remarked that in Smollett's translation 'Jervas's translation was very freely drawn upon, and very little or probably no heed given to the original Spanish'.[23] In the course of the twentieth century, scholars would go so far as to deny Smollett any hand in the translation or indeed any knowledge of Spanish at all, charges that have been thoroughly refuted by Martin Battestin.[24] The recent critical edition thus allows us to savour the intricacies of Smollett's relationships with his predecessors and with Cervantes's text, plus the relationships among the other texts, almost as if we had all the books open before us at once. Jervas's high-minded seriousness and Ozell's humour become part of our conversation with Smollett.

Like generations, translations age. As Ormsby observed of Shelton, however, this is not always to their disadvantage. Smollett's language, for example, is not so far from us as to seem alien, nor so close as to create jarring incongruities. Language change becomes acutely visible in translation, which foregrounds the temporality of the act of reading.

The successive versions of *Don Quixote* also point toward changes in the concept of authorship throughout the period. It is not entirely the case, as George Steiner argued, that translators have only recently begun 'emerging from a background of indistinct solitude'.[25] While the translators of earlier centuries whom he cites — among them Motteux, Smollett, and Tieck as translators of *Don Quixote* — may no longer spark instant associations with Cervantes for today's readers, they certainly were visible to the readers of their own day. The neoclassical translators may have called for texts that made the author 'speak' like a compatriot, but far from rendering the translator 'invisible', such practice lent power and creative authority to the translator. Rival translations such as those by Stevens, Motteux, Jervas, and Smollett enhanced the status of individual translators through competition in the literary marketplace. So while it may be the case that, during this period, 'increased authorial prestige [...] undermined the durable institution of literary imitation',[26] as Joseph Loewenstein has argued, the equally durable institution of literary translation — whose boundary with imitation had long been mobile and indistinct — takes on new lustre as it participates in the emergence of individual authorship. Of course, translation and authorship never merge, however prominent particular translators, from Cowley to Smollett to Gregory Rabassa and Eliot Weinberger, may become. The continuing 'difference' inherent in translation and retranslation, the awareness that one is engaged in what Smollett termed 'a task already performed' (p. 20), and the unavoidable awareness that we have seen among all our translators of other versions, revisions, and languages, point toward another understanding of writing — as repetition, revision, and rewriting — and hence a disenchanted notion of originality, often unacknowledged, but quietly present, an ongoing alternative to Romantic notions of textual production. 'Several hands' are always present in the making of a translation, not only the author's and translator's, but also those of previous translators, editors, and readers. For all the ease with which *Don Quixote* was welcomed and naturalized into the local environment, as much in France as in England, the very multiplication of versions and adaptations prevents any monolithic construction of it as a 'uniform monument'; the 'hostile dynasties' of successive translators remind us of the slippages and insecurities attendant on even the most fluent of translations.[27]

Over the course of the first 150 years of translations of *Don Quixote*, we also see the rise of a new phenomenon, the modern classic, which is concurrent with the emergence of the modern use of the word *literature* in English over the course of the eighteenth century. Tytler's reliance on examples of translations from modern languages in order to justify his theoretical principles bespeaks a profound change. Prior to 1700, it would have been unheard of to consider such translations worthy of critical analysis or to see them accorded the sort of scholarly treatment reserved for the Greek and Latin classics, or scripture: critical preface, author's biography, explanatory notes. Just as in earlier centuries the advent of moveable type consolidated vernacular culture and conferred an air of historicity and truthfulness on the printed word, so the production of elegant editions, with illustrations and editorial apparatus, now lend to works from the living languages a kind of cultural authority that had previously belonged only to the Ancients. The translator's footnote marks a small, but telling step in this process, by denoting that the text cannot be instantly seized in the entirety of its meaning, but requires — and merits — gloss and commentary.[28]

Notes to Chapter 5

1. Franco Moretti, *Atlas of the European Novel, 1800–1900* (London: Verso, 1998), pp. 171–74. See also the editors' introduction and essays in Margaret Cohen and Carolyn Dever, *The Literary Channel: The Inter-National Invention of the Novel* (Princeton, NJ: Princeton University Press, 2002).

2. Moretti, *op. cit.*, p. 171.

3. I develop this approach in the longer project from which this article is drawn: *Translation, Subjectivity, and Culture in France and England, 1600–1800* (Stanford, CA: Stanford University Press, 2008).

4. See J. A. G. Ardila, *Cervantes en Inglaterra: el Quijote en los albores de la novela británica* (Liverpool: Liverpool University Press, 2006), pp. 32–48; Edwin B. Knowles, 'Cervantes and English Literature', in *Cervantes across the Centuries*, ed. by A. Flores and M. J. Benardete (New York: Dryden Press, 1947), pp. 267–93. Needless to say, the literature on *Don Quixote*'s reception is immense. See Dana B. Drake, *Don Quijote in World Literature: A Selective, Annotated Bibliography* (New York: Garland, 1980).

5. John Stevens, 'Preface', in *The History of the most Ingenious Knight Don Quixote de la Mancha. Written in Spanish by Michael de Cervantes Saavedra. Formerly made English by Thomas Shelton; now Revis'd, corrected, and partly new Translated from the Original, by Capt. John Stevens*, 2nd edn (London, 1706), p. A3[r]. In the Stevens volume and in most of the early texts cited, the translators' prefaces have signature page numbers, such as A1, A2, etc. I have retained these numbers, adding only the indication 'recto' ([r]) or 'verso' ([v]). References to all translations will appear in the text.'

6. John Phillips, trans., *The History of the most Renowned Don Quixote of Mancha: and his Trusty Squire Sancho Pancha* (London, 1687).

7. Interestingly, Victorian Cervantist John Ormsby's translation project also began with a return to Shelton: 'Shelton's racy old version, with all its defects, has a charm that no modern translation, however skilful or correct, could possess. Shelton had the inestimable advantage of belonging to

the same generation as Cervantes; 'Don Quixote' had to him a vitality that only a contemporary could feel; it cost him no dramatic effort to see things as Cervantes saw them; there is no anachronism in his language; he put the Spanish of Cervantes into the English of Shakespeare'. John Ormsby, 'Translator's Preface', in Miguel de Cervantes, *The Ingenious Gentleman Don Quixote of La Mancha*, trans. by John Ormsby, 2 vols (New York: Century, 1907), I, p. v.

8. Peter Anthony Motteux, 'Dedication', in *The History of the Renown'd Don Quixote De la Mancha. Written in Spanish by Miguel de Cervantes Saavedra. Translated from the Original by several Hands: and publish'd by Peter Motteux, Servant to his* Majesty, 2 vols (London: Sam Buckley, 1700), I, A2^{r}–A3^{v}.

9. Knowles, 'Cervantes and English Literature', pp. 280–81; Ardila, *Cervantes en Inglaterra*, pp. 55–56.

10. Charles Jervas, 'The Translator's Preface', *The Life and Exploits of the ingenious gentleman Don Quixote de la Mancha. Translated from the Original Spanish of Miguel Cervantes de Saavedra*, 2nd edn, 2 vols (London: Tonson and Dodsley, 1749), I, p. iv; Ormsby, 'Preface', I, pp. vii–viii.

11. One critic decries second-hand translation as 'the Adulteration of the noblest Wines'. Henry Felton, *A Dissertation on reading the classics, written in the year 1709*, 4th edn (London: B. Motte, 1730), p. 126.

12. Charles Jervas, 'The Translator's Preface', I, p. iii. The first Italian translation of *Don Quixote* is Franciosini's *L'ingegnoso cittadino don Chisciotte della Mancia* (Venetia: A. Baba, 1622).

13. The Oudin and Rosset French translations of Parts I (1614) and II (1618) also predate Franciosini's translation. While Jervas may have been referring to the 1678 translation by Filleau de Saint-Martin, which was undoubtedly known to Motteux, it seems unlikely that Filleau's version, which calls attention to its freedom and 'modernity', would correspond sufficiently to Shelton's — best known, like the Oudin-Rosset version, for its literal qualities — as to permit Jervas to imagine a common link with Franciosini. Jervas's references to Franciosini thus appear gratuitous, serving simply to discount the earlier translators.

14. Ormsby, 'Translator's Preface', I, p. ix; Martin C. Battestin, 'Editor's Introduction', in Miguel de Cervantes, *The Life and Adventures of the Renowned Don Quixote*, trans. by Tobias Smollett, ed. by Martin C. Battestin and O. M. Brack (Athens: University of Georgia Press, 2003), p. xxxv. Ormsby, while noting that Jervas consulted Shelton, felt that he was nevertheless an 'incomparably' better scholar than the latter (p. ix), but Battestin attributes Jervas's accuracy to his 'dependence on Shelton' (p. xxxv).

15. Ozell, 'Avertisement', in Miguel de Cervantes, *The History of the Renowned Don Quixote De la Mancha*. 4th edn, 4 vols (London: Knaplock, Midwinter, Tonson, Churchill, 1719), n. pag.

16. *The History of the Renowned Don Quixote de la Mancha. Written in Spanish by Miguel de Cervantes Saavedra. Translated by Several Hands: and published by the Late Mr. Motteux. Revis'd a-new from the best Spanish Edition, By Mr. Ozell: Who has likewise added Explanatory Notes from Jarvis, Oudin, Sobrino, Pineda, Gregorio, and the Royal Academy dictionary of Madrid*, 2 vols (Glasgow: Robert and Andrew Foulis, 1771). Ozell died in October of 1743; the extent of his use of Jervas in the new *Don Quixote* edition suggests that this project occupied him intensely in the last year of his life.

17. Here is Jervas's footnote to the phrase: 'The original is *duelos y quebrantos*, literally *griefs and groans*. It is a cant-phrase for some fasting-day-dish in use in *La Mancha*. Some say, it signifies *brains fry'd with eggs*, which the church allows in poor countries in defect of fish. Others have guess'd it to mean some windy kind of diet, as peas, herbs, &c. which are apt to occasion cholicks; as if one shou'd say, *greens and gripes on Saturdays*. As it is not easy to settle its true meaning, the translator has substituted an equivalent dish better known to the *English* reader'. Jervas (trans.), *Don Quixote*, p. 1, note 2.

18. See *Don Quijote de la Mancha*, ed. by Francisco Rico and Joaquín Forradellas, 2 vols (Barcelona: Instituto Cervantes, 1998), p. 1, note 36.

19. For an overview, see Bruce W. Wardropper, '*Duelos y Quebrantos*, Once Again', *Romance Notes*, 20 (1980), 413–16.

20. Alexander Tytler, *Essay on the Principles of Translation* (London: T. Cadell and W. Creech, 1791), pp. 178–79.

21. Tytler, p. 180.

22. For this reason, Tytler draws heavy fire from Lawrence Venuti, who sees in the *Essay* a key document in the constitution of strongly adaptative, 'hegemonizing' translation norms. See Venuti, *The Translator's Invisibility: A History of Translation* (London: Routledge, 1995), pp. 68–74.

23. Ormsby, 'Translator's Preface', p. x.

24. See Battestin, 'Introduction', p. xxxiv, and his article, 'The Authorship of Smollett's *Don Quixote*', *Studies in Bibliography*, 50 (1997), 295–321. For a general account of Smollett's career as a translator, see Leslie A. Chilton, 'Introduction', in *The Adventures of Telemachus, the Son of Ulysses*, by Fénelon, trans. by Tobias Smollett, ed. by Leslie A. Chilton and O. M. Brack (Athens: University of Georgia Press, 1997), pp. xvii–xxxv.

25. George Steiner, *After Babel: Aspects of Language and Translation*, 2nd edn (Oxford and New York: Oxford University Press, 1992), p. 285.

26. Joseph Loewenstein, *The Author's Due: Printing and the Prehistory of Copyright* (Chicago: University of Chicago Press, 2002), p. 87.

27. I borrow both expressions from Jorge Luis Borges: 'The *Quixote*, due to my congenital practice of Spanish, is a uniform monument, with no other variations except those provided by the publisher, the bookbinder, and the typesetter; the *Odyssey*, thanks to my opportune ignorance of Greek, is an international bookstore of works in prose and verse'. 'The Homeric Versions', trans. by E. Weinberger, in *Selected Non-Fictions*, ed. by E. Weinberger (New York: Viking, 1999), p. 70; and 'Lane translated against Galland, Burton against Lane; to understand Burton we must understand this hostile dynasty'. 'The Translators of *The Thousand and One Nights*', trans. by Esther Allen, also in Borges, *Selected Non-Fictions*, p. 92.

28. Portions of this article originally appeared in my article 'Tobias Smollett and the Translations of the *Quijote*', *Huntington Library Quarterly*, 67. 4 (2001), 651–68; permission to re-use them is gratefully acknowledged.

CHAPTER 6

The Modern Translations of
Don Quixote in Britain

Michael J. McGrath

The marriage of Henry VIII to Catharine of Aragon in 1509 had a significant impact upon the popularity of English translations of sixteenth-century Spanish literature. Translations of the poetry of Juan Boscán and Garcilaso de la Vega, among other poets, and the spiritual writings of Fray Luis de Granada introduced the English-speaking world to Spain's rich literary heritage. Anthony Munday's translation of *Amadís de Gaula* (1589–95) paved the way for the first English translation of *Don Quixote* by Thomas Shelton, whose edition appeared in 1612. The novel and its characters have had a profound impact upon British readership. Irish author James Joyce alludes to *Don Quixote* in *Ulysses* (1922):

> They [Irish novelist George Moore and Edward Martyn, Moore's cousin] remind me of don Quixote and Sancho Panza. Our national epic has yet to be written, Dr. Sigerson says. Moore is the man for it. A knight of the rueful countenance here in Dublin. With a saffron kilt? O'Neill Russell? O, yes, he must speak the grand old tongue. And his Dulcinea? James Stephens is doing some clever sketches. We are becoming important, it seems.[1]

Since the beginning of the nineteenth century, six more translations of Cervantes's masterpiece became available to new generations of readers in Britain. The aim of this study is to illustrate how modern British translators of *Don Quixote* interpreted Cervantes's masterpiece.

Alexander James Duffield's translation of *Don Quixote* began as a collaborative endeavour with Henry David Watts, but each embarked upon his own translation when their relationship became strained. The title of Duffield's translation is *The Ingenious Knight Don Quixote de la Mancha, A New Translation from the Originals of 1605 and 1608, with some notes of Bowle, J. A. Pellicer, Clemencin and others*. In the same year (1881), Duffield also published *Don Quixote, his Critics and Commentators, with a Brief Account of the Minor Works of Cervantes and a Statement of the Aim of the greatest of them all*. Duffield's translation exhibits the seriousness with which residents of Victorian Britain approached their lives. The burlesque humour and satire of previous translations are absent, replaced by a more sober interpretation. Duffield aimed to produce a translation of *Don Quixote* that reflects the sensibilities and tastes of Victorian Britain:

> It seems to me that the time has come when his [Cervantes's] great work should
> be read not only for the beauty of its excellence, the charm of its style, for its
> sweet humour and tender compassion, but in order to perceive more clearly
> and enjoy more thoroughly 'the gross and scope' of that jest, as well as for the
> honour of its author, and the glory of the work which he wrought. For he was
> one of the most renowned refiners of taste and manner of whom Christendom
> can boast, and though dead, yet speaks in all the languages of the polite nations
> of the world.[2]

Serena Roybal Huffman notes that the serious tone of Duffield's translation
produces a version that 'departs markedly from the original. The tone is much more
chaste, and as a result, much of the original humor is lost'.[3] In I, 52, for example,
Don Quixote displays the intensity of his anger after the goatherd insults him: 'Sois
un grandísimo bellaco y vos sois el vacío y el menguado; que yo estoy más lleno que
jamás lo estuvo la muy hideputa puta que os parió'.[4] Duffield's translation, however,
does not capture the essence of Don Quixote's sentiments: 'Thou art a great villain
and thy skull is vile and empty; mine is more pregnant than ever was the gill-flirt
drab which bore thee' (II, 405). Duffield's polite translation of Cervantes's vulgarity
must have pleased Britain's Protestants, who were, for the most part, emotionally
restrained. Huffman, however, views this conservatism as a flaw in Duffield's
translation: 'He senses impurity where there is none more often than not, revealing
that his translation does not represent much more than the work of a stereotypically
prudish Victorian'.[5] Knowles also views Duffield's Victorian conservatism as
problematic: 'This Victorian bias for the chaste and the moral throws some of
Duffield's comments and parts of his translation off center'.[6]

The title of John Ormsby's translation is *The Ingenious Gentleman Don Quixote
of La Mancha* (1885). In 1980, Joseph R. Jones and Kenneth Douglas edited *Don
Quixote, The Ormsby Translation, Revised, Backgrounds and Sources*. According to
Jones, 'Ormsby's knowledge of Spanish was quite remarkable, and he produced
the first truly accurate English translation of Cervantes' great novel'.[7] Ormsby's
theory of translation is 'to avoid everything that savours of affectation. The book
itself is, indeed, in one sense a protest against it, and no man abhorred it more
than Cervantes'.[8] Ormsby's translation of the knight's angry words to the goatherd
recreates with accuracy the syntactical and semantic nuances of the original: ' "You
are a great scoundrel", said Don Quixote, "and it is you who is empty and a fool. I
am fuller than ever was the whorish bitch that bore you" ' (p. 397). Ormsby's desire
to produce a translation that was as accurate as possible to the original, however,
deprives the reader at times of the spirit of Cervantes's text. Cervantes describes
the dialogue that takes place between Don Quixote and the licentiate's cousin,
who agrees to lead the knight to the Cave of Montesinos: 'En el camino preguntó
don Quijote al primo de qué género y calidad eran sus ejercicios, su profesión y
estudios. A lo que él respondió que su profesión era ser humanista, sus ejercicios y
estudios, componer libros para dar a la estampa, todos de gran provecho y no menos
entretenimiento para la república' (p. 213). Ormsby's translation of this passage is
stilted and convoluted: 'On the way Don Quixote asked the cousin of what sort
and character his pursuits, avocations, and studies were, to which he replied that he
was by profession a humanist, and that his pursuits and studies were making books

for the press, all of great utility and no less entertainment to the nation' (p. 240). In spite of this occasional flaw, Ormsby's translation is superior to Duffield's and Watts's versions, as Huffman observes: 'Because he [Ormsby] emphasized fidelity to the letter so much, the spirit of the novel suffered, yet he was still able to recreate the original more accurately than either of his Victorian competitors'.[9] Even though Ormsby's translations of certain passages are faulty, his version was by far more popular than Duffield's and Watts's translations. Ormsby's knowledge of translation theory and Cervantean scholarship contributed significantly to the success of his translation, which was the first annotated translation of *Don Quixote* since Jervas's version in 1742.

In the preface to his translation (1888), Henry Edward Watts addresses Duffield's and Ormsby's translations: 'As to the two recent translations, which are more directly the competitors with this for the favour of all faithful Cervantists, it would be unbecoming of me to speak. That I am not content with them sufficiently appears in this present undertaking'.[10] Watts believed that a translator should endeavour to recreate with as much accuracy as possible the original text (I, 15). Furthermore, Watts affirmed that translators should not violate the spirit of the original with a translation that reflects the ideology of the society in which they live: 'To intrude one's own Nineteenth-Century personality into such a book as DON QUIXOTE, is an offence as gross against good manners as against art' (I, 16). Watts's translation of Don Quixote's insult of the goatherd is evidence of his decision not to bow to the religious and social ideologies of his day in order to respect the true spirit of the knight's words: '"You are a very great rascal", cried Don Quixote at this; "and it is you who are empty and deficient; for I am fuller than ever was the whore, — offspring of a whore, — that brought you forth"' (III, 402).

Watts's many insightful footnotes provide the reader with the necessary information to appreciate the literary, cultural, and historical elements of the novel. Cervantes describes Don Quixote's diet as consisting of 'Una olla de algo más vaca que carnero, salpicón las más noches, duelos y quebrantos los sábados, lantejas los viernes, algún palomino de añadidura los domingos' (p. 113) ['A mess of somewhat more beef than mutton, a salad on most nights, a hotch-potch on Saturdays, lentils on Fridays, with the addition of a pigeon on Sundays] (II, 32). Watts's detailed footnote allows the reader to gain a true appreciation of the cultural significance of the knight's diet:

> The diet of Don Quixote may be taken as that of a small country gentleman of the period. The olla was, and is, the standing dish, more or less savoury according to its contents. The salad (salpicori) was one of meat cut into small pieces and dressed with vinegar, oil, and pepper. The dish I have ventured, for want of a better equivalent, to translate ' hotch-potch', *duelos y quebrantos*, has been a fertile subject for the commentators, and a hard bone for the translators to pick. *Duelos y quebrantos*, Pellicer has explained, arose out of the custom in the pastoral districts of Spain for the shepherds to bring home to their masters, at the end of the week, the remains or prime pieces of the animals which had come to a violent end, either from wolves or accidents in the field. Out of these was made the dish called *duelos y quebrantos* — literally, 'griefs and breakings' — the first word expressive of the sentiment of the master at his loss, the second

denoting the condition of the animal. This dish, as being meagre and little appetising, good Spaniards, by a special dispensation, were permitted to eat on Saturdays. On that day abstinence from meat used to be strictly observed throughout Spain, in commemoration of the great and crowning victory of Las Navas de Tolosa, gained in 1212, over the Moors, when Santiago in person helped the Christian host. The custom lasted till the middle of the Eighteenth century, when it was abolished by a Bull of Pope Benedict XIV. The name *duelos y quebrantos* as well as the dish, appears to be now obsolete in Spain, — at least, I never could hear of it; but it still survives in the Spanish countries of America (II, 32).

Watts's translation was the last by a British translator until the middle of the twentieth century. First published in 1950, John Michael Cohen's translation remained in print until the 1970s.[11] His stated aim was to translate *Don Quixote* with 'the task of reconciling faithfulness to Cervantes with the writing of contemporary English'.[12] Cohen's translation of Don Quixote's insult of the goatherd in I, 52 is quite similar to Watts's translation: '"You are a very great rascal", cried Don Quixote at this point, "and it is you that is vacant and deficient. For I am a good deal fuller than ever that whore's daughter, the whore that bore you, was"' (p. 451). While Cohen recognizes that earlier translations resemble the original in spirit, he also believed that previous translators failed to capture the genius of Cervantes's language. With the exception of episodes in which the Spanish is archaic for effect, Cohen modernizes both vocabulary and syntax.

While Cohen translates the majority of Sancho's sayings with his own words, he inserts occasionally English sayings that resemble closely the original. After the barber abandons his donkey in I, 25, Sancho comments to Don Quixote how much he likes the animal: 'Y ¡para mis barbas, si no es bueno el rucio!' (p. 297). Cohen elects to utilize an English colloquialism to express the strong sentiment that Cervantes communicates with the word *barbas* [beard]. 'And I'll be blowed if the dapple is not a good ass' (p. 164). Cohen anglicizes the names of the characters and suggests that the reader pronounce them in the 'English way', because Spanish pronunciation has changed considerably since Cervantes's day.

Cohen points out that the 'stilted language' (p. 19) of the pastoral narratives makes it difficult to achieve a translation that flows freely. Faced with a dearth of suitable translations, Cohen adapts oaths and expletives: 'Some of the oaths and expletives have had to be toned down, as in this respect the richness of our vocabulary has been considerably depleted since the seventeenth century, and such a literal rendering as "By God's hand!", or "Woe is me!" is now merely funny' (p. 19). He admits that a lack of faith in his own ability to translate effectively the interpolated poems is the reason he relies on earlier translators' versions of them.

Cohen's footnotes are scanty, and he explains that 'the obscurities are few, and no attempts to explain them do much more than pile up indigestible historical references, that prevent the reader from getting along with the book' (p. 20). Too few footnotes, however, can distort Cervantes's intent and possibly diminish the reader's appreciation of the novel. In the Prologue to Part II, Cervantes responds to the accusation by Alonso de Avellaneda, who published in 1614 a spurious edition of Part II, that Cervantes disparages the playwright Lope de Vega in Part I: 'no tengo yo de perseguir a ningún sacerdote, y más si tiene por añadidura ser familiar del Santo Oficio; y si él lo dijo por quien parece que lo dijo, engañóse de todo en todo; que del tal adoro el ingenio, admiro las obras, y la ocupación continua y virtuosa' (p. 26); 'I am not likely to persecute any priest, particularly if he is a familiar of the Holy Office to boot. And if it was on behalf of a certain person that he wrote what he did, he is absolutely mistaken; for I revere that man's genius, and admire his works and his virtuous and unceasing industry' (p. 468). Cohen's failure to explain that Lope de Vega had many affairs after he became a priest, as well as the lack of any reference to Cervantes's jealously of Lope de Vega's success as a playwright, deprives the reader of the knowledge required to appreciate Cervantes's ironic tone.

After publishing Cohen's translation in 1950, and taking it through some nine printings, Penguin replaced it with John Rutherford's translation in 2000. Rutherford summarizes his approach to his translation in the following way: 'What I tried to do was different: to let the Spanish words construct in my mind's eye the world of the novel, and to live in that world; to see and hear Don Quixote and Sancho and to make them my best friends (some loss of sanity is a price that any artist has to pay); and only then to search for the English words with which to describe what I found in my imagination'.[13] Rutherford rejects the idea of the 'invisible translator'. Just as Cervantes used the language of his day, Rutherford believes a translation should use the language of its day (p. xxix). Rutherford's translation of Don Quixote's angry words for the goatherd are representative of what a reader might expect from a twenty-first-century translator: ' "You are a villainous wretch", Don Quixote burst out, "and you are the one who is empty and a fool, and I am fuller than the whore of a bitch who bore you ever was" ' (p. 468).

Rutherford's use of vocabulary that a reader who lives outside of Britain would probably not understand, makes it difficult to appreciate fully the virtues of his translation. Rutherford's translation of the epitaph that appears on the grave of Don Quixote is one example of this. In his translation, Rutherford employs British English vocabulary:

> Aquí yace el caballero
> bien molido y mal andante
> a quien llevó Rocinante
> por uno y otro sendero.
> Sancho Panza el majadero
> yace también junto a él,
> escudero el más fiel
> que vio el trato de escudero.

> Here lies a knight, a man of pluck,
> Rich in thumpings, poor in luck,
> Who, perched on Rocinante's back,
> Rode up this path and down that track.
> And Sancho Panza is the dolt
> Who lies beside him in t his vault:
> The loyallest man in our empire
> Who ever earned the name of squire (p. 478).

Additional examples include 'weeds' (p. 694) to describe mourning clothes, 'farthing' (p. 851) to refer to money, and 'twenty stone' (p. 936) to describe a villager's weight. Sancho Panza speaks with Cockney slang, which, as T. Lathrop has pointed out, is a variation of English that does not correspond to the linguistic register of Sancho's Spanish: 'Sancho, even though he was an illiterate fellow, really spoke a rather standard Spanish, and not a substandard variant, and Cockney English is substandard.'[14] In expressing his anger with the way the author of the second part of *Don Quijote de la Mancha* portrays him, Sancho declares, 'I'll be blowed, gents, if the author of that book you've got there doesn't want to get on bad terms with me — and if he calls me a greedy-guts, as you say he does, I only hope he doesn't call me a boozer into the bargain' (p. 889).

While Rutherford admits that it would be easy to shorten complex sentences and correct grammatical inaccuracies, he does neither to preserve Cervantes's literary style: 'El lecho, que era un poco endeble y de no firmes fundamentos, no pudiendo sufrir la añadidura del harriero, dio consigo en el suelo, a cuyo gran ruido despertó el ventero, y luego imaginó que debían de ser pendencias de Maritornes, porque, habiéndola llamado a voces, no respondía' (p. 244) becomes 'The bed, being some-what fragile and insecurely founded, couldn't bear the addition of the muleteer and came crashing to the floor and awoke the innkeeper, who immediately assumed that it must be some of Maritornes' goings-on, because he yelled out to her and there was no reply' (p. 147). Cohen's translation of the same sentence is vastly different: 'The bed was rather weak and supported on no firm foundations. So, unable to bear the additional weight of the carrier, it gave way with a great crash. This woke the innkeeper, who called for Maritornes and, getting no reply, suspected that she must be the cause of the noise' (p. 123). Rutherford describes the process of translating as an 'impossible goal' (p. xxxii), for translators are unable to achieve the perfection they desire. Yet he believes that translators should not feel inferior to the author of the original: 'If, as we've been told over and over again, we're attempting the impossible, it follows that we aren't humble hacks but heroes. So I had to try to write as Cervantes did, and to be as creative and as playful with language as he was. By undertaking this translation I'd chosen to rub shoulders with the great man, so that was what I had to do, not grovel at his feet' (p. xxvii). Like a modern knight errant, he adds, translators must aspire to come as close as possible to the perfect translation.

Edith Grossman was neither born in Britain nor educated there, yet her 2003 translation of Cervantes's masterpiece has contributed significantly to the state of English translations of the novel in Britain.[15] In the 'Translator's Note to the Reader', Grossman informs the reader that she aspires to recreate as much as possible the genius of Cervantes's prose using contemporary English:

> When Cervantes wrote *Don Quixote*, his language was not archaic or quaint. He wrote in a crackling, up-to-date Spanish that was an intrinsic part of his time (this is instantly apparent when he has Don Quixote, in transports of knightly madness, speak in the old-fashioned idiom of the novels of chivalry), a modern language that both reflected and helped to shape the way people experienced the world. This meant that I did not need to find a special, anachronistic, somehow-seventeenth-century voice but could translate his astonishingly fine writing into contemporary English.[16]

Furthermore, Grossman speaks to the enormous challenge of translating *Don Quixote*, a task she refers to as a 'daunting and inspiring enterprise' (p. xviii).

Grossman's translation of the opening line of the novel is representative of her ability to translate Cervantes's difficult prose in such a way that neither content nor rhythm is sacrificed: 'En un lugar de La Mancha, de cuyo nombre no quiero acordarme, vivía un hidalgo de los de lanza en astillero, adarga antigua, rocín flaco y galgo corredor' (p. 113) becomes 'Somewhere in La Mancha, in a place whose name I do not care to remember, a gentleman lived not long ago, one of tose who has a lance and ancient shield on a shelf and keeps a skinny nag and a greyhound for racing' (p. 19). Her recreation of Don Quixote's vitriolic words directed toward the goatherd is both faithful to the original and easy to understand: '"You are a villain and a scoundrel", said Don Quixote, "and you are the one who is vacant and foolish; I have more upstairs than the whore who bore you ever did"' (p. 439). Grossman's translation of the epitaph on the grave of Don Quixote also illustrates (as Fuentes has put it) her 'plain but plentiful contemporary English':[17]

> Here lies the famous knight
> errant and badly bruised
> and borne by Rocinante
> down many a primrose path.
> Sancho Panza the simple
> lies here, too, beside him,
> the squire most loyal and true
> who ever plied the trade (p. 448).

There have been nine translations of *Don Quixote* published in Britain and in the United States since 1881.[18] Readers who depend upon a translation to appreciate the knight errant's adventures may end up reading a novel that is linguistically and culturally inferior to the original. Furthermore, the reader's first exposure to *Don Quixote* may be markedly different to the original. Duffield's Protestant sensibility and Victorian mentality were responsible for a translation void of Cervantean humour. Ormsby and Watts, who were contemporaries of Duffield, also misrepresented at times the spirit of the novel because of the era in which they lived. Furthermore, Ormsby attempted to recreate the Spanish language of the seventeenth century by incorporating obsolete language into his translation.[19] Cohen, like Ormsby and Watts, aspired for a translation that was as faithful as possible to the original. The quality of Cohen's translation, however, suffers at times due to Cohen's desire to be too faithful to the original. Rutherford aspired to recreate Cervantes's text as closely as possible, but he did so with a keen awareness of the potential pitfalls of such an endeavour. Watts, Rutherford and Grossman seemed to understand better than Duffield, Ormsby, or Cohen how important a true appreciation of the genius of the novel was to a translation that was faithful both in letter and in spirit. Each translator's version of *Don Quixote* contributed to the popularity and critical acclaim of the novel in Britain.

Notes to Chapter 6

1. James Joyce, *Ulysses* (New York: Random House, 1946), p. 190.
2. Alexander James Duffield, 'Introduction', in Miguel de Cervantes, *The Ingenious Knight Don Quixote de la Mancha*, 2 vols (London: C. K. Paul & Co., 1881), p. vi. References to the Duffield translation are to this edition.
3. Serena Roybal Huffman, 'A Victorian Don Quixote: Cervantes in England' (unpublished doctoral thesis, University of New Mexico, 1983), p. 62.
4. Miguel de Cervantes Saavedra, *El ingenioso hidalgo don Quijote de la Mancha*, ed. by John Jay Allen (Madrid: Cátedra, 2005), p. 652. All references to the original Spanish version of *Don Quixote* are to Allen's edition.
5. Huffman, p. 72.
6. Edwin K. Knowles, 'Cervantes and English Literature', in *Cervantes Across the Centuries*, ed. by Ángel Flores and M. J. Bernadete (New York: The Dryden Press, 1948), pp. 267–93 (p. 290).
7. Joseph R. Jones, 'Introduction', in Miguel de Cervantes Saavedra, *Don Quixote, The Ormsby Translation, Revised, Backgrounds and Sources*, ed. by Joseph R. Jones and Kenneth Douglas (New York: W. W. Norton, 1980), p. ix.
8. Miguel de Cervantes Saavedra, *The Ingenious Gentleman Don Quixote of La Mancha*, trans. by John Ormsby (London: Smith, Elder & Co., 1885), p. 8. References to Ormsby's translation are to this edition.
9. Huffman, p. 73.
10. Miguel de Cervantes Saavedra, *The Ingenious Gentleman Don Quixote of La Mancha*, I, trans. by Henry Edward Watts, 5 vols (London: Bernard Quaritch, 1888), p. 13. References to Watts's translations are to this edition.
11. Portions of my discussion of Cohen's translation, as well as the forthcoming discussion of Rutherford's and Grossman's translations, appear in my article 'Tilting at Windmills: *Don Quijote* in English', *Cervantes*, 25. 1 (2006), 1–40. In the article, I compare and contrast Cohen's and Rutherford's translations with all of the translations published since 1949, beginning with Samuel Putnam's version. I am grateful to the editor for permission to reprint this material.
12. Miguel de Cervantes Saavedra, *The Adventures of Don Quixote de la Mancha*, trans. by J[ohn] M[ichael] Cohen, 1950 (Harmondsworth: Penguin, 1975), p. 11. References to Cohen's translation are to this edition.
13. Miguel de Cervantes Saavedra, *The Ingenious Hidalgo Don Quixote de la Mancha*, trans. by John Rutherford, with an Introduction by Roberto González Echevarría (Harmondsworth: Penguin, 2001), p. xxvii. References to Rutherford's edition are to this edition.
14. Tom Lathrop, 'Review of *The Ingenious Hidalgo Don Quixote de la Mancha*, trans. by John Rutherford, with an Introduction by Roberto González Echeverría', *Cervantes*, 22. 2 (2002), p. 177.
15. A. S. Byatt, 'Windmills of the Mind', *The Guardian*, 24 January 2004: 'Edith Grossman's translation has been described as a masterpiece. It has energy and clarity, and she has invented a robust style which is neither modern nor ancient [...] and the rhythm of the telling is compelling'.
16. Miguel de Cervantes Saavedra, *Don Quixote*, trans. by Edith Grossman, with an Introduction by Harold Bloom (New York: Ecco, 2003), p. xx.
17. Carlos Fuentes, 'Tilt: The Errant Knight of La Mancha Rides Again in a New English Translation', *New York Times*, 2 November 2003, p. 15.
18. The translations published in United States are the following: Samuel Putnam (New York: Random House, 1949); Burton Raffel (New York: W. W. Norton, 1995); Edith Grossman (New York: HarperCollins, 2003); and T. Lathrop (Newark, DE: Juan de la Cuesta Hispanic Monographs, 2005).
19. Huffman, 'A Victorian Don Quixote: Cervantes in England', p. 64.

CHAPTER 7

Englishing Cervantes's *Exemplary Novels*

Frances Luttikhuizen

In the summer of 1613, Cervantes published his *Novelas ejemplares* [Exemplary Novels], twelve delightful short stories. Long before the stories appeared in English, playwrights such as John Fletcher, Francis Beaumont, Thomas Middleton, William Rowley and Philip Massinger read them in the French and adapted some of the plots to their own advantage. In 1640, six of the twelve stories appeared in English. The translator, James Mabbe (1572–1642), or Don Diego Puede-Ser as he called himself, was one of the great Elizabethan translators.

Over the centuries, three complete renderings (1846, 1902, 1992) and seventeen noteworthy partial renderings (1640, 1687, 1694, 1709, 1720, 1728, 1741, 1811, 1822, 1832, 1928, 1950, 1961, 1962, 1963, 1972, 1998, 2006) have appeared in English. Like all great foreign literature of the past that has continued to interest readers and translators, the English versions of Cervantes's short stories have had several periods of excellence: the Elizabethan period, the Restoration period, that of the Romantics and the Victorians, and the Modern and Postmodern periods. It is only in the light of the prevailing literary tastes of these various periods that they can be properly assessed. The object of this chapter, therefore, is not simply to judge the merits of a given translation through its variant readings — omissions, additions and mistranslation — but rather to focus on the parallels between the translation and the literary tastes and style in vogue at the time, and thus discuss each one in its unique cultural context.

The Elizabethan period (1560–1660), which extended from the reign of Henry VIII to the mid-seventeenth century, was a time of expansion in all respects. It coincided with the emergence of a whole new generation of what we might call 'lay-scholars' — men who had spent time abroad and who later in life set themselves to the task of translating. Their aim was 'to English' the works of foreign writers. Although Mabbe's translation of the *Exemplary Novels* (London, 1640) appeared at the close of this splendid period, his formative years fell within it and consequently his work is full of those rhetorical devices so typical of that age: repetition, assonance, alliteration, puns and witty conceits. The first thing that strikes the reader is his passionate delight in words and sounds. Nouns, adjectives and even verbs often come in carefully paralleled and balanced pairs, or Euphuistic doublets, as they are sometimes called: 'fair and beautiful'; 'quick and nimble'; 'storm and tempest'; 'peace and quiet'; 'dark and duskie'; etc. The person that marked the beginning of this style was Lord Berners, whose rendering of Antonio de Guevara's *Reloj de Príncipe* (1535) provided the germ for that exaggerated style with its quaint metaphors, witty conceits and tricky word play, so characteristic of the Elizabethan translations, that became known as 'euphuism' — it would find its maximum expression in John Lyly's *Euphues* (1578), from which it takes its name.

Aware that they were not writing for the learned, the Elizabethan translators took special care to explain references to foreign history or culture unfamiliar to their readers by incorporating clarifications by way of side notes, or even detailed insertions. For example, where Cervantes briefly states that Carrizales's house was 'una casa que tenía agua de pie y jardín con muchos naranjos' [a house with a spring and a garden full of orange trees] (p. 363),[1] Mabbe renders: 'a house with a curious Garden belonging unto it, in the midst whereof was a fountaine, beautified round about with grapes, oranges and lemons; diversified with sundry sorts of flowers and fruits both pleasing to the eye and pleasant to the taste' (p. 276).[2]

One distinctive quality the translators shared with the dramatists of their day was an extraordinary appreciation for the visual and the audible. We think of them as enthusiastic storytellers as they inserted additional adjectives and adverbs to give the text a liveliness and vigour not always present in the original: *boisterous* billows; a *flaming* fire; *drooping* melancholy; *all-seeing* eyes; *heaven-menacing* towers; *swift-gliding* time; *awe-moving* fierceness; etc. Mabbe could not resist the temptation of adding occasional stage directions: 'y sacando un escudo de oro' [taking out a gold *escudo*] (p. 480) becomes 'and putting his hand into his Pocket, and taking out a Crowne of gold' (p. 2); '*abrió a la justicia* [he opened the door for the authority]' (p. 484) becomes 'removing the chairs and unlocking the door, he opened it to the Justice' (p. 5). Mabbe also drew freely from his own rich store of colloquial phrases and proverbs when the occasion arose: 'Carrizales resolved to change his former course of life and *turn over a new leaf*' (p. 270); 'Loaysa was *quite off the hinges* and fully resolved with himself to...' (p. 273), and so on.

One of the popular literary themes of this period was unrequited love, which explains Mabbe's choice of stories: *The two Damsels, The Ladie Cornelia, The liberall Lover, The force of Bloud, The Spanish Ladie, The jealous Husband*. His rendering of *The Spanish Lady* deserves mention. It is a story of personal conflict, of the plight of crypto-Catholics in England. As an Anglican and a staunch royalist, he could not consent to having his country spoken of as the home of pirates and plunderers, or his queen upholding secret Catholics in her army. To resolve this problem he resorted to garbling. He carefully and systematically omitted the words England, English, Catholic, etc. substituting them for 'a famous northern island', 'the inhabitants of the island', 'the language spoken on the island', 'secret Christians'. Even the title, *La española inglesa* [The Spanish Englishwoman] becomes simply The Spanish Lady. As secretary to the English ambassador in Madrid, Mabbe may have met Cervantes and furnished him with details concerning London and the court, which would later appear in the novel. Years later, in times of political and religious turmoil, he may have wanted to take Cervantes's story one step further. By placing the story in some 'famous northern islands' he moved the story from the local realm into the universal, making local acts of religious tolerance universal acts of tolerance.

The Elizabethans were followed by a new generation of translators, mainly journalists and hack writers, who advocated simplicity of language. The Restoration (1660–1700) was greatly influenced by contemporary French literature, to the point that most foreign literature came into England through retranslations from the French by translators who practised Dryden's theory of translation — that is, that the foreign author should speak such English as he would himself have spoken if he had been born in England, and that a translator worth reading must be a master of the languages he translates out of, and that he translates into; but if a deficiency be allowed in either, it is in the original.[3] In 1687, while still holding the position of licencer of the press, Sir Roger L'Estrange (1616–1704) — best remembered for his rendering of Quevedo's *Sueños* — published a series of ten unattributed short stories entitled *The Spanish Decarmeron* [*sic*] (London: Simon Neale, 1687). Having omitted the names of the authors of the stories, they passed unrecognized until Sir Henry Thomas, keeper of printed books in the British museum, discovered the source, in 1919, quite by accident.[4] The title, *The Generous Lover*, had at once suggested to him Cervantes's *El Amante Liberal*. In effect, the first five stories were from Cervantes's *Exemplary Novels*, the same ones translated by James Mabbe in 1640 and reissued anonymously in 1654 — *Delight in Several Shapes* (London: William Sheares, 1654). The other five stories were from Castillo Solorzano's *La Garduña de Sevilla* (London: John Starkey, 1665), translated by John Davies of Kidwelly, and licenced by L'Estrange.

In the Preface to *The Spanish Decarmeron*, L'Estrange justifies his endeavour thus:

> As to this Decarmeron of Novels, they are Spanish relations, written by a famous author of that kingdom. One of the most refin'd wits of France thought it worth his pains to render it into the language of his country with all the graces and advantages it might derive from either. I have done it out of the latter, with the freedom of alteration and addition as my fancy led me to make it the most divertive I could in ours, which is the only recommendation of things of this nature... I have no more to satisfie the Reader at the present, only that the Englishing of them has been a Diversion to me, and I hope to others they will not be unpleasant.[5]

L'Estrange's 'freedom of alteration and additions' included numerous spicy digressions in the form of bawdy songs or interpolated stories. The Libertine alone contains four additional stories, all taken from the *Heptameron; or, Contes de la Reine de Navarre*. He also changed the names of all the characters in the stories. One name he didn't bother to change, however, was Mundalin — Mabbe's garbled name for London in *La española inglesa*. In short, L'Estrange's version was not done from the French, as he states, but was simply a paraphrased appropriation of Mabbe's 1640 rendering, or its unattributed 1654 reprint, stripped of all the delightful paired words and phrases.

Another restoration translator, Walter Pope (1630–1714), a professor of astronomy at Gresham College and founding member of the Royal Society, also changed the names of the characters in his rendering of the *novelas* (*Select Novels*, 1694). He justifies this procedure by adducing his desire to 'English' the story:

> I have not endeavour'd to render my author word for word, but my concern

was to make him speak ENGLISH. In [The Spanish–English Lady] I have taken
more liberty, for its scene lying for the greatest part in England, the laws and
customs whereof, Cervantes was not very well skill'd in. I have changed the
names of some persons, and places which are such in the original as were never
heard of in England.[6]

Pope, who had spent long periods in Italy and was better versed in Italian than in
Spanish, used for his source text the Italian version, *Novelliere Castigliano de Michiel
de Cervantes Saavedra* (Venetia: Barezzi, 1626). His fascination with Italy is seen in
his choice of novels and, like Mabbe, he took every opportunity to enlighten his
readers regarding things Italian. One curious example is in *El Licenciado Vidriera*
where Novillieri, the Italian translator, had already added seven wines to the list of
twenty the tavern keeper set before the weary soldiers: Pope added four more.

The first half of the eighteenth century brought a shift in literary trends and
literary awareness. It also marked the first great age of English literary criticism.
It was also the age of satire. Three names stand out among the translators of
Cervantes's *Exemplary Novels* during this period: John Ozell (1675–1743), Samuel
Croxall (1695–1752) and Robert Goadby (1721–1778). Ozell, a zealous Whig
and an accountant by profession, translated several of the Cervantes's stories and
published them in his *Monthly Magazine* (London: D. Midwinter, 1709). He is best
remembered, however, for his translation of Molière's *Works* and his 1719 revision
of Motteux's earlier rendering of *Don Quixote*.

It is beyond the scope of this essay to discuss the merits of Cervantes's twelve
short stories.[7] Nevertheless, it should be pointed out that they vary considerably
with regard to content, and even style. This is also clearly reflected in the choice
of novels in each literary period. The seventeenth-century translators opted for
stories of pirates, sea battles, love, jealousy, wrongdoing, forgiveness and reward.
Ozell's choice of stories reflects a shift in interest, producing the first rendering of
La gitanilla and *El coloquio de los perros*. Robert Goadby, in response to the growing
taste for prose satire, also opted for the more picaresque and satirical stories in his
Two Humorous Novels (London: Ward and Chandler, 1741). Consistent with the idea
of 'belle-infidele', a French concept that valued adaptation over verbal accuracy —
the guiding principle of the Augustan translators — Goadby states: 'greater care
hath been taken to give the sense of my author than a close adherence to his words'.[8]
His occasional additions and transformations are reminiscent of Mabbe: 'one of [the
boys] had a piece of a shirt, which just cover'd his shoulders and breast, *and that
was so black, that one would have sworn it had not been wash'd since the days of Noah*' (p.
118). There are also several passages that are euphemistic or evasive. For example,
where the hospital dog, Berganza, tells how he overheard an old man saying that it
was because so many girls were turning to bad occupations, rather than becoming
servants, that the hospitals were filling up each summer with infected men, Goadby
alters the passage to say simply: '[young girls] who, by not going into service, fall
into divers ills, at last are oblig'd to go into the hospitals' (p. 113). He could hardly
have failed to appreciate Cervantes's direct allusion to syphilis; nor that it was not
the girls who landed in hospital, but their unfortunate customers. On the other
hand, literary sensibilities of the Augustan age tended to suppress erotic elements.

Another curious omission is the reference to Monopodio's hairy chest: 'moreno de rostro, *cecijunto*, barbinegro y muy espeso, los ojos hundidos. Venía en camisa, y por la abertura de delante descubría un bosque, tanto era el vello que tenía en el pecho' [a dark face, eyebrows closely knit together, a thick black beard and sunken eyes. He was wearing a shirt and through the opening in the front there appeared as it were a forest, so thick was the hair on his chest] (p. 198) becomes '[he had] a swarthy complexion, his eyes sunk in his head, his beard black and very thick' (p. 142). Even Gananciosa's habit of spitting before singing is given a euphemistic rendering: 'la Gananciosa ha escupido, señal que quiere cantar' [Gananciosa has just spit, a sign she wants to sing] (p. 221) becomes 'Gananciosa is humming, I suppose she is going to sing' (p. 168).

The most noteworthy of these three Augustan translators was Samuel Croxall, remembered for his translation of Aesop's *Fables*. His six-volume *A Select Collection of Novels and Histories* (London: John Watts, 1720) contained 26 short stories from the French, the Italian and the Spanish, 'All new translated from the originals, by several eminent hands'. The Spanish stories include two episodes from *Don Quixote* and eight of the novellas. This collection of short stories is considered one of the most important anthologies of the period; it helped to define the genre and to equip it with a canon. The title itself reflects the literary debate of the period: novel versus romance. For Croxall, Cervantes offered an alternative to the heroic and the satiric modes in vogue at the time. He told stories of adultery, jealousy and crime — observation of human motives and behaviour. Cervantes was well aware of this difference, when he wrote: 'Soy el primero que ha novelado en lengua castellana [I am the first to have written novellas in Spanish]' (p. 15). Croxall's preface to his collection became a standard reference in vindicating Cervantes as one of the great European short story writers:

> It is somewhat surprising that this learned writer [Huet], who displays with so much pomp his deep reading in romances and is so lavish in praise of the French romancers and novelists, should pass by in silence the novels of Cervantes; this is a remarkable instance of his fond partiality of his own countrymen. Monsieur Fontenelle is guilty of the like omission ... he mentions with applause [others], without one word about Cervantes. But (not to detract from the merit of the French is this kind of writing) we cannot however help thinking that the novels of Cervantes will be esteemed the richest jewel in this collection. These are enliven'd by the same spirit which animated *Don Quijote*, and shine in the fairest light by a brilliancy of thought and elegant invention, tender sentiments, and a thorough insight into human nature.[9]

As stated on the title page, they were all new translations done from the original. Croxall himself does not appear to have had a hand in the translations. The 'most eminent hands' referred to may have included any one of the literary men with whom he associated: John Dryden, Joseph Addison, Samuel Garth, John Mainwaring, William Congreve, Alexander Pope, Laurence Eusden, Nicolas Rowe, Naham Tate, etc. There is a conscious effort to 'English' the stories by inserting typical English phrases such as 'not worth a Goat' (p. 184), 'make your bones rattle in your skin' (p. 189), 'thresh'd him like stockfish' (p. 194), 'skittish as a colt' (p. 222), and so on.

'Englishing' also involved waiving theological controversy. For example, the important Catholic doctrine of salvation by works — the main tenet of the Council of Trent against the Protestant *sola fide* — is substituted by a colloquial saying without doing violence to the text, hence, the Spanish phrase 'tan imposible será apartarme de ver el rostro de esta doncella como no es posible ir al cielo sin buenas obras' [it will be as impossible to stop me from seeing the face of this girl as it is to go to heaven without good works] (p. 421) becomes 'I can no more be drawn away from this beautiful maid than a miser from his gold' (p. 187). Generally speaking, however, there are relatively few instances of substitution, transformation, hedging, adaptation, or omission.

Shortly after Croxall's publication, there appeared a translation of the four novels Croxall had not included in his selection: *A collection of select novels, written originally in Castillian by Don Miguel Cervantes Saavedra, author of the History of Don Quixote de la Mancha* (Bristol: S. Farley, 1728). The translator, Harry Bridges (1645–1730), a wealthy landed gentleman who had spent several years in Spain in his youth, seems to have undertaken the enterprise as a pastime in his old age; he used as his source text a very defective 1705 French version. The errors of his source text, together with Bridges's own carelessness, disqualify this rendering from further discussion.

In general, Romantic literature, and by implication Romantic translation, is characterized by its personal nature, its strong emphasis on feeling, and the belief that it should be spontaneous and imaginative. In 1822, there appeared an anonymous translation of nine of Cervantes's short stories that epitomizes this definition: *The Exemplary Novels of Miguel de Cervantes Saavedra, the author of Don Quixote de la Mancha; published at Madrid in 1613, so called because in each of them be proposed useful examples, to be either imitated or avoided* (London: T. Cadell, 1822). The source text was a combination of a defective French rendering printed in Amsterdam in 1731 and Charles-Pierre Coste d'Arnobat's *Nouvelles imitées de Michel Cervantes et autres auteurs espagnols* (Paris: Gérard, 1802). Despite the fact that the English rendering is a very free adaptation of the above, it is well worth analysing. It belongs to the general nineteenth-century movement of literary expurgations, more specifically, to the period Rachel Howard calls female-authored Moral–Domestic fiction,[10] a genre that had its heyday between 1820 and 1834. Although Moral–Domestic fiction shared similarities with both Romantic and Victorian fiction, its strong evangelical message was at odds with contemporary female authors such as Mary Wollstonecraft or Mary Hays. Some representatives of this evangelical group included Hannah More, Harriet Bowdler, Maria Edgeworth, Sarah Trimmer, Catherine Sinclair, Hesba Stretton, and Mary Martha Sherwood.

Exactly who the anonymous translator was remains a mystery. Women translators were relatively prominent among the Victorians, mainly because translation was considered more compatible with female modesty than original writing. In the Preface, Thomas Cadell, the editor, who in 1818 brought out Mary Smirke's rendering of *Don Quixote*, describes the translator as 'a fair friend possessing a dignified, masculine, comprehensive mind, with all its accomplishments' who was so delighted with the stories, she thought they 'ought not to continue lost on a humble stall in the streets in a foreign language; and was induced to become their disinterested patroness and usher to English society, in an English dress'.[11]

From the strong evangelical tone of the digressions, this 'fair interpreter' was very likely one of the educational theorists who endorsed Rousseau's didactic theories but at the same time believed that the prime reason for education was religion. Her lengthy digressions and rewritings make the stories nearly unrecognizable at times. Though both Hannah More and Sarah Trimmer were particularly active in the campaign to produce suitable works of literature for young readers; nevertheless, Mary Martha Sherwood seems to be the most likely candidate. Sherwood, who wrote over a hundred short stories herself, strongly defends the novel as a means to communicate Christian and educational themes that otherwise might be unpalatable to young readers. She was always looking for new reading material for her all-girls boarding school. This 'moralized' 1822 rendering fits Sherwood's profile — in 1820 she thoroughly edited Sarah Fielding's *Governess,* and the following year she rewrote *Pilgrim's Progress*.

In 1832, a slightly abridged version of *Rinconete y Cortadillo* and *El amante liberal* appeared in Thomas Roscoe's 'Novelists' series, *The Spanish Novelists* in three volumes (London: Richard Bentley, 1832). Roscoe's choice reflects the prevailing Victorian taste for stories overflowing with drama, humour, realistic characters and complicated plots. Shortly after this, in 1846, the first complete rendering of all twelve of Cervantes's stories appeared as part of the Henry G. Bohn's Standard Library series. According to the translator, Walter Keating Kelly (1810–1870), three of the stories had already been translated when he took over the project. Whereas the first translator had worked from Louis Viardot's recently published a French translation entitled *Les Nouvelles de Miguel de Cervantes Saavedra* (Paris: Dubochet, 1838), Kelly worked directly from the Spanish, namely, Salvador Faulí's 1797 Valencia edition. As part of Bohn Library, Kelly's rendering was reissued again and again. Indeed, so successful was Bohn's attempt to provide good literature at a low price that it is said that Bohn's Library did for literature what railroads did for industry.

Despite its popularity, Kelly's rendering was severely criticized by Fitzmaurice-Kelly:

> Frankly, his performance is not one to be proud of. In the First place he began by making a fatal mistake, adopting as the basis of his translation the corrupt text of the Valencia edition published by Faulí in 1797 instead of following the *princeps*. In the second place he frequently fails to grasp his author's meaning and in many passages his translation is positively misleading. In the third place — and this is an unpardonable fault — he systematically omits whole paragraphs of prose, and ballads entire, without a word of warning, while he occasionally interpolates original matters of his own. Judged by the most lenient standard, Kelly's version must be emphatically condemned as altogether inadequate to the needs of the scholar and the general reader alike.[12]

The nineteenth century was a period of contrasts, as far as translation theory is concerned. In an age when translators often seemed to consider themselves authors, or co-authors, it was common practice to abridge texts, to expand them, to paraphrase them; in short, to 'improve' them, as title-pages often boasted. Though the majority of Kelly's additions and mistranslations can be traced back to his source texts, what stands out in his work are the numerous omissions and clippings. Most omissions appear at the end of the stories, suggesting weariness or editorial pressure. On the other hand, Kelly was a master at paraphrasing which allowed him to skip ballads and entire episodes without the reader even suspecting something was missing. An eloquent example is found in *La ilustre fregona* where a four-page omission is bridged thus: 'Astruiano played for the dancers with such spirit and precision of touch that they all vowed he made the guitar speak, [four-page omission] but just as he was doing his best'.[13]

In 1901, James Fitzmaurice-Kelly, who had made his mark in Spanish studies with the publication of his *Life of Miguel de Cervantes Saavedra* (1892), *History of Spanish Literature* (1898), and as editor of John Ormsby's rendering of *Don Quixote* (1899), began the ambitious project of editing *The Complete Works of Cervantes* in English translation. The series was to have twelve volumes, but only eight saw completion. *The Exemplary Novels* (*Complete Works*, vols 7 and 8) appeared in 1902. The translator was Norman MacColl (1843–1904), editor of *Select Plays of Calderon* (London: Macmillan, 1888) and editor in chief of *The Athenaeum* (1871–1900).

Although Fitzmaurice-Kelly acknowledged that 'hundreds and perhaps thousands of readers must have lived and died without even a superficial knowledge of the Exemplary Novels' (p. xliii), he duly informed the reader:

> Mr MacColl has adopted the only sound plan in such undertakings: he has taken [the *editio princeps* of 1613] as the basis of his rendering [...] Mr MacColl starts with the same superiority over all other translators of the Novelas ejemplares that Mr Ormsby has over all other translators of Don Quixote: while not despising the light thrown on defective passages by other editions, both are alone in choosing an authentic text on scientific principles and keeping to it as closely as the genius of our speech allows. To render Cervantes's text as he wrote it, without either additions or suppressions, is in itself an exceeding merit. And there is another point upon which stress should be laid. It is an almost incredible fact that there exists no annotated edition of the Novelas and consequently the translator of these stories is at an immense disadvantage [...] He must solve all his puzzles alone and unaided. All the more, therefore, is Mr MacColl to be congratulated on his very successful achievement (pp. xliii–xliv).

In effect, MacColl could pride himself on bringing out the first unexpurgated version in English, but, unfortunately, occasional additions or omissions found in the text evidence the fact that his source text was not the 1613 *princeps* but the 1876 Madrid edition issued by the Biblioteca Universal Ilustrada.

Though MacColl's translation appeared in the Edwardian period, he was greatly influenced by Francis Newman's Victorian theory, applied to the classics, that 'the translator should retain every peculiarity of the original, so far as he is able, with the greatest care the more foreign it may be'.[14] MacColl made every effort to retain the 'peculiarity of the original' using quaint and even archaic forms such as the use of 'thee' and 'thou'. Contrary to earlier translators, who made every effort to 'English' the text with short monosyllabic Anglo-Saxon words, MacColl preferred Latin-based words. 'The little English words, like the little English ships that have a way of getting around their powerful opponents',[15] as J. B. Trend would come to describe them, gave life to the text while MacColl's three and four-syllabic words sounded stilted and lifeless. Despite a nearly flawless rendering, a few errors did manage to slip through, mainly by way of false cognates. One, however, deserves mention. As a shy bachelor, not well-versed in the wiles of naughty *dueñas*, MacColl misinterprets the word *gracias* and gives the following passage a totally euphuistic twist: 'no quiso la buena dueña perder la coyuntura que la suerte le ofrecía, de gozar, primero que todas, las gracias que ella se imaginaba que debía tener el músico [the good duenna didn't want to miss the opportunity that good luck was offering her to enjoy, before any of the others, the charms that she imagined the musician must have]' (p. 395) becomes 'the opportunity of enjoying, before anyone else, the gratitude which she conceived that the musician ought to feel' (p. 2.22). His *gracias* were his enchantments, his charms, his sexual attributes. She was interested in enjoying him.

The old conflict between 'domesticating' — or 'Englishing' as the early trans-lators called it — and 'foreignizing' continued throughout the twentieth century. Whether author-oriented or reader-oriented, the dominant tendency has been toward 'domestication', that is, rendering the text so smooth, so invisible, that the reader often fails to realize that the work is a translation at all.

In 1928, the renowned Hispanist John Brande Trend (1887–1958), who had published widely on Spanish music, theatre, history and poetry, produced a rewrite of two of Mabbe's 1640 stories, 'endeavouring, by discreetly pruning his English and by restoring what he left out, to bring his version more into agreement with what Cervantes actually wrote, taking care, however, to preserve the balance of the sentences and the rhythm of phrase, as being two of the qualities which make the Elizabethan translators of the old Spanish novelists the great masters of their craft that they are' (p. xii).

After completing his translation of *Don Quixote* in 1949, the American journalist, translator and scholar Samuel Whitehall Putnam (1892–1950) set to work on the *Exemplary Novels*. He died suddenly in 1950 having completed only three of them: *El licenciado Vidriera*, *Rinconete y Cortadillo* and *El coloquio de los perros*. Putnam's approach contrasted drastically with MacColl's as he made every effort to 'domesticate' the text. He even took the liberty of finding equivalents for some of the nicknames: Cariharta becomes Chubby Face; Silguero becomes Finch; Desmochado becomes Lop-Eared, etc. Putnam's rendering ushered in a new era of colloquial, everyday, unaffected language. It was followed by Harriet de Onís (1961), John Michael Cohen (1962), Walter Starkie (1963), Cyril Albert Jones (1972), Barry W. Ife et al. (1992), Leslie Lipson (1998), and Stanley Appelbaum (2006). All these contemporary renderings — profusely annotated and with scholarly introductions — are partial renderings except for Ife's 1992 dual-language edition: *Exemplary Novels*, 4 vols, ed. by B. W. Ife (Warminster: Aris & Phillips, 1992).

Despite the more scholarly approach to translation, there continued to exist curious examples of euphemistic renderings. Gananciosa's spitting before singing, rendered 'humming' by Goadby in 1741, and 'blowing her nose' by Kelly in 1846, was rendered 'clearing her throat' by Starkie in 1963. R. M. Price, one of Barry Ife's translators, also showed a sense of decorum in discreetly rendering 'basket' (p. 72) for 'vasera de orinal' [a basket-like container where chamberpots are kept] (p. 306) in *El licenciado Vidriera*. We might venture to state that 'domesticating' the *Exemplary Novels*, that is, minimizing the foreignness of the target text, had its heyday in the 1960s with John M. Cohen. Whereas Putnam reserved the change of names to minor characters, Cohen changed them all: Rinconete y Cortadillo become Big Sharp and Little Snip, Monopodio becomes Big Boss, Escalanta becomes Shady, Gananciosa becomes Meg the Money, and so on. This trend was reversed by Ife's team of translators in 1992, who restored all the names to the originals and resorted to a slightly more archaic style.

In conclusion, the Elizabethan translators did not pride themselves on making meticulous imitations of the original, their aim being to dress them in English garb. The eighteenth-century translators made them conform to their own aristocratic standards, pruning away former digressions. The Romantics, believing that literary art, like any other art, had to speak directly to the emotional side of man's nature, sacrificed fidelity to the original to achieve this response. The Victorians continued to clip anything that offended their sensibilities. The Edwardians tried to fix that, but not entirely. Our own Postmodern age, like the Elizabethan period, must cater to a new set of readers. Nevertheless, to compare the work of the Elizabethan translators to that of a modern translator is to compare a painting to a photograph. Their tales, full of rhythms and rhymes and repetitions, like those of the ancient Celtic bards, may have caused many a head to nod in drowsiness as they were read aloud on long winter nights; nevertheless, they carried their hearers into realms of imagination and fantasy as few have been capable of since.

Notes to Chapter 7

1. Page references for the Spanish text refer to the *Novelas ejemplares*, ed. by Frances Luttikhuizen (Barcelona: Planeta, 1994).
2. *Exemplarie Novells; in six books. Full of various accidents both delightfull and profitable by Miguel de Cervantes Saavedra, one of the prime wits of Spaine, for his rare fancies, and wittie inventions. Turned into English by Don Diego Puede-Ser* [James Mabbe] (London: R. M., 1640). Page references for the English translations will be given in the text after bibliographical data has been provided.
3. The essential elements of Dryden's famous theories can be found in 'To Sir Richard Fanshaw Upon his Translation of Pastor Fido' (1644), his Preface to the *Eneida* (1697) and his Preface to *The Destruction of Troy* (1656).
4. Henry Thomas, 'Bibliographical Notes', *Revue Hispanique*, 45 (1919), 5–15.
5. R. L'Estrange, 'Preface', in *The Spanish Decameron* (London: Simon Neale, 1687), p. 3.
6. Walter Pope, 'Preface', in *Select Novels* (London: Charles Brome, 1694).
7. The most recent study is *A Companion to Cervantes's 'Novelas ejemplares'*, ed. by Stephen Boyd (Rochester: Tamesis, 2005); see also Francisco Rico, 'Presentación' and Javier Blasco, 'Estudio preliminar', both in Miguel de Cervantes, *Novelas ejemplares*, ed. by Jorge García López (Barcelona: Galaxia Gutenberg, 2005).
8. Robert Goadby, 'Preface', in *Two Humorous Novels. I. A diverting Dialogue between Scipio and Berganza, two dogs belonging to the Hospital of the Resurrection, in the city of Valladolid; II. The comical history of Rinconete and Cortadillo* (London: Ward and Chandler, 1741).
9. S. Croxall, 'Preface', in *A Select Collection of Novels and Histories* (London: John Watts, 1720), p. viii.
10. Rachel A. Howard, 'Domesticating the Novel: Moral–Domestic Fiction, 1820–1834', *Cardiff Corvey Articles*, 13 (Winter 2004). *http://www.cf.ac.uk/encap/corvey/articles/cc13_n03.html>* [accessed 2 January 2007].

11. Thomas Cadell (trans.), *The Exemplary Novels of Miguel de Cervantes Saavedra, the author of Don Quixote de la Mancha*, 2 vols (London: T. Cadell, 1822), I, p. xi.

12. James Fitzmaurice-Kelly, *The Exemplary Novels of Miguel de Cervantes Saavedra*, trans. by N. MacColl (Glasgow: Gowans & Gray, 1902), p. xliii.

13. W. K. Kelly, *The Exemplary Novels of Miguel de Cervantes Saavedra* (London: Henry G. Bohn, 1846), p. 384.

14. F. W. Newman, 'Homeric Translation in Theory and Practice', in *Essays*, ed. by M. Arnold (Oxford University Press, 1914), pp. 313–77 (p. 315).

15. J. B. Trend, *Spanish Stories of the Sixteenth Century in Contemporary Translation* (Oxford: Oxford University Press, 1928), p. v.

PART III

CERVANTES AND THE BRITISH NOVEL

CHAPTER 8

The Cervantic Legacy in the Eighteenth-Century Novel

Brean Hammond

In 1725, Jonathan Swift, at the height of his fame gained through the *Drapier's Letters* campaign, used his influence on Lord Carteret (Lord Lieutenant of Ireland) to procure for his friend Thomas Sheridan the curacy of Rincurran near Cork. Sheridan blew it, however. Being asked to preach a sermon on 1 August, the anniversary of the King's coronation, he had nothing more suitable on his person than a sermon on the text 'Sufficient unto the day is the evil thereof' from Matthew 6. 34. He was duly reported by a spy in the congregation and never gained the post.[1] Consoling him afterwards, Swift wrote: 'Too much advertency is not your talent, or else you had fled from that text, as from a rock. For as Don Quixote said to Sancho, what business had you to speak of a halter, in a family where one of it was hanged?'[2] As this anecdote shows, Cervantes was on the tip of the tongue for eighteenth-century writers. Swift is quoting a little inaccurately, from memory. It is in fact Sancho Panza who says to the Don: 'Nay, I am an Ass to talk of an Ass; for 'tis ill talking of Halters i'th' House of a Man that was hang'd', in the text of the Motteux translation (1700–03) as revised in 1725 by Ozell.[3]

The mid-1720s represent a moment of exceptional interest in Cervantes. Ozell's revision of Motteux was the most available printed edition, but for some time previously the merits of Cervantes had become a topic for critical discussion. In his essay 'Of Poetry', Sir William Temple made a comparison between Rabelais and Cervantes to the effect that the latter is more acceptable in polite society: 'The Matchless Writer of *Don Quixot* is much more to be admired [than Rabelais], for having made up so excellent a composition of Satyr or Ridicule, without those Ingredients [malicious, smutty and profane remarks], and seems to be the best and highest Strain that ever was, or will be reached by that Vein'.[4] The quality of refinement or purification of discourse valued by Temple was one measure of a changing taste that led the artist Charles Jervas (sometimes rendered Jarvis) to think that Peter Motteux's translation required to be superseded. Jervas's translation was motivated by his dissatisfaction with the burlesque inflection given to the narrative by Motteux, who failed to appreciate that the comedy of *Don Quixote* lies precisely in taking Quixote as seriously as he takes himself, with the gravity that any would-be Spanish *hidalgo* does himself the credit of according. Although Jervas's translation was not published until 1742, it was apparently finished by 1725 when Pope mentions it in a letter to Swift: 'Jervas and his Don Quixot are both finish'd'.[5] Swift's interest in Cervantes may have derived from Temple, whom he served as secretary in the 1690s and whose works he saw through the press in the early 1700s. Recent scholarship strongly suggests that at around this same period — mid-to-late 1720s — Swift had approached the Dublin publisher John Hyde with his own translation of eight chapters of *Don Quixote*; and that his hand is to be found in the machinery of the actual Dublin translation issued by Hyde's widow Sarah in 1733.[6] For one major eighteenth-century writer, then, whom Pope apostrophized in his *Dunciad* of 1728 as in the tradition of Cervantes, the Spanish writer remained an enduring influence throughout his writing career.

In the theatre, interest in Cervantes was well established before the turn of the century. Shakespeare was amongst the writers bitten by the Cervantic bug, as we shall see shortly. It was Shelton's translation that inspired Thomas D'Urfey's fully staged version, in three separate parts performed at the Queen's Theatre, Dorset Garden and published in 1694. Inevitably, representing the antics of the Don and Sancho onstage in embodied form would impart a lowbrow, pantomimic aspect to the action: and this guaranteed D'Urfey's success in the repertoire for many years to come.

Part II of D'Urfey's *Comical History* was revived, for example, at Lincoln's Inn Fields in the 1727/8 season, the same season that witnessed a remarkable premiere of Cervantic provenance. In December 1727, the Shakespearean scholar Lewis Theobald claimed that his play *Double Falshood* was a further adaptation of a lost original play by none other than Shakespeare, based on the Cardenio story as presented in Thomas Shelton's translation. Since Theobald could not have known that Shakespeare, in collaboration with John Fletcher, had indeed produced a play called *The History of Cardenio* subsequently lost, it has seemed very probable to recent scholars that this was a genuine Jacobean fossil.[7] Theobald's play became something of a *succès de scandale*, pilloried by his enemies with Alexander Pope in the vanguard; and as Theobald became less and less certain that it was a single-authored play by Shakespeare, he sold the rights to the publisher John Watts and went very quiet on his discovery. Don Quixote and Sancho Panza make no appearance in Theobald's dignified tragicomedy. This was no doubt a deliberate omission by an aspiring editor of Shakespeare reluctant to have his own version of what he thought of as Shakespeare's Cardenio play look like a direct competitor with an established low-comedy musical that dealt with the same material, albeit in an entirely different style.[8] The *Double Falshood* debacle probably inspired Henry Fielding's dramatic interest in Cervantes, which began with the play *Don Quixote in England*, drafted in 1728 though not acted or published until 1734. A document in anti-Walpolean political opposition, this play deploys Don Quixote in a straightforwardly satirical fashion. His knight errantry is understood by the locals in a country borough on the eve of an election as a desire to stand for Parliament. This enables his idealism to be brought up sharp against financial, trading, commercial, and professional forms of self-interest; against a society poisoned by money, as the opposition inspired by Bolingbroke claimed England to be in 1734. Quixotism is exploited to do the work of the social satirist, as it will be later by Smollett. Thus the Don's opponent, the knight of the Long-Purse, is not, as Don Quixote believes him to be, 'a deflowerer of virgins, a destroyer of orphans, a despoiler of widows, a debaucher of wives', but actually Sir Thomas Loveland, 'a good-natur'd [...] civil Gentleman'.[9] Terms that express Don Quixote's code of honour are translated into the shabbiest nonce metaphors for political venality, and his timeless quest to combat injustice is skewed towards specific contemporary conditions.

However popular *Don Quixote* was in the theatre, it was in prose fiction — in the development of the early novel — that Cervantes was most influential in the eighteenth century. By mid-century, the 'first wave' of the novel's efflorescence in the writings of Daniel Defoe, Eliza Haywood, Jane Barker, Mary Davys, Elizabeth Rowe and Penelope Aubin was over, and the mission to make the novel a serious art form was well under way. The novel's endeavour to theorize itself really gets under way after 1740, in the wake of Fielding's 1742 preface to *Joseph Andrews*: this new degree of theoretical awareness separates mid-century from earlier prose fiction, requiring us to modify Ian Watt's 'rise of the novel' hypothesis and to speak of two rises of the novel rather than one.[10] Fielding's preface famously accepts the term 'romance' for what he is writing, but argues for a comic form that, though not in metre, can be 'referred' (his term) to Homer's lost comic epic, the *Margites*. The resultant formula, the 'comic Epic-Poem in Prose', is a generic confection, the main utility of which is to banish such writing as is represented by 'those voluminous Works commonly called *Romances*, namely, *Clelia, Cleopatra, Astraea, Cassandra*, the Grand *Cyrus*, and innumerable others which contain, as I apprehend, very little Instruction or Entertainment'.[11] In the opening chapter to book III, Fielding reinforces the distinction between such outmoded French romances and his own aspirations when he revisits the old topic of the varying potentials of history and fiction to tell truth. Here, Fielding defends 'biographical' fiction as having greater imaginative truth than supposed history, and Cervantes is presented as the supreme example:

> Tho' it may be worth the Examination of Critics, whether the shepherd *Chrysostom*, who, as *Cervantes* informs us, died for Love of the fair *Marcella*, who hated him, was ever in *Spain*, will any one doubt but that such a silly Fellow hath really existed? Is there in the World such a Sceptic as to disbelieve the Madness of *Cardenio*, the Perfidy of *Ferdinand*, the impertinent Curiosity of *Anselmo*, the Weakness of *Camillo*, the irresolute Friendship of *Lothario*; tho' perhaps as to the Time and Place where those several Persons lived, that good Historian may be deplorably deficient.[12]

Although Fielding finds the terms 'novel' and 'romance' equally contaminated and inadequate as generic descriptors of his new species of writing, he communicates a very powerful idea of writing that is more general in its application to life, and more credible, than all the prose fiction currently being written. Cervantes is the originator of it.

To write prose fiction after 1750, then, was to be involved in an enterprise that was increasingly self-aware, that made revitalized claims to seriousness and divorced itself from earlier forms of French writing, but also from English writing indebted to it. That such pretensions to moral weight were convincing was largely due to the colossal achievement of Samuel Richardson. At the same time as Fielding is rediscovering a Cervantic legacy for the novel, Samuel Richardson is also being hailed as a writer to whom the terms 'novel' and 'romance' are alike unsatisfactory in doing justice to the probability and conviction of his writing. Joseph Spence wrote to Richardson that 'one might, for instance, as well judge of the beauties of a prospect by the rules of architecture, as of your Clarissa by the laws of novels and romances. A piece of a quite new kind must have new rules'.[13] If, around 1750, a new chapter in the story of the English novel's development centres around the greater degree of self-consciousness with which Fielding and Richardson, the leading practitioners, were writing fiction, there was fundamental division between them on the question of how the cultural elevation of the novel was to be achieved. Richardson pinned massive hopes on the probability gained from his method of 'writing to the moment': nothing less than the defence of the Christian religion and its key tenets of 'self-denial and mortification' depends on it.[14] The effect of *Clarissa* upon novelists who wrote in its wake is immediate, and novels as disparate as Fielding's *Amelia* and Haywood's *The History of Miss Betsy Thoughtless* testify to it. Readers from all social echelons testify to the absorptive power of Richardson: to read about Pamela and Clarissa was to be at once converted to, or affirmed in, their way of thinking. Betty Schellenberg provides insight into the nature of the mechanism at work.[15] In novels such as the continuation of *Pamela* and in *Sir Charles Grandison*, Richardson constructs conversational circles, the purpose of which is to limit individual action and subsume it to a group consensus. Such fictions replace conflict by consensus and mutual reinforcement. Richardson's narrative structures are typically centripetal and static rather than linear or goal-orientated, turning not upon the actions of an isolated, misunderstood protagonist pitted against society, but on an intimate circle dominated by a centrally authoritative persona such as Grandison. In this respect, Richardson's life imitated his art. He placed himself at the centre of a group of influential readers, a kind of focus group who provided feedback to the author while he was in the process of composition. By the 1750s, Richardson's success had created an impasse for other writers — a vast barrier that seemed well-nigh impossible for other writers to negotiate.

   Mid-century reinscriptions of *Don Quixote* were vital in enabling a form of fiction that, while it still qualified as 'serious', nevertheless provided the readerly satisfactions that — as readers from Samuel Johnson to Sir Walter Scott have testified — it appeared to be Richardson's express purpose to deny. Fielding's writing was new, he would claim, because it was old. He distanced himself from the new species of writing inaugurated by Samuel Richardson precisely by allying himself with carefully selected previous practitioners, the most important of whom was, as we have seen, Cervantes. Cervantes's ironic, intrusive narrative self-consciousness, physical comedy and episode-based exposition were the features that attracted him as a means of rendering the vraisemblance of life. From *Don Quixote*, Fielding and Smollett drew the licence to incorporate into their works the kinds of 'low' material, incidents, and idioms that represented the 'impolite other' of Richardsonian fiction. By mid-century, and in the wake of Fielding's theorizing of a new biographically based fiction with serious credentials, Cervantes began to serve as a very direct source of inspiration for the novel. While many novels written after *Joseph Andrews*, such as *Tom Jones*, *Roderick Random* and *Humphry Clinker*, display this Cervantic inheritance, a more specific sub-species of Cervantic novel also developed at this time, the foremost examples of which are Lennox's *The Female Quixote; or, The Adventures of Arabella* (1752), Smollett's *The Life and Adventures of Sir Launcelot Greaves* (1760–61), and Graves's *The Spiritual Quixote* (1773).

Lennox's *The Female Quixote*, a work which Fielding himself praised as superior to *Don Quixote* in certain respects, offers the most fully developed representation of a key contemporary image: that of a young woman led astray by reading too many French romances. Although Lennox's feminized reinscription of Don Quixote required a decorum that denied her access to some of the Cervantic aspects of which Smollett in particular would take advantage — Ronald Paulson sees her as 'from the camp of Richardson'[16] — Lennox's recasting of Dulcinea *as* Quixote involved an especially apposite reworking of Cervantes's model. For, by contrast to the situation that subsisted in early seventeenth-century Spain, in eighteenth-century Britain the reading of romances was identified almost entirely with women. Emulating Cervantes's tale of 'the bad Effects of a whimsical study' (as her opening chapter heading puts it), *The Female Quixote* thus portrayed romance-reading as the modern woman's quixotism.[17]

In very broad terms, the development of Quixotism in the later century was from the satirical to the romanticized: writers who stressed the buffoonish side of Don Quixote, his insane pride and the absurdity of the literature that provokes his quest would lean towards satire, whereas those who see him as an exemplary figure who refuses to allow his high ideals to be tainted by a fallen world would be casting him almost as a prototype Byronic hero.[18] More specifically, I would emphasize five aspects of Cervantic fiction, deployed by writers of English fiction in the decades immediately following the mid-century, to establish a powerful line of narrative energy that revalidates process against stasis, incident against conversation: (i) the typical narrative structuring of specific incidents; (ii) the Quixote and Sancho Panza character types; (iii) the collision between a set of 'spiritual' or 'idealistic' values derived from a body of literature and the earthiness of quotidian incidents; (iv) dominant themes of madness and the law; and (v) epistemological questions raised on the levels of narrative content (appearance and reality as perceived by Quixote) and of narrative form — the intertextual references that emphasize the novel as artefact, documentary record and illusion. As E. C. Riley comments, this final factor indicates a side of the fiction 'very congenial to the age of Borges and Eco, Barthes and Derrida'.[19] Cervantes proves a fecund influence for Smollett and Fielding in the quest to write serious, ethical fiction that is not painted into a Richardsonian corner of overt Christian moralism and the eschewal of narrative pleasure. The final part of this article will suggest how the embodiment of those Cervantic features assisted novelists of the mid-to-late century to negotiate the Richardsonian monolith.

In further elaboration of the first point, one might select the incident at the inn with the serving maid Maritornes, 'remarkable for her capacious countenance, beetle-brow'd, flat-nosed, blind of one eye, and bleared in the other', who has set up an assignation with a carter in the dark garret that Don Quixote and Sancho have been allocated as their sleeping-quarters.[20] Stumbling her way to bed, Maritornes is seized by Don Quixote, who is convinced that she is a gentlewoman possessed by lust for his body, and she has to endure a high-sounding speech explaining why Don Quixote cannot submit to her embraces. This oration being overheard by the frustrated carter, a fracas ensues that involves Sancho when Maritornes seeks refuge in his bed. Incidents structured in this fashion echo their way through Fielding's inn at Upton (in *Tom Jones*) and the novels of Smollett. Comic slapstick of this kind thumbs its nose at the decorous gavottes of Richardsonian posture. That prose narratives of this period take over the Quixote–Sancho pairing of characters locked into a sado-masochistic, manic-depressive dynamic in which they become complementary in their strengths and deficiencies, but ultimately entirely loyal to one another, requires little substantiation. It appears in the relationship between Martinus Scriblerus and Crambo in Pope, Swift, Gay and Arbuthnot's *Memoirs of Martinus Scriblerus* (1742), in that of Abraham Adams and Joseph Andrews, Tom Jones and Partridge, Roderick Random and his man Strap, Peregrine Pickle and his sidekick Tom Pipes, Matthew Bramble and Humphry Clinker, Launcelot Greaves and Timothy Crabshaw, Squire Wildgoose and his acolyte Tugwell, Uncle Toby and Corporal Trim, and doubtless many others.[21] What this relationship enables is the articulation of the human body in grotesque forms that Bakhtin would term 'carnivalized'. This is particularly true of Smollett's writing, in respect of which it became at once the central node of controversy. We should not overlook Cervantes, however, in favour of seeing Smollett's interest in the endangered body as the product of eighteenth-century philosophical and political discourses of the nervous system and Humean sympathy. Perhaps the single most memorable incident in *Don Quixote* occurs when the Don mistakes a flock of sheep for a hostile army, and is attacked by their guardian shepherds. An olio of scatological violence in which Sancho and the Don are covered in each others' excrement, the incident authorizes such 'low' events as Peregrine Pickle's perforation of Mrs. Trunnion's chamber-pot, making it into a kind of colander for the benefit of Captain Trunnion occupying the lower berth; or the nauseatingly graphic account in *Roderick Random* of a naval engagement with the French in which Roderick reports: 'I concealed my agitation as well as I could, till the head of the officer of Marines, who stood near me, being shot off, bounced from the deck athwart my face, leaving me well-nigh blinded with brains', after which he is covered in the entrails of a dying drummer.[22] From Cervantes assuredly, if also from various other sources, Smollett took the licence to incorporate low material, incidents, and idioms that affronted the decorum of Richardsonian fiction.

Thematically, Cervantes's *Don Quixote* is dominated by two topics, madness and the law — closely connected, since one main form of Don Quixote's madness is his constant disregard for state law. Whenever he perceives cruel treatment, his chivalric code dictates that he must intervene. Eighteenth-century imitators of Don Quixote perceived that they would have to 'naturalize' his madness and go a different way to work with the law. Smollett's *Sir Launcelot Greaves* is the clearest example. A pathology is supplied for Greaves's madness — it is the result of a nervous disorder following rejection in love — and his chivalry takes the form of redressing wrongs that are actually the result of the biased and unjust legal system. Greaves's confrontation with the hideous Justice Gobble is the most salient case. The point is not to transcend the law but to return it to its proper functioning as a protector of the interests of ordinary citizens against the powerful. Greaves distinguishes himself explicitly from the delusional aspects of Quixotic madness: 'I have not yet encountered a windmill for a giant; nor mistaken this public house for a magnificent castle'.[23] This cues us in to one of the less successful aspects of eighteenth-century Quixotic prose. One of the fascinations of Don Quixote's character is that when he is not suffering from delusion, he holds entirely lucid and indeed strikingly intelligent discussions of the burning issues of the day. Imitators *try* to take this on board: so that in Lennox's *The Female Quixote* we are *told* that this is true of Arabella, but not a single intelligent syllable of her conversation is ever actually represented. In *Don Quixote*, there is a constant fascination with the ontological status of what our hero experiences. His presumed dementia does actually put him above state prosecution because he would be dismissed as *non compos*. Eighteenth-century versions cannot stomach the subversive aspects of Don Quixote being taken at his own estimate, and as with Lennox's *The Female Quixote* tutored, it is said, by Samuel Johnson, they put much energy into the dehumouring of their Quixotic figures, ending in restoration to sanity, marriage and social control.

Finally, *Don Quixote* is a work that problematizes not only the distinction between what is true and not, 'real' experience and delusion, but also the formal means by which such questions can be raised. *Don Quixote*'s ludic juggling with the terms of the narrative contract upon which the reader agrees to read, has received some attention.[24] Readers familiar with it must have been sensitized to those metafictional elements that can disrupt the narrative surface, leaving coherence to be manufactured only with difficulty by the reader. One might perceive in sites as widely different as the antiquarian posturing in the first preface to Horace Walpole's *The Castle of Otranto* (1764) and the tantalizing unfinished 'Fragment' in Sterne's *A Sentimental Journey* (1768) a Cervantic concern with the epistemological status of the object being perceived. Such a concern would dominate in the publishing sensation of the era, Sterne's *Tristram Shandy*.

Notes to Chapter 8

1. The full story is amusingly told in Irvin Ehrenpreis, *Swift: The Man, his Works and the Age*, 3 vols (London: Methuen, 1962–83), III, 362–65.
2. Swift to Thomas Sheridan, 11 Sep. 1725, in *The Correspondence of Jonathan Swift, D.D.* ed. by David Woolley, 4 vols (Frankfurt: Peter Lang, 1999–2007), II, 594. Swift had the 1652 folio reprint of Shelton's translation on his shelves.
3. Miguel de Cervantes Saavedra, *The History Of The Renowned Don Quixote De La Mancha. Translated By Several Hands: And Publish'd By Peter Motteux*, revised by J. Ozell, 4 vols, 5th edn (London, 1725), I, 272.
4. *Miscellanea. The Second Part. In Four Essays. I. Upon Antient And Modern Learning. ... IV. Upon Poetry. By Sir William Temple* (London, 1705), p. 353.
5. Pope to Swift, 14 December 1725. *The Correspondence of Alexander Pope*, ed. by George Sherburn, 5 vols (Oxford: Clarendon Press, 1956), II, 350.

6. See the remarkable essay by A. C. Elias, 'Swift's *Don Quixote*, Dunkin's *Virgil Travesty*, and Other New Intelligence', *Swift Studies*, 13 (1998), 27–104.

7. The whole story will be told in my forthcoming edition of the play for Arden Shakespeare. It is too complex to offer more than a brief mention in this chapter.

8. There is no similarity between D'Urfey's burlesque treatment of the Cardenio story in *The Comical History of Don Quixote Part One* (1694) and the version of it presented in *Double Falshood*. D'Urfey has Fernando rescue Luscinda from her convent and bring her to an inn, where Dorothea [*sic*] is already present. In the course of III. 1, Fernando is reconciled to Dorothea and the rest of the action concerning this trio takes the form of recovering Cardenio and reuniting him with Luscinda. Cardenio in this version is heavily involved with Don Quixote. In the course of the dialogue between them excerpted above (IV. 1), Cardenio ridicules the Don and his mistress Dulcinea, without knowing that it is the Don he addresses.

9. Henry Fielding, *Don Quixote in England* (London, 1734), p. 24.

10. As does J. Paul Hunter in *Before Novels: The Cultural Contexts of Eighteenth-Century Fiction* (New York and London: W. W. Norton, 1990), p. 11. The reference to Ian Watt is of course to *The Rise of the Novel: Studies in Defoe, Richardson and Fielding* (London: Chatto and Windus, 1957).

11. Henry Fielding, *Joseph Andrews*, ed. by Martin C. Battestin (Oxford: Clarendon Press, 1967), p. 4.

12. Henry Fielding, *The History of the Adventures of Joseph Andrews, and his Friend Mr Abraham Adams*, 2 vols (London, 1743), II, 2–3.

13. *Polymetis; Or, An Enquiry Concerning The Agreement Between The Works Of The Roman Poets, And The Remains Of The Antient Artists* (London, 1747), cited by Elizabeth Heckendorn Cook, *Epistolary Bodies: Gender and Genre in the Eighteenth-Century Republic of Letters* (Stanford: Stanford University Press, 1996), p. 75.

14. Samuel Richardson, 'Postscript' to *Clarissa; or, the History of a Young Lady* [London, 1751], 4 vols (London: Dent, 1932), IV, 552–65.

15. Betty A. Schellenberg, *The Conversational Circle: Re-Reading the English Novel 1740–1775* (Lexington: Kentucky University Press, 1996).

16. Ronald Paulson, *Don Quixote in England: The Aesthetics of Laughter* (Baltimore: Johns Hopkins University Press, 1998), p. 174.

17. Charlotte Lennox, *The Female Quixote; or, The Adventures of Arabella*, ed. by Margaret Dalziel (London: Oxford University Press, 1970), pp. 7, 5.

18. See Susan Staves, 'Don Quixote in Eighteenth-Century England', *Comparative Literature*, 24 (1972), 193–215 (p. 194).

19. E. C. Riley, 'Introduction', in Miguel de Cervantes Saavedra, *Don Quixote de la Mancha*, trans. by Charles Jarvis, ed. by E. C. Riley (Oxford: Oxford University Press, 1992), p. xi.

20. Miguel de Cervantes Saavedra, *The History And Adventures Of The Renowned Don Quixote. Translated From The Spanish Of Miguel De Cervantes Saavedra. By T. Smollett, M.D.*, 2 vols (London, 1755), I, 86.

21. The novels from which those pairings come are: Henry Fielding, *The History Of The Adventures Of Joseph Andrews, And His Friend Mr. Abraham Adams* (1742); Henry Fielding, *The History of Tom Jones, a Foundling* (1749); Tobias Smollett, *The Adventures of Roderick Random* (1748); Tobias Smollett, *The Adventures of Peregrine Pickle* (1751); Tobias Smollett, *The Expedition of Humphry Clinker* (1771); Tobias Smollett, *The Adventures of Sir Launcelot Greaves* (1762); Richard Graves, *The Spiritual Quixote; or, The Summer's Ramble of Mr. Geoffry Wildgoose* (1773); Laurence Sterne, *The Life and Opinions of Tristram Shandy, Gentleman* (1760–67).

22. Tobias Smollett, *The Adventures of Roderick Random*, ed. by Paul-Gabriel Boucé (Oxford: Oxford University Press, 1979), pp. 167–68.

23. Tobias Smollett, *The Life and Adventures of Sir Launcelot Greaves*, ed. by Peter Wagner (Harmondsworth: Penguin, 1988), p. 50.

24. See, for example, Wayne C. Booth, 'The Self-Conscious Narrator in Comic Fiction before *Tristram Shandy*', reprinted in *Tristram Shandy: Contemporary Critical Essays*, ed. by Melvyn New (Basingstoke: Macmillan New Casebooks, 1992), pp. 36–59.

CHAPTER 9

The Quixotic Novel in
British Fiction of the
Nineteenth and Twentieth Centuries

Howard Mancing

The three most important, original, and influential British novelists in the early nineteenth century are Jane Austen, Walter Scott, and Mary Wollstonecraft Shelley. All three are writers profoundly influenced by Cervantes and *Don Quixote*. They represent the first phase of the Cervantic novel in nineteenth-century England, and thus this essay opens with a consideration of some of their major writings. Next, I will turn to other British novelists of the nineteenth century, then take a look at Cervantic fictions in twentieth-century Britain, and finish with some contextualizing summary comments.[1]

I will use the term 'quixotic novel' to refer to any work that bears some clear relationship (mostly or exclusively in character and themes) to Cervantes's novel.[2] Most often the relationship is seen in characters who may be based on or simply resemble the imaginative knight errant Don Quixote, his pragmatic squire Sancho Panza, or the non-existent lady of incomparable beauty, Dulcinea del Toboso. At other times the relationship is based on certain themes that find definitive expression in *Don Quixote*: appearance vs. reality,[3] the power of literature in the human imagination, an impractical and idealistic attempt to change one's life, and so forth. Whilst quixotic novels are Cervantic in their characters and themes, the nineteenth and twentieth centuries did also revisit the self-conscious, metafictional innovations that characterized the eighteenth-century Cervantean novel (*Don Quixote* is, after all, the first true postmodern novel).[4] As in the eighteenth century, although to a lesser extent, the quixotic and the Cervantean come together. I will return to the concept of the quixotic novel at the end of this essay in order to contextualize my analysis of individual writers.

Jane Austen (1775–1817) may be considered the last of the great eighteenth-century enlightenment novelists; her limited output (six major works) of restrained, understated, subtle domestic novels were mostly written and published (perhaps a little anachronistically) between 1811 and 1818. Her work, like that of Samuel Richardson and others in the great British novelistic tradition dating back to the seventeenth century, combines psychological realism with Romantic concerns and the conventions of Romance; they are what Walter L. Reed has called 'romanticized novels,' a hybrid genre that has its roots simultaneously in the medieval tradition of the sentimental romance and in the social and psychological realism of works like *Don Quixote*.[5] *Northanger Abbey* was Austen's very first attempt at long fiction, written in the final years of the eighteenth century but unpublished until 1818, the year after her death. Usually considered less polished than some of her other works (*Emma, Mansfield Park, Persuasion*), it is also somewhat more exuberant (if still quite restrained) than they are. In many ways, it is Austen's most delightful book.

Catherine Morland, protagonist of *Northanger Abbey*, is a female Quixote in the mould of Arabella (from Charlotte Lennox's *Female Quixote*, 1752),[6] Dorcasina (from Tabitha Tenney's *Female Quixotism*, 1801), Cherubina (from Eaton Stannard Barrett's *The Heroine*, 1809), and — later — Emma (of Gustave Flaubert's *Madame Bovary*, 1856–57), the most famous of all quixotic women protagonists.[7] Catherine is an avid reader of gothic fictions, especially those of Ann Radcliffe, and dreams of having the same sort of thrilling and dangerous adventures that the heroines of these novels experience. As a teenager, she avidly reads books like Radcliffe's *The Mysteries of Udolpho* (1794), and she considers herself to be 'in training for a heroine; she read all such works as heroines must read'.[8] When she is invited to spend some time at a remote estate — Northanger Abbey — she begins to perceive and understand everything in terms of her literary models. As she tries to discover the terrifying secrets she assumes to be hidden in the old country house, she consistently misinterprets what she sees and transforms reality in the most quixotic of manners. The delightful, satiric, way in which she complicates her own life and those of others by reading certain ordinary events as extraordinary adventures from a gothic plot is the essence of the quixotic premise. At the end of the novel, as at the end of *Don Quixote*, the heroine overcomes her book-inspired vision of the world and is reconciled with reality: 'The visions of romance were over. Catherine was completely awakened' (p. 164). There is a certain degree of quixotism in other Austen characters — especially Marianne Dashwood in *Sense and Sensibility* (1811), but also Elizabeth Bennett in *Pride and Prejudice* (1813) and Emma Woodhouse in *Emma* (1816) — but none comes close to Catherine Morland in replicating the quixotic model.[9]

Walter Scott (1771–1832), meanwhile, is the first great Romantic historical novelist of European literature and the most popular and most imitated writer of his time. Prolific (he wrote some thirty novels, along with his many poetic works, numerous works of non-fiction, and several plays) where Austen is limited, and exuberant where she is restrained, the two could hardly provide a greater contrast. Yet they both find their roots in Cervantes, for whom Scott had the 'most unbounded admiration'.[10] Scott read Spanish, as a teenager began a translation of *Don Quixote*, and had seven copies of the novel in Spanish (including the elaborate 1780 edition of the Spanish Royal Academy) in his personal library.[11] As Michael Gerli has shown, Scott identified with Cervantes as he struggled with the concept of the novel, and particularly how one was to distinguish between fiction and historical truth.[12] Furthermore, he clearly saw that the history of the novel, very specifically including his own contributions to it, was a long and continuous one from the days of the Spanish picaresque and Cervantes onward.

References and allusions to Cervantes and his works, especially (but not limited to) *Don Quixote*, can be found throughout his fictional writings.[13] Importantly, in his first novel, *Waverley* (1814), Scott writes that he intends 'not to follow in the steps of that inimitable author [Cervantes], in describing such total perversion of the intellect as misconstrues the objects actually presented to the senses, but that more common aberration from sound judgment which apprehends occurrences indeed in their reality, but communicates to them a tincture of its own romantic tone and colouring'.[14] Scott is making a relatively subtle distinction, and a legitimate one, but, in the end, one of degree. Nowhere is the Cervantine presence seen in Scott's work than in *Waverley* itself, where Edward Waverley is by all standards a quixotic character, reading his way 'through the sea of books, like a vessel without a pilot or a rudder' (p. 13). There is one scene in the novel that is an explicit rewrite of a famous scene in Chapter 5 of the first part of *Don Quixote*, when Pedro Alonso brings Don Quixote back home after his first sally. Fergus says, 'Open your gates, incomparable princess, to the wounded Muslim Abindarez, when Rodrigo de Narvez [*sic*], constable of Antiquera [*sic*], conveys to your castle, or open them, if you like better, to the renowned Marquis of Mantua, the sad attendant of his half-slain friend, Baldovinos of the Mountain. Ah, long rest to thy soul, Cervantes! without quoting thy remnants, how should I frame my language to benefit romantic ears!' (p. 121). It is difficult to imagine what sort of fiction — if any — Walter Scott might have written without the theoretical and pragmatic model of Cervantes.[15]

Finally, Mary Wollstonecraft Shelley (1797–1851) maintained an interest in Cervantes throughout her life; her biography of him is the longest essay in her *Lives of the Most Eminent Literary and Scientific Men of Italy, Spain, and Portugal* (1837); references to Cervantes, Don Quixote, and Sancho Panza appear frequently in her writings. She most often compared herself to Sancho, and both her husband Percy and her father (William Godwin)[16] to Don Quixote, particularly in her journal *History of a Six Weeks' Tour* (1817), a trip she described in terms of romance and adventure. Significantly, during this trip she and her husband were reading and discussing *Don Quixote*, as they were again during the time when she was writing *Frankenstein, or the Modern Prometheus* (1818).

In *Frankenstein*, the Cervantine element centres around the character of Safie, a Muslim, or 'Arabian', woman, who is found in a key episode at the centre of the novel. Safie is based directly on Zoraida, the love-interest in the embedded 'Captain's Tale' in *Don Quixote* (I, 39–41). Both stories involve love between a gallant Christian man and a Muslim woman who is secretly a Christian, betrayal of the protective father, theft of jewels and money, letters that must be translated, significant non-verbal communication, and eventual reunion of the separated lovers. This key episode was inserted by Shelley when the draft of the novel was otherwise nearly complete, and when she had just recently finished reading *Don Quixote*.[17] In 1820, Shelley again read *Don Quixote*, this time in Spanish. In two of Shelley's other novels — *Lodore* (1835) and *Falkner: A Novel* (1837) — the influence of Cervantes's work is also evident. Perhaps no British writer since Fielding has been more intimately connected in so many ways to Cervantes than Mary Shelley.

After Austen, Scott, and Shelley, the remainder of the nineteenth century in

England (as well as in the rest of Europe and America) continues to find thematic, technical, and stylistic inspiration in *Don Quixote*. In the limited space of this essay, I can only comment briefly on a limited number of writers and mention even more briefly some others. Suffice it to say that at no point in the nineteenth century is the influence of Cervantes in the English novel absent.

England's greatest and most popular novelist of the century is the prolific Charles Dickens (1812–1870). Dickens had read *Don Quixote* as a boy, and the formative Cervantine influence on his work is evident in his first two novels: *The Posthumous Papers of the Pickwick Club* (1837) and *Oliver Twist* (1837–38).[18] *The Pickwick Papers*, first published in twenty monthly instalments beginning in April 1836, is Dickens's overt attempt to rewrite/adapt *Don Quixote* (as was Oliver Goldsmith's quixotic *Vicar of Wakefield*, 1766) in a contemporary British context.[19] The novel's popularity has faded over the years, perhaps at least partly to its lack of technical innovation. The kindly, genial, optimistic Pickwick is, like Don Quixote, an older man who sets out on adventure (even if his inspiration is at first less literature than science).[20] Both protagonists are naive interpreters of the world in which they find themselves, which makes them both objects of ridicule and practical jokes. Pickwick soon acquires a down-to-earth, folkloric, and loyal sidekick named Sam Weller, who, like Sancho Panza, often acts as the 'reality instructor' to his master.[21] The two form perhaps the most consciously created Quixote–Sancho pair in nineteenth-century literature. Weller's difficulties with the English language explicitly recall Sancho's (although Sam's 'Wellerisms' are formally and thematically quite unlike Sancho's proverbs drawn from folk wisdom) and makes the former one of the latter's most famous and loveable literary progenies.

If Dickens is the most popular and influential novelist of the century, George Eliot (Mary Ann Evans, 1819–1880) is the author of the novel often considered the best English fiction of the time: *Middlemarch* (1871–72). Eliot read *Don Quixote* in its entirety in Spanish, so there is no question of her familiarity with Cervantes's work; she even uses a quotation, in Spanish, from *Don Quixote* as an epigraph at the beginning of the second chapter of *Middlemarch*. Although this novel abounds in quixotic characters — the idealistic and altruistic Dorothea Brooke and the Reverend Casaubon, whose quest for the key to the understanding of all mythologies is most obviously and explicitly quixotic[22] — it is another of Eliot's novels that, it seems to me, best captures the author's quixotic spirit.

In *The Mill on the Floss* (1860), Maggie Tulliver's vivid imaginative powers, together with her passion for books and fantasies, make her Eliot's best Don Quixote figure: 'But I can tell you almost everything there is in my books, I've read them so many times'.[23] Like Don Quixote, she contrasts literature and life: 'In books there were people who were always agreeable or tender [...] The world outside the books was not a happy one, Maggie felt' (p. 205). When she runs away to live with the gypsies and be their queen, Maggie characteristically finds little resemblance between reality and her romantic fantasy of gypsy life.[24] Later, her reading of Thomas à Kempis's *The Imitation of Christ* sparks a second quixotic phase in Maggie's life. This time she strives to remodel herself in imitation of exemplary moral, rather than romantic, figures. In this she follows in a long line of female would-be saints, of whom the greatest exemplar is Saint Teresa of Avila.[25] In addition, Eliot also compares, at some length, the previously mentioned Dorothea Brooke with Saint Teresa.

Finally, the most prominent novelist of the late-nineteenth century is the Anglicized (and Anglophile) American Henry James (1843–1916), who became a naturalized English citizen shortly before his death. James's meticulous drawing-room realism makes him the worthiest successor of Jane Austen in his production of a series of tightly-structured, serious, subtly ironic, realistic fictions. These qualities are farthest from the overtly comic, laughter-filled, exuberant, self-reflexive characteristics one associates with *Don Quixote*. Yet, like Austen, he is the author of one novel, sometimes considered his best, with a clearly quixotic heroine, *The Portrait of a Lady* (1881), whose protagonist, Isabel Archer, is in every way a quixotic character whose youthful reading and flights of imagination are her most important characteristics:

> To say that she was so occupied [i.e., that she was reading] is to say that her solitude did not press upon her; for her love of knowledge had a fertilizing quality and her imagination was strong. [...] Her reputation of reading a great deal hung about her like the cloudy envelope of a goddess in an epic. [...] The girl had a certain nobleness of imagination which rendered her a good many services and played her a great many tricks. She spent half her time in thinking of beauty, and bravery, and magnanimity.[26]

Cervantean themes — appearance vs. reality, literature and life — and quixotic characters — Quixotes, Sanchos, Dulcineas — abound, either explicitly or implicitly, in literature in general, and certainly in other novelists of the nineteenth century. They are to be found in the work of significant writers like Elizabeth Gaskell, William Makepeace Thackeray, Anthony Trollope, Lewis Carroll, and Thomas Hardy, as well as in the work of less well-known novelists like Justin McCarthy and John Buchan. But in the twentieth century, the Cervantean and the quixotic are even more evident in British fiction.

Our survey of twentieth-century quixotic fiction will, arbitrarily, be limited to a brief discussion of half a dozen novelists, writers who span the period from beginning to end, whose work is widely varied, and all of whom pay homage in their own way to *Don Quixote*. The survey will begin with Wyndham Lewis (1884–1957), who lived and travelled extensively in Spain. His long literary career in the first half of the century includes several novels that feature characters who are either explicitly or implicitly inspired, at least in part, by *Don Quixote*. For example, in his first novel, *Tarr* (1918), Frederick Tarr is described by the narrator as a curious sort of reverse-Don Quixote:

> His sardonic dream of life got him, as a sort of quixotic dreamer of inverse illusions, blows from the swift arms of windmills and attacks from indignant and perplexed mankind. He, instead of having conceived the world as more chivalrous and marvelous than it was, had conceived it as emptied of all dignity, sense and generosity. The drovers and publicans were angry at not being mistaken from legendary chivalry or châtelains. = The very windmills resented not being taken for giants![27]

Self-Condemned (1954) is probably Lewis's best and most quixotic novel. The protagonist René Harding imposes a romantic penance upon himself, in a manner that very much recalls Don Quixote's deeds in Sierra Morena (I, 25). At several key points in the novel he is referred to as being quixotic, a dreamer, a fanatic, 'a man apt to become possessed of some irrational idea'.[28]

G. K. Chesterton (1874–1936) was a flamboyant figure and a prolific writer whose Father Brown mysteries have proven to be his most popular works. An early essay titled 'The Divine Parody of Don Quixote' (1901) is significant in that it both shows his early interest in Cervantes's novel and his sense that Don Quixote is in some ways a prototype of modern man.[29] His novel *The Return of Don Quixote* (1927) is one of the early 'namesakes' of Cervantes's hero. It is a political, polemical novel in which there is more than one Quixote and more than one Sancho.[30] The novel culminates when librarian Michael Herne, who is playing the role of Richard the Lion-Hearted on stage, walks out of the theatre with his lance in hand, followed by a friend, Douglas Murrel, who offers to be his Sancho Panza, mounts a horse pulling a handsome cab and rides off to perform quixotic deeds. Herne describes the new quixotism of the twentieth century:

> All your machinery has become so inhuman that it has become natural. In becoming a second nature, it has become as remote and indifferent and cruel as nature. The Knight is once more riding in the forest. Only he is lost in the wheels instead of in the woods. You have made your dead system on so large a scale that you do not yourselves know how or where it will be hit. That's the paradox! Things have grown incalculable by being calculated. You have tied men to tools so gigantic that they do not know on whom the strokes descend. You have justified the nightmare of Don Quixote. The mills really *are* giants.[31]

L. P. Hartley (1895–1972), a talented but generally neglected mid-century novelist, is best known for his *Eustace and Hilda* trilogy (1944–47). Probably his least appreciated, and certainly his least typical, novel is *The Love-Adept* (1969), a self-conscious and wryly humorous novel about novel-writing in the tradition of *Don Quixote*. At the beginning of the novel, James Golightly is struggling with the ending of his novel entitled *The Love-Adept*. After he manages to finish it, he sends pre-publication copies to four friends, all named Elizabeth (the novel is dedicated to 'Elizabeth'). Most of the novel consists of correspondence between James and the Elizabeths about his novel, especially the ending (which three of the Elizabeths never manage to read). In a letter to Elizabeth II, James cites Cervantes, 'the wisest and the most humane of novelists', and his 'extraordinary' ending for *Don Quixote*.[32] Later, in a letter to Elizabeth IV, James praises Homer, in the *Iliad* and the *Odyssey*, and then adds, 'Of all the novelists comparable to Homer in stature, only Cervantes, I think, *improvises* the ending. *Don Quixote* is not constructed, according to any canons of art; it doesn't work up to anything; it hasn't a dénouement or a climax, the logical issue of what has gone before, unless Don Quixote's disillusion with Dulcinea (which no doubt was always in the author's mind) could be counted as an anti-climax' (p. 135). Finally, in the last chapter, James writes to Elizabeth IV, discusses his theory of an ending, and calls her his Dulcinea. Then, in a closing epilogue, the four Elizabeths meet at a cocktail party and it is revealed that James is marrying Elizabeth IV. The whole point of *The Love-Adept*, whose ending is discussed down to the very last lines of the novel, is the nature of novelistic endings, and the model throughout is *Don Quixote*. It is one of the more interesting and original metafictions of the mid-century, as well as one of the most overtly quixotic novels ever written.

A much better-known example of metafiction, and a quixotic novel in a very different way is *The French Lieutenant's Woman* (1969), by John Fowles (1926–). The heroine, Sarah Woodruff, is a quixotic dreamer in the line of Catherine Morland. She would 'lay awake at nights imagining scenes from the more romantic literature of her adolescence, scenes in which starving heroines lay huddled on snow-covered doorsteps or fevered in some bare, leaking garret. [...] she had read far more fiction and far more poetry, those two sanctuaries of the lonely, than most of her kind. They served as a substitute for experience'.[33] Her lover, Charles, is more prosaic and realistic, but he does conceive of his servant, Sam (derived to some extent from Dickens's Sam Weller) as 'his Sancho Panza, the low comedy that supported his spiritual worship of Ernestina-Dorothea' (p. 52; perhaps he means Dulcinea). In fact, Sam is not very much like Sancho, in spite of the explicit connection.

What most recalls Cervantes in this novel, however, is the frequent self-conscious metafictional narrative play. Fowles as narrator accompanies Charles on a train ride; he provides multiple endings for the story; he ruminates on the nature of the novel. Typical is a chapter which begins, 'I do not know. This story I am telling is all imagination. These characters I create never existed outside my own mind [...] But I live in the age of Alain Robbe-Grillet and Roland Barthes; if this is a novel, it cannot be a novel in the modern sense of the word' (p. 104). It is not clear what Fowles means here, because metafiction of the sort he is writing is precisely what the 'modern sense' of the (postmodern) novel consists of. In other words, *The French Lieutenant's Woman* is a novel in the original, Cervantean, sense of the word, a sense which provides the basis for fiction throughout the centuries. Later in the chapter the author/narrator sums up the original Cervantean insight concerning the conflict between the imagination and reality that has inspired literature throughout the centuries: 'We are all in flight from the real reality. That is a basic definition of *Homo sapiens*' (p. 107).

Graham Greene (1904–1991) is the author of perhaps the most celebrated rewriting of Cervantes's novel in the late twentieth century: *Monsignor Quixote* (1982), the culmination of his very long interest in things Spanish and particularly *Don Quixote*. Greene was a great admirer of philosopher and novelist Miguel de Unamuno and was much influenced by his romantic concept of Don Quixote.[34] Quixotic characters appear in several of Greene's earlier works, but Cervantes's novel and its characters become the focus of *Monsignor Quixote*. Father Quixote, parish priest in El Toboso, who claims to be a direct descendant of Don Quixote, suddenly finds himself promoted to monsignor and, in the company of the town's atheist Marxist ex-mayor, named Enrique Zancas (whom the monsignor calls 'Sancho' after Cervantes's squire)[35], sets out in his old Seat 600 — which of course he has named Rocinante — on a journey to Madrid. The sometimes doubting priest[36] and the sometimes believing atheist consume large quantities of wine as they engage in long conversations about theology, political theory,[37] and, of course, Cervantes and *Don Quixote*; each one influences the other increasingly as the novel progresses. Some of the adventures they have during the course of the trip recall specific characters and scenes from *Don Quixote*: windmills–Holy Brotherhood/Guardia Civil; Sansón Carrasco/Father Herrera; Don Diego de Miranda/Señor Diego; penitents/church procession. When priest and politician visit the city of Salamanca, they pay homage to Greene's much admired Unamuno, as they contemplate his monument in that city and Sancho remarks to Father Quixote, 'You know how he loved your ancestor and studied his life'.[38] This is not the most profound retelling of the story of Don Quixote, but it is an intelligent and entertaining one, with thoughtful religious, philosophical, and political themes. It is one of Greene's better novels.[39]

The last novelist I want to mention specifically is the celebrated Anglo-Indian writer Salman Rushdie (1947–). Rushdie was already a respected novelist in the early 1980s, but he suddenly burst into international fame and became a *cause célèbre* with the publication of *The Satanic Verses* (1988) and has since gained prominence as the most important 'postcolonial' writer in the world. His novel *The Moor's Last Sigh* (1995) is a long and complex family saga of the spice trade in India. It is also Rushdie's most quixotic novel to date, as it resonates throughout with references and allusions to *Don Quixote*. The family's patriarch, Francisco da Gama, for example, is specifically compared to Don Quixote. Rushdie has explicitly named Cervantes as one of his 'literary parents.'

The novel's title is significant on at least three counts. First, it evokes the story of Boabdil, the last Muslim king of Granada, who surrendered to Christian forces in 1492. Upon leaving his beloved land, he turned and looked one last time at the Alhambra, gave a great sigh, and burst into tears. His mother is supposed to have admonished him that he did well to weep like a woman for that which he could not defend as a man. The site from which he gazed this final time upon Granada is known in Spanish as *El último suspiro del moro* [*The Moor's Last Sigh*]. Boabdil was sometimes known as *el zogoybi* [the Unfortunate], and this is the source of the name of the protagonist, Moraes 'Moor' Zogoiby.[40]

Second, *The Moor's Last Sigh* is the title of the most famous painting done by the protagonist's artist mother, Aurora Zogoiby. The painting is described in detail at the beginning of Chapter 13, at the very centre of the novel: 'It was a picture which, for all its great size, had been stripped to the harsh essentials, all its elements converging on the face at its heart, the Sultan's face, from which horror, weakness, loss and pain poured like darkness itself, a face in a condition of existential torment reminiscent of Edvard Munch'.[41] In this work Aurora manages both to depict the famous historical scene and imply her understanding of her treatment of her only son. 'Moor' thus takes on here a double meaning: Boabdil and Moraes Zogoiby.[42]

And third, the final section of the novel is also titled 'The Moor's Last Sigh.' In these final chapters, Moraes Zogoiby takes refuge at the clan's ancestral home, the village of Benengeli, located in the borderland between Andalusia and La Mancha. And here is where the Cervantine and quixotic aspects of the novel become most prominent. Rushdie's novel frequently calls its own veracity into question, commenting on the relationship between fact and fiction, reporting and interpreting, reminding us constantly that storytelling is at the heart of living. Cervantes does the same, particularly through his meticulous Muslim historian, Cide Hamete Benengeli, whom Christians would take to be a congenital liar. This ironic self-undermining narrative is almost certainly the reason why the village is named Benengeli (a neighbouring village is named Avellaneda, after the author of the apocryphal continuation of Cervantes's novel, and another is Erasmo, the Spanish version of Erasmus). This section is full of commentary on Spanish history and culture, and especially *Don Quixote*, which is mentioned and/or alluded to several times. On one occasion the narrator tries to recall the last names of a couple of characters: 'Lorenço, del Toboso, de Malindrania, Caraculiambro?' (p. 417). Don Quixote's beloved (and imaginary) Dulcinea is from El Toboso and is inspired by the peasant woman Aldonza Lorenzo. In the first chapter of the 1605 *Don Quixote*, the protagonist imagines a future battle with a giant named Caraculiambro, who comes from the kingdom of Malindrania. *The Moor's Last Sigh* is arguably the last great quixotic novel of the twentieth century. It underscores once again the inexhaustible source of ideas, characters, themes, and narrative techniques that Cervantes bequeathed to all subsequent novelists.

Space does not permit further examination of quixotic novels of the twentieth century. Throughout the scholarly works cited at various times in this essay one will find further commentary on British authors who have writen sequels to *Don Quixote*, novels whose main characters are reincarnations (or, at least, namesakes) of Don Quixote, are explicitly or implicitly (but obviously, for one who looks) inspired in or otherwise comparable to Cervantes's hero, and/or display the sort of self-conscious metafiction first explored in depth by Cervantes. Even a short list of such major (and very minor) novelists and short story writers is an impressive one: Max Beerbohm, Anthony Burgess, Robin Chapman,[43] Joseph Conrad, Isobel Fitzroy, George Gissing, Geoffrey Household, Eyre Hussey, James Joyce, Malcolm Lowry, W. Somerset Maugham, Kenneth Morris, George Orwell, J. B. Priestley, Muriel Spark, Elizabeth Taylor, J. R. R. Tolkien, Peter Ustinov, T. H. White, and Virginia Woolf.

At the beginning of this essay I mentioned briefly the forms that a 'quixotic novel' might take. *Don Quixote* has frequently been called the prototype for the novel in general — by writers as distinct as José Ortega y Gasset, Harry Levin, Lionel Trilling, and Harold Bloom.[44] The case is often made that it is the first, as well as the best, of all novels. M. M. Bakhtin has theorized that the novel first 'emerged' in the Renaissance with Rabelais and Cervantes, and that *Don Quixote* is 'the classic and purest model of the novel as genre'.[45] It is not accidental that the great satiric novelists of the eighteenth-century — Fielding, Sterne, Diderot — all recognize *Don Quixote* as their model; that the greatest realist novelists of the nineteenth century — Flaubert, Dostoevsky, Pérez Galdós — all acknowledge Cervantes as their master; that the major modernist novelists of the early twentieth century — Woolf, Proust, Kafka — all made use of Cervantes's novel and his characters; or that the great post-modern novelists of the late twentieth and early twenty-first centuries — Fuentes, Kundera, Auster — all look to Cervantes as the first of their kind.

As I have done previously, I would like here to compare the novel to language, as conceived by Noam Chomsky. Chomsky has often stated that if Martians were to come to earth they would conclude that earthlings spoke but one language. That is, that at the most profound level all languages are essentially the same; the obvious differences are but surface manifestations. The novel, I suggest, may present a similar case. There is really only one novel (the quixotic), in the most profound sense of the word, but with many surface variations. Therefore, if the presence of *Don Quixote* is found throughout the British novel of the nineteenth and twentieth centuries, it is only because *Don Quixote* is found throughout the novel of all times and places.[46]

Notes to Chapter 9

1. This overview will be brief and superficial, as an in-depth study would occupy the pages of a lengthy book. In recent years, my interest in the history and theory of the novel, and in Cervantes's central role in both, has been a dominant theme in much of my research. Because of this, I have previously dealt with some — but by no means all — of the material included in this essay in other publications. Therefore, throughout this essay I draw heavily on three previous works: *The Cervantes Encyclopedia*, 2 vols (Westport, CT: Greenwood Press, 2004); *Miguel de Cervantes' 'Don Quixote': A Reference Guide* (Westport, CT: Greenwood Press, 2006) and 'The Quixotic Novel in British and American Literature', *CIEFL Bulletin*, New Series, 15. 2 (2005) and 16. 1 (2006): Special Double Issue: *Cervantes and His Legacy in Contemporary Fiction*, ed. by A. Robert Lauer and Sonya S. Gupta (Hyderabad, India: Central Institute of English and Foreign Languages, 2007), pp. 1–18. In all cases, the material is contextualized somewhat differently than it is in those sources.
2. See my *Reference Guide*, pp. 166–70, and 'The Quixotic Novel', pp. 3–5, for a fuller discussion of what I consider to be included within the concept of the 'quixotic novel'. In comparison with my expansive and inclusive concept, see Alexander Welsh, *Reflections on the Hero as Quixote* (Princeton, NJ: Princeton University Press, 1981), pp. 3–16, for a more limited and restrictive approach.
3. In a famous essay, Lionel Trilling proposed that the basic theme of literature in general is 'the old opposition between reality and appearance, between what really is and what merely seems' and then concludes that 'all prose fiction is a variation on the theme of *Don Quixote*': *The Liberal Imagination: Essays on Literature and Society* (New York: Viking Press, 1950), pp. 207, 209. See my *Reference Guide*, pp. 95–96, for an attempt to elaborate on Trilling's idea and explain why in fact *Don Quixote* can legitimately be considered the prototype for the appearance vs. reality theme.
4. American postmodern novelist John Barth, the author of several outstanding quixotic fictions himself, calls Cervantes 'the real inventor of postmodern fiction': *Further Fridays: Essays, Lectures, and Other Nonfiction 1984–1994* (Boston: Little, Brown, 1995), p. 46.
5. See Walter L. Reed, *An Exemplary History of the Novel: The Quixotic versus the Picaresque* (Chicago: University of Chicago Press, 1981), pp. 152–56; see also pp. 135–36.
6. On Austen's debt to Lennox's novel and her quixotic protagonist, see Elaine M. Kauvar, 'Jane Austen and *The Female Quixote*', *Studies in the Novel*, 2 (1970), pp. 211–21.
7. Emma Bovary may also be the greatest of all female Quixotes, but Benito Pérez Galdós's Isidora Rufete, protagonist of *La desheredada* (1881) might also make a good case to lay claim to the title.
8. Jane Austen, *Northanger Abbey* (London: J. M. Dent & Sons, 1950), p. 3.
9. See John A. G. Ardila, 'Cervantes y la *Quixotic fiction*: La parodia de géneros', *Anales Cervantinos*, 34 (1998), p. 145–68 (pp. 162–68), on Austen's protagonist as the culmination of a series of female quixotic parodies in English fiction.
10. Quoted by Clara S. Wolfe, 'Evidences of Scott's Indebtedness to Spanish Literature', *Romanic Review*, 23 (1932), pp. 301–11 (p. 301).

11. Scott referred to Cervantes's 'inimitable romance,' but, according to W. U. McDonald, Jr., 'Scott's Conception of *Don Quixote*', *Midwest Review*, 1 (1959), pp. 37–42 (p. 40), did not intend the term 'romance' to carry any of the negative connotations it often has when compared to 'novel.'

12. Michael E. Gerli, '"Pray, landlord, bring me those books": Notes on Cervantes, Walter Scott, and the Social Legitimacy of the Novel in Early Nineteenth-Century England', in *'Corónente tus hazañas': Studies in Honor of John Jay Allen*, ed. by Michael J. McGrath (Newark, DE: Juan de la Cuesta, 2005), pp. 231–42.

13. Wolfe, 'Evidences of Scott's Indebtedness to Spanish Literature', p. 301, says there are over a hundred allusions to *Don Quixote* in Scott's novels. See also Aubrey Bell, 'Scott and Cervantes', in *Walter Scott To-day: Some Retrospective Essays and Studies*, ed. by H. J. C. Grierson (London: Constable & Co., 1932), pp. 69–90, on Scott's interest in Cervantes and other Spanish writers.

14. Walter Scott, *Waverley; or, 'Tis Sixty Years Since*, ed. by Claire Lamont (Oxford: Clarendon Press, 1981), p. 18.

15. See Patricia S. Gaston, 'The Waverley Series and *Don Quixote*: Manuscripts Found and Lost', *Cervantes*, 11. 1 (1991), pp. 45–59, on Scott's use throughout the Waverley novels of devices such as 'the journey and inn motifs, the found manuscript device, and the strategy of self-conscious textual referentiality' (p. 48), all of which she traces back to Cervantes.

16. Godwin himself very much admired *Don Quixote* and was the author of *The Adventures of Caleb Williams* (1794), a quixotic novel. He then became the butt of the satire in Charles Lucas's *The Infernal Quixote* (1801); see Mancing, *Encyclopedia*, I, 339. It would seem much more likely than not that his daughter's life-long concern for Cervantes and his novel had its origin in Godwin's interest in the same subjects.

17. For more on the quixotic elements in *Frankenstein*, and on the Shelley–Cervantes relationship in general, see Erin Webster Garrett, 'Recycling Zoraida: The Muslim Heroine in Mary Shelley's *Frankenstein*', *Cervantes*, 20. 1 (2000), pp. 133–56. See also Jeanne Moskal, '"To speak in Sanchean phrase": Cervantes and the Politics of Mary Shelley's *History of a Six Weeks' Tour*', in *Mary Shelley in Her Times*, ed. by Betty T. Bennet and Stuart Curran (Baltimore: Johns Hopkins University Press, 2000), pp. 18–37.

18. *Oliver Twist* is indebted less to *Don Quixote* than to Cervantes's novella titled *Rinconete y Cortadillo* (1613), in which the character of Monipodio (based on an actual historical figure whom Cervantes may have known), the leader of a criminal ring in Seville that featured cutpurses and cape-stealers, is the acknowledged model for Fagin, head of the gang of thieves populated by such picaresque figures as Bill Sikes and the Artful Dodger. For a good presentation of the influence on the Spanish picaresque novel tradition on subsequent Continental realist novelists, see the important book by Reed, *An Exemplary History of the Novel*. See also Pamela H. Long, 'Fagin and Monipodio: The Source of *Oliver Twist* in Cervantes's *Rinconete y Cortadillo*', *Dickensian*, 90 (1994), pp. 117–24, and María Teresa Vázquez de Prada , 'El *Quijote* y *Oliver Twist*,' *ES*, 21 (1998), pp. 129–43.

19. Surprisingly, although *The Pickwick Papers* is almost universally compared to *Don Quixote*, and virtually no one doubts Dickens's profound and direct indebtedness to Cervantes, there is no mention of either Cervantes or his novel in Dickens's work. In fact, although the Quixote–Pickwick identity is obvious and was frequently made in Dickens's time, he himself never explicitly made the comparison. Long, however, states that 'Dickens himself admitted to having based his character Mr Pickwick almost directly on the Manchegan knight' (p. 117). See Welsh, *Reflections*, pp. 11–12; Angus Easson, 'Don Pickwick: Dickens and the Transformation of Cervantes', in *Rereading Victorian Fiction*, ed. by Alice Jenkins, Juliet John and John Sutherland (New York: Macmillan, 2000), pp. 173–88; and María Teresa Vázquez de Prada Merino, 'Ecos del *Quijote* en Charles Dickens', in *La huella de Cervantes y del 'Quijote' en la cultura anglosajona*, ed. by José Manuel Barrio Marco, and María José Crespo Allué (Valladolid: Universidad de Valladolid, Secretariado de Publicaciones e Intercambio Editorial, 2007), pp. 197–208, on the question of Dickens's degree of familiarity with Cervantes. See also Paul Goetsch, 'Charles Dickens's *The Pickwick Papers* and *Don Quixote*', in *Cervantes in the English-Speaking World*, ed. by Darío Fernández-Morera and Michael Hanke (Kassel: Edition Reichenberger, 2005), pp. 143–58 (pp. 143–45) on the genesis of Dickens's novel, which did not begin as a consciously quixotic

or Cervantine work but which clearly evolved into exactly that, and the early critical reception which often saw *Pickwick* in those terms.

20. María Teresa Vázquez de Prada acknowledges the Quixote–Pickwick similarity but also compares Dickens's protagonist to Sancho Panza: 'Sancho Panza y Mr. Pickwick: Una Nueva Comparación', *Cuadernos de Estudios Manchegos*, 18 (1988), pp. 21–33.

21. Mercedes Potau, 'Notes on Parallels between *The Pickwick Papers* and *Don Quixote*', *Dickens Quarterly*, 10. 2 (1993), pp. 105–10 (p. 105) suggests that it was the introduction of Sam Weller into the story that made clear the similarities between Dickens's serialized story and Cervantes's novel.

22. Pedro Javier Pardo García, 'La heroína quijotesca en la novela inglesa del siglo XIX: Jane Austen, George Eliot y otros novelistas', in *Cervantes y el ámbito anglosajón*, ed. by Diego Martínez Torrón and Bernd Dietz (Madrid: Trivium, 2005), pp. 356–75 (p. 371, note 2), compares Casaubon to what he calls 'quijotesque pedants' of the type found in the works of Swift and Sterne. For a more extended comparison of the two figures, see also Chester St. H. Mills, 'Eliot's Spanish Connection: Casaubon, the Avatar of Quixote,' *George Eliot–George Henry Lewes Studies*, 26/27 (1994), pp. 1–6.

23. George Eliot, *The Mill on the Floss*, ed. by Gordon S. Haight (Oxford: Clarendon Press, 1980), p. 95.

24. Eliot read *Don Quixote* with George Henry Lewes in 1864, and in 1866 she and Lewes toured Spain, where she was particularly interested in gypsy life. Maggie's dalliance with the gypsies almost certainly also owes something to Cervantes's 1613 novella titled *La Gitanilla* [The Little Gypsy Girl], a work whose influence can also be seen in her poem 'The Spanish Gypsy' (1868); see Lina Sierra Ayala, 'Miguel de Cervantes y George Eliot: *La Gitanilla* y *The Spanish Gypsy*', in *La huella de Cervantes* (see Vázquez de Prada Merino, above), pp. 172–230.

25. Saint Teresa herself, like Don Quixote, was a fond reader of chivalric romances in her youth and even plotted with her brother to run off together to fight against the Muslim infidels in Africa. Perhaps the best literary example of this sort of religious quixotism can be found in the figure of María in Armando Palacio Valdés's novel *Marta y María* (1883); see Mancing, *Encyclopedia*, II, 538–39.

26. Henry James, *The Portrait of a Lady* (New York: Modern Library, 1951), pp. 27, 45, 68.

27. Wyndham Lewis, *Tarr* (New York: Alfred A. Knopf, 1918), p. 285.

28. Wyndham Lewis, *Self-Condemned* (London: Methuen, 1954), p. 27. For more on quixotic elements in novels and essays by Lewis, see Alberto Lázaro Lafuente 'Estampas del *Quijote* en la novela británica contemporánea', in *La huella de Cervantes* (see Vázquez de Prada Merino, above), pp. 253–77 (pp. 260–64).

29. See Elmar Schenkel, 'G. K. Chesterton: *The Return of Don Quixote*', in Fernández-Morera and Hanke (eds), *Cervantes in the English-Speaking World*, pp. 169–80, on Chesterton's expressed interest in Cervantes and his novel in essays and fictions other than *The Return of Don Quixote*.

30. See Pilar Vega Rodríguez, '*El regreso de Don Quijote* de Chesterton. Tradición y Utopía', *Anales Cervantinos*, 37 (2005), pp. 239–51 (pp. 246–48) on the various Quixotes and Sanchos in the novel.

31. G. K. Chesterton, *The Return of Don Quixote* (Philadelphia: Dufour, 1963), p. 218.

32. L. P. Hartley, *The Love-Adept* (London: Hamish Hamilton, 1969), p. 30.

33. John Fowles, *The French Lieutenant's Woman* (Boston: Little, Brown, 1969), pp. 60, 62.

34. Unamuno valued Don Quixote over Cervantes and saw him as the very incarnation of the Spanish spirit. This is expressed most famously in his rewrite of Cervantes's novel, titled *Vida de Don Quijote y Sancho* (1905), and in a series of short essays; see Mancing, *Encyclopedia*, pp. 748–50. For more on Greene's interest in the philosophy and fictions of Unamuno, see Eric J. Ziolkowski, *The Sanctification of Don Quixote: From Hidalgo to Priest* (University Park: Penn State University Press, 1991), pp. 215–16, and Jae-Suck Choi, 'A Knight of Faith: *Monsignor Quixote*', in *Greene and Unamuno: Two Pilgrims to La Mancha* (New York: Peter Lang, 1990), pp. 187–200.

35. Zancas is a surname ascribed once to Sancho in *Don Quixote* I, 9.

36. Monsignor Quixote is an important contribution to the tradition of linking Don Quixote and Jesus Christ; others are found in the works of Dostoevsky and Kierkegaard, as well as Unamuno and even the poet W. H. Auden. See Ziolkowski, especially pp. 236–39, 247–62; and Mancing, *Encyclopedia*, I, 240.

37. The political setting in the novel, as well as the socio-political context of its writing and reception are studied by Berta Cano Echevarría, 'La España anacrónica del *Monsignor Quixote* de Graham Greene', in *La huella de Cervantes*, pp. 291–99.

38. Graham Greene, *Monsignor Quixote* (Toronto: Lester & Orpen Dennys, 1982), p. 98.

39. *Monsignor Quixote* was also made into a film in 1985, directed by Rodney Bennett, with Alec Guinness as Don Quixote and Leo McKern as Sancho Panza. See Caytano Estébanez Estébanez, '*Don Quijote*, de hidalgo de la Mancha a monseñor: Cervantes, Graham Greene y Rodney Bennett', in *La huella de Cervantes*, pp. 301–10 (pp. 308–09), and Leopoldo Durán, *Graham Greene, amigo y hermano* (Madrid: Espasa, 1996), pp. 265–74.

40. For more on the Spanish background and context of Rushdie's novel, see Paul A. Cantor, 'Tales of the Alhambra: Rushdie's Use of Spanish History in *The Moor's Last Sigh*', *Studies in the Novel*, 29 (1997), 323–41.

41. Salman Rushdie, *The Moor's Last Sigh* (New York: Vintage Books, 1995), p. 218.

42. Aurora's painting is, at least to some extent, a response to a more sentimental painting of the same scene by another character, Vasco Miranda: 'I have called it *The Artist as Boabdil, the Unlucky (el-Zogoybi), Last Sultan of Granada, Seen Departing from the Alhambra*', said Vasco with a straight face. 'Or, *The Moor's Last Sigh*' (p. 160).

43. Chapman is probably the English writer most profoundly concerned with *Don Quixote*. He established the relationship with his highly original novel *The Duchess's Diary* (1980), bringing to life an important character from the second part of *Don Quixote*. Very recently, he has written two more novels inspired directly by Cervantes's novel: *Sancho's Golden Age* (2004), a sequel that takes place about five years after the death of Don Quixote, and *Pasamonte's Life* (2005), a picaresque tale narrated in the first person by the galley slave Ginés de Pasamonte, who has a role in both parts of Cervantes's novel.

44. José Ortega y Gasset, *Meditaciones del 'Quijote' e ideas sobre la novela* (Madrid: Revista de Occidente, 1956), p. 134; Harry Levin, 'The Quixotic Principle: Cervantes and Other Novelists', in *The Interpretation of Narrative: Theory and Practice*, ed. by Morton W. Bloomfield (New York: Gordian Press, 1970), pp. 45–66; Trilling, cited previously; and Harold Bloom, *The Western Canon: The Books and School of the Ages* (New York: Harcourt Brace, 1994), p. 441.

45. M. M. Bakhtin, *The Dialogic Imagination: Four Essays*, ed. by Michael Holquist, trans. by Caryl Emerson and Michael Holquist (Austin: University of Texas Press, 1981), p. 324. Bakhtin's brilliant essay-within-an-essay, the long section of 'Discourse in the Novel' titled 'The Two Stylistic Lines of Development in the European Novel', pp. 366–422, can be read as the proposal that Cervantes's novel is indeed the prototype of the novel in general. In it, Cervantes and *Don Quixote* are mentioned and discussed in some detail no fewer than nineteen times; no other author or work is cited nearly as often as Cervantes in this segment of Bakhtin's writings that is most crucial for an understanding of his theory of the novel.

46. For the comparison with Chomsky, see Mancing, *Reference Guide*, pp. 166–70.

CHAPTER 10

The American Sources in Cervantes and Defoe

Stelio Cro

The claim that Cervantes was at all influential upon Defoe is intrinsically contro-versial and impossible to prove — there is simply not enough textual evidence to sustain such a hypothesis. However, besides the proven fact that Defoe wrote sheer picaresque novels, a number of scholars (*infra*) have suggested that he was influenced by Cervantes. The first of these was Samuel Taylor Coleridge, who identified Cervantes's *Persiles y Segismunda* as a likely source for Defoe's *Robinson Crusoe*. Nearly two hundred years later, Ronald Paulson suggested that to English Protestants 'the story of Don Quixote could have been read as a spiritual pilgrimage', and underlines Defoe's admiration for Cervantes's masterpiece, which he considered 'an allegorical representation of the life of the duke of Medina-Sidonia'.[1] This identification of the novel as an allegorical allusion offers a rich perspective to modern criticism. In *Cervantes, the Novel, and the New World*, Diana de Armas Wilson endeavours to establish the role of Cervantes in the development of the modern novel. This critic rejects Ian Watt's thesis contained in *The Rise of the Novel*, as a prejudicial and nationalistic attempt 'to install Daniel Defoe as "the first key figure in the rise of the novel" — not merely the English novel, as Hispanists were surprised to learn, but the novel'.[2] In order to overcome the pitfalls of a nationalistic thesis on the rise of the novel, Wilson believes that it is time to study the influence that the New World had in providing what we might call the breeding ground for the novel, a source of the strong influences arising from 'the geopolitics swirling around the matter of America — its conquest and colonization by a series of European nations, most indelibly by Spain and England'.[3] Recalling Coleridge's suggestion that Cervantes's *Persiles* might have provided the germ of Defoe's *Robinson Crusoe*, Wilson develops a comparative study of Cervantes novel, its American sources and how both played their part in the elaboration of Defoe's masterpiece.

These scholarly contributions have advanced the study of the relationship between Defoe and Cervantes to unprecedented levels, utilizing an array of methodologies, such as comparative literature, postcolonial theories, sociological theories for literary genres, multinational systems and aesthetics, interdisciplinary methods. What remains to be done is a rereading of *Don Quixote* and *Robinson Crusoe*, regardless of academic narrow specialization, taking into consideration what these great books have done to strengthen the rise of the modern novel in the western tradition.

In order to understand the extent of Cervantes's model in the conception of Defoe's *Robinson Crusoe* it might be necessary to recall the American sources, a comparative and historical method already invoked by Wilson. This becomes necessary to understand the Spanish influence in general and to locate in a more complete way the presence of Cervantes within that larger study. However it must be understood that the two sources are intimately intertwined. Thus, although one could argue that the adventures with Friday and with the newcomers to Crusoe's island undoubtedly belong to an interest in the New World, the permanent appeal of Defoe's masterpiece stems from a unique combination at his time of exotic sources, as well as Cervantes's intuition of the powerful effect of reading. There is an original and new dimension of the book as an independent object, an intuition first fully realized by Cervantes in Part I of *Don Quixote*, when the country gentleman Quijano goes mad from reading the chivalry books; an intuition that opened a never-ending debate on the real intention of the author, a topic first debated by Unamuno in his *Vida de Don Quixote y Sancho*.[4] Defoe seized on that intuition and transferred it to the episode of Crusoe's reading of the Bible.[5]

Religious behaviour in *Robinson Crusoe* means moral, practical conduct that brings with it a sense of interior appeasement and a sense of reconciliation with one's own fate. After an illness and a dream in which he sees a burning man who threatens to kill him because he has not repented of his sins, Robinson Crusoe begins to pray, for the first time in his life, at regular times during the day. He also, for the first time, asks the Lord's blessing for his food (p. 91). His view of the world will gradually adhere to that natural religion in order to come to some kind of acceptance of his situation. It is at this point in the account that Robinson Crusoe starts reading the Bible regularly. The first reading occurs when he is cooking some tobacco leaves in order to prepare a potion for his cold. He meditates upon the first words he reads on opening the Bible: 'Call on me in the Day of Trouble, and I will deliver, and thou shalt glorify me'; he then drinks the potion and falls asleep soon after, but not before kneeling and praying to the Lord as he has never done before. When he wakes up, having slept all night and perhaps all the subsequent day, he is well, although weak. His readings of the Bible increase over the next few days and he is now ready to convert to Christianity and pray according to Christian principles and virtues, faith and hope: 'This was the first Time that I could say, in the true Sense of the Words, that I pray'd in all my life; for now I pray'd with a Sense of my condition, and with a true Scripture View of Hope founded on the Encouragement of the Word of God; and from this Time, I may say, I began to have Hope that God would hear me' (p. 96). In fact, had it not been for his shipwreck and his life on the island, Crusoe might have never known true Christianity: 'My Condition began now to be, tho' not less miserable as to my Way of living, yet much easier to my Mind; and my Thoughts being directed, by a constant reading the Scripture, and praying to God, to things of a higher nature: I had a great deal of Comfort within, which till now I knew nothing of' (p. 97).

The tobacco signifies the healing power of nature; body and soul can be cured by nature and religion, especially the Christian faith because it is so close to nature, provided that one is prepared to accept it and has gone through a crisis, either physical or spiritual. As the body needs to recover from illness with the aid of nature, so the soul longs for religious guidance. From here on Robinson Crusoe's life grows materially and spiritually for the next fifteen years; he is thankful to the Lord for having given him the opportunity to understand divine providence: 'I had now brought my State of Life to be much easier in itself than it was at first, and much easier to my Mind, as well as to my Body. I frequently sat down to my Meat with Thankfulness, and admir'd the Hand of God's Providence which had thus spread my Table in the Wilderness' (p. 130). This is really a new life, in the Christian sense of being reborn: 'In the first Place, I was remov'd from all the Wickedness of the World here. I had neither the Lust of the Flesh, the Lust of the Eye, or the Pride of Life. I had nothing to covet' (p. 128). There is a symbolic and providential meaning to the coincidence of both dates, his birthday and his shipwreck on the deserted island: 'The same Day of the Year I was born on (viz.) the 30th of September, that same Day, I had my Life so miraculously saved 26 Years after, when I was cast on Shore in this Island, so that my wicked Life, and my solitary Life begun both on a Day' (p. 133).

The happy state of Crusoe acquires a negative connotation in that it is possible only on the island. In fact, his first reaction, upon discovering a man's footprint, after fifteen years of exile in the island, is fear. Far from expressing jubilation or even relief that other human beings may be close at hand and he might actually be rescued, his instinctive reaction is fear. And this is even prior to his discovery that the people who occasionally land on the island are cannibals: 'I came home to my Fortification, not feeling, as we say, the Ground I went on, but terrify'd to the last Degree, looking behind me at every two or three Steps, mistaking every Bush and Tree, and fancying every Stump at a Distance to be a Man' (p. 154). Fearing the presence of man, he even wonders if the print he discovered was not the print of the Devil himself, coming for his soul. But after a more serene observation, he concludes that the creature who had left the footprint was more dangerous than the Devil himself (p. 155). This changes Robinson's life and also gives the reader a clear indication of his perception of the extreme polarization of human nature as he says, upon learning that cannibalistic banquets are held at a site at the opposite extreme of his island residence: '(I) gave God thanks that had cast my first Lot in a Part of the World where I was distinguish'd from such dreadful Creatures as these [...] been comforted with the knowledge of himself, and the Hope of his Blessing' (p. 165). The adventures are thus propelled into a theological dimension with endless allegorical reverberations.

Of course Cervantes is not the only Spanish source of Defoe. He probably knew Peter Martyr's *De Orbe Novo* in Richard Eden's translation. The first edition, published in 1555, included the first three Decades, with the account of the cannibals. A complete translation of the eight Decades, by Eden, was published in 1597 and reprinted in 1612, 1620 and 1626. The title of this translation evoked the adventure and mysteries awaiting the reader.[6]

Defoe's historical sources, although based on witnesses' accounts, functioned in the story as the fantastic creatures evoked by the chivalry books of Don Quixote's library. Between *Don Quixote* and the *Persiles*, Cervantes attempted to bring the 'material de Indias' within the scope of the novel of adventures. Critics have already underlined the utilization of the chronicles of America in the elaboration of the *Persiles*.[7]

In *Persiles*, the allusions to shipwrecks and to their survivors at the beginning of the novel, and to the accounts by those survivors of islands inhabited by natives who have great wealth in gold and pearls, are reminiscent of the chronicles of America, especially Garcilaso el Inca's *Comentarios reales*. In the third chapter of this work Garcilaso tells the story of the pilot, Alonso Sánchez de Huelva, who in 1484 was surprised by a storm 'tan recio y tempestuoso que, no pudiendo resistirle, se dejó llevar de la tormenta y corrió veinte y ocho o veinte y nueve días sin saber por dónde ni adónde, porque en todo este tiempo no pudo tomar el altura por el sol ni por el Norte' [so swift and violent that, unable to resist it, let the storm carry him sailing with it for twenty-eight or twenty-nine days without knowing where he was going, because during all this time he had been unable to fix his position by observing the sun or the North star].[8] The episode, with its digressions and its fictitious elements is suited to the digressive nature of the *Persiles*. As we will see, the episode of Pedro Serrano in the *Comentarios reales* acquires the nature of a narrative, capable of inspiring a writer like Cervantes. In this episode we are decidedly faced with a historical event that challenges the reader's willingness to believe it. In *Don Quixote*, the defect of chivalry books is that their plot is not believable, their situation defies the measure of belief required to be an essential ingredient in a good story. And even if these books have no other aim but to entertain, they cannot achieve it with these crude means. Fiction is good when it has a truthful component: 'tanto la mentira es mejor cuanto más parece verdadera' [the lie is much better when it sounds more truthful], and 'tanto más agrada cuanto tiene más de lo dudoso y posible' [it is much more pleasant when it is more doubtful and possible].[9] To this we could add what Cervantes said in the *Viaje del Parnaso*: 'que a las cosas que tienen de imposibles / siempre mi pluma se ha mostrado esquiva; / las que tienen vislumbre de posibles, / de luces, de suaves y de ciertas, / esplican mis borrones apacibles' [my pen never felt at ease with things that seemed impossible. On the other hand, things that could offer a possible truth, a dim light of hope, explain my best scripts].[10]

An example of the characteristic overlapping of truth and fiction is the topos of the island in Spanish literature. It is a topos that begins with an Italian book, the *Libretto de tutta la nauigatione de Re de Spagna et de le isole nouamente trouate*, published in Venice in 1504. It is possible that because it is based on an early draft of Peter Martyr's *De Orbe Novo* Spanish scholars refrained from considering it as part of their literary heritage.[11] The number of editions published in Europe in the decades following 1504, including the change of title in order to disguise its real author, is an eloquent proof of the popularity of a new literary genre which never died out and that includes, among its most prominent authors, Cervantes, Defoe and Stevenson.[12]

Schevill and Bonilla have discussed Cervantes's debt to the Bizanthyne Novel of Heliodoro and of other Renaissance authors, such as Aquiles Tacio and to the fictitious voyage of Niccolò Zeno, published in Venice in 1558, Olao Magno's the

Opera breve, la quale demostra e dechiara ouero da il modo facile de intendere la charta ouer delle terre frigidissime di Settentrione [A brief work that demonstrates and explains, providing an easy way to understand the map of the very cold lands in the Northern Hemisphere] (Venice, 1539) and *Historia de gentibus septentrionalibus* [A History of the Northern People] (Rome, 1555), Antonio de Torquemada's *Jardín de flores curiosas, en que se tratan algunas materias de Humanidad, Philosophia, Theologia y Geographia, con otras cosas curiosas y apazibles* [A garden of curious flowers, in which are discussed some subject matters of Humanity, Philosophy, Theology and Geography, with other curious and delectable subjects] (Leyden, 1573; Salamanca, 1577), Francisco Thamara's *El libro de las costumbres de todas las gentes del mundo* [The book of the customs of the people of the world] and Julio Solino's *De las cosas maravillosas del mundo* [Of the marvellous things in the world], besides the chronicles of America. To this source these scholars dedicate several pages, singling out Garcilaso's *Comentarios reales* as the main source of Cervantes. They mention other sources, namely the chivalry books, the pastoral genre and a novel by Giovanni Giraldi Cinzio. Schevill and Bonilla also underline the importance of the topos of the island in the fictitious voyage of the Zeni brothers. This work includes a false map of the island of Frislanda, name that appears in the title: *Dello scoprimento dell'isole Frislanda, Eslanda, Engrouelanda, Estotilanda et Icaria, fatto sotto il polo artico da' due fratelli Zeni, M. Nicolò il Caualiere, et M. Antonio* [Of the discovery of the islands of Frisland, Iceland, Greenland, Estotiland and Icaria, made under the Arctic Pole by the two Zeni brothers, M. Niccolò, a Knight, and M. Antonio] (Venice, 1558).

It is quite significant that the topos of the island is intimately connected with the character of Sancho. After making its appearance in I, 7, where Don Quixote mentions to Sancho the possibility of him becoming the governor of an island (I, 7; p. 85), the topos reappears towards the end of the 1605 Part I, in Chapter 47, when the barber, disguised as a fictitious character, reproaches Sancho for his insistence of becoming some day governor of an island: 'en mal hora se os entró en los cascos la ínsula que tanto deseáis' [It was not a good occurrence to get so worked up over that island that you want so much] (I, 47; p. 516).

The next time the island reappears as a central topos in the story is in the 1615 Part II, with the treatment of Barataria, the false 'island' of Sancho in Chapters 42–45, with its utopian ramifications. The selection of these chapters could be justified because of their symmetry:

Chapters 42–44: Don Quixote and Sancho meet before the latter departs for the island.

Chapter 44, first half: farewell and departure of Sancho.

Chapter 44, second half: the Duchess offers four damsels to Don Quixote. Altisidora tries to seduce Don Quixote, but the knight proclaims his fidelity to Dulcinea. This episode is an act that separates the two parts of the utopian project.

Chapter 45: oral tradition, represented by the judgments of Sancho, a true judicial reform.

With the episode of Barataria, Cervantes might have shown another profound and original interpretation of Thomas More's *Utopia*. Only by accepting the ambiguity of More's work we can perceive the depth and influence of this little book, published in 1516. The dogmatic reading of this text on the part of a certain critical tradition, interested in limiting the text to radical and revolutionary movements, limits its interest and ignores the Erasmian spirit that inspired it.[13]

Cervantes, like More, believed that a text that denies all the values of its readers does not entertain them; it rejects them or bores them. But a text where those values are considered under a new light entertains and educates. This is the meaning of the Barataria episode and that of Crusoe's island. The topos is an allegory of England, an island that 'can be better governed with less laws and a more rational use of raw materials and industry.

Both Cervantes and Defoe chose the overlapping of true and fiction as their method of narrative, in order to entertain and educate. The probability of truth in fiction was their guiding method, as Cervantes reminds us in a passage of *Persiles*: 'puesto que es excelencia de la historia que, qualquiera cosa que en ella se escriuia, puede passar al sabor de la verdad que trae consigo; lo que no tyiene la fabula, a quien conuiene guissar sus acciones con tanta puntualidad y gusto, y con tanta verissimilitud, que, ha despecho y pesar de la mentira, que haze dissonancia en el entendimiento, forme vna verdadera armonia' [in fact an excellent aspect of history is that what is written in it is generally believed as truthful, something that fiction cannot claim; for this reason the latter must arrange its narrative in such a way that, with much care and delight might obtain so much plausibility that, in spite of the fact that it is fiction, and that it defies reason, produces a certain harmony] (II, 100).

One could still ask this question: what did Defoe see in Cervantes that might signify for him what Virgil meant to Dante? Recalling the Dante–Virgil relationship might shed light on Defoe and Cervantes. Like Dante, Defoe was determined to recreate an epic, although a new and different one, something never attempted previously. He read the adventures of the immortal Manchego with the naïve and avid curiosity of his English contemporaries, moved by Don Quixote's noble ideals, by his faithfulness to a lost cause. Defoe transformed the medieval ideals of Don Quixote into the English ingenuity of Crusoe, a new man, the new hero of a new mercantile empire in which England would prove to be the supreme achiever. Once the allegory of the new hero took hold the English novel was born, but it would not have been possible without the tale of Don Quixote, depicted at the twilight of a declining age.

Notes to Chapter 10

1. See *Don Quixote in England: The Aesthetics of Laughter* (Baltimore and London: The Johns Hopkins University Press, 1998), pp. 158–59.
2. Diana de Armas Wilson, *Cervantes, the Novel, and the New World* (Oxford: Oxford University Press, 2003), p. 46.
3. Wilson, p. 59.
4. Miguel de Unamuno, *Vida de Don Quixote y Sancho* (Madrid: Espasa-Calpe, Austral, 1964), pp. 155–56 'y es que Don Quixote vio de veras lo que dijo había visto en la cueva de Montesinos — a pesar de las maliciosas insinuaciones de Cervantes en contrario — y Sancho no vio lo que dijo haber visto en las esferas celestes yendo en lomos de Clavileño, sino que lo inventó

mintiendo' [the truth is that Don Quixote really saw what he said he saw in the Montesinos' cave — in spite of Cervantes' malicious insinuations to the contrary — and Sancho did not see what he said that he saw in heaven while riding on Clavileño, because he lied]. This passage indicates a disagreement between the author and an illustrious reader.

5. References to Defoe's *Robinson Crusoe* are from Daniel Defoe, *Robinson Crusoe*, ed. by J. Donald Crowley (Oxford: Oxford University Press, 1985).

6. *The decades of the New World or West India, conteyning the navigations and conquests of the Spanyards, with the particular description of the most ryche and large landes and islands lately found in the west ocean parteyning to the inheritance of the kings of Spayne. In the wich the diligent reader may not only consyder what commodities may herby chance to the hole christian world in tyme to come, but also learn many secreates touchynge the land, the sea and the starres, very necessarie to knowe to all such as shal attempt any navigations or otherwise have delite to behold the strange and wonnderffull woorkes of God and Nature.* Written in the latine tounge by Peter Martyr of Angleria, and translated in to englyshe by Richarde Eden. Londini in aedibus Guilhelmi Powell, anno 1555.

7. The first scholars who suggested the influence of Garcilaso de la Vega, el Inca's *Comentarios reales* on the *Persiles* were Rodolfo Schevill and Adolfo Bonilla in 'Introducción', in Miguel de Cervantes, *Persiles y Segismunda*, in *Obras Completas* (Madrid: Imprenta de Bernardo Rodríguez, 1914), IX/X, 337. References to the *Persiles* are to this edition, in two volumes, with the volume and page number in parentheses. A complete review of the bibliography on this subject can be found in Rafael Osuna's 'El olvido del *Persiles*', *Boletín de la Real Academia Española*, 48 (1968), 55–75. The first article that examined the presence of the chronicles of America in Cervantes is José Toribio Medina's 'Cervantes americanista', in *Estudios Cervantinos* (Santiago de Chile: Fondo histórico y bibliográfico José Toribio Medina, 1958), pp. 507–37; see also Stelio Cro, 'Cervantes, el *Persiles* y la historiografía indiana', *Anales de Literatura Hispanoamericana*, 3. 4 (1975), 5–25. However, other critics, considering the date of publication of the *Comentarios Reales* by Garcilaso de la Vega, el Inca, in 1609, deny knowledge by Cervantes by arguing that the *Persiles* was written before 1609; see Max Singleton, 'El misterio del *Persiles*', *Realidad*, 2 (1947), 237–53; Juan Bautista Avalle Arce, in 'Introducción biográfica y crítica', in Miguel de Cervantes, *Persiles* (Madrid: Castalia, 1969), pp. 7–32, disagrees with Schevill and Bonilla for chronological reasons, arguing that the two first books of the *Persiles* were written between 1599 and 1605, a few years before the publication of Garcilaso's work.

8. Garcilaso de la Vega, el Inca, *Comentarios reales de los Incas*, ed. by José Durand (Lima: Reproducción de la primera edición hecha por la Universidad Mayor de San Marcos, 1967), p. 69. References in parenthesis in the body of the text.

9. References to *Don Quixote* indicate part and chapter.

10. Miguel de Cervantes, *Viaje del 'Parnaso'*, in *Obras Completas*, ed. by Germán de Argumosa (Barcelona: Editorial Juventud, 1964), p. 1535. All other references to this edition in parentheses.

11. Cf. Stelio Cro, 'La Princeps y la cuestión del plagio del *De Orbe Novo*', *Cuadernos para Investigación de la Literatura Hispánica*, 28 (2003), 15–24.

12. The second edition of *Libretto* changed the title to *Paesi nouamente ritrouati e Nouo Mondo per Americo Vesputio intitulato*; published in Vicenza in 1507, in the same year of the publication of *Cosmographie Introductio* by Martin Waldseemüller, it suggested in the title the paternity of the discovery by Americo Vespucci that consecrated the name of Americo as that of the father of America, thus underlining the extraordinary nature of the overlapping between truth and fiction even at the most climatic moment of the history of the New World. *Paesi* was a bestseller, being reprinted in 1508 and again in 1512 in Milan; it was translated into Latin and published in 1508, also in Milan; then into German and published, also in 1508, in Nuremberg; and then into French, published in 1512 in Paris. It continued enjoying great popularity and underwent several translations and publications in the sixteenth century.

13. For the radicalization of More's masterpiece and the utopian genre, see Karl Mannheim, *Ideology and Utopia* (New York: Harvest Books, 1936); for Erasmus's influence see Achille Olivieri (ed.), *Erasmo e le utopie del cinquecento: l'influenza della Moria e dell'Enchiridion* (Milan: Edizioni Unicopli, 1996).

CHAPTER 11

Henry Fielding: from Quixotic Satire to the Cervantean Novel

J. A. G. Ardila

Henry Fielding was one of the most accomplished men in eighteenth-century England; having been educated at Eton and at the University of Leyden, he enjoyed a successful career as a playwright, became justice of the peace in Westminster and Middlesex, established the first London police force, edited a number of newspapers and magazines (namely *The Champion*, 1739–41, *The True Patriot*, 1745–46, *The Jacobite Journal*, 1747–48, and *The Covent Garden Journal*, 1752), and finally took to novel writing. He is nowadays remembered as one of the finest English novelists; Walter Scott christened him 'the father of the English novel',[1] and Anthony Burgess has called him 'The greatest novelist of the [eighteenth] century'[2] and 'England's greatest novelist'.[3] Fielding's best novels evince his interest in Cervantes's *Don Quixote*, which he regarded as the canon of the novel. So closely did Fielding follow Cervantes that Smollett claimed that 'The genius of Cervantes was transfused into the novels of Henry Fielding', and his contemporaries compared his pre-eminence among English novelists to that of Cervantes in Spanish literature.[4] But whilst *Joseph Andrews* is mainly a parody and a satire acted by quixotic characters, *Tom Jones* emulates the narrative structure of *Don Quixote*.

On his return to London from Holland, Fielding tried his hand at writing for the stage. His first play, *Love in Several Masques* (1728), was followed by two adaptations from Molière, *The Mock Doctor* and *The Miser*. All of his subsequent plays boasted a satirical vein: *The Author's Face* takes on the literary world; *Rape upon Rape* criticizes English justice; and *Tom Thumb* is a parody of contemporary literature. Satire in Fielding's plays included unequivocal political attacks, especially against the Prime Minister, Robert Walpole. When, in 1737, Fielding published *Pasquin* and *The Historical Register for 1736*, the government closed all theatres in London (except the one in Covent Garden and that in Drury Lane), and passed the Stage Licensing Act, which enabled censors to prohibit the staging of Fielding's plays. Fielding's theatrical works include *Don Quixote in England*, a piece in which Don Quixote and Sancho visit England in search of new adventures. Although Walpole's legislation forced Fielding to give up play-writing, he soon started to publish novels — *Shamela* (1741), *Joseph Andrews* (1742), *Jonathan Wild* (1743), *Tom Jones* (1749), and *Amelia* (1751). His novels retained the parody and the satiric strain of his plays. *Shamela* was a parody of Samuel Richardson's *Pamela*, a popular novel which, in Fielding's view, exalted a spurious perception of virtue. His second novel was entitled *The Adventures of Joseph Andrews and his Friend, Mr Abraham Adams, Written in Imitation of Cervantes, Author of Don Quixote*. In another attempt to parody Richardson's works, Fielding had introduced Joseph as the brother of Pamela Andrews.

Fielding's novels stand out in the history of English literature, not only for their exceptional literary quality, but also because they illustrate the eighteenth-century eagerness to establish a canon of the English novel. This he strove to achieve by following an archetypical text: Cervantes's *Don Quixote*. Albeit many scholars have studied Cervantes's influence on *Joseph Andrews* (*v. infra*), very little attention has been paid to his plays and to *Tom Jones*. However, the impact of Cervantes on Fielding's oeuvre progresses through three stages: *Don Quixote in England* from his time as a playwright; *Joseph Andrews* from his early years as a novelist; and his *magnum opus*, *Tom Jones*.

Satire in Fielding's plays abides by the artistic fashion of the time. English theatres had remained closed during the Puritan Republic; during the Reformation and well into the eighteenth century satire became commonplace. Swift, Pope and Gay were members of the Scriblerus Club, a society against inappropriate forms of learning. Gay, Pope and Arbuthnot wrote *Three Hours after Marriage*, a prime example of the period's satirical mind. Plays often questioned social stereotypes and morality: William Wycherly's *The Country Wife*, Richard Sheridan's *The Critic* and John Gay's *The Beggar's Opera* attest to this satirical fashion which permeated the stage and the arts. Hence Fielding's plays are far from innovatory; they conform to the early-eighteenth-century trends. Neither are his literary sources pioneering: he adapted from Molière, as Wycherly had in *The Plain Dealer* (which is believed to be based on *The Misanthrope*). A well-known source for satire in the seventeenth century was *Don Quixote*, most notably after the publication of Butler's *Hudibras*, in 1663, 1664, and 1678.

Before *Don Quixote in England* (staged in 1733, although Fielding declared in the preliminaries that it was begun in 1728), Fielding had sketched a quixotic character in his first play, *Love in Several Masques* (1728), namely Helena, the country girl whose only knowledge of city life is drawn from fiction.[5] In bringing the Knight of La Mancha and his squire over to England and confronting them with English society and human types, Fielding was aligning his work with the sign of the times — he was presenting his audience with a satirical play based on a notorious foreign model. *Don Quixote in England* is, above all, a literary gem, an intriguing play written by one of the masters of English literature, which also corroborates Cervantes's status as a renowned and respected model in eighteenth-century England. *Don Quixote in England*, however, has failed to attract the attention of literary critics; we have only Gnutzmann's article and a number of allusions in the books by Paulson and Canavaggio.[6]

Don Quixote in England is a three-act ballad opera that includes a total of fifteen songs. This play opens with Don Quixote and Sancho in the English countryside. The Spanish knight has travelled to England because in 'a search of adventure [...] no place abounds more with them'.[7] There are similarities with the Spanish novel from the very beginning, e.g. the first act opens with Don Quixote refusing to pay the inn-keeper. Fielding's knight errant is also a madman who lives in a distorted world — inns are castles, a gentleman in the inn is the giant Toglogmoglogog, and when Don Quixote hears a girl singing he immediately assumes that she is a princess in distress. Fielding portrays Sancho in the same comical and degrading vein of former English writers, namely Thomas D'Urfey in *The Comical History of Don Quixote* and Edmund Gayton in *The Pleasant Notes upon Don Quixote*. Knowles has observed that Fielding's knight is endowed with the insane–sane duality of the Spanish model, although in the English play, this duality is so extreme that it lacks verisimilitude.[8] Knowles pinpoints the poor psychological development of Fielding's characters; however, the author did not intend to develop the notorious Cervantic characters, but merely to exploit them for his satirical purposes. Social criticism is spoken by the main character, who ponders on the hypocrisy of some professionals, saying for example that physicians are hypocrites uninterested in their patients, and the rich are free to take from others without fear of justice. In addition to the satirical elements in the play, Fielding endeavoured to paint the English social landscape. Sancho, for instance, becomes enchanted with English food and beer. Squire Badger, a precursor of Western in *Tom Jones*,[9] typifies the English country nobleman in his penchant for hunting and drinking — he is, however, the villain of the play, who stands between Dorothea and Fairlove. Fielding had given his play a secondary plot, as Cervantes had in *Don Quixote* with Marcela's story. In *Don Quixote in England*, the main characters come across Dorothea Loveland, a lady whose father has arranged her marriage to Squire Badger, although she is in love with Fairlove.

In his first novel, entitled *Shamela*, Fielding reacted against the morality in Richardson's *Pamela*. The eponymous heroine in Richardson's novel is a servant who rejects the sexual advances of his master, Mr. B. As the subtitle of the novel indicates, Pamela has her *virtue rewarded* when Mr. B marries her. In *Shamela* those same characters behave very differently as they are moved (according to Fielding) by real impulses — Shamela is a cunning woman who pretends to be virtuous so as to marry the naïve Mr. Booby. Fielding's second novel, *Joseph Andrews*, purports to have the same aim: to ridicule and parody Richardson's *Pamela*.[10] In order to do so, Fielding narrated the adventures of Pamela's brother, Joseph, who lives his life according to the moral maxims given by his sister in her letters. *Joseph Andrews* is Cervantic because it presents a character whose demeanour is drawn from anachronistic moral values that clash with his society, bringing forth comical situations. But *Joseph Andrews* is Cervantean and quixotic in many ways — as Alexander Welsh has pointed out, the subtitle of the novel, i.e. 'Written in Imitation of the Manner of Cervantes, Author of Don Quixote', alludes to 'method, manner, and the heroe'.[11] Indeed Fielding's debt to Cervantes is manifold and has been acutely discussed by several scholars.[12]

In the preface to *Joseph Andrews*, Fielding expresses his literary consciousness and intentions. He begins: 'As it is possible the mere English reader may have a different idea of romance with the author of these little volumes; and may consequently expect a kind of entertainment, not to be found, nor which was ever intended, in the following pages; it may not be improper to premise a few words concerning this kind of writing, which I do not remember to have seen hitherto attempted in our language' (p. 25).[13] In the subsequent paragraphs the reader finds a brief but clear discussion of contemporary prose. Fielding explains that 'The epic as well as the drama is divided into tragedy and comedy' (p. 25).[14] Fielding acknowledges that Homer's *Iliad* illustrates how a text may partake of both, and suggests that epic can be written in either verse or prose. But he is also expressing Cervantes's premise (spoken by the canon of Toledo) that epic can be written in either verse or prose. He mentions Cambray's *Telemachus* as an example of prose epic, and observes that some 'voluminous works', such as *Clelia*, *Cleopatra*, *Grand Cyrus*, are called 'romances' (p. 25). These romances, Fielding argues, 'contain [...] very little instruction or entertainment'. He then proposes to consider the 'comic romance' as 'a comic epic-poem in prose'. Fielding explains:

> [The comic romance] differs from the serious romance in its fable and action [...] that as in the one these are grave and solemn, so in the other they are light and ridiculous: it differs in its characters, by introducing persons of inferior rank, and consequently of inferior manners, whereas the grave romance, sets the highest before us; lastly in its sentiments and diction, by preserving the ludicrous instead of the sublime. In the diction [...] burlesque itself may be sometimes admitted; of which many instances will occur in this work (p. 26).

The burlesque or comic romance is therefore different from the fashionable romances and also from the plays commonly referred to as burlesque. Fielding sought to ridicule lowness and coarseness by showing 'affectation'.[15] *Joseph Andrews* thus established itself as the point of departure for a new prose genre, and Fielding insists at the end of his preface: 'Having thus distinguished *Joseph Andrews* from the productions of romance writers on the one hand, and burlesque writers on the other, and given some few very short hints [...] of this species of writing, which I have affirmed to be hitherto unattempted in our language; I shall leave to my good-natur'd reader to apply my piece to my observations' (30). In presenting himself as the first author of comic romances in English, Fielding echoes Cervantes's claims in the *Exemplary Novels* to be the first Spanish writer to have written novellas,[16] and reveals his desire to innovate, as Cervantes had done before him. In so doing, Fielding knowingly emulated Cervantes's conception of the novel as a counter-genre or anti-romance.

In addition to the literary discussion contained in the preface, in the first chapters of Books I, II, III Fielding introduces a metafictional discussion of literary theory. In Chapter I, 1, entitled 'Of writing lives in general, and particularly of Pamela; with a Word by the bye of Colley Cibber and others', he discloses (in a very ironic tone) the didactic aim of his novel — *Joseph Andrews* is to serve as an exemplum against Richardson's novels. Chapter II, 1 is entitled 'Of divisions of Authors' and explains the advantages of dividing a book into chapters. Chapter III, 1 is the most interesting of these three metafictional chapters. In this chapter, the title of which is 'Matter prefatory in Praise of Biography', Fielding, referring to the novel as a literary genre, argues that 'the truth is only to be found in the works of those who celebrate the lives of great men, and are commonly called biographers' (183)

— i.e. that a novel must comply with verisimilitude or realism and narrate the life of a remarkable character. Novelists are therefore called *biographers*. Realism is a fundamental feature of Fielding's new genre. The novel (as opposed to the romance) must present historical reality, and it must do so to an even greater extent than history books. Fielding chooses *Don Quixote* in order to exemplify this when he wonders: 'is not such a book as that which records the achievements of the renowned Don Quixotte, more worthy the name of a history than even Mariana's [*Historia general de España*]' (185). For Fielding, the works written by *biographers* (i.e. novelists) are to be trusted because although they may not be entirely accurate at times, they present historical truth. He argues (183) that the story of Grisóstomo in *Don Quixote* could have taken place in any country or century without depriving the passage of its verisimilitude. He mentions Grisóstomo before enumerating several characters from Cervantes's novel:

> Tho' it may be worth the examination of critics, whether the shepherd Chrysostom, who, as Cervantes informs us, died for love of the fair Marcella, who hated him, was ever in Spain, will any one doubt but that such a silly fellow hath ever existed? Is there in the world such a sceptic as to disbelieve the madness of Cardenio, the perfidy of Ferdinand, the impertinent curiosity of Anselmo, the weakness of Camilla, the irresolute friendship of Lothario; tho' perhaps as to the time and place where those several persons lived, that good historian may be deplorably deficient (183–84).

Fielding thus describes the very nature of the novel as being the only genre that conforms to realism. Time and place are important in the stories of Grisóstomo, Cardenio and the curious impertinent because they cause them to conform to reality and turn them into 'the history of the world in general' (185). Realism was Fielding's aim, as he declares in the same paragraph: 'I describe not men, but mankind; not an individual, but a species' (185). The manner of Cervantes consisted, primarily, in writing a realistic tale that accurately depicted mankind.

   In addition to literary technique and aspirations, *Joseph Andrews* abides by the manner of Cervantes in two ways — its quixotic characters, and the many passages which Fielding drew from *Don Quixote*. Countless situations in *Joseph Andrews* are taken from (or, at least, pungently resemble) those in *Don Quixote*.[17] The most obvious similarity is that the action in both novels take place on the roads, in inns, and in houses.[18] As Stephen Gilman has pointed out, Joseph's adventures on the roads are 'reminiscences of the *Quijote*: an adventurous journey punctuated by inns and unscrupulous keepers thereof'.[19] The heroes find themselves involved in quarrels on the road: Don Quixote in Chapter I, 45; Joseph in Chapter III, IX, where 'he fought like a madman, and looked so black with the impressions he had received from the mop, that Don Quixote himself would certainly have taken him for an enchanted Moor' (245). Mancing has noted that, generally speaking, 'Some of the comic inn scenes, with naughty romps in the sack, mistaken identities, and brawls, are directly modelled on DQ's [Don Quixote's] and SP's [Sancho Panza's] adventures'.[20] The situations in the inns include the following: Fanny recognizing Joseph's own voice when he sings (II, XII) and Doña Clara recognizing that of his lover (I, 43); Betty's sympathy for Joseph (I, XIII) and Maritornes's sympathy for Sancho (I, 12); the commotion in the inn with Maritornes (I, 16) and in Lady Booby's house. The following passages take place in houses: the jokes on Don Quixote during his stay at the ducal manor, and the jokes on Adams at Mr. Wilson's house (III, IV); the situations lived by Don Quixote and Sancho at don Diego's house (II, 18), and those lived by Joseph and Adams at Mr. Wilson's.

Whilst there is a general consensus on the Cervantic nature of the aforementioned passages, scholars have held different opinions regarding the quixotic qualities of Joseph. Generally speaking, some think that both Joseph and Adams are Quixotes, whereas others maintain that Adams is a Quixote and Joseph is a Sancho. Although A. R. Penner recognized that Joseph is not a straight imitation of any Cervantine character, but a compound of several personalities, he also suggested that 'Andrews does, in a limited sense, play the role of Sancho to the quixotic Adams'.[21] This theory was subsequently elaborated by Paulson. Although Paulson recognizes that Fanny (who is Joseph's love) is the equivalent to Dulcinea, he presents the eponymous protagonist as 'the Sancho of the story'.[22] Because Joseph has read religious literature, e.g. *The Whole Duty of Man* and the Bible, and believes in the New Testament, Paulson argues that 'In this way he is defined as a Sancho to Adams's Quixote; therefore as an un-Quixotic character'.[23] This scholar also accounts for Fielding's admiration for Sancho Panza, whom he had introduced as 'a Masterpiece in Humour of which we never have, nor ever shall see the like',[24] and explains that Sancho was the main character in *Don Quixote in England*. Indeed the Manchegan squire was an extremely popular character in England during the eighteenth century and after;[25] however, the many differences noted by Penner[26] as well as any close reading of the text prove that in *Joseph Andrews* Fielding drew two different quixotic figures: Joseph and Adams, each one conceived with a specific purpose.[27]

Joseph is a Quixote because he lives and acts according to the obsolete values he has read in *Pamela*. In both novels, literary idealism clashes with the harsh real world — Joseph, like Don Quixote behaves awkwardly and foolishly because his demeanour does not correspond to what is done and expected in his society. As Fielding intended to denounce in *Shamela*, Pamela's values are feigned and hypocritical. In *Joseph Andrews*, Pamela's attitude is further ridiculed as it is upheld by a man: not only does Joseph seem ridiculous because he staunchly observes by the hypocritical Richardsonian values, but also because he is a man conforming to female etiquette. Joseph's prudish feminine ways trigger his misunderstanding with Lady Booby, who will immediately expel him from her house. Lady Booby has admonished Joseph that a kiss is 'a prologue to a play' (58) and asked him whether he would continue his kissing. He replies at once, 'I hope I should be able to control them to get the better of my virtue' (58). Such a response sparks off Lady Booby's reaction: 'Your virtue! (said the lady after recovering after a silence of two minutes) I shall never survive it. Your virtue. Intolerable confidence! Have you the assurance to pretend, that when a lady demeans herself to throw aside the rules of decency, in order to honour you with the highest favour in her power, your virtue should resist her inclination?' (58). Yet Joseph is adamant in upholding the obsolete views of his sister: 'I can't see why her having no virtue should be a reason against my having any. Or why because I am a man or because I am poor, my virtue must be subservient to her pleasures' (58). Whereas in Richardson's novel Pamela's virtue is rewarded when she finally weds her master, in *Joseph Andrews*, Richardsonian virtue goes unrewarded early in the novel (in Chapter I, 8) when Lady Booby expels him from the house.

Some critics[28] have also noted that Joseph rejects women in the same manner as Don Quixote rejects Maritornes and Altisidora. Finally, there is a change in Joseph's psychology which also resembles that in Don Quixote. The passage, in Chapter I, 12, where Joseph is assaulted by two thieves who rob him and beat him up while the coach passengers laugh at him, is analogous to Chapter I, 4 in *Don Quixote*, where the knight is bludgeoned by two muleteers in the presence of the silent Toledo merchants.[29]

Despite all the analogies between Joseph and Don Quixote, Fielding's character cannot be regarded as a proper Quixote,[30] since he is not a psychotic monomaniac. Withal, *Joseph Andrews* is a parody of Richardson's novels (of *Pamela* in particular), in the same way that *Don Quixote* is a parody of chivalric romances. In *Joseph Andrews*, however, Fielding borrowed the Cervantean device of using a main character who imitates a literary character. In this sense, *Joseph Jones* is a straightforward Cervantean parody, and also the first English Cervantean novel — since it draws on Cervantes's technique of literary parody.

All critics have regarded Adams as quixotic[31] — John Skinner, for example, has called him 'the most striking metamorphosis of Don Quixote in English literature'.[32] Indeed, Fielding found the epitome of human righteousness in the character of Don Quixote.[33] In the light of Fielding's assertion in *The Coffey-House Politician* (1730) that 'Good nature is Quixotism', Battestin has adroitly claimed that 'It was only natural that Fielding should fashion Parson Adams, the incarnation of good man, after the manner of Don Quixote'.[34] Indeed the description of Adams resembles Don Quixote:

> Mr Abraham Adams was an excellent scholar. He was a perfect master of the Greek and Latin languages; to which he added a great share of knowledge in the oriental tongues, and could read and translate French, Italian and Spanish. He had applied many years to the most severe study, and had treasured up a fund of learning rarely to be met in a university. He was besides a man of good sense, good parts, and good nature, but was at the same time as entirely ignorant of the ways of this world, as an infant just entered into it could possibly be [...] He was generous, friendly and brave to an excess; but simplicity was his characteristic (43).

Like Alonso Quijano, Adams has read his books time and again. Like Alonso, he is sensitive and generous. Like Don Quixote, Adams is ignorant of the world. However, Don Quixote is so because of his insanity, which causes his chivalric behaviour, while Adams is ignorant because of his high moral values. Fielding's character is not a madman, but lives on much higher moral ground than the rest of his society.[35] When Fielding's parson encounters other people, he, like Don Quixote, is ridiculed. Adams thus becomes Fielding's means to do what he had done so successfully as a playwright — to satirize eighteenth–century English society. As Paulson has put it, 'By making Quixote a clergyman, Fielding has found an equivalent for Quixote's spiritual dimension and problematized the clericalism of *Pamela*'.[36] Like Joseph, Adams cannot be regarded as a Quixote because he is not insane.

In sum, Fielding presented two quixotic characters in *Joseph Andrews*: Joseph, whose reading of *Pamela* causes him to behave awkwardly; and Adams, who adopts a set of dated moral values. This novel thus conveys both the parody and the satire which Cervantes intended in *Don Quixote*. So much did Fielding crave to emulate Cervantes that, in order to give his novel the full flavour of the Spanish text, he split Don Quixote's psychology into two different characters. The result proves most successful because *Joseph Andrews* is both a parody of Richardson's novels and a satire of English society. Hence Fielding succeeded in writing a novel in the manner of Cervantes. And this manner is made up of as many Cervantine elements as Fielding could possibly assemble: most notably the parody and the satire with the Quixotic characters, the metafictional level where the theory of the epic romance is fully explained, and the imitation of situations and characters. In addition to the above Cervantean features, Mancing has pointed out others: 'the "true history" device, the intrusive narrator, the search for sources, comic character names, comic chapter titles, links from one chapter to the next, and a variety of embedded narrations'.[37] For Acosta these borrowings include: the familiarity with which the narrator addresses the reader; metafiction; the incursion in the both novels of characters from other texts (don Álvaro de Tarfe from Avellaneda's *Don Quixote*, and Pamela from Richardson's eponymous novel); the parody of the poetic diction; and the style in the descriptions, especially of landscape and sunrise.[38]

Tom Jones, Fielding's best work and perhaps the greatest novel of Augustan England, exemplifies in many ways the state of the novel as a new and emerging genre at this time. Indeed, Fielding was concerned about establishing the canon of the English novel, and in *Tom Jones* he endeavoured to fulfil his literary ambition. Unlike *Joseph Andrews*, *Tom Jones* is not a parody. Past were the days when Fielding opposed Walpole or despised Richardson's concept of virtue. He had succeeded in his political satires and literary parodies and was aiming at something of greater consequence. When he wrote *Tom Jones* he still found inspiration in *Don Quixote*.

For decades, scholars had criticized *Joseph Andrews* for (in Northrop Frye's terminology) its *and-then* narrative structure, i.e. that its episodes had been put together randomly, lacking a cause–effect order. Ethel Thornbury[39] suggested that the imperfections of *Joseph Andrews* were a result of Fielding's admiration for *Don Quixote*, and that the perfect narrative structure of *Tom Jones* must to be taken as evidence of Fielding's ruling out Cervantes as his model. Albeit some still refuse to accept that in *Don Quixote* most chapters are a consequence of the precedent ones, no Cervantes scholar accepts this theory today.[40] The views of Thornbury resulted partly from Fielding's own criticism of *Don Quixote* in a review of Charlotte Lennox's *The Female Quixote*. In his critical essay, Fielding considered Lennox's novel superior to Cervantes's on the grounds that Lennox complied with the laws of epic regularity, laid out by the Frenchman René Le Bossu in a book published in English as *Treatise on the Epic Poem* in 1719. According to Le Bossu, when epic was written in prose instead of verse, it should have an episodic plot, and any interpolated stories not linked to the main plot should be excluded. In Fielding's opinion, *Don Quixote* did not abide by these rules, whereas *The Female Quixote* did. Thornbury and others did not realize that Fielding was comparing Cervantes's novel to Lennox's, not to his own *Tom Jones*. And indeed, twentieth-century Cervantes scholarship has demonstrated that *Tom Jones* differs from Le Bossu's laws and emulates the narrative structure of *Don Quixote*.[41] The narrative structure of *Tom Jones* was inspired by *Don Quixote*, and Fielding made extensive use of the following Cervantic features: an episodic plot, parallel strands, *analepsis*, *prolepsis*, interpolated stories, focalization, and *deus ex machina*.[42] Other Cervantic borrowings in *Tom Jones* include the psychology of Tom and Partridge, the psychological development of Tom, and the use of metafictional passages.[43]

There are very few interruptions in the plot of *Don Quixote* — merely the month the protagonist spends at home (at the end of Part I and beginning of Part II). Likewise, the adventures of *Tom Jones* are only interrupted between Books II and III (where twelve years are omitted). This narrative structure makes *Don Quixote*, as well as *Tom Jones*, a narrative entirety. In Fielding's novel, the omission of twelve years may be justified because time bears no relation to the purpose of the story, which is to narrate the developments in Tom and Sophia's love. Cervantes divided his narrative into 116 chapters. Generally speaking, each chapter contains an adventure, and they are narrated without any interruptions. In some instances, a chapter includes two adventures, e.g. I, 4 and I, 8. Sometimes an adventure is told in more than one chapter, e.g. II, 36–41. In order to achieve this, Cervantes uses two techniques: by linking the end of a chapter with the beginning of the next; and by announcing the beginning of a new chapter before the preceding one is finished. *Tom Jones* is divided into 208 chapters. Each adventure is usually narrated in a chapter, and very seldom in two or more (like in the adventure of the Man of the Hill, or the confusion in Upton). In order to achieve a continuous narrative, Fielding uses three techniques: (1) he indicates at the end of a chapter that a new one is about to begin, or he opens one chapter indicating that the former one is finished; (2) he uses the adverb *now* at the beginning of a chapter to indicate that the action is continued; and (3) he indicates with *soon*, *no sooner* and *not long* at the beginning of a chapter that the action is continued from the former one.

The titles of many chapters in *Tom Jones* bear a conspicuously Cervantic tone. When, in *Don Quixote*, an adventure spans several chapters, the titles in the second and subsequent chapters indicate that the adventure 'se sigue' [is continued] (e.g. I, 30; I, 40; I, 44, etc.). Similarly, Fielding uses the formula '[the story] is continued' (e.g. VIII, 12; VIII, 13; XI, 5; XVIII, 5; XVIII, 6; XVIII, 7; XVIII, 8; XVIII, 9). Other titles in Fielding's novel indicate that the chapter contains a dialogue (e.g. VI, 6; IX, 6; X, 3, etc.), as in Cervantes's (e.g. I, 49; II, 3; II, 5, etc.). In many other instances, the hyperbolic vocabulary used by the English novelist in the titles of chapters follows that in *Don Quixote*. Such usage in Cervantes is, of course, deeply ironic, because the great adventures are merely chance meetings with the commonest of people. This device is frequent in Fielding's novel, and although he did not intend to parody the chivalric romances (simply because they were no longer fashionable), it enhances the ironic nature of his novel. Examples of this in *Don Quixote* and *Tom Jones* include 'la grande aventura' [the great adventure] (II, 22) and 'this great history' (III, 9), 'la espantable [...] adventura' [the dreadful ... adventure] (I, 8) and 'a dreadful accident' (VII, 14) or 'las más raras adventuras' [the strangest adventures] (I, 23) and 'An odd accident' (I, 4), and many others with the words 'extraño' [strange] (in I, 43; II, 11; II, 12; II, 36) and 'strange' (VII, 7; XIV, 9; XVIII, 3). The other examples of hyperbolic vocabulary in *Don Quixote* are 'famoso' [famous], 'estupenda' [fabulous], 'innumerable' [countless], 'discreta' [discreet], 'brava' [brave], 'descomunal' [enormous], 'inaudito' [unheard of], 'admirable' and 'memorable', and in *Tom Jones* 'sage', 'curious', 'whimsical', 'heroic', 'generous and greatful', 'tempestous' and 'bloody'.[44]

Finally, the foil countryside–city in Fielding's novel also bears the Cervantean label. Most adventures in Part I of *Don Quixote* are set in the countryside, and many in Part II take place in the ducal palace. And whilst in the open fields Don Quixote takes the lead in his adventures, in the duke's palace and realms his actions are subject to the aristocrats' jokes. Sancho's adventures in Barataria have also been carefully planned by the duke's servants. The adventures of Tom occur in three different settings: Books I to VI in rural Somerset; Books VII to XII on the roads to London; and Books XIII to XVIII in London. It is in London that the two lovers have to confront the intrigues orchestrated by Lady Bellaston and Lord Fellamar. Conversely, in Somerset and on the roads Tom always takes the initiative, helping Mrs. Waters and aiding the Man of the Hill.

Don Quixote tells of the adventures of the knight and his squire; *Tom Jones* tells of the adventures of Tom (and, to a lesser extent, of Sophia). When, in both novels, the main characters part from each other, the narration gives an account of the adventures that happen to each of them. The plot of *Don Quixote* has been described as a river,[45] where the main plot is the river itself and the interpolated stories are streams that flow into it. When Sancho leaves the palace to take up his governorship in Barataria, the *river* splits in two courses that join together again when he comes across his master. Cervantes narrates an adventure of Don Quixote in the palace and then one of Sancho in Barataria, and so forth. In Fielding's novel, the plot takes place in Somerset, where Tom and Sophia live, until Book VII, when Tom is expelled from Allworthy's house. Thereafter, the novel narrates the adventures of both characters until they finally merge together in the denouement. For most of the novel, therefore, the plot is narrated in parallel actions, which come together in Book X, which takes place in Upton, and in Book XIV in Lady Bellaston's house. Unlike Cervantes, Fielding could not structure his parallel strands in chapters. In *Tom Jones*, the individual adventures of Tom and Sophia are narrated in groups of chapters.

Cervantes makes extensive use of *analepsis*. This device allows him to omit certain details and create some suspense: for example, only at the end of the Maese Pedro episode does the narrator reveal that Maese is Ginés de Pasamonte. The *analepsis* is used in four instances (namely in II, 5; II, 27; II, 50; II, 65). All in all, this device results from the use of an unreliable narrator (*v. infra*). *Analepsis* becomes an integral part of Fielding's narrative in the same way. For example, Book IX begins with Honour discovering Tom's love for Sophia, continues with Tom saving Mrs. Waters, and ends with an *analepsis* explaining how Mrs. Waters became the victim of such a violent aggression. (There are other instances of *analepsis* are in Books III, VII, and X.)

Analepsis sometimes combines with a *deus ex machina*. In *Don Quixote*, Dorotea happens to be involved in Cardenio's story (I, 28), the thief who stole Sancho's donkey happens to be Ginés (I, 30), the party of people who arrive at the inn happen to be Luscinda and Fernando with their escort (I, 35), etc. Similarly, in *Tom Jones* the Fitzpatricks happen to be related to Sophia (X, 7), the barber–surgeon happens to be Partridge (VIII, 6), the man who has attacked Waters happens to be Northerton (IX, 2), the lady who arrives at the inn happens to be Harriet's saviour in Ireland (XI, 8), the highwayman happens to be Mrs. Miller's nephew (XII, 14) and Waters happens to be Jenny Jones (XVIII, 1).

Le Bossu ruled that no interpolated story should be included unless it was thematically interlinked to the main plot. In early-seventeenth-century Spain, however, readers expected interpolated stories,[46] and writers considered them an Italian fashion worth imitating.[47] Very recently, some scholars have convincingly argued that these interpolated stories form part of the entirety of *Don Quixote*.[48] There are twelve interpolated stories in *Don Quixote* and in *Tom Jones* there are five, all of which infringe Le Bossu's laws: the story of the Man of the Hill (VIII, 11–15); Mrs. Fitzpatrick's story (XI, 4–5, 7); Nightingale's (XIII, 5); Mrs. Miller's (XIV, 5); and Partridge's (XVIII, 6). These do not conform to epic regularity. The story of the Man of the Hill is told in Book VIII, but it could have been inserted anywhere between Books VII (when Tom begins his journey) and XII (when Tom arrives in London). Surprisingly, the narrator apologizes in XII, 13 for the short adventure of the gypsy wedding in XII, 12, but does not apologize for or explain the long story of the Man of the Hill.

As the plot progresses, so does Don Quixote's psychology; his madness weakens, giving way to his most lucid discourses, and he comes to epitomize the most noble of virtues.[49] Tom's psychological development, from naughtiness to repentance, leads him to his existential goal — marriage with Sophia. This change can be noticed in the sermons spoken in the novel: whilst the first books contain sermons by Allworthy, in the last books it is Tom who enunciates the sermons and therefore comes to embody morality — likewise, *Don Quixote* Part II abounds with the knight's sensible speeches. The psychological development of the hero characterizes the novel (as opposed to the romance) and it is one of the literary innovations in the novels *Lazarillo de Tormes* (1554) and *Guzmán de Alfarache* (1599 and 1604), and also in other texts, e.g. Parmeno in *Celestina* (1499). This feature can also be observed in Defoe's novels, in *Moll Flanders*, *Colonel Jack*, *Roxana* and *Robinson Crusoe*.

Despite the opinions of some critics,[50] Tom cannot properly be classed as a *pícaro* (i.e. the main character of a picaresque novel). As has been proved elsewhere,[51] Tom does not possess any of the features of the rogue.[52] He is simply and merely a badly behaved youngster. On the other hand, Fielding endowed Tom with some of Don Quixote's most notorious psychological features[53] — he is the only character who acts in a knightly fashion, rescuing the Man of the Hill and ladies in distress, forgiving those thieves who steal out of necessity, and aiding those in need. In acting so, the main character opposes the meanness of his society, best exemplified by Blifil. Like the Spanish knight, Tom seems an anachronistic figure in a changing society — he stands for such values as generosity and loyalty, whereas others are driven by greed and lust. Tom's love for Sophia differs from Don Quixote's love for Dulcinea in that the English youngster is not faithful. His wantonness, however, becomes an essential feature of his juvenile naivety, one which he loses gradually. Sophia is a Dulcinea-like character — she is portrayed as a picture of perfection that matches Tom's knightly character. The reader will find in *Tom Jones* the same contrast between platonic love and earthy love (or lust) exposed in *Don Quixote*. Dulcinea is perfect and hence loved by the knight. The prostitutes who welcome him to the first inn are viewed by Don Quixote as ladies, whose coquetry he ignores. He is also adamant in rejecting Maritormes's love. In *Tom Jones*, Molly is a coarse country-girl who is the opposite of Sophia's fineness, as the prostitutes are the opposite of Dulcinea. However, he succumbs to Molly's sexual determination, while rejecting Lady Bellaston's advances, as Don Quixote rejects Maritornes's. Indeed, Tom lives in the real world, and Don Quixote lives in an imaginary one. Yet Fielding's character confronts the same foil as Cervantes's did: the platonic love he feels for his lady against the temptations from other women. Although Tom is clearly not a madman, his dignified generosity makes him a *rara avis* in his society. Just like the Caballero del Verde Gabán regards Don Quixote as a sane madman but also as a mad man (II, 17), some characters discuss Jones's mental health. In XII, 7, Tom is thought to be a madman when the puppet-show man says, 'the gentleman has surprised me very much, when he talked so absurdly [...] indeed he had a strange wildness in his eyes'; and the landlord states: 'no one but a madman would have thought of leaving so good a house, to ramble in the country at that time of night'. The travellers discuss the possibility of sending the mad Jones back home to his relations, just as Don Quixote's neighbours plotted to bring him back home. Later in that chapter of *Tom Jones*, some characters discuss the limits between sanity and insanity: 'Madness was sometimes a difficult matter for a jury to decide' warns the exciseman. This is a very interesting psychological feature which places Tom, within his society, in a similar position to Don Quixote — his insanity alienates him from society and prevents him from acting according to contemporary values; paradoxically, however, he is the only character who proclaims and acts according to the highest moral values.

One of the most intriguing Cervantean features of *Tom Jones* is its metafictional dimension. Don Quixote has been called the best commentary of Spanish Golden-Age literature,[54] for its metafictional reflections on the qualities of sixteenth-century prose — most notably in the burning of Alonso Quijano's books and the dialogue between the curate and the canon, but also in memorable passages like Marcela's speech to the shepherds, when she makes *tabula rasa* of the pastoral tradition and of platonic love. Likewise, Fielding consciously endeavoured to establish a new genre, the novel. And like Cervantes stated in his *Exemplary Novels*, Fielding proudly proclaimed himself 'the founder of a new province of writing' (II, 1). *Tom Jones* comprises eighteen books. The first chapter of each book is entirely devoted to discussing a specific issue, most of them literary issues, e.g. the role of the hero in fiction (IV, 1), comedy (V, 1), theatre as a reflection of real life (VII, 1), realism in literature (VIII, 1), the critics (XI, 1), etc. Other chapters present the reader with reflections of issues such as culture (III, 1), love (VI, 1), and virtue (XV, 1). The first chapter of the novel is entitled 'Showing what kind of a history this is; what it is like, and what it is not like'. In this chapter, and in the rest of his novel, Fielding refers to *Tom Jones* as a 'history', and discerns two categories of historians: the 'painful and voluminous historian', i.e. the scholar who writes history books; and 'those writers who profess to disclose the revolutions of countries'. For Fielding, the latter corresponds to the novel, hence novel-writing conforms to historical realism. This idea is further developed in subsequent books. In Book IX, the 'historic kind of writing' (409) is opposed to 'what is false and counterfeit' in the romance.

The combination of historical realism and fiction had been achieved more than a century earlier by some Spanish novelists, namely by the anonymous author of *Lazarillo de Tormes* and by Mateo Alemán in *Guzmán de Alfarache*.[55] Following in the footsteps of Mateo Alemán, Cervantes does refer to *Don Quixote* as a true 'historia', as opposed to the make-believe stories told in the chivalric romances.[56] There is in *Tom Jones* the same fiction–metafiction duality as in *Don Quixote*, albeit in Fielding's novel the two levels are clearly distinguished, since the metafictional level takes the first chapter of each book. And as in Cervantes's novel, in Fielding's there is a very clear indication that the text, although patently fictional, is historical, that is, that it conforms to historical realism.[57]

Nonetheless, *Don Quixote* is not a truly historical account of a truly historical character. The reader immediately realizes so, partly because this is a literary work, partly because of the historical inaccuracies it contains (e.g. the many names given to Alonso Quijano and to Cardenio), and also because of the use of an unreliable narrator. The author of *Lazarillo de Tormes* presented this novel as the true autobiography of Lazarillo; however, in writing his novel, the author relied heavily on folklore. Hence any reader would realize that Lazarillo could not have lived such a chain of adventures known to virtually everyone as folk tales.[58] In a recent book, Juan Bautista Avalle Arce[59] has examined the role of the unreliable narrator in Spanish fiction, suggesting that (although there are examples of it in some mediaeval texts such as Juan Ruiz's *Libro de Buen Amor* and also in *Celestina*, *Lazarillo de Tormes* and *Guzmán de Alfarache*) Cervantes, in *Don Quixote* Part II, was the first author to use an unreliable narrator. The reader may be confused by the amalgam of narrative voices in Part I, where the narrators include Cide Hamete, the Arabic translator, the Spanish editor and a fourth narrator. The instances of unreliable narration are numerous in Part II; Avalle Arce suggests that the false promise made by Sansón Carrasco to Don Quixote marks the birth of the unreliable narrator in modern fiction.[60]

Likewise, eighteenth-century readers were aware that *Tom Jones* was a work of fiction. Ian Watt pointed out that the passage of the conciliation between Jones and Sophia is far from believable.[61] It is also worth noting that the narrator himself acknowledges the unreliability of his story: 'I do not, therefore, deliver the following as a certain truth, for indeed I can scarce credit it myself; but the fidelity of an historian obliges me to relate what hath been confidently asserted' (X, 9).

This means that it was an unreliable narrator that told Jones's story to the narrator of the novel. Although much more simple than the four narrators in *Don Quixote*, *Tom Jones* is also an unreliable narration. The pair Cide Hamete–Arab translator in Cervantes's novel is transfused to *Tom Jones*, where the reader reads a *second-hand* story. Cervantes's unreliable narrator was preceded by those in *Lazarillo de Tormes* and *Guzmán de Alfarache*; Fielding had an immediate predecessor in Defoe, whose roguish narrators in *Moll Flanders*, *Roxana* and *Colonel Jack*, like in the Spanish picaresque novels, are seldom reliable. Yet Fielding's efforts to present fiction as 'history' were explicitly encouraged by Cervantes in *Don Quixote*.

Jones cannot be regarded as a Quixote. His noble values certainly alienate him from his society and he is quixotic in as much as his generosity and knightly ideals confront the meanness of society; so amiss he seems in his society that he is believed to be a madman by some characters. However, Jones does not analogize Don Quixote's psychology and his story should not be labelled as quixotic. Conversely, owing to the use in *Tom Jones* of a significant number of narrative techniques which were previously used by Cervantes in *Don Quixote*, Fielding's novel must be regarded as an example of the Cervantean novel — in conceiving the narrative structure of *Tom Jones*, Fielding clearly emulated *Don Quixote*. His use of the episodic plot, parallel strands, interpolated stories, and other devices such as *analepsis* and a *deus ex machina* is not coincidental: they all result in a narrative structure that emulates *Don Quixote*.

From an understanding of the quixotic (in *Don Quixote in England* and *Joseph Andrews*), Fielding managed to read *Don Quixote* as a complex literary master piece in which Cervantes achieved what Fielding himself craved for: to have established a new genre that transcended the romance. And in emulating Cervantes, Fielding succeeded in writing the best novel of Augustan England.

Notes to Chapter 11

1. Walter Scott, *Lives of the Novelists* (London: J. M. Dent, 1820), p. 46.
2. Anthony Burgess, *English Literature* (Harlow: Longman, 1996), p. 159.
3. Anthony Burgess, 'Fielding's Life', *The Observer*, 29 October 1989, p. 45.
4. Quoted in Roland Paulson and Thomas Lockwood (eds.), *Henry Fielding: The Critical Heritage* (London: Routledge & Kegan Paul, 1969), p. 403. The eighteenth-century quotations in Paulson and Lockwood's volume include Coventry's claim that Fielding was 'our English Cervantes' (p. 269) and Murphey's calling him 'the ENGLISH CERVANTES' (p. 428).
5. Cf. Roland Paulson, *Don Quixote in England: The Aesthetics of Laughter* (Baltimore: Johns Hopkins University Press, 1998), pp. 59–60. Paulson suggests that 'the early fools in Fielding's plays are Quixotic characters such as Politic, Sir Avarice, Pedant, and Sir Simon Raffler' (p. 60).
6. Rita Gnutzmann, 'Don Quixote in England de Henry Fielding con relación al *Don Quijote* de Cervantes', *Anales Cervantinos*, 22 (1984), 77–101; Paulson, *Don Quixote in England*, pp. 4, 60, 161; Jean Canavaggio, *Don Quichotte du livre au mythe. Quatre siècles d'errance* (París: Fayard, 2005). Also Edwin K. Knowles, 'Cervantes and English Literature', in *Cervantes across the Centuries*, ed. by Á. Flores and M. J. Benardete (New York: Gordian Press, 1947), pp. 277–303 (p. 292); J. A. G. Ardila, *Cervantes en Inglaterra: el Quijote en los albores de la novela británica* (Liverpool: Liverpool University Press, 2006); Raimund Borgmeier, 'Henry Fielding and his Spanish Model: "Our English Cervantes"', in *Cervantes in the English Speaking World*, ed. by Darío Fernández-Morera and Michael Hanke (Barcelona and Kassel: Edition Reichenberger, 2005), pp. 43–64; and the

entries to Fielding in Howard Mancing, *The Cervantes Encyclopedia* (Westport and London: Greenwood Press, 2004) and in the *Gran Enciclopedia Cervantina*, ed. by Carlos Alvar (Madrid: Castalia, 2005–07).

7. Henry Fielding, *Don Quixote in England A Comedy. As it is Acted in the New Theatre in the Hay-Market* (London: J. Watts, 1734), p. 3.

8. Knowles, 'Cervantes and English Literature', p. 292.

9. Cf. F. Homes Dudden, *Henry Fielding: His Life, Works, and Times* (Hamden, CT: Archon Books, 1966), p. 129.

10. Nonetheless, the differences between these two novels are many. As R. F. Brissenden, 'Introduction', in Henry Fielding, *Joseph Andrews* (Harmondsworth: Penguin, 1985), pp. 7–18, has pointed out, '*Shamela* is nothing but a burlesque [...] *Joseph Andrews*, however, was intended from the beginning to be much more than this — to be, in fact, as Fielding states in his Preface, a comic epic-poem in prose' (p. 11). See also Martin Battestin, *The Moral Basis of Fielding's Art: A Study of Joseph Andrews* (Middleton, CT: Wesleyan University Press, 1967).

11. Alexander Welsh, 'The Influence of Cervantes', in *The Cambridge Companion to Cervantes*, ed. by Anthony Cascardi (Cambridge: Cambridge University Press, 2002), pp. 80–99 (p. 80).

12. Most notably Santiago Acosta Aide, 'El influjo del *Quijote* en *Joseph Andrews*', *Revista Canaria de Estudios Ingleses*, 11 (1985), 69–80; and Mancing, *The Cervantes Encyclopedia*, p. 293.

13. References to *Joseph Andrews* are to the Penguin Classics edition (Harmondsworth, 1985).

14. In *Don Quixote in England*, Fielding had attempted to combine both. Cf. Paulson, *Don Quixote in England*, p. 161: 'The two plots of *Don Quixote* — comic and romantic — are usually connected by a figure like Marcela who rhymes with Quixote's particular folly, acting out what she reads in a book. Thus Fielding's *Don Quixote in England* includes, alongside Quixote and Sancho [...] the love intrigue of Fairlove and Dorothea'.

15. Paulson in *Don Quixote in England* (p. 59) has argued that 'the Manner of Cervantes', which Fielding announces in the subtitle of his novel, is characterized by affectation.

16. Miguel de Cervantes, 'Prólogo al lector', in *Novelas ejemplares*, 2 vols (Madrid: Espasa-Calpe, 2004), I, 75: 'yo soy el primero que he novelado en lengua castellana' [I am the first one to have written novellas in the Spanish language].

17. Pointed out in Battestin, *The Moral Basis of Fielding's Art*, p. 176; Aurelien Digeon, *The Novels of Fielding* (New York: Russell and Russell, 1962), p. 64; Ernest Baker, *Intellectual Realism: From Richardson to Sterne* (New York: Barnes and Noble, 1970), p. 93; Emile Pons, 'Fielding, Swift et Cervantes. De *Don Quichotte in England* à *Joseph Andrews*', *Studia Neophilologica*, 15 (1942–43), 305–33; Acosta, 'El influjo del *Quijote* en *Joseph Andrews*', pp. 71–75. Some critics have noted that many of the details given in some of these passages of *Joseph Andrews* analogize those in *Don Quixote*. For example, McKillop et al., *The Early Masters of English Fiction* (Lawrence: University Press of Kansas, 1968), p. 114, have pointed out that the Slipslop's bad breath resembles that of Maritornes. Acosta (p. 74) has explained that in both Mr. Wilson's and don Diego's houses, the hosts, from being uneasy by the presence of the extravagant protagonists, gradually become at ease when they realize their sincerity. In both novels, the characters talk about the same topics — in *Don Quixote* about chivalry and poetry; in *Joseph Andrews* about classic literature.

18. Acosta Aide, 'El influjo del *Quijote* en *Joseph Andrews*', p. 73.

19. Stephen Gilman, 'On Henry Fielding's Reception of *Don Quixote*', in *Medieval and Renaissance Studies in Honour of Robert Brian Tate*, ed. by Ian Michael and Richard A. Cardwell (Oxford: Dolphin, 1986), pp. 27–38 (p. 30).

20. Mancing, *The Cervantes Encyclopedia*, p. 293.

21. A. R. Penner, 'Fielding's Adaptation of Cervantes' Knight and Squire: The Character of Joseph', *Revue de Littérature Comparée*, 41 (1967), 508–14 (p. 509).

22. Paulson, *Don Quixote in England*, p. 147. This theory may have been prompted by Andrew Wright, *Henry Fielding: Mask and Feast* (London: Chatto and Windus, 1968), p. 29, who suggested that although Fielding wrote his novel in the manner of Cervantes, there was no Sanchoesque character in it.

23. Paulson, *Don Quixote in England*, p. 149.

24. In her review of Charlotte Lennox's *The Female Quixote*. Cited in Paulson, *Don Quixote in England*, p. 148.

25. Apud J. A. G. Ardila, 'Sancho Panza en Inglaterra: *Sancho at Court* de Ayres y *Barataria* de Pilon', *Bulletin of Hispanic Studies*, 82 (2005), 551–69. Also see J. A. G. Ardila, *Cervantes en Inglaterra*, pp. 43–44, for a discussion of the anonymous *Barataria: A Select Collection of Fugitive Political Pieces: Consisting of Letters, Essays, & c.* (Dublin, 1772) and in particular the letter 'The Answer of the Inhabitants of BARATARIA, to the Speech of Sancho Pança their Governor'.

26. Penner, 'Fielding's Adaptation of Cervantes' Knight and Squire', p. 511.

27. Dudden described Adams as 'a thoroughly English incarnation or embodiment of the basic idea of Cervantic quixotism' (p. 338). Walter Reed, *An Exemplary History of the Novel: The Quixotic versus the Picaresque* (Chicago: Chicago University Press, 1981), p. 129, pointed out that the 'Quixotic figure is really double: Parson Adams and Joseph Andrews'. For Reed, Adams is an ethical Quixote whose alienation from society lies in his anachronistic Christian moral values rather than in romance reading. This idea was taken by Isolina Ballesteros, 'La presencia de *Don Quijote* de Cervantes en *Joseph Andrews* de Fielding', *Anales Cervantinos*, 27 (1989), 215–24 (p. 218). Pedro Javier Pardo García, in 'Formas de imitación del *Quijote* en la novela inglesa del siglo XVIII: *Joseph Andrews* y *Tristram Shandy*', *Anales Cervantinos*, 33 (1995–97), 133–64, follows Dudden very closely: where Dudden suggests that Adams is 'a thoroughly English incarnation or embodiment of the basic idea of Cervantic Quixotism' (p. 337), Pardo claims that Adams is 'la figura quijotesca por excelencia de toda la obra de Fielding' [Fielding's most quixotic character] (p. 69).

28. Penner, 'Fielding's Adaptation of Cervantes' Knight and Squire', and Juventino Caminero, 'Joseph Andrews y Don Quijote: dos castos varones', *Letras de Deusto*, 9 (1979), 95–129.

29. Cf. M. Johnson, *Fielding's Art of Fiction* (Philadelphia: University of Pennsylvania Press, 1965), pp. 51–52.

30. According to the definition given in Ardila, *Cervantes en Inglaterra*, p. 27, i.e. a character whose psychology is drawn from Don Quixote's, including the knight's insanity.

31. Susan Staves, in 'Don Quixote in Eighteenth-Century Fiction', *Comparative Literature*, 24. 3 (1972), 193–215, suggests that 'Parson Adams, the true hero of Fielding's novel [...] stands half-way between the two possible extremes of the quixotic figure' (p. 206) — these extremes being the Quixote as a fool in satire versus the Quixote becoming wholly sympathetic. A comparison in greater detail may be found in Knowles, 'Cervantes and English Literature', p. 293.

32. John Skinner, '*Don Quixote* in Eighteenth-Century England: A Study in Reader Response', *Cervantes*, 7 (1987), 45–57 (p. 53).

33. In Ardila, *Cervantes en Inglaterra*, pp. 3–5, I have argued that goodness is one of the fundamental psychological characteristics of Don Quixote. I agree with Michael Predmore, *The World of Don Quixote* (Cambridge, MA: Harvard University Press, 1967), p. 105, who pointed out a number of similarities between Christ's speech (apud Matthew 7. 13–14) and Don Quixote's (II, 6; II, 18; II, 27). Don Quixote's Christian values have been recently examined in Francisco Layna, *La eficacia del fracaso. Representaciones culturales de la Segunda Parte del Quijote* (Madrid: Ediciones Polifemo, 2005).

34. Battestin, *The Moral Basis of Fielding's Art*, p. 181.

35. Dudden summarized Adams's quixotism by drawing the following group of similarities between Adams and Don Quixote: each is an honourable, high-minded, simple hearted Christian gentleman, ardently devoted to ideals which are entirely unintelligible to the commonplace people round him; each is a student of ancient books, interprets the world in the light of a by-gone age, and is incapable of seeing contemporary persons and things as they are; each is accordingly scoffed at and victimized by the worldly-wise; each, again, is animated by an abounding charity, and generously constitutes himself the champion of the weak and oppressed; each is indomitably brave and fearless, delights in fighting (in the literal sense) for a good cause, and is tough enough to stand drubbings; each has a pronounced taste for adventure, and meets with strange experiences in the course of his wanderings; each, also, though often placed in ridiculous situations and subjected to unseemly usage, wonderfully retains his native dignity and never for an instant forfeits our respect and sympathy (p. 338).

36. Paulson, *Don Quixote in England*, pp. 146–47. And therefore, Paulson claims, 'Joseph follows the New Testament and the teachings of Jesus. In this way he is defined as a Sancho to Adam's Quixote' (p. 149). Paulson refers to 'the clericalism of Pamela' because Richardson had somehow

sought to endow his heroine with the morals of the Church so as to parody the excesses of former sentimental romances. Fielding, however, believed that Richardson had kept up with the romance tradition, and that *Pamela* was not a parody. Richardson's attempt at parody is, in Paulson's words, 'un-Quixotic' (p. 149).

37. Mancing, *The Cervantes Encyclopedia*, p. 293. Likewise, Gilman had pointed out that he manner of Cervantes consisted in 'this kind of superbly controlled comic narration'. See Stephen Gilman, *The Novel According to Cervantes* (Berkeley: University of California Press, 1989), p. 176.

38. Acosta Aide, 'El influjo del *Quijote* en *Joseph Andrews*', p. 79.

39. Ethel M. Thornbury, *Henry Fielding's Theory of the Comic Prose Epic* (Madison: University of Wisconsin Press, 1931).

40. Among those who proclaim the hypothetical *and-then* plot of *Don Quixote* is one of its recent English translators, John Rutherford, in 'Introduction', in Miguel de Cervantes, *The Ingenious Hidalgo Don Quixote de la Mancha*, trans. John Rutherford (London: Penguin, 2000), pp. vii–xxi. The latest to advocate the contrary is Layna Ranz in *La eficacia del fracaso*. The first critic was Alexander A. Parker in 'Fielding and the Structure of *Don Quixote*', *Bulletin of Hispanic Studies*, 33 (1956), 1–16. Although Parker did not prove the influence of *Don Quixote* on *Tom Jones*, he did correct the arguments of Thornbury and his followers. Parker's opinions have been seconded in Bruce Wardropper, 'Don Quijote: ¿ficción o historia?', in *El Quijote*, ed. by George Haley (Madrid: Taurus, 1984), pp. 237–52, and in Stanislav Zimic, *Los cuentos y las novelas del 'Quijote'* (Madrid and Frankfurt: Iberoamericana and Vervuert, 1998), pp. 21–22. Anthony Close has further viewed *Don Quixote* as a *comic epic*, in Anthony Close, 'Don Quixote as the Burlesque Hero: A Reconstructed Eighteenth-Century View', *Forum for Modern Language Studies*, 10 (1974), 365–78.

41. Apud Ardila, 'Cervantes y la *quixotic fiction*: sucesión episódica y otros recursos narrativos', *Cervantes*, 21. 1 (2001), 43–65; J. A. G. Ardila, 'La horma narratológica: *Tom Jones* de Henry Fielding', in J. A. G. Ardila, *Cervantes en Inglaterra*, pp. 49–79. Henceforth I will follow the latter study, where a detailed discussion and textual examples can be found. Cervantes's influence on *Tom Jones* had been pointed out (but not proved) in Knowles, 'Cervantes and English Literature' (p. 293), and Wayne C. Booth, 'The Self-Conscious Narrator in Comic Fiction before *Tristram Shandy*', *PMLA*, 47. 2 (1952), 163–85 (p. 176). Walter F. Starkie, 'Miguel de Cervantes and the English Novel', *Essays by Diverse Hands*, 34 (1966), 159–79 (p. 169), mentions *Tom Jones* but does not assign it any Cervantine features.

42. Cf. Ardila, 'La horma narratológica', p. 50.

43. Cf. Ardila, 'La horma narratológica', p. 50. Other isolated coincidences have been pointed out by various critics: Edward C. Riley in *Introducción al Quijote* (Barcelona: Crítica, 1990), p. 194, suggested that both Cervantes and Fielding use two narrative voices, e.g. in *Don Quixote* II, 16 and in *Tom Jones* XII, 5; Edwin Williamson in *El Quijote y los libros de caballerías* (Madrid: Taurus, 1991), p. 266, believes that *Don Quixote* inspired the irony in *Tom Jones*; Ronald Paulson in *Don Quixote in England*, p. 157, pointed out that the puppet show in *Tom Jones* XII, 5 was inspired by Maese Pedro.

44. For a complete list of examples see Ardila, 'La horma narratológica: *Tom Jones* de Henry Fielding', pp. 59–64.

45. Apud Ardila, 'La horma narratológica: *Tom Jones* de Henry Fielding', p. 64.

46. Cf. Jorge Urrutia, 'Narración y bloques narrativos en Miguel de Cervantes', in *Estudios sobre el Siglo de Oro. Homenaje al profesor Francisco Ynduráin* (Madrid: Editora Nacional, 1984), pp. 499–518.

47. Riley, *Introducción al Quijote*, p. 100.

48. Zimic, *Los cuentos y las novelas del 'Quijote'*, p. 36; José C. Nieto, *Consideraciones del Quijote. Crítica. Estética. Sociedad* (Newark, DE: Juan de la Cuesta, 2002).

49. Parker in 'Fielding and the Structure of *Don Quixote*' (p. 14) explained the psychological evolution of Don Quixote. Despite Anthony Close's refusal to acknowledge the knight's noble qualities (as highlighted by the late-eighteenth- and early-nineteenth-century writers), Francisco Layna has recently studied Don Quixote's psychological progression and the exaltation of his noble values. For Close's arguments vide Anthony Close, *The Romantic Approach to 'Don Quixote': A Critical*

History of the Romantic Tradition in 'Quixote' Criticism (Cambridge: Cambridge University Press, 1978), and Anthony Close, *Cervantes and the Comic Mind of his Age* (Oxford: Oxford University Press, 2000).

50. E.g. Pedro Javier Pardo García, 'La otra cara de Cervantes en la novela inglesa del siglo XVIII: *Tom Jones* y *Humphry Clinker*', in *Actas del II Congreso Internacional de la Asociación de Cervantistas*, ed. by Giuseppe Grilli (Naples: Instituto Universitario Orientale, 1995), pp. 839–54.

51. Apud J. A. G. Ardila, 'Textos y contextos de la novela picaresca, 1554–1753' (unpublished doctoral thesis, Universidad Autónoma de Madrid, 2005).

52. The rogue in the picaresque novel has been studied by many scholars, for a complete review of those studies see Ardila, *El género picaresco en la crítica literaria* (Madrid: Biblioteca Nueva, 2008). The most complete of those studies are Carlos Blanco Aguinaga, 'Cervantes y la picaresca: notas sobre dos tipos de realismo', *Nueva Revista de Filología Hispánica*, 11 (1957), 313–42; Antonio Rey Hazas, *La novela picaresca* (Madrid: Anaya, 1990); Florencio Sevilla, 'Presentación', in *La novela picaresca española*, ed. by Florencio Sevilla (Madrid: Castalia, 2001).

53. Cf. Ardila, 'Cervantes y la *quixotic fiction*: sucesión episódica y otros recursos narrativos', p. 44.

54. Apud Alberto Blecua, 'Prólogo', in Miguel de Cervantes, *El ingenioso hidalgo Don Quijote de La Mancha* (Madrid: Espasa-Calpe, 2005), pp. xviii–xxiv (p. xxiii).

55. The presentation of fiction as history or, to be more precise, the writing of fiction that is presented as true to emphasize its realism, was attempted by the anonymous author of *Lazarillo de Tormes* (1554). In 1599 Mateo Alemán published his novel *Guzmán de Alfarache*, to which he referred to as a 'poética historia' [poetic history], because, like Fielding's concept of epic prose, the 'poética historia' was literary fiction presented as truth. For a detail discussion of Alemán's 'poética historia' see Henri Guerreiro, '*Guzmán de Alfarache*: una "poética historia" al servicio de un realismo sin lindes', in *La invención de la novela moderna*, ed. by Jean Canavaggio (Madrid: Casa de Velázquez, 1999), pp. 207–33; Pedro M. Piñero, 'La publicación del *Guzmán de Alfarache* (Madrid, 1599) y la invención de la novela moderna', in *Atalayas del Guzmán de Alfarache*, ed. by Pedro M. Piñero (Seville: Universidad de Sevilla and Diputación de Sevilla, 2002), pp. 13–26; Edmond Cros, '*Guzmán de Alfarache* y los orígenes de la novela moderna', in *Atalayas del Guzmán de Alfarache*, pp. 167–76.

56. On the literary impact of Alemán on Cervantes see, *inter alia*, José María Micó, 'Prosas y prisas en 1604: el *Quijote*, el *Guzmán* y la *Pícara Justina*', in *Hommage à Robert Jammes*, ed. by Francis Cerdan, 3 vols (Tolouse: Presses Universitaires de Mirail, 1994), III, 827–48; Antonio Rey Hazas, 'El *Guzmán de Alfarache* y las innovaciones de Cervantes', in *Atalayas del Guzmán de Alfarache*, 177–218. A recent and detailed discussion of realism in *Don Quixote* can be found in Francisco Rico, '*Don Quijote*, Madrid, 1604, en prensa', *Bulletin Hispanique*, 101 (1999), 415–34, and also in Riley, *Introducción al Quijote*, p. 323.

57. For the most recent discussion of realism in *Don Quixote* vide Antonio Garrido Domínguez, *Aspectos de la novela en Cervantes* (Alcalá: Centro de Estudios Cervantinos, 2007).

58. As explained by Fernando Lázaro Carreter, *Lazarillo de Tormes en la picaresca* (Barcelona: Ariel, 1972). The most recent analyses of folklore in *Lazarillo* can be found in Maxime Chevalier, 'Folklore y literatura: *Lazarillo de Tormes*, otra vez', in *La invención de la novela*, pp. 159–69, and J. A. G. Ardila, 'Novela y folclore en *Lazarillo de Tormes*', in *Actas del Congreso de Literatura y Cultura Popular*, ed. by Jesús Cañas et al. (Cáceres: Universidad de Extremadura, 2008).

59. Juan Bautista Avalle Arce, *Las novelas y sus narradores* (Alcalá de Henares: Centro de Estudios Cervantinos, 2006).

60. Avalle Arce, *Las novelas y sus narradores*, p. 199.

61. Ian Watt, *The Rise of the Novel: Studies in Defoe, Richardson and Fielding* (London: Chatto & Windus, 1957), p. 311.

CHAPTER 12

Heroic Failure: Novelistic Impotence in *Don Quixote* and *Tristram Shandy*

Christopher Narozny and Diana de Armas Wilson

Any attempt to collect the abundant commonalities[1] between *Don Quixote* and *Tristram Shandy* under a single heading would be doomed to failure, but the heading of impotence[2] might comprise the largest number. In *Tristram Shandy* the protagonist narrator is both literally and rhetorically impotent; in *Don Quixote* the protagonist lives by a defunct moral and rhetorical code. But out of such powerlessness there emerges a new kind of text, one that works with instead of against failure, one whose primary narrative strategy is in fact an aesthetic sublimation of the failure from which no author can escape. Such a text privileges inquiry over certainty, signifiers over signs. Such a text is typically called postmodern, but, as Steve Coogen somewhat awkwardly says in the recent film version[3] of Sterne's novel, '*Tristram Shandy* was post-modern before there was anything to be post about'. This is, of course, an overstatement, or maybe an oversight: there was Cervantes 'to be post about', and Sterne, throughout his novel, pays frequent homage to his 'master'. In order to determine how impotence becomes, for Sterne, a primary source of invention, it is necessary to look more closely at the impotence itself, which we will do by firstly discussing authorship, identity, rhetoric, and narrative.

Both Don Quixote and Tristram Shandy are rendered impotent by their avowed objectives: we know in advance that Don Quixote will not succeed in reinstating knight errantry as Spain's dominant moral discourse, and we quickly realize that Tristram will fail to deliver his life and opinions. These objectives are not, however, the real source of impotence, but rather a 'hobbyhorsical', to borrow Sterne's term, response to a pervasive, almost transcendental real-world impotence. They are, in Terry Eagleton's words, 'displacement activities' which serve as 'substitute manhood[s] to make up for real-life humiliations'.[4] Sterne, like Cervantes before him, assigns each of his male characters a 'substitute' activity: just as Don Quixote has knight errantry, Uncle Toby and Trim have model battlefields, Walter has the Tristrapaedia, and Tristram has the act of writing.

The reality these characters seek to evade is, as Bakhtin might argue, central to the novel as a genre.[5] For Bakhtin, the novel peaks at moments when dominant ideologies and powers are actively crumbling. In other words, the novel thrives at moments of systemic impotence. Don Quixote lived at a time when caste values were giving way to class values, when a feudal economy was rapidly disappearing before the onslaught of capitalism. Alonso Quijano, a middle-aged man of modest means, is of little worth under this new regime. He is, at best, a cog in a machine he cannot comprehend, and in this way he functions as a sad double for knight errantry. Neither Alonso Quijano nor knight errantry can properly exist in the wake of feudalism. By attempting to restore knight errantry, Don Quixote seeks to reinstate a caste system and hence to reclaim his identity. Knight errantry is then a particularly apt hobbyhorse, one that makes Don Quixote something of an admirable anti-hero: he is not just fighting windmills and puppets, he is, more importantly, fighting history. As the reader might suspect, he cannot win.

In *Tristram Shandy*, literal impotence — Toby's war wound and Tristram's unfortunate circumcision — serves as a close double for figurative impotence. The impotence of each male character, moreover, doubles another character's impotence. Tristram's failure to deliver his life and opinions and Uncle Toby's failure to reconstruct meaningfully the battle where he was rendered literally impotent are both failures of representation. They are also failures at living: Tristram, in his career as narrator, learns that there simply is not enough time to write about life *and* experience it: 'at this rate I should just live 364 times faster than I should write'.[6] Similarly, Walter learns that he cannot, at once, both write a dissertation on the education of his son and actually educate his son: as Tristram observes, 'the misfortune was, that I was all that time totally neglected and abandoned to my mother' (p. 368). In all three cases, the inability to live life while representing it is far from undesirable: for Toby, building mock battlefields becomes a means of not experiencing his impotency; for Walter, planning the education of his son becomes a way of not educating him in the contingent real world; for Tristram, writing about his life becomes a means of avoiding it. Cumulatively, Sterne's trio projects a world in which the individual is simply not up to the task.

If the characters depicted lack agency, the authors who pen them suffer from a similar dysfunction. In both *Don Quixote* and *Tristram Shandy* the authors fail to control the flow as well as the meaning of their texts. As early as Chapter 9 of Part I we meet the first few in what becomes a parade of authors: the marketgoer who seeks out the authentic history of Don Quixote, the Arab historian who wrote it, and the hired translator who provides the Spanish version. They are joined by the tellers of numerous interpolated stories and the author of the counterfeit second volume. Few if any of these authors appear to be vying for control; rather, they seem to be collectively relinquishing control. This makes sense in a text that aims to shatter the authority of all those stories of chivalry. One way to shatter authority is to divide the central authorial voice into multiple, competing voices.

Sterne also employs multiple authors, but Tristram's voice struggles vociferously for control. What is implicit in Cervantes's text becomes explicit in Sterne's. In *Don Quixote*, particularly in Part I, the interpolations disrupt the main narrative without apology; no central consciousness labours to make sure that all pertinent voices appear in proper order and on equal footing. In *Tristram Shandy*, Tristram's role as narrator and author is to orchestrate the kind of multiplicity of voices found in *Don Quixote*, and he often doubts himself equal to the challenge: 'I have been at

it these six weeks, making all the speed I possibly could, — and am not yet born'
(p. 65). The harder he tries to drive his narrative forward, the further behind he
finds himself.

The humour and pathos in *Don Quixote* depend on the protagonist's strict
adherence to an antiquated and effete rhetorical model — a loyalty that leaves him
vulnerable to all manner of drubbings and manipulations. But Cervantes's parody
of chivalric romance belies a deeper rhetorical crisis: Don Quixote, through his
internalization of chivalric discourse, seeks to turn signifiers into signs. Meaning is
fixed in chivalric romance: evil is evil, good is good, and if something is not what
it seems, this has nothing to do with an overarching crisis of representation; rather,
it is obvious that an evil sorcerer has meddled in human affairs.

In *Tristram Shandy*, Sterne widens the parodic scope by targeting not a particular
generic discourse, but rather the whole of formal rhetoric. This parodying is the
thrust of many of the text's more overt heteroglossic moments: a given rhetorical
apparatus either fails in its objective and/or is made to look ridiculous. An apt
example is the *Mémoire présenté á messieurs les docteurs de Sorbonne* and the doctors'
Réponse. This is a clear instance of deliberative rhetoric that fails to deliberate, leading
Tristram to comment that he 'hopes they all rested well the night after so tiresome
a consultation' (p. 86). The interpolations in *Tristram Shandy* are humorous in large
part because the rhetorical situation so seldom suits the text or speech delivered.
This is nowhere more evident than during the long period of time which Walter
and Uncle Toby spend — accompanied variously by Trim, Dr. Slop, and Obadiah
— awaiting Tristram's birth, a period which offers the reader a thorough if desultory
critique of classical and contemporary rhetorical practices. Walter and his entourage
invent ways of passing the time; each of their inventions introduces a new text
into the larger narrative, and each new narrative appears singularly ill-suited to
the impending miracle of childbirth. First, there is Parson Yorick's sermon (in
reality, Sterne's sermon borrowed from his own ecclesiastical career), delivered by
Trim, a sermon on conscience which, read in the parlour rather than the pulpit,
becomes a mere rhetorical object, one that persuades its audience to do nothing
more than critique it as such. The critique begins with an unfavourable assessment of
Trim's delivery and ends with a favourable critique of the sermon's diction (p. 156).

Sterne takes this same occasion to parody the Elocutionary movement then
in vogue throughout Britain. Thomas Sheridan's *British Education*, published
three years earlier, claimed that persuasive preaching must be 'accompanied by a
corresponding look, and gestures, which naturally result from a man who speaks
in earnest'.[7] There is a reciprocal and pervasive relationship in *Tristram Shandy*:
characters are used to make the rules of rhetoric appear ridiculous, but the use and
misuse of rhetorical principles also make these same characters delightfully comic.
This, too, Sterne learned from his beloved master Cervantes, whose muledrivers
and prostitutes and innkeepers' wives stare blankly at Don Quixote as he expounds
on the chivalric code.

This same period of waiting offers a second parody of rhetorical principles: in
order to expedite Dr. Slop's efforts to curse Obadiah over the affair of the knots,
Walter, with 'Cervantic Gravity', refers him to a composition which includes all 'fit

forms of swearing suitable to all cases, from the lowest to the highest provocations which could possibly happen' (p. 181). He does so as Dr. Slop stands with his thumb bleeding and Mrs. Shandy moans with labour pains above. Tristram then provides the reader with the original Latin text and its English translation. Here, as elsewhere, Sterne parodies the topoi. In this instance, not only are the topics themselves absurd, but so is the attempt to employ them. During a particularly painful and obstreperous moment, Dr. Slop is asked to stop and search through a book of execrations in order to select the most appropriate. Don Quixote uses chivalric codes to displace his own authentic experience and reasoning.[8] Cervantes sets out to reclaim individual authenticity by shattering 'the authority of all those tales of chivalry, and their influence upon people, especially common people, all around the world' (p. 11). Sterne and Cervantes are in solid agreement with Plato's critique of rhetoric in the Gorgias: a rhetorician will not hesitate to argue either for or against a subject about which he is thoroughly ignorant.[9] Sterne echoes this criticism most directly by having Walter gleefully declare: 'Didst thou ever see a white bear? — But thou couldst discourse about one' (p. 396).

Sterne's overarching complaint is, like Plato's, that formal rhetoric prefers style to substance, but that is not the extent of his complaint. Formal rhetoric ostentatiously believes that it can accomplish its objectives — that it can communicate accurately in order to persuade, move, and cajole. In other words, formal rhetoric is to the practitioner what knight errantry is to the knight: a code which, once mastered, will guide him safely through life. Sterne, like Cervantes 150 years before him, and like the modernists 150 years after him, seeks to disprove the efficacy of any such code. Kirsten Pederson, who views this destabilization as Sterne's primary goal, calls Tristram Shandy 'a literary dissertation on the impossibilities of communication where language — like so many other things in the work — is impotent and unable to express anything at all'.[10]

Sterne parodies not only formal rhetoric, but also narrative — particularly the autobiographical fiction of the preceding decades. The problems with Richardson's technique of writing to the moment are, in Sterne's view, multiple: in order to write to the moment one would have to spend long periods in writing hibernation in order to catch up with his life; second, writing to the moment does not necessarily account for the past or the future, of which the present is largely composed; and third, the goal of writing to the moment does not take into consideration the many interruptions which will inevitably derail the author — namely, other people's stories.

Once again, Sterne's strategies for exposing (or maybe exploiting) Richardson's technique are adapted from Don Quixote. His principal method is one earlier alluded to: Tristram experiences the act of writing his life story as a dilemma, even a kind of neurosis. He is not fit to produce a Cervantine text by himself. In Chapter 14 of Part I, he confesses that, 'when a man sits down to write a history [...] he knows no more than his heels what lets and confounded hindrances he is to meet with on the way' (p. 64). These hindrances often involve the past; whatever moment Tristram happens to be recounting is inevitably at the mercy of an anterior moment; hence, his life story begins (and continues for several hundred pages) prior to his birth.

Writing to the moment requires adhering to the moment, and, as Michael Bell observes, Tristram invariably chooses 'private association at the expense of narrative progress'.[11]

If the individual is destined to failure, if rhetoric and narrative are destined to failure, and if the author no longer exercises any control over his text, then it becomes difficult to imagine why anybody would take up a pen. The answer is that all of this perceived, if not flaunted, impotence becomes the source of a new kind of power, one that privileges *inventio* over *narratio*, the efficient over the final cause. If formal rhetoric is rendered impotent by its belief that words can communicate accurately, then the novel, as practised by Cervantes and Sterne, is made potent by its recognition that words can do no such thing. Jonathan Lamb, in his essay 'Sterne and Irregular Oratory', describes the first part of this equation when he writes, 'the risible failure of reading as a decisive interpretive act leads to a narrative whose stake is no longer an accurate decoding of signs, but the plausible representation of a series of scenes which dramatize the comic futility of thinking that that there is one correct reading'.[12] But as Cervantes and Sterne might argue, a new (novel) kind of power emerges for reader and author alike.

In order to understand this upstart power, we might begin by looking at Ian Watt's arguments for why the novel took hold in eighteenth-century England.[13] While Watt denies *Don Quixote* the status of novel (he labels it a myth), his criteria for the novel — for what the novel is and why it came into being — often seem tailored to Cervantes's text. In short, the novel (both its authorship and readership) was made possible by a new and distinctively middle-class kind of experience.[14] What is striking, at least in the context of the current discussion, is that Cervantes, in his Prologue to Part I, imagines a very similar set of criteria for *Don Quixote*. The similarities are telling, and it is worth looking at them more closely.

With the Prologue's first words, 'Desocupado lector [Leisurely reader]', Cervantes seems to be addressing a new class of people who have the time and opportunity to read. He makes this clear when he addresses the problem of finding suitable prefatory matter (p. 8). Over one hundred years before Defoe's *Robinson Crusoe*, Cervantes addresses the Wattian 'division of labour' and exhibits the 'new emphasis on ordinary life' (p. 71). In essence, Cervantes offers a new way of filling those leisure hours (both by writing and reading), and, as everything new in the world must define itself against what is already in circulation, he devotes a good portion of the Prologue to telling us what his novel is not: it is not crammed full 'of Aristotle's wisdom, or Plato's, and the whole mob of philosophers' (8); and it is not one of those 'useless books about chivalry' (p. 11). In other words, Cervantes's novel is no advocate of 'universals' — neither those of ancient philosophers nor those of medieval knights.

The relation of author to reader becomes one of the dominant concerns of the eighteenth-century novelist, and Sterne is no exception. Thomas Keymer views this relationship as a major source of Sterne's invention.[15] Sterne, in the guise of his narrator, answers this question for himself: 'The truest respect which you can pay to the reader's understanding is to halve the matter amicably, and leave him something to imagine, in his turn, as well as yourself' (p. 127). This explains why

Sterne exhibits an even lower tolerance for universals than his master: they leave the reader nothing to imagine. As we mentioned earlier, Walter's primary narrative function is to deliver this anti-universal message. Walter believes in chains of cause and effect (hence his distress over Tristram's smashed nose, accidental naming, and impromptu circumcision), and Tristram rebels against this philosophical naiveté through the practice of writing. 'Is a man to follow rules', Tristram asks, 'or rules to follow him?' (p. 282).

If, as Cervantes's Prologue seems to claim, the novel is neither a daunting intellectual enterprise nor another empty manifestation of a dangerous ideological status quo, then an alternate definition is needed. Cervantes provides this definition by creating the character of his friend and transcribing their conversation. The idea of public conversation (of the dialogic), with the explosion of coffee houses and public spaces in London, becomes central to the 'rise of the novel' in eighteenth-century England (authors such as Fielding and Defoe talk about it explicitly in their work), but Cervantes seems to be describing a similar phenomenon more than one hundred years earlier in Spain. Contemporary social and technological innovations made public dialogue possible on a larger scale than ever before. It seems significant, then, that Cervantes renders the bulk of his Prologue as a conversation, and that within this conversation his friend advises him to let his ideas be understood 'without making them complicated or obscure' (p. 11). In other words, Cervantes is making a kind of dual argument for the vernacular — for a kind of direct and accessible intelligence, a meeting ground somewhere between unobtainable erudition and thinly veiled propaganda, something his working class friends could both enjoy and profit from. At the same time, he argues for the dialogic by envisioning a kind of text his friends could not only consume, but also construct.

Sterne enthusiastically adopts this agenda. 'Writing', Tristram tells us, 'when properly managed (as you may be sure I think mine is) is but a different name for conversation' (p. 127). This principle is later reiterated in a dialogue between Toby and Trim: 'If I should differ from your honor...', Trim begins, and Toby interrupts, 'Why else do I talk to you, Trim?' (p. 555). Sterne, like Toby, sees no value in labouring over a text that will elicit complacent nods. And indeed, given the new diversity of the reading public, such a text is no longer possible.

If Watt succeeds in identifying the conditions prerequisite to the novel's rise, or at least its rise to power, then Bakhtin identifies the methods by which the novel responded to those conditions; specifically, he explains how the novel achieves heteroglossia. He does this most directly by proposing five 'compositional unities': (1) direct authorial literary-artistic narration (in all its diverse variants); (2) stylization of the various forms of oral everyday narration; (3) stylization of the various forms of semiliterary (written) everyday narration (the letter, the diary, etc.); (4) various forms of literary but extra-artistic authorial speech (moral, philosophical or scientific statements, oratory, ethnographic descriptions, memoranda and so forth); (5) the stylistically individualized speech of characters.[16] Bahktin looked for and located each of these 'unities' in *Don Quixote*, a fact that makes the novel appear as a natural and almost necessary invention of the Renaissance. This is true specifically of the degree to which place logic (or commonplaces, or topoi) dominated Renaissance intellectual life, and the degree to which the humanists valued a kind of investigative inclusiveness (examining a given issue, person, place, or thing from every conceivable angle) over and above the act of defining. Of course, any such investigation is, in Bakhtinian terms, necessarily dialogic: the individual topics speak to one another. And of course Bakhtin's compositional-stylistic unities are a kind of topical system, a means of approaching a given subject from multiple perspectives. If, as Watt asserts, the eighteenth century required a literary form capable of accounting for all the varieties of human experience, it seems only logical that the topoi would play a role in that form's inception and development.

Whilst it is true that Sterne parodies the topoi, he limits his parody to specific applications; in particular, he parodies the rhetoricians who use place logic as a method of finding 'fit forms suitable to all occasions', and of discoursing 'on a white bear' without ever having seen one. These objectives reduce place logic to a means to an end: they require the practitioner to begin, as it were, with the final cause. Place logic's real value, for Sterne as for Cervantes, lies in the field of invention: 'The machinery of my work', says Tristram, 'is of a species by itself; two contrary motions are introduced into it, and reconciled, which were thought to be at variance with each other' (p. 95). Sterne supplies the motions (or topics); it is up to us to reconcile them. Tristram's self-proclaimed mission — 'to point out to the curious, different tracts of investigation' (p. 89) — is reminiscent of Cide Hamete's famous injunction: 'Reader, you decide' (p. 487).

The reader is not required to decide which of the juxtaposed voices speaks the truth, which is lying, which is good, or which is bad. Rather, the reader must decide how so many voices within a single text speak to each other, contradict each other, reflect on each other. The reader is not obliged to ponder about what they mean, but about how they mean. How these voices combine to make, or maybe subvert, meaning is the process Bakhtin describes when he talks about dialogized heteroglossia.

Sterne has often been called a protomodernist precisely because he makes such demands on the reader. Like the Cervantes of *Don Quixote* Part I, Sterne places what Anthony J. Cascardi calls a 'particular emphasis [...] on the strange visibility of exclusions, gaps, and lacks'.[17] Again like Cervantes, Sterne has been criticized for this reason: according to F. R. Leavis, *Tristram Shandy* is nothing more than 'irresponsible trifling'.[18] Jonathan Lamb vehemently defends Sterne when he asks us to consider it as 'an unstable series of seized initiatives, designed not for interpretive symmetry but for local practical advantages in the engagement with the reader'.[19] This might be said not only of Sterne and Cervantes, but also of James Joyce, Gertrude Stein, Samuel Beckett, Jorge Luis Borges, and many others.

Sterne's primary revision to the Cervantine enterprise is deceptively simple: he chose to write *Tristram Shandy* in the first person. Writing a Cervantean novel in the first person requires more than just entering Don Quixote's point of view, it requires centring (or maybe decentring) Cervantes's narrative play in a single mind; an individual consciousness must navigate the interpolations, the digressions, the multiplicity of authors, and the competing texts found in *Don Quixote*.

In this way, Tristram's *I* has far more in common with the multifarious authors of *Don Quixote* than it does with the epistolary *I*'s of Clarissa. For Sterne, the conflict enters through the illusion which Richardson (who loathed *Tristram Shandy*) laboured to conceal: specifically, the division in time between the *I* doing the writing and the *I* being written about. The problem, as Eagleton observes, is that 'the writing "I" interprets (rather than simply recalls or reflects) the self it writes about, and thus puts a distance between the two'.[20] Tristram himself experiences this dichotomy as a source of tension; if the writing *I* were not there to interpret the narrative, the story would hardly be worth telling, but the interpretation often seems to prevent the story from actually being told.

Provided that, for Cervantes, success in writing meant creating a new kind of experience for the reader, then for Sterne, success meant not only creating a unique experience, but also performing its construction. Tristram the narrator is not merely a constant double for his text, he is at the same time a double for the reader. The success for both parties lies in the effort: both are confronting an impotence far greater than themselves. Melvyn New describes the reader's success when he writes, 'Sterne shows us [...] that the instinct or desire to order the story is always more powerful than our capacity to rest in muddle'.[21] In other words, the act of reading elicits a survival instinct in the reader. The same is true for the writer: while the act of writing might begin as a means of avoiding life, it becomes, by the end, a way of being in an epistemologically hostile world. This almost religious function of writing constitutes the primary link between Sterne and the twentieth century, when writers such as Samuel Beckett continues representing the aesthetics of failure.

Writing, like our obligation to continue existing, is all failure, but there is 'progress' (digressive though it may be), and there is something potentially heroic (if not religious) in that progress, in the willingness to confront the fact that nothing is certain or perfect. The art of living is possibly nothing more than the will to fail, and one practises that art through writing and reading, through constant invention and investigation. Don Quixote's effort to revive knight errantry in the face of all odds is not unlike Tristram's ceaseless effort to write himself into his own life story. The heroism lies in the effort — in the efficient rather than the final cause.

Notes to Chapter 12

1. The protagonists of both novels are driven by a singular obsession (knight errantry for Don Quixote, autobiography for Tristram); both narrators appear self-consciously preoccupied with the publication of their book; both novels include numerous embedded texts; both feature similar pairings of characters (Don Quixote and Sancho Panza, Toby and Trim); both are anti-romantic in tone. For a more thorough account of the points in common between *Don Quixote* and *Tristram Shandy*, see Felicitas Kleber's, 'Laurence Sterne's *Tristram Shandy* and *Don Quixote*', in *Cervantes in the English-Speaking World: New Essays*, ed. by Darío Fernández-Morera and Michael Hanke (Kassel: Edition Reichenberger, 2005), pp. 65–81.
2. By 'impotence' we mean the inability to achieve a goal which one has clearly envisioned. Don Quixote seeks to help others, but in the real world he makes very little progress. Tristram conceives of writing his life's story, but in reality he recounts only the smallest portion. For interesting commentary on the impotence of language in *Tristram Shandy*, see Kirsten Pedersen,

'How to Recognize a Novel When You See One: A Story about *Tristram Shandy* and Tristram Shandy's Story', in *Reinventions of the Novel*, ed. by Karen-Margrethe Simonsen, Marianne Ping Huang and Mads Rosendahl Thomsen (Amsterdam: Rodopi, 2004), pp. 33–48.

3. *A Cock and Bull Story*, director Michael Winterbottom (BBC Films, 2005).

4. Terry Eagleton, *The English Novel: An Introduction* (Malden: Blackwell Publishing, 2005), p. 89.

5. See *The Dialogical Imagination: Four Essays by M. M. Bakhtin*, ed. by Caryl Emerson and Michael Holquist (Austin: University of Texas Press, 1982).

6. Laurence Sterne, *Tristram Shandy*, ed. by Christopher Ricks and Graham Petrie (New York: Penguin, 1967), p. 286. All subsequent citations to this text will appear parenthetically in our text.

7. Quoted in James A. Herrick, *The History and Theory of Rhetoric* (Boston, MA: Pearson, 2005), p. 181.

8. Miguel de Cervantes, *Don Quijote: Norton Critical Edition*, trans. by Burton Raffel, ed. by Diana de Armas Wilson (New York: W. W. Norton, 1999), p. 45. All subsequent English translations are to this edition and will be noted parenthetically in our text.

9. Plato, *Gorgias*, trans. by W. C. Helmbold (Indianapolis, IN: Bobbs-Merrill, 1952). Plato, through the character of Socrates, argues that rhetoric as practised by the Sophists is little more than an ethically suspect form of manipulation.

10. Pedersen, 'How to Recognize a Novel', p. 40.

11. Michael Bell, 'Laurence Sterne and the Twentieth Century', in *Laurence Sterne in Modernism and Postmodernism*, ed. by David Pierce and Peter de Voogd (Amsterdam: Rodopi, 1996), pp. 39–54 (p. 44).

12. J. P. Lamb, 'Sterne and Irregular Oratory', in *The Cambridge Companion to the Eighteenth-Century Novel*, ed. by John Richetti (New York: Cambridge University Press, 1996), pp. 153–74 (p. 157).

13. Ian Watt, *Rise of the English Novel* (Berkeley: University of California Press, 1957). Citations to this text appear parenthetically in the text.

14. Grand theorists such as Michael McKeon complicate Watt's assertion that the novel was born out of formal realism by observing that many early novels still incorporated stock characters from romance tales., While paying great respect to Watt's thesis, McKeon contends that Watt is perhaps overly invested in equating the rise of the novel with the rise of the middle class. Certainly, Watt's classification of *Don Quixote* as myth is too convenient. Nevertheless, Watt's criteria remain useful in any examination of the novel's origins. See Michael McKeon, *The Origins of the English Novel: 1600–1740* (Baltimore, MD: Johns Hopkins University Press, 1987).

15. Thomas Keymer, *Sterne, the Moderns, and the Novel* (Oxford: Oxford University Press, 2002), p. 34.

16. Bakhtin, *The Dialogical Imagination*, p. 262.

17. Anthony J. Cascardi, 'The Archeology of Desire in *Don Quixote*', in *Quixotic Desire: Psychoanalytic Perspectives on Cervantes,* ed. by Ruth Anthony El Saffar and Diana de Armas Wilson (Ithaca, NY: Cornell University Press, 1993), pp. 37–58 (p. 81).

18. Quoted in Lamb, 'Sterne and Irregular Oratory', p. 153.

19. Lamb, 'Sterne and Irregular Oratory', p. 154.

20. Eagleton, *The English Novel*, p. 86.

21. Melvyn New, 'Sterne and the Narrative of Determinateness', in *Critical Essays on Laurence Sterne*, ed. by Melvyn New (London: Prentice Hall, 1998), pp. 127–39 (p. 128).

CHAPTER 13

Tobias Smollett, *Don Quixote* and the Emergence of the English Novel

J. A. G. Ardila

The excellence of Smollett's prose has conferred upon him a pre-eminent place in the history of English literature. Smollett distinguished himself as one of the prototypical writers of eighteenth-century England — he edited the newspapers *The Briton* (1762–63), *The Critical Review* (1756–63) and (with Oliver Goldsmith) *The British Magazine* (1760–63); he translated Cervantes's *Don Quixote* (1755), Lesage's *Gil Blas* (1748), Félenon's *The Adventures of Telemachus* (1776) and parts of Voltaire's complete works (1761–63); as a historian he authored *The Complete History of England* (1757; 1758), *Continuation of the Complete History of England* (1760; 1765), and *The Present State of all Nations* (1768); and he wrote several poems. He was also a registered physician and the author of *An Essay on the External Use of Water* (1752). Yet he is best known for his six novels: *Roderick Random* (1748), *Peregrine Pickle* (1751), *Ferdinand Count Fathom* (1753), *Sir Launcelot Greaves* (1760), *The History and Adventures of an Atom* (1769), and *Humphry Clinker* (1771). His vast knowledge of English society, as a historian, a journalist, a physician and a translator, enabled him to endow his novels with the minute details that made them as realistic as those by Defoe and Fielding. Most of Smollett's works are satirical; he was a Scotsman who opposed the 1707 Act of Union but lived in England, of whose society he was always most critical.

Smollett grew fascinated with *Don Quixote* in as much as he was obsessed with writing the first canonical novel in the English language. He may have started working on his translation of *Don Quixote* before or approximately at the time he began his first novel. In one way or another Cervantes's influence glows in Smollett's novels; *Roderick Random* and *Humphry Clinker* are Cervantean fictions, *Sir Launcelot Greaves* is quixotic, and *Peregrine Pickle* incorporates Cervantic vocabulary and characters. Surprisingly, however, Smollett scholars have traditionally focused on the extent to which his novels belong with the Spanish picaresque genre. Indeed *Ferdinand Count Fathom* is one of the latest picaresque novels in European literature, and *Roderick Random* borrows from the so-called picaresque myth (i.e. that it partakes of a limited number of picaresque features).[1] But despite Smollett's zeal for Spanish picaresque literature, his Cervantean and quixotic novels make him (alongside Fielding) the English-speaking author of greatest indebtedness to Cervantes.[2]

Smollett's English translation of *Don Quixote* appeared in 1755, and its subsequent editions outnumbered any other English version in the eighteenth century. Although some scholars have doubted Smollett's authorship,[3] critics today concur that this translation is Smollett's own work,[4] and some even consider it the best *Don Quixote* in English.[5] The 1755 translation sheds much light on Smollett's indebtedness to Cervantes in two ways: (1) because Smollett's biography of Cervantes (included in the preliminaries) provides a thorough account of his own admiration for Cervantes; and (2) because Smollett worked on his translation and on *Roderick Random* simultaneously.

The first biography of Cervantes had appeared in Lord Carteret's edition of 1738. The biographer was Gregorio Mayans. Lord Carteret's edition attests to the admiration of the English for *Don Quixote* and its author.[6] Smollett intended to endow his translation with a critical appeal and his biography is the first in a language other than Spanish. This account of the life of Cervantes bears enormous significance to the reception of Cervantes in England: whilst in the seventeenth century *Don Quixote* had been read as a comic book and in the first half of the eighteenth century as a satire, in 1755 Smollett presented Cervantes as the epitome of all noble values and virtues. His praises for the Spanish author include the following passage: 'Cervantes, whether considered as a writer or a man, will be found worthy of universal approbation and esteem; as we cannot help applauding that fortitude and courage which no difficulty could disturb, and no danger dismay; while we admire that delightful stream of humour and invention, which flowed so plenteous and so pure, surmounting ludicrous all the mounds of malice and adversity'.[7] In turning the knight of La Mancha into an exemplary character, Smollett's translation precedes the reception by the late-eighteenth- and early-nineteenth-century Romanticists.[8]

It is uncertain how Smollett was commissioned to write the work and when exactly he carried it through. Edgar Allison Peers[9] suggested that on seeing the success of Jarvis's translation, the future publisher of Smollett's translation realized the selling potential of a new English version, and decided to look for a renowned novelist who could translate the Spanish original; a famous translator would undoubtedly appeal to the readers and bring forth the expected revenue. Before 1755, Smollett had published *Roderick Random*, *Peregrine Pickle* and *Ferdinand Count Fathom*, a group of successful novels which met the publisher's requirements. If Peers's hypothesis is correct, Smollett would have started working on his translation long after *Roderick Random* was published in 1748. This theory was subsequently contended by Lewis Knapp, who suggested that Smollett translated at the same time as he wrote *Roderick Random*.[10] It seems very likely that Smollett wrote his first novel and his translation simultaneously. In the light of Freud's theories on dreams, it has been suggested[11] that Cervantes's influence on *Roderick Random* may have been unconscious (as well as conscious) because, as a translator, Smollett became a proto-reader of Cervantes. This influence can be inferred from the striking similarities between Don Quixote's first stay in an inn and Roderick's stay in another on his way to London.

In sum, further to reconfiguring the perception of Cervantes in England, the 1755 rendering of *Don Quixote* evinces Smollett's profound admiration and respect for the Spanish author and his *opera prima*, and also provided the Scotsman with a deep knowledge of *Don Quixote*. Smollett therefore accounted for Cervantes's work in his mission to transcend the romance.

In the preface to his first novel, Smollett reflected upon the nature of prose fiction. Those academics (*supra*) who have refuted the picaresque qualities of Smollett's novels, took the preface in *Roderick Random* to provide textual evidence for their assumptions. Smollett therein proclaimed, 'The following sheets I have modelled on his [Lesage's] plan, taking the liberty, however, to differ from him in the execution' (p. 4).[12] Smollett writes that *Gil Blas* 'not only deviates from probability, but prevents that generous indignation which ought to animate the reader, against the sordid and vicious disposition of the world' (pp. 4–5), i.e. that Lesage failed to endow his text with realism and with a satiric intention which exposed the lack of values in society. Indeed, in the preface Smollett unmistakably stated his intention not to follow Lesage, which does not necessarily imply a rejection of the picaresque genre, since, *sensu stricto*, *Gil Blas* is not a picaresque novel.[13] Until very recently,[14] however, scholars did not realize that, in addition to renouncing Lesage, Smollett was implicitly and explicitly extolling Cervantes and vowing to take *Don Quixote* as the literary canon. In addition to several allusions to Cervantes and *Don Quixote*,[15] Smollett offers in his preface a brief history of prose fiction, in which he mentions three authors: Jenofont, Lesage, and Cervantes. He declares: 'I believe I need not trouble myself in vindicating a practice authorized by the best writers in this way, some of whom I have already named' (p. 5). But he has condemned Jenofont for having written romances, and has rebutted Lesage for being much too complacent with human vices. The only author mentioned in the preface who escapes Smollett's criticism is Cervantes, of whom he writes that 'by an inimitable piece of ridicule, [he] reformed the taste of mankind' (p. 4). The Spanish author is thus commended for having exposed and ridiculed the romances, and *Don Quixote* is implicitly presented as the canonical novel.

The Cervantic influence on *Roderick Random* took form in: (1) the transgression from romance to novel within the plot; (2) the use of the word *Dulcinea*, and others of Cervantine origin; (3) Strap, who is a Sanchoesque character; (4) the use of a *deus ex machina*; (5) and the use of comic satire.

As Smollett states in his preface (*supra*), he considered realism to be one of the chief characteristics of the novel. Many twentieth-century scholars[16] have agreed that the novel becomes a new literary genre when the elements of the romance are used and transcended simultaneously. The romance in *Don Quixote* appears in the form of interpolated stories. Cervantes's method of converting romance idealism into novelistic realism is simple: a story in the romance fashion, told by a secondary character, becomes realistic when it flows into the main plot. For example, in Part I the knight comes across a group of shepherds who are about to bury Grisóstomo. One of the shepherds tells Don Quixote how Grisóstomo fell in love with Marcela, a shepherdess of unmatched beauty who rejected his love; Grisóstomo wrote very fine verses for her and succumbed to an unrestrained melancholy which drove him to an early grave. This story contains all the elements of the pastoral romance; however, it is told within the realistic frame of Don Quixote's story. Romance is turned into realism when Marcela appears at the funeral and delivers a long and cogent speech slating pastoral love and making *tabula rasa* of the pastoral romance. For Marcela, pastoral love is simply nonsensical and also unfair to beautiful women like her, who should not feel obliged to love all those who fall for them.[17]

In *Roderick Random*, Smollett includes two romance stories: 'The History of Miss Williams' and the story of John Brown in Sussex. Like many characters in *Don Quixote*, Miss Williams is a secondary character who tells of her adventures. Miss Williams, a young learned woman, connoisseur of philosophy and sentimental literature, is rescued by Lothario when an aristocrat tried to rape her. They fall in love with each other before she learns that he has vowed to marry another woman; Miss Williams's honour is finally restored when another gentleman slays Lothario. The story is told in the hyperbolic tone of the romances and conveys all the thematic conventions of the romance — namely, love triangles, ravishers, knightly saviours, perfect love, revenge, etc. However, Miss Williams undergoes a psychological change, from behaving in the romantic fashion to developing a disparaging attitude towards men and love. In her progress from idealism to realism, Miss Williams exposes, in the most Cervantean fashion, the preposterous nature of the romance.

The story of John Brown forms part of the main plot. John Brown is the false name used by Roderick Random when he becomes the servant of a rich lady in Sussex. On his return to England from Cartagena de Indias, Random's ship sinks. He manages to reach the shore, and is sheltered by a good witch who recommends him to a lady. His stay at this lady's manor contains all the themes of the romance. There he meets Narcissa, the lady's daughter and a woman of extreme beauty, who is engaged to the perfidious Sir Timothy. John Brown writes poems that soon conquer her heart. Driven by jealousy, Sir Timothy attempts to rape her, but John comes to her rescue. Fearing Sir Timothy's wickedness, the witch advises John to flee the place, which he does. The adventures of John Brown are not merely an interlude in the novel. The parody in this passage differs from the parody in 'The History of Miss Williams'; its plot is less hyperbolic, more realistic, but Roderick enters the world of the romance to leave it behind. The denouement does not conform to the romance conventions: the hero of a romance would have confronted the villain and defeated him. Because neither the witch nor Roderick acts like the witch and the hero in a romance, this romance progresses from an idyllic situation to a credible one.

Smollett employs the following words and names taken from *Don Quixote*: *duenna* (p. 304), Dulcinea (pp. 42, 303, 327, 334), and Lothario. The Dulcineas in Smollett's first novel are: the lady who travels to London in the same coach as Roderick (p. 42), Mrs. Winthers (p. 303), and Miss Snapper (pp. 327, 334). *Duenna* had been included as a noun in the *Oxford English Dictionary* in 1708, and *Dulcinea* in 1748. Lothario was, alongside Don Juan and Casanova, the typical name for a seducer in eighteenth-century England due to the popularity of *El curioso impertinente*.[18] Although *Dulcinea* was included, as a noun, in the English lexicon, by using it, Smollett establishes two levels of reality: he refers to a seemingly perfect lady with the word *Dulcinea* when that woman is not actually perfect. Smollett thus presents low characters as idyllic, in the same ironic tone as Cervantes did.

Roderick cannot be regarded as a Quixote. Yet his companion Strap is a Sanchoesque character.[19] Roderick calls Strap 'my faithful squire' (p. 371) clearly referring to Sancho. Like the Spanish squire, Strap is cowardly, stingy, and simple — e.g. when they are attacked by the highwaymen (p. 45–46) he falls on the ground and everyone assumes he has been shot; when he needs to use the toilet he says that his 'bowels [are] disordered' (p. 58); and he refuses to pay the innkeeper (p. 52).[20]

It has been suggested[21] that Smollett's usage of a *deus ex machina* was inspired by *Don Quixote*. Whilst Strap reappears providentially on several occasions (allowing Roderick to continue his adventures), Roderick's finding his father in Argentina forms the basis of the *anagnorisis* which places the main character in the social place he deserves. (The episode where Roderick comes across his father in Argentina resembles Moll Flanders's meeting her mother in Virginia.) A *deus ex machina* was a common device in prose fiction and cannot be strictly attributed to Cervantes's influence; however, it adds to the many Cervantic characteristics which cause *Roderick Random* to be a Cervantean novel.

Satire is a sign of the Restoration and the eighteenth century. Nonetheless, satire in *Roderick Random* is achieved by Cervantine means, since Smollett resorted to what Sterne called 'Cervantic tone', i.e. narrating 'silly and trifle events, with the Circumstantial Pomp of Great Ones'.[22] *Roderick Random* contains numerous instances of Cervantic tone; the most memorable examples of this are the orders of Captain Oagum (pp. 162–63), Roderick's conversation with Captain Whiffle (p. 199) or his interview with Lord Straddle (p. 313).

All these features — especially Smollett's presentation of romance plots which flow into the main plot — make *Roderick Random* a Cervantean novel. Although some critics have pointed out a number of Cervantic elements in Smollett's *Peregrine Pickle*,[23] it cannot be considered a Cervantean novel. After the publication of *Roderick Random*, Smollett developed an aversion towards Fielding — *Roderick Random* had been published anonymously and the general opinion was to attribute it to Fielding; subsequently, Fielding accused Smollett of plagiarism, on the grounds that Straps resembles Partridge (in *Tom Jones*). Smollett might have also felt offended by Fielding's disdainful remarks about Scotland, and in writing *Peregrine Pickle* he sought to expose the vices of English society. Indeed, the interpolated story 'Memoirs of a Lady of Quality', a long digression based on real fact in which the worst vices of the London aristocracy are revealed, became a scandal at the time of its publication. Smollett's satire cannot be deemed Cervantean; however, there are a number of Cervantic elements which bear evidence of Smollett's admiration for *Don Quixote* and his zeal to pay homage to Cervantes, namely the use of *Dulcinea* as a noun and the usage of a pseudo-Sanchoesque character,

Like *Roderick Random*, *Peregrine Pickle* contains some Cervantic vocabulary. A *duenna* is again a chaperone and appears seven times (p. 312, four times; p. 313, twice; p. 314)[24] to refer to the old lady who travels with the Catholic newlywed woman courted by Peregrine. A *Dulcinea* is a young beautiful lady, and is used nine times (pp. 166, 193, 204, 213, 288, 314, 318, 389, 597). The main character addresses his friend Pipes as 'trusty squire' (p. 315), clearly alluding to Sancho Panza. Unlike Straps, Pipes cannot be considered a Sanchoesque character, simply because he does not conform to Sancho's psychology. Pipes only resembles Sancho when Peregrine trusts him to deliver a letter to Emilia; like Sancho with Don Quixote's message for Dulcinea, Pipes fails to give the letter to the addressee in a very comical passage (p. 126).

Although Peregrine is not a Quixote, there are some characters who resemble the Spanish knight. The narrator describes Mr. M's former life as 'military Quixotism' (p. 695). Early in the text appears 'a thin meagre swarthy figure gasping in all the agony of fear, under the hands of a squat, hard-feature man' (p. 181), a description which resembles that of Lismahago (in *Humphry Clinker*), who has been regarded as quixotic.[25] The narrator describes another character as 'This phantome [...] was a tall, long-legged meagre, swarthy fellow, that stooped very much; his check-bones were remarkably raised, his nose bent into the shape and size of a powder-horn, and the sockets of his eyes as raw around the edges, as if the skin had been pared off' (pp. 194–95). In sum, albeit *Peregrine Pickle* is a long satire whose randomly presented episodes cause it to be more a romance than a novel, it makes use of several Cervantic elements with the only intention of expressing the author's interest in *Don Quixote*.

Smollett's third novel, *Ferdinand Count Fathom*, is a picaresque novel[26] with no trace of Cervantes's influence. In his fourth novel, *Sir Launcelot Greaves*, Smollett attempted to imitate *Don Quixote*. *Launcelot Greaves* is a quixotic fiction with a quixotic character, a monomaniac who thinks himself a knight and whose extravagant adventures serve as the vehicle for Smollett's satire. *Launcelot Greaves* includes a number of episodes taken from *Don Quixote* (*v. infra*). Notwithstanding its striking indebtedness to Cervantes, critical judgements on this novel have varied dramatically — after many scholars (*v. infra*) regarded it as a specimen of quixotic fiction, others highlighted a number of differences so as to deprive it of its Cervantic status. Nonetheless, the studies published in the past twelve years (*v. infra*) have treated *Launcelot Greaves* as an imitation of *Don Quixote*.

The characters and plot of *Launcelot Greaves* imitate *Don Quixote*. When Launcelot, a young gentleman, finds out that his beloved Aurelia will wed someone else, he is seized by desperation and loses his senses; he believes that he is a knighterrant on a mission whereby he will ultimately conquer Aurelia's heart. After being knighted in a bogus ceremony, he asks a farmer, Timothy Crabshaw, to become his squire and accompany him on his adventures. Once on the road, Launcelot and Crabshaw engage in a succession of quixotic adventures. Launcelot names his horse Bronzomarte. Crabshaw's psychology resembles Sancho in virtually everything — he argues with his master, and is often admonished by Launcelot for of his simplicity and avarice. Other Cervantic characters are Squire Sycamore, who, in the manner of Sansón Carrasco, pretends to be the Knight of the Griffin, and Aurelia, whose idealization analogizes Dulcinea.

When Smollett wrote *Launcelot Greaves* he did not intend to write a parody, because there was no genre worth parodying — *Joseph Andrews* had ridiculed Richardsonian literature, and *The Female Quixote* (1752) was a successful parody of the sentimental romances. Smollett therefore intended to write a quixotic satire. From the beginning of the eighteenth century, *Don Quixote* had been read as a satire, and Smollett's *Launcelot Greaves* opened the way for the publication of a cascade of satiric quixotic fictions — *Tarrataria; or, Don Quixote the Second* (1761), Richard Graves's *The Spiritual Quixote* (1773), *The Philosophical Quixote; or, Memories of David Wilkins* (1782), *The Country Quixote* (1785), *The Amicable Quixote; or, The Enthusiasm of Friendship* (1788), Jane Purbeck's *William Thornborough, the Benevolent Quixote* (1791), *The History of Sir George Warrington; or, The Political Quixote* (1797) and Charles Lucas's *The Infernal Quixote* (1801). In his adventures, Launcelot comes across a number of social types whom the author uses to expose the faults of English society — Tom Clarke, Dolly Cowslip, Mr Ferret, Justice Gobble, Isaac Vanderpelf, and Sir Valentine Quickset. This scheme, conceived as a means for satire, is taken from the Spanish picaresque novels.[27]

Owing to the aforementioned analogies with *Don Quixote*, critics studied *Launcelot Greaves* as a close imitation of Cervantes's work. In her study of *The Female Quixote* and eighteenth-century quixotic fiction, Miriam Small acknowledged that Smollett 'borrows from Cervantes not in idea but in actual incident and character'.[28] Small believes that Smollett took the general plan of *Don Quixote*, copied a number of passages from Cervantes's novel, which he embellished with descriptions of the English landscape and with stereotyped English characters, to which he added some other adventures. Edwin Knowles provided a very unfavourable critical account of this novel. In his survey of Cervantic literature in England, he brands *Launcelot Greaves* 'one of the most unsuccessful of [Smollett's] writings'.[29] He further suggests that Launcelot was modelled on Butler's *Hudibras* rather than on the Spanish knight, and also that Crabshaw is as selfish as D'Urfey's Sancho in *The Comical History of Don Quixote*. More recently, Canavaggio[30] has regarded Sir Launcelot as a Quixote.

The tendency within English literary studies was to demote *Launcelot Greaves* for being an imitation of *Don Quixote*.[31] This perception stems from Smollett's times. In 1764, James Beattie wrote, 'Sir Launcelot Greaves is of Don Quixote's kindred, but a different character. Smollett's design was, not to expose him to ridicule; but rather to recommend him to our pity and admiration'.[32] Such views persisted until the 1970s, when a number of scholars (*infra*) argued that *Launcelot Greaves* ought to be considered a novel of very little indebtedness to Cervantes. For these critics, Smollett accomplished a praiseworthy satire of English society hardly comparable to *Don Quixote*. This thesis was disseminated by Lewis Knapp, Robert Mayo, and by Paul-Gabriel Boucé,[33] a French scholar who has stubbornly refuted the influence of Spanish Golden-Age novels upon British literature.[34] A summa of their arguments was drawn by Peter Wagner, who also proposed to relate Launcelot with the Arthurian Lancelot and with Shakespeare's Hamlet. Wagner's arguments exemplify these scholars' complete unawareness of Cervantes scholarship.

Wagner begins his discussion of *Don Quixote* by noting that, when Ferret describes Launcelot as a modern Don Quixote, 'Launcelot's reply, which can also be read as Smollett's defence of the plot and structure of the novel, has often been ignored: he refutes Ferret's implication that he, Launcelot, is a modern Don Quixote, and explains that he is perfectly sane and intends to fight the "foes of virtue and decorum"'.[35] Nonetheless, Wagner only cites parts of a passage that, read in its whole, shows a completely different picture:

'What! (said Ferret) you set up for a modern Don Quixote? — The scheme is rather too stale and extravagant. — What was an humorous romance, and well-timed satire in Spain, near two hundred years ago, will make but a sorry jest, and appear equally insipid and absurd, when really acted from affectation, at this time a-day, in a country like England.

   The Knight, eying this censor with a look of disdain, replied in a solemn lofty tone: 'He that from affectation imitates the extravagances recorded of Don Quixote, is an impostor equally wicked and contemptible. He that counterfeits madness, unless he dissembles like the elder Brutus, for some virtuous purpose, not only debases his own soul, but acts as a traytor to heave, by denying the divinity that is within him. — I am neither an affected imitator of Don Quixote, nor, as I trust in heaven, visited by that spirit of lunacy so admirably displayed in the fictitious character exhibited by the inimitable Cervantes. I have not yet encountered a windmill for a giant; not mistaken this public house for a magnificent castle. Neither do I believe this gentleman to be the constable; not that worthy practitioner to be master Elizabat, the surgeon recorded in Amadis de Gaul, nor you to be the enchanter Alquife, nor any other sage of history or romance. — I see and distinguish objects as they are discerned and described by other men. I reason without prejudice, can endure contradiction, and, as the company perceives, even bear impertinent censure without passion or resentment. I quarrel with none but the foes of virtue and decorum, against whom I have declared perpetual war, and them I will every where attack as the natural enemies of mankind...' The tone in which these words were pronounced, and the indignation that flashed from the eyes of the speaker, intimidated every individual of the society, and reduced Ferret to a temporary privation of his faculties (p. 50).[36]

Indeed, Launcelot repudiates being associated with Don Quixote; however, as Sarah Wood has noted, 'his overly formal response to Ferret's remarks, delivered "in a solemn lofty tone" and accompanied by "a look of disdain", suggest that his debt to Don Quixote runs deeper than he would care to admit'.[37] Even more so, although Launcelot taxes Don Quixote with being a madman, Launcelot's own speech and gestures are those of a madman, so much that it frightens his interlocutors. In sum, he claims that he is not a Don Quixote because he is not insane, yet his words and gestures attest to his very insanity. To make his point even more incongruent, Wagner recognizes Launcelot's insanity,[38] analysed by several critics.[39] When Wagner argues that 'One of the more important functions madness assumes in *Launcelot Greaves* is that of a mask, a sort of disguise which, ironically, discovers or uncovers social and political reality',[40] he also ignores that this was exactly the same function that Cervantes assigned to Don Quixote's insanity — which he drew from Erasmus's *Praise of Folly* and also applied to *El licenciado Vidriera*.

   From his partial reading of the above passage, Wagner goes on to exaggerate the un-quixotic qualities of Launcelot pointed out by others.[41] Launcelot differs from Don Quixote, Wagner argues, in as much as 'unlike Cervantes's sad, grotesque, deluded and unsuccessful knight, Launcelot is the handsome romantic hero who inspires awe and pity but not laughter'.[42] He also relates Launcelot's lunacy to the Arthurian knight Lancelot and to Hamlet — although in his edition of the novel fourteen notes refer to *Don Quixote*, whereas none refers to the Lancelot story. This leads him to relate *Launcelot Greaves* to Celtic mythology, and to present it as

Smollett's attempt at the melancholic literature of the times. But this hypothesis fails to realize Smollett's perception of *Don Quixote*. Wagner claims that Launcelot's name 'immediately establishes the connection between myth and the eighteenth-century (fictional) reality',[43] but does not realize that *greaves* (which is a piece in an armour) translates into Spanish as *quijote*.[44] His portrayal of a Don Quixote who inspires 'laughter' corresponds to the sixteenth-century perception, not to the second half of the eighteenth century. And it was precisely Smollett, in his 'Life of Cervantes', who did most to overcome the laughable image and to start the romantic perception of a Don Quixote who arose, like Launcelot, 'awe and pity'. This development and change in the reception and understanding of Cervantes and Don Quixote in England was explained by Stuart Taves and A. P. Burton long before Wagner published his study.[45] Also before Wagner, Anthony Close[46] explained the Romanticists' reading of *Don Quixote*. Cervantes scholarship has further explained how Smollett preceded the Romantic perception of *Don Quixote*.[47] Paulson's study of the artistic representations of Don Quixote provided enough evidence to conclude that, as Paulson puts it, 'Smollett's nominal Quixote was Sir Launcelot Greaves [...] a handsome and idealized descendant of the Hogarth–Vanderbank illustrations'.[48] Paulson refers to John Vanderbank's pictures for the 1738 London edition of *Don Quixote* by Tonson, commonly known as Lord Carteret's edition, in which, Paulson points out, the images were 'to idealize, elevate, and dignify the Cervantean action'.[49] In the works of Hogarth and Vanderbank, the Spanish knight is painted as a man in his thirties or even in his late twenties.[50]

The other un-Cervantic elements mentioned by Wagner include: 'The chapter endings are, more often than not, crucial in the maintaining of the reader's interest in that they seem to forebode disaster or simply break off in mid-action like the novels of Dickens',[51] but also like those in *Don Quixote*.[52] Wagner states, 'Smollett introduces incidents and accidents to avoid monotony in longer sections, as in Chapter IV, where Tom Clarke is simply interrupted when his narrative about Launcelot's life risks getting too long'.[53] But so did Cervantes in *Don Quixote*, for example when he interrupts the long story of Anselmo and Lotario by inserting the adventure of the bags of wine. Wagner argues, 'On occasion, Smollett appears as the omniscient author in the manner of Henry Fielding, who was also a great master in the handling of chapter units, opening and closing them with formal and histrionic flourishes',[54] but Fielding borrows this technique from Cervantes.[55] Wagner claims that 'Smollett owes to him [...] also such literary devices as "deus ex machina"',[56] but Fielding takes this device from *Don Quixote*.[57]

All the differences pointed out by Knapp, Niehus, Mayo, Boucé and ultimately Wagner are not relevant enough to detach *Launcelot Greaves* from the Cervantic tradition. Those who take into consideration Smollett's perception of Cervantes will realize that these hypothetical differences are deceptive. *Launcelot Greaves* is much more quixotic than most critics have conjectured — e.g. even Christoph Ehland's thesis that Launcelot is unquixotic owing to his 'anxiety about the sometimes reckless transformation of the British socio-economic system at the threshold of an even more radical transformation: the industrial age',[58] ignores the fact that Cervantes and also the Spanish picaresque novelists used the figure of the squire to illustrate the change in Spain from a feudal and military society to modern times.[59] *Launcelot Greaves* is a satire of English society built upon characters and situations taken from *Don Quixote*. Its quixotic characters (the knight-errant and his squire) and the many situations drawn from Cervantes's novel, in the same vein as all the other imitations of the second half of the eighteenth century, merit the category of quixotic fiction.[60]

Smollett's fifth novel, *The History and Adventures of an Atom*, bears no trace of Cervantes's influence. However, Smollett's last novel, *Humphry Clinker*, is a Cervantean novel. When *Humphry Clinker* was published in 1771, the sentimental romance had been successfully parodied by Charlotte Lennox in *The Female Quixote* (1752), and both Smollett and Fielding had published a number of novels. Even so, Smollett found in *Don Quixote* the main inspiration for his last novel. In *Roderick Random*, he had attempted, successfully, to emulate Cervantes's method of transforming the romance into the novel. In *Humphry Clinker* he accumulated examples of all the contemporary varieties of prose fiction, as Cervantes had done in *Don Quixote*. Smollett's novel exemplifies Bakhtin's theory of the emergence of the novel and the novelization of the romance, according to which the novel emerges, as a new genre, when the romance traditions merge together in one text.[61] Cervantes does so by including the interpolated stories which represent the different variants of the romance. Because in 1771 it was no longer necessary to novelize prose fiction, the concatenation of all the varieties of prose fiction in *Humphry Clinker* is clearly an attempt to emulate the hybrid nature of *Don Quixote*.

Some academics[62] have discussed the intermingling of all the romance traditions in *Don Quixote*, and concluded that these apparently independent parts form an entirety, thus proving that the process of novelization, as theorized by Bakhtin, takes place in Cervantes's masterwork.[63] *Humphry Clinker* is an epistolary novel in which some letters and plots conform to different novel traditions. This novel comprises the following forms of the eighteenth-century English novel: the travel book, the history book, the sentimental novel, the Gothic novel, and the novel of manners.

Smollett did not seek to novelize the romance, because the romance had been overcome in many novels since Fielding; Smollett's only reason to create this literary universe in his novel was to emulate Cervantes, which he had done in *Roderick Random*. Cervantes — the author whom Smollett had translated and of whom he had written a panegyric biography — was the main influence upon his works. In his last novel Smollett once again endeavoured to pay homage to Cervantes by emulating him. And not only did the Scotsman transfuse Cervantes's narrative method of novelization into *Humphry Clinker*, thus creating a Cervantean novel, he also created a quixotic character: Lismahago, a quixotically eccentric character, is first described as 'A tall meagre figure, answering, with his horse, the description of Don Quixote mounted on Rozinante' (p. 222). Later in the novel, 'The lieutenant [Lismahago] charged himself with this commission, and immediately set out a horseback for his lordship's house, attended, at his own request, by my man Archy Macalpine, who had been used to military service; and truly, if Macalpine had been mounted upon an ass, this couple might have passed for the knight of La Mancha and his squire Panza' (p. 322). Like the Spanish knight conjured up with Erasmian folly, Lismahago allows the author to express his satirical views with the excuse that they are uttered by an eccentric man; Lismahago acrimoniously rejects the 1707 Act of Union (pp. 316–17) because it is detrimental to the Scots and only the English will profit from it.

From his passionate translation of *Don Quixote* and his eulogistic 'Life of Cervantes', Smollett developed an overpowering enthusiasm for Cervantes which left a profound mark in most of his novels. *Roderick Random* and *Humphry Clinker* are Cervantean novels in distinct ways and in their own right; while *Sir Launcelot Greaves* is the only imitation of *Don Quixote* by an eighteenth-century author which has stood the test of time.[64] Smollett played an indispensable role in the emergence of the English novel in the eighteenth century; his contribution to the English novel is particularly Cervantean and quixotic. Smollett's novels are, alongside Fielding's, the most Cervantean in British literature.

Notes to Chapter 13

1. Amongst those who consider Smollett an author of picaresque novels are M. A. Goldberg, *Smollett and the Scottish Tradition* (Albuquerque: University of New Mexico Press, 1959); Philip Stevik, 'Smollett's Picaresque Games', in *Tobias Smollett: Bicentennial Essays Presented to Lewis M. Knapp*, ed. by G. S. Rousseau and P. G. Boucé (New York: Oxford University Press, 1971), pp. 111–30; Donald Bruce, *Radical Dr. Smollett* (London: Houghton Mifflin, 1964), p. 167; Jerry C. Beasley, '*Roderick Random*: The Picaresque Transformed', *College Literature*, 5 (1979), 211–20; Alice G. Fredman, 'The Picaresque in Decline: Smollett's First Novel', in *English Writers of the Eighteenth Century*, ed. by John H. Middendorf (New York and London: Columbia University Press, 1971), pp. 189–207; Alexander A. Parker, *Literature and the Delinquent: The Picaresque Novel in Spain and Europe, 1599–1753* (Edinburgh: Edinburgh University Press, 1967); Frederick Monteser, *The Picaresque Element in Western Literature* (University, AL: University of Alabama Press, 1975), p. 51; Richard Bjornson, *The Picaresque Hero in European Fiction* (Madison: University of Wisconsin Press, 1977), p. 244.

2. The first critic to point out the similarities between *Don Quixote* and *Humphry Clinker* was James Fitzmaurice-Kelly, 'Cervantes in England', *Proceedings of the British Academy*, 3 (1905–06), 11–30 (p. 25), noticing the similarities between Don Quixote and Lismahago. After Fitzmaurice-Kelly, Walter Starkie, 'Miguel de Cervantes and the English Novel', *Essays by Diverse Hands*, 34 (1966), 159–79 (p. 171). Clive T. Probyn, *English Fiction of the Eighteenth Century, 1700–1789* (London: Longman, 1987), p. 108, suggested that the melting of genres in *Don Quixote* was later emulated by Smollett in his novels. In a different manner, Pedro Javier Pardo García, 'La otra cara de Cervantes en la novela inglesa del siglo XVIII: *Tom Jones* y *Humphry Clinker*', in *Actas del II Congreso Internacional de la Asociación de Cervantistas*, ed. by Giuseppe Grilli (Naples: Instituto Universitario Orientale, 1995), pp. 839–54, focused on the picaresque and Cervantean elements in Fielding's *Tom Jones* and in *Humphry Clinker*. *Humphry Clinker* was later studied in J. A. G. Ardila, 'Cervantes y la *quixotic fiction*: el hibridismo genérico', *Cervantes*, 21. 2 (2001), 5–26, and in J. A. G. Ardila, 'La novelización del romance: *Humphry Clinker* de Tobias Smollett', in *Cervantes en Inglaterra. El Quijote en los albores de la novela británica* (Liverpool: Liverpool University Press, 2006), pp. 80–101. At the same time of the publication of Ardila's article on *Humphry Clinker* appeared Pilar Rotella, 'Cervantes y Smollett: una relectura de *The Expedition of Humphry Clinker*', in *Actas del IV Congreso Internacional de la Asociación de Cervantistas, Lepanto, 1 / 5 de octubre de 2000*, ed. by Antonio Pablo Bernat Vistarini, 2 vols (Palma: Universidad de las Islas Baleares, 2001), II, 1267–74. The influence of Cervantes upon Smollett's *Roderick Random* was first analysed by Ardila in 'La teoría cervantina de la novela en *Roderick Random*', *Bulletin of Spanish Studies*, 79 (2002), 543–61, and later in J. A. G. Ardila, 'Un ejemplo señero de la *Cervantean fiction*: *Roderick Random* de Tobias Smollett', in *Cervantes en Inglaterra*, pp. 133–55.

The subsequent studies of Cervantes and Smollett include Pedro Javier Pardo García, 'Tobias Smollett's *Humphry Clinker* and the Cervantine Tradition in Eighteenth-Century England', in *Cervantes in the English-Speaking World: New Essays*, ed. by Darío Fernández-Morera and Michael Hanke (Kassel and Barcelona: Edition Reichenberger, 2005), pp. 81–106, and Christoph Ehland, 'Tobias Smollett's Quixotic Adventures', in *Cervantes in the English-Speaking World: New Essays*, pp. 107–26. Pardo's study takes on issues already tackled in Ardila's articles. Ehland's paper examines the combination of picaresque and Cervantean elements in Smollett's works. Pardo does not mention such relevant studies as Walter Reed, 'The Problem of Cervantes in Bakhtin's Poetics', *Cervantes*, 7. 2 (1987), 29–37, and Ardila's findings; Ehland ignores all relevant criticism on the picaresque novel and also the seminal work by Walter Reed, *An Exemplary History of the Novel: The Quixotic versus the Picaresque* (Chicago: Chicago University Press, 1981). For a more detailed discussion of Pardo and Ehland see J. A. G. Ardila's review in *Revista de Literatura*, 68 (2006), 646–50.The Cervantean in Smollett's works has been acknowledged in general studies such as Roland Paulson, *Satire and the Novel in Eighteenth-Century England* (New Haven, CT: Yale University Press, 1967), pp. 167–80; Brean Hammond, 'Mid-Century Quixotism and the Defence of the Novel', *Eighteenth-Century Fiction*, 10. 3 (1998), 247–68 (p. 164); Roland Paulson, *Don Quixote in England: The Aesthetics of Laughter* (Baltimore, MD: Johns Hopkins University Press, 2005), p. 185; and Jean Canavaggio, *Don Quichotte du livre au mythe. Quatre siècles d'errance* (Paris: Fayard, 2005), p. 110.

3. Many critics tried to prove that Smollett's *Don Quixote* was a reworking of Jarvis's. The most detailed study was Carmine Rocco Linsalata, *Smollett's Hoax: Don Quixote in English* (Stanford, CA: Stanford University Press, 1956), who denied Smollett's authorship.

4. Julie C. Hayes, 'Tobias Smollett and the Translations of the *Quijote*', *Huntington Library Quarterly*, 67. 4 (2001), 651–68; Martin Battestin, 'The Authorship of Smollett's Don Quixote', *Studies in Bibliography*, 50 (1997), 295–312; Martin Battestin, 'Introduction', in Miguel de Cervantes, *The History and Adventures of the Renowned Don Quixote*, trans. by Tobias Smollett (Athens, GA: University of Georgia Press, 2003), pp. 11–42.

5. Carlos Fuentes, 'Introduction', in Miguel de Cervantes, *The History and Adventures of the Renowned Don Quixote* (New York: Random House, 2001), pp. vii–xxvii. Anthony Pym has also extolled the style of this translation in 'The Translator as Author: Two Quixotes', *Translation and Literature*, 14. 1 (2005), 71–81.

6. The biography by Smollett has been praised by A. P. Burton, 'Cervantes the Man Seen Through English Eyes in the Seventeenth and Eighteenth Centuries', *Bulletin of Hispanic Studies*, 45 (1968), 1–15 (p. 11), and J. A. G. Ardila, 'Traducción y recepción del *Quijote* en los siglos XVII y XVIII', in *Cervantes en Inglaterra*, pp. 32–48 (pp. 40–41).

7. Tobias Smollett, 'The Life of Cervantes', in *The History and Adventures of the Renowned Don Quixote* (New York: Random House, 2001), p. 19.

8. Cf. Burton, 'Cervantes the Man Seen Through English Eyes in the Seventeenth and Eighteenth Centuries'; Susan Staves, '*Don Quixote* in Eighteenth-Century England', *Comparative Literature*, 24 (1972), 193–215; J. A. G. Ardila, 'Traducción y recepción del *Quijote* en Gran Bretaña, 1612–1776', *Anales Cervantinos*, 37 (2005), 253–65; José Manuel Lucía Megías, *Leer el Quijote en imágenes. Hacia una teoría de los modelos iconográficos* (Madrid: Calambur, 2006).

9. Edgar Allison Peers, 'Cervantes in England', *Bulletin of Spanish Studies*, 25 (1947), 226–38.

10. Lewis Knapp, *Tobias Smollett: Doctor of Men and Manners* (New York: Russell & Russell, 1963), pp. 93–108. Knapp noticed that in a letter dated 7 June 1748, Smollett mentioned that he had agreed with the editors to translate *Don Quixote*, and that on 21 November 1748, the *General Advertiser* confirmed this.

11. J. A. G. Ardila, 'Intertextualidad general y restringida en el *Don Quixote* de Smollett', *Anuario de Estudios Filológicos*, 25 (2002), 137–51; J. A. G. Ardila, 'Un ejemplo señero de la *Cervantean fiction*:', in *Cervantes en Inglaterra*, pp. 140–43.

12. All subsequent references to *Roderick Random* are taken from the Penguin Classics edition (Harmondsworth, 1995).

13. Cf. Monteser, *The Picaresque Element in Western Literature*, p. 52; Alexander Blackburn, *The Myth of the Picaro* (Chapel Hill: University of North Carolina Press, 1979), p. 118.

14. Until the publication of Ardila, 'La teoría cervantina de la novela en *Roderick Random*'.

15. See Ardila, 'La teoría cervantina de la novela en *Roderick Random*', pp. 143–48.
16. Most notably Gérard Genette, *La littérature au second degree* (Paris: Seuil, 1982). For the English novel see Michael McKeon, *The Origins of the English Novel 1600–1740* (London and Baltimore: Johns Hopkins University Press, 1987), pp. 25–64; for the Spanish novel see Edward C. Riley, 'Cervantes: Una cuestión de género', in *El Quijote*, ed. by George Haley (Madrid: Taurus, 1980), pp. 37–51.
17. On Marcela's speech see T. Hart and S. Rendall, 'Rhetoric and Persuasion in Marcela's Address to the Shepherds', *Hispanic Review*, 46 (1978), 287–98. On the interpolated stories in *Don Quixote* see Stanislav Zimic, *Los cuentos y las novelas del Quijote* (Madrid and Frankfurt: Iberoamericana and Vervuert, 1998).
18. Cf. Howard Mancing, *The Cervantes Encyclopedia* (Westport and London: Greenwood Press, 2004), p. 629.
19. Hammond has even considered Roderick–Strap as a Quixote–Sancho pair. Ardila, 'Un ejemplo señero de la *Cervantean fiction*', in *Cervantes in Inglaterra*, p. 150, does not consider Roderick a Quixote since he does not suffer any form of dementia nor behave in an eccentric manner.
20. For a complete list of examples see Ardila, 'Un ejemplo señero de la *Cervantean fiction*', pp. 150–53.
21. Apud Ronald Paulson, 'The Pilgrimage and the Family: Structures in the Novels of Fielding and Smollett', in *Tobias Smollett. Bicentennial Essays Presented to Lewis M. Knapp*, ed. by G. S. Rousseau and P. G. Boucé (New York: Oxford University Press, 1971), pp. 57–78; Ardila, 'Un ejemplo señero de la *Cervantean fiction*', p. 153.
22. Cf. Melvyn New, 'Editor's Introduction', in Laurence Sterne, *The Life and Opinions of Tristram Shandy, Gentleman* (Harmondsworth: Penguin, 1997), pp. xxvii–xli.
23. Hammond (p. 264) has suggested that the comical low incidents are Cervantic. Knowles, 'Cervantes and English Literature', presented Hawser Trunnion as a 'quixotic eccentric' (p. 294). R. K. Britton, 'Don Quixote's Fourth Sally: Cervantes and the Eighteenth-Century English Novel', *New Comparison*, 15 (1993), 21–32, indicates that 'in both *Joseph Andrews* and *Tom Jones* [Fielding] adopts some typically Cervantine methods' (p. 28), and that 'In *Tom Jones*, Fielding observed that in an history of the kind he was writing, time was like a continuous line along which the author could move either backwards or forwards at will' (p. 31).
24. All references to *Peregrine Pickle* are taken from James L. Clifford's edition for Oxford University Press (Oxford, 1983).
25. Apud Ardila, 'Cervantes y la *quixotic fiction*: el hibridismo genérico', p. 17.
26. Cf. Ardila, 'Textos y contextos de la novela picaresca, 1554–1753', unpublished doctoral thesis, Universidad Autónoma de Madrid, 2005.
27. The most recent discussions of the picaresque novel as a genre can be found in Florencio Sevilla, 'Presentación', *La novela picaresca española* (Madrid: Castalia, 2001) and in J. A. G. Ardila, *El género picaresco en la crítica literaria* (Madrid: Biblioteca Nueva, 2008).
28. Miriam Rossiter Small '*The Female Quixote* and Other Quixotic Imitations of the Eighteenth Century', *Charlotte Ramsey Lennox: An Eighteenth-Century Lady of Letters* (New Haven, CT: Yale University Press, 1935), pp. 64–117 (p. 97).
29. Knowles, 'Cervantes and English Literature', p. 294.
30. Apud Canavaggio, *Don Quichotte du livre au mythe*.
31. Vide David Evan, 'Introduction', in Tobias Smollett, *The Life and Adventures of Sir Launcelot Greaves* (Oxford: Oxford University Press, 1973), p. x; Robert Giddings, *The Tradition of Smollett* (London: Methuen, 1967), p. 136; Milton A. Goldberg, *Smollett and the Scottish School: Studies in Eighteenth-Century Thought* (Albuquerque: University of New Mexico Press, 1959), p. 108; Robert D. Spector, *Tobias George Smollett* (New York: Twayne Publishers, 1968).
32. James Beattie, 'An Essay on Laughter and Ludicrous Composition', in *Essays* (Edinburgh: Creech, 1776), pp. 581–705 (p. 605).
33. Lewis Knapp, *Tobias Smollett, Doctor of Men and Manners* (Princeton, NJ: Princeton University Press, 1949); Robert D. Mayo, *The English Novel in the Magazines, 1740–1815* (Oxford: Oxford University Press, 1962); Paul-Gabriel Boucé, *The Novels of Tobias Smollett* (London: Longman, 1976).
34. And he has done so while ignoring all research published in Spanish.

35. Peter Wagner, 'Introduction', in Tobias Smollett, *The Life and Adventures of Sir Launcelot Greaves* (Harmondsworth: Penguin, 1988), pp. 7–28 (p. 9).

36. All references to *Launcelot Greaves* are taken from the Penguin Classics edition (Harmondsworth, 1988).

37. Sarah F. Wood, *Quixotic Fictions of the USA, 1792–1815* (Oxford: Oxford University Press, 2005), p. 20.

38. Wagner, 'Introduction', p. 13: 'it may be rewarding to explore Launcelot's lunacy'.

39. Boucé, *The Novels of Tobias Smollett*, pp. 175–86; Max Byrd, *Visits to Bedlam: Madness and Literature in the Eighteenth Century* (Columbia: University of South Carolina Press, 1974), p. 133; Paul F. Saagpakk, 'A Survey of Psychopathology in British Literature from Shakespeare to Hardy', *Literature and Psychology*, 18 (1968), 135–65 (p. 148); Denise Bulckaen-Messina, 'Symptomes cliniques de la folie dans les romans de Smollett', in *Folie, folies, folly dans le monde anglo-américain aux xviie et xviiie siècles* (Aix-en-Provence: Presses universitaires de Provence, 1984), pp. 43–55 (p. 43).

40. Wagner, 'Introduction', p. 13.

41. Namely by Paul-Gabriel Boucé, *The Novels of Tobias Smollett*, pp. 93–96, and Edward L. Niehus, 'Quixotic Figures in the Novels of Smollett', *Durham University Journal*, 71 (1978–79), 233–43 (p. 238).

42. Wagner, 'Introduction', p. 13.

43. Wagner, 'Introduction', p. 14.

44. This was pointed out by Harry Levin, 'The Quixotic Principle: Cervantes and other Novelists', *Harvard English Studies*, 1 (1970), 45–66.

45. Stuart M. Tave, *The Amiable Humorist: A Study in the Comic Theory and Criticism of the Eighteenth and Early Nineteenth Centuries* (Chicago: University of Chicago Press, 1960); A. P. Burton, 'Cervantes the Man Seen Through English Eyes in the Seventeenth and Eighteenth Centuries'.

46. Anthony J. Close, *The Romantic Approach to 'Don Quixote': A Critical History of the Romantic Tradition in 'Quixote' Criticism* (Cambridge: Cambridge University Press, 1978).

47. Ardila, 'Traducción y recepción del *Quixote* en los siglos XVII y XVIII', pp. 40–45.

48. Paulson, *Don Quixote in England*, p. 185.

49. Paulson, *Don Quixote in England*, p. 49.

50. The most recent study of the artistic representations of Don Quixote is José Manuel Lucía Megías, *Leer el Quijote en imágenes. Hacia una teoría de los modelos iconográficos* (Madrid: Calambur, 2006), pp. 315–70 for Vanderbank and the English artists. The largest collection of Don Quixote's pictures is available in www.qbi2005.com, edited by José Manuel Lucía Megías.

51. Wagner, 'Introduction', p. 11.

52. As proved in J. A. G. Ardila, 'Cervantes y la *quixotic fiction*: sucesión episódica y otros recursos narrativos', *Cervantes*, 21. 1 (2001), 43–65; J. A. G. Ardila, 'La horma narratológica: *Tom Jones* de Henry Fielding', in *Cervantes en Inglaterra*, p. 49–79.

53. Wagner, 'Introduction', p. 11.

54. Wagner, 'Introduction', p. 11.

55. Cf. Ardila, 'La horma narratológica: *Tom Jones* de Henry Fielding'.

56. Wagner, 'Introduction', p. 12.

57. Cf. Ardila, 'La horma narratológica: *Tom Jones* de Henry Fielding'.

58. Ehland, 'Tobias Smollett's Quixotic Adventures', p. 123.

59. Cf. Antonio Rey Hazas, 'El *Quijote* y la picaresca: la figura del hidalgo en el nacimiento de la novela moderna', *Edad de Oro*, 15 (1996), 141–60.

60. After Wagner, Kenneth Simpson, 'The Importance of Tobias Smollett', in *The History of Scottish Literature: Volume 2, 1660–1800*, ed. by Andrew Hook (Aberdeen: Aberdeen University Press, 1989), pp. 101–21, regretted the unimpressive quality of *Launcelot Greaves*.

61. See the following studies by M. Bakhtin: *Esthétique et théorie du roman* (Paris: Gallimard, 1978); *The Dialogic Imagination: Four Essays* (Austin: University of Texas Press, 1981); *Problems of Dostoevsky's Poetics* (Minneapolis: University of Minnesota Press, 1984); *Rabelais and his World* (Bloomington: Indiana University Press, 1984); *Speech Genres and Other Late Essays* (Austin: University of Texas Press, 1986).

62. Zimic, *Los cuentos y las novelas del Quijote*, p. 35; Bruce Wardropper, 'Don Quijote: ¿ficción o historia?', in *El Quijote*, ed. by George Haley, pp. 237–52 (p. 252); Michel Moner, 'Cervantes y la "invención de la novela": estado de la cuestión', in *La invención de la novela*, ed. by Jean Canavaggio (Madrid: Casa de Velázquez, 1999), pp. 233–67 (p. 249). For the novelization of the romance in Cervantes and how Smollett emulated Cervantes's technique see Ardila, 'Cervantes y la *quixotic fiction*: el hibridismo genérico'; Ardila, 'La *novelización* del romance: *Humphry Clinker* de Tobias Smollett'.

63. Asunción Rallo Gruss, 'Montemayor, entre *romance* y novela: hibridismo de géneros y experimentación narrativa en *La Diana*', in *La invención de la novela*, pp. 129–57, has argued that the novelization was attained before Cervantes in the pastoral novels by Spanish and Portuguese authors *Florisel de Niquea* (1551), *Menina e moça* (1554), *Los amores de Clareo y Florisea* (1552), and *Los siete libros de la Diana* (1559?).

64. All other authors of quixotic fictions have been largely forgotten, with the sole exception, perhaps, of *The Female Quixote*. Jane Austen's *Northanger Abbey* must be regarded as a Cervantean novel, as proved by J. A. G. Ardila, 'Cervantes y la quixotic fiction: la parodia de géneros', *Anales Cervantinos*, 34 (1998), 145–68, and J. A. G. Ardila, 'La parodia de géneros: *The Female Quixote* de Charlotte Lennox y *Northanger Abbey* de Jane Austen', in *Cervantes en Inglaterra*, pp. 102–32.

CHAPTER 14

Feminine Transformations of the *Quixote* in Eighteenth-Century England: Lennox's *Female Quixote* and Her Sisters

Amy J. Pawl

The appearance in 1752 of Charlotte Lennox's *Female Quixote* brought a new figure to the attention of the English reading public: the female literary Quixote. This figure was to persist over the next half century, emerging recognizably from works such as George Colman's *Polly Honeycombe*, Maria Edgeworth's 'Angelina', Jane Austen's *Northanger Abbey*, Tabitha Tenney's *Female Quixotism*, and Eaton Barrett's *The Heroine*. The female Quixote, as presented by Lennox, has much in common with the male Quixote: her delusions, like Alonso Quixano's, arise from her reading; her attempts to interpret the world in terms of her literary models make her both ridiculous and noble; and her kind, generous nature makes her beloved despite her follies. Thus far, she might be a Quixote of either sex. There are, however, special difficulties involved in being a female Quixote in a society that limits a woman's access to mobility, autonomy, and self-determination. One of the tasks of this essay will be to demonstrate the surprising ways in which Lennox and other authors overcome these difficulties to create female Quixotes who become vehicles for fantasies of female power and importance. Its other task will be to set these successes in context by examining the ways in which female power is redirected, corrected, or undercut by characters who attempt the heroines' seduction or reform.

Charlotte Lennox's Quixote is, like Cervantes's, above all a devoted reader. The daughter of a wealthy and reclusive Marquis, Arabella immerses herself in her deceased mother's books, mostly French romances which have been placed in her father's library and upon which she forms her ideas of the world.[1] Arabella's father dies soon after the novel opens, having lived just long enough to approve Arabella's cousin, Mr. Glanville, as her suitor. Arabella, unsurprisingly, finds paternal fiat to be an insufficiently romantic way of proceeding, expecting rather that a lover of hers should 'purchase her with his Sword from a Croud of Rivals; and arrive to the Possession of her Heart by many Years of Services and Fidelity' (p. 27). The rest of the book focuses on this impasse, pitting Arabella's desire to live the life of a heroine against the desire of Mr. Glanville (and his father) to see her restored to reason. As Arabella is independently wealthy, highly intelligent, and convinced of the historical truth of the romances she has read, reforming her is no easy task. A Quixote armed with quotations is a formidable opponent, as Don Quixote's priest and barber well knew.

Both Arabella and Don Quixote govern their lives according to literary precedent. When Sancho Panza attempts to challenge the wisdom of Don Quixote's vow to lead an ascetic life until he wins himself a new helmet, Don Quixote insists, 'I know very well what precedent I am following', thus justifying himself in his own eyes.[2] Similarly, Arabella, when she receives her first love letter (from a secret admirer), 'search[es] the Records of her Memory for a Precedent', but 'not finding, that any Lady ever opened a Letter from an unknown Lover' (p. 13), she orders the letter returned. Time and again, Don Quixote and Arabella attempt to match their actions to those of their literary heroes and heroines, often citing verse and chapter in their own justification. In addition, they both employ literary precedents in an effort to understand the world and to explain or predict the actions of those around them. Their notions of probability are based on their reading. Both, for example, find it impossible to imagine that a hero would be subject to the laws of his country, simply because such an occurrence has never appeared in their reading. 'Where have you ever heard or read of a knight errant being brought before a judge, however many homicides he may have committed?' (p. 80) asks the knight rhetorically. Arabella concurs: 'The law has no Power over Heroes; they may kill as many Men as they please, without being called to any Account for it' (p. 128).

Most importantly, perhaps, both Quixotes use literary precedent as a mechanism to protect their illusions. Much of the pleasure of both books, indeed, comes from observing the ingenuity with which the protagonists sift and twist their literary sources in order to come up with an explanation that accommodates their romantic vision and prevents reality from obtruding itself upon their notice. Don Quixote, as his delusions are more extreme than Arabella's (she may be wrong about a person's motives or status, but she does not go so far as to mistake sheep for soldiers, or windmills for giants), needs a more powerful mechanism to protect them, which he finds in the ever-present actions of his evil enchanter, whose envy leads him to change people's faces and forms. Arabella, for her part, must rely on ever subtler applications of her reading. When she sends the unopened missive back to her secret admirer, Arabella expects to learn 'that the Return of his Letter would make her Lover commit some very extravagant Actions' (p. 14), and she quizzes her maid Lucy, the messenger, for a description. Lucy answers (accurately, as the reader knows) that Mr. Hervey, the unknown lover, had kissed the letter several times, because he thought it contained an answer from Arabella. Arabella shows her creative reading ability in the following response: 'Foolish Wench! [...] How can you imagine he had the Temerity to think I should answer his Letter? A Favour, which, though he had spent Years in my Service, would have been infinitely greater than he could have expected. No, Lucy, he kissed the Letter, either because he thought it had been touched at least by my Hands, or to shew the perfect Submission with which he received my Commands' (p. 15). Thus far Arabella has succeeded in making life conform to romance, but when she expresses aloud her fear (or hope) that the despairing lover will 'commit some desperate Outrage against himself' she receives a new hermeneutic challenge in Lucy's unwelcome assurance that 'There is no Fear [...] that he will do himself a Mischief; for when he discovered his Mistake, he laughed heartily' (p. 15). This is harder to explain away, but Arabella rises to the occasion, and though it takes her 'a little Time to consider of so strange a Phaenomenon', she insists that 'he laughed because his Reason was disturbed at the sudden Shock he received' (p. 15).

At least this episode involved a real love letter; a later incident in Bath poses a greater threat to Arabella's romantic expectations, as she receives not one but two letters that explicitly deny the 'crime' of which she has accused the authors, that of being in love with her. As Arabella believes that 'all Letters directed to me must contain Matters of Love and Gallantry' (p. 293) she expects to find declarations of love enclosed. Her surprise and chagrin are evident when her cousin, Miss Glanville, snatches the first letter and reads it aloud, noting with some malice that 'Mr. Selvin utterly denies the Crime of loving you' (p. 295). But once again, Arabella is saved by literary precedent. Her 'Spirits [...] rais'd by recollecting an Adventure in her Romance, similar to this' (p. 295), Arabella cites the example of 'Seramenes; who being in Love with the beautiful Cleobuline, Princess of Corinth, took all imaginable Pains to conceal his Passion, in order to be near that fair Princess', concluding, 'In these Cases therefore, the more resolutely a Man denies his Passion, the more pure and violent it is' (p. 295). As a strategy, this is brilliant; by invoking the double-bind of love, in which a lover's silence or denial is as revealing as a declaration, Arabella has ensured that she won't encounter disappointment or enlightenment. Rather like Freud's Dora, Arabella's presumed suitors have no way to say no.

But Arabella and Don Quixote do more than simply live according to the rules of their literary predecessors; they expect to be immortalized among them. Blended with concern for their present reputations is the assurance that their deeds, thoughts, and words will be preserved as models for later generations. Don Quixote's expectations in this regard are playfully validated by the author, who gives his character the satisfaction of knowing (in Part II of *Don Quixote*) that his earlier adventures have already been recorded. In an imaginative bit of literary frame-breaking that anticipates more postmodern pleasures, Cervantes proceeds to introduce characters within the narrative who have read Part I of *Don Quixote*, and who react to the knight and his squire accordingly. Don Quixote's 'fame' is thus definitively established within the text, though its nature is not what Don Quixote himself might wish.

Arabella is no less desirous of present and future fame. Her concern upon one occasion that her kindness to her cousin and suitor Mr. Glanville might be construed as 'an Indulgence, for which I may haply be blamed in After-ages' (p. 111) is less important as an expression of anxiety than as the expression of her confidence that readers in 'After-ages' will be eagerly scrutinizing the text of her life. When her surprised confidante asks Arabella how her story will be transmitted, and whether she herself plans to write it, Arabella replies calmly: 'I shall not write it [...] tho', questionless, it will be written after my death' (p. 110). Arabella's most violent action, and the one that puts an end to her career as a heroine, also underscores her commitment to futurity. Believing that she sees several would-be ravishers approaching on horseback, she attempts to imitate the virtuous heroines of antiquity by hurling herself into a river (the Thames, in her case) in order to preserve her virtue.

If Arabella and Don Quixote see their beloved romances as sources of power and inspiration, those around them agree — but draw very different conclusions about the matter. Arabella's father and her suitor Mr. Glanville resemble the priest, the barber, the niece and the housekeeper in *Don Quixote*: all tacitly attest to the power of romance by believing that destruction of the books might be enough to liberate the affected Quixote from their influence. In a scene that directly echoes the great book-burning in *Don Quixote*, Arabella's father exclaims, 'These foolish books [...] have turned her Brain! Where are they? [...] I'll burn all I can lay my Hands upon' (p. 55). But while Mr. Glanville is capable of 'cursing Statira and Orontes a thousand times, and loading the Authors of those books with all the Imprecations his Rage could suggest' (p. 52), he realizes that he can make a virtue of interceding on this occasion, and so persuades the enraged Marquis to allow him to return Arabella's books to her unharmed.

The real danger to the literary Quixote, however, lies not with those who dismiss or fear the literature of romance, but with those whose knowledge of it allows them to co-opt its power. While both Don Quixote and Arabella are capable of an eloquent defence when their beliefs are challenged, they are comparatively defenceless when their predilections appear to be shared. Arabella is taken in by the fine language and romantic gestures of her neighbour and would-be suitor, Sir George. A reader of romances himself, he can suit his style to her expectations, pleasing her with his judicious and elegantly phrased observations on love and beauty. So extreme is his language that her cousins assume he is in jest; Arabella, on the other hand, finds that he 'speak[s] very rationally upon these Matters' (p. 144). His interpolated life's history, told to the assembled company on a rainy evening, is taken literally by Arabella, who easily credits his claim to be a dispossessed prince capable of killing five hundred men in armed combat. But like the manipulative Duke and Duchess in the second part of *Don Quixote*, Sir George is more adept at imitating form than at understanding content. His story contains, for him, a fatal flaw — he has unintentionally proven himself to be a faithless lover, and Arabella considers him by rights the property of another woman, the beautiful Philonice of his own invention. He has failed to appreciate the sincerity and rigour of Arabella's belief system, which requires eternal constancy, not merely 'several Years' (p. 250) spent lamenting the loss of an abducted lady.

Sir George's actions here do resemble in a number of ways those of the Duke and Duchess in *Don Quixote*. Like Sir George, they go to great lengths to stage scenes for their Quixote, employing and costuming numerous other persons; like Sir George, they are selfishly motivated. Perhaps most importantly of all, like Sir George, the Duke and the Duchess have usurped the Quixote's privilege of creating his or her own visions. The enchanted Dulcinea, the case of the bearded lady-in-waiting, the episode of the lady dead of love and revived — all are assaults on the agency of the Quixote; they are asking him to play to their script. Both Don Quixote and Arabella are vulnerable to assaults of this kind, as these and other episodes like them show. But unlike Quixotes we will see later in the eighteenth century, both Arabella and the Don maintain their dignity by refusing to compromise their beliefs. Ridiculous as their actions may be, they cannot be tricked into revealing a single self-interested, petty, or sordid motivation for them — which is more than can be said for their persecutors.

This laudable consistency and nobility of character is perhaps the most important similarity between Arabella and Don Quixote. The belief system that has evolved from their romance reading is expressed in a highly admirable personal character. The old knight and the young lady are reliably generous, noble, and honourable. Appeals to their generosity are certain to succeed; attempts at intimidation likely to fail. Both are eager to relieve distress in others, no matter what class of person they encounter. In fact, class confusion is another distinctive trait in both novels: Arabella mistakes jockeys at a race course for 'Persons of great distinction' (p. 84), Don Quixote mistakes innkeepers for castellans, and both mistake prostitutes for highborn ladies. The Quixote's gaze, while imperfect, is always charitable in its effects.

The nobility of their respective Quixotes' characters brings us to a larger structural similarity between *Don Quixote* and the *Female Quixote*: the identically vexed relationship in both texts between parody and satire. Both books begin by mocking a literary genre, chivalric romance, through the creation of a character who exemplifies (and exaggerates, where possible) the salient traits of the genre. But each work rapidly reveals that it has an equal if not greater investment in satire, as the 'real world' of the text is paraded before the reader and made to look petty, foolish, and even grotesque, especially as seen through the virtuous and defamiliarizing eye of the Quixote. The satiric force of Don Quixote had long been appreciated by the eighteenth century, and it was often seen primarily as a satiric work. In her imitation, Lennox seems to enjoy preserving this aspect of the original. But the very straightforwardness of the satire complicates the position of the Quixote as its vehicle. By using the virtues promulgated by the romance genre as a way to castigate the failings of the real world, the authors have given legitimacy to their Quixotes' views, which are presumably themselves the target of authorial mockery. As parody and satire collide, the reader may be forgiven for being confused. The result in both cases is the ambiguity for which Don Quixote has long been famous: a central character who is either a lunatic, a hero, or both.

Similar as they are, however, Don Quixote and Arabella are crucially distinguished as the result of their difference in gender. Henry Fielding, writing in the *Covent Garden Journal* in the year of *The Female Quixote*'s publication, points to sexual difference to explain Cervantes's advantage over Lennox. The difference reduces to kinds of action: men 'perform', while women 'provoke' and 'admire'. Obviously, the stories written to accommodate these verbs will be very different ones, and it is important to note that the distinction is not invented by Fielding, but sustained by the sources. Arabella, after all, does not want to be a female knight. She wants to be a lady out of romance.

One of the first problems faces by a female Quixote who is determined to be ladylike is finding any adventures at all. The peripeteia of a male Quixote is out of her reach: Arabella simply can't traipse all over the countryside, as Don Quixote and Sancho Panza do. One of Arabella's solutions is to imagine an enforced and therefore feminine type of mobility, in which confinement and abduction are the keys to adventure and the world. Abduction, because it leaves the woman's consent out of the question, is, oddly enough, the most respectable way to leave home. Arabella makes use of this strategy throughout the novel. She is continually imagining herself to be the target of abduction plots or rape attempts. This delusion gives her the opportunity not to act, which would be unfeminine, but to react, which allows her to remain true to her romance models while still generating adventures. Thus her suspicion that Edward the gardener (a nobleman in disguise, she believes) is about to break into her house to carry her off allows her to flee from her home into the surrounding countryside at nightfall, an event which invites further incidents. Another kind of action seemingly closed to Arabella because of her sex is the purely physical. Not only will she never lift a lance, she will never even be on the receiving end of physical violence. The kind of sadistic abuse visited upon Don Quixote and Sancho Panza has no parallel in Lennox's novel. While Don Quixote is often surrounded by spectators who jeer and cheer as he is pummelled, bloodied, and humiliated, Arabella is almost never aware of even the mildest derision of those around her. Her creator, interestingly, protects her from the consequences of her follies.

While Cervantes's hero falls short of the physical ideal in many ways, Lennox cannot afford to let her heroine do so. In a sense this makes Lennox's undertaking much more conservative than Cervantes's, but the terms of comparison are not equal. Because of the difference of gender, different standards apply. While a male might be allowed to overcome an unfortunate appearance by virtue of a noble soul, a female's identity has historically been too closely tied to her appearance and to her body for this to be possible. If Lennox wants her heroine to be taken seriously at all, she must preserve her beauty. Over fifty years later, Jane Austen comments on the unfair but potent effect of appearance when she describes the 'large fat sighings' of an amply-proportioned matron over the memory of her deceased son.[3] As we will see, female Quixotes whose appearance is ridiculed do not succeed in sustaining any readerly respect. In endowing Arabella with beauty and a graceful set of limbs, Lennox has, perhaps wisely, avoided the unbecoming conjunction of romance ideals and a plain female face.

Arabella's power, however, does not stop with her beauty. Despite the restrictions on her action dictated by romance form and discussed above, Arabella's romances and her romance delusions are indeed sites of female power.[4] To begin with, Arabella concentrates on the actions — whether large or small — that are available to her literary heroines. While a lady of romance may seem passive in comparison to her bold and venturesome knight, it turns out that she can command others with nothing more than a slight gesture of her hand. These small actions are made much of in the novel, as those around Arabella learn to read and respond to her 'dumb signs' (p. 36). Even larger actions, if undertaken in self-defence, are also permissible, such as Clelia's heroic swimming of the Tiber.

But perhaps more potent than her actions are the romance heroine's words. Arabella is a firm believer in their efficacy: with her words a heroine can command a lover to live or die, banish him from the country, or allow him to hope. At various points in the novel, Arabella acts on these beliefs. When Mr. Glanville is sick (of love, she presumes), she commands him to recover. And when offended at what she sees as Mr. Selvin's presumption, she banishes him from England, much to his surprise. In short, Arabella has taken literally the conventions of courtly romance, a form attractive to women precisely because it seems to place them in a position of importance. Arabella repeatedly refers to women as 'that Sex which merits all your Admiration and Reverence' (p. 107), and men are expected to show 'obedience' to her and 'submission' to her commands. Viewed from this angle, it is no wonder that romance is appealing — it seems to depict a utopian gynocracy.

These, then, are Arabella's assumptions. Arabella's success is evident on two levels. Interpersonally and socially, she is in control: her uncle and cousin continually seek to accommodate her. Arabella's power is in an important sense negated by her reform at the end of the novel. The reform brackets her power, finally disavowing it. Arabella's repudiation of her romance delusions, like Don Quixote's, is made from a sick bed; but unlike Don Quixote, Arabella recovers, and marries. By giving her heroine a conventionally happy ending, a romance ending in fact, Lennox does a great deal to discredit the subversive powers Arabella has embodied. They were not, it seems, so important after all, if she can give them up and still live. Don Quixote, in contrast, has the advantage here: death lends an unmistakable éclat to his reform; the loss of his romance ideals is nearly coterminous with the loss of his life and character.

The female Quixotes who follow Arabella are in one important respect a new breed: they are reading not antique romances but the latest and most popular of literary genres — the novel. George Colman's *Polly Honeycombe*, a comic play subtitled 'A Dramatick Novel of One Act', draws attention to this shift in taste on the part of the reading public.[5] The genealogy Colman establishes is clear. The novel, while not identical to the romance, is closely related. Lennox's audience was no doubt easily able to extend her satire of the misguided romance reader to include novel readers as well. Because the novel's 'drift [is] the same', the novel-reading Quixote has much in common with the romance-reading Quixote. Both expect adventures, admirers, coincidences, noble or sentimental friendships, and a happy ending. But the novel-reading Quixote must adhere to the new standards of realism that her genre embraces: she must not expect her heroes to mow down their enemies by the hundreds, and if she is abducted (which is still likely), it will be by an ordinary baronet and not a prince or a giant. The verisimilar is now valued above the marvellous by readers, as many contemporary writers were to note.[6]

The female Quixotes that populate the second half of the eighteenth and early part of the nineteenth century are amusing and in some ways heterogeneous. Colman's *Polly Honeycombe* (1760) presents a stage version of the Quixote, a merchant's daughter whose novel-reading makes her reject the prosperous and pompous Mr. Ledger, a suitor proposed by her father, in favour of the poetically inclined Mr. Scribble. The tone of the play is light and the moral inconclusive: the irrepressible Polly escapes marriage altogether, her father is thrown into impotent confusion, and the play concludes with an ironic encomium on the virtues of novels. Maria Edgeworth's novella 'Angelina' (1801) targets the sentimental novel specifically, and is unique in focusing on the heroine's desire for a female friend. Having been begun a correspondence with 'Araminta', the author of a popular novel, Angelina is persuaded to run away to 'Angelina's Bower', a rustic cottage whose picturesque charms are soon discovered to be no compensation for 'the want of double refined sugar, of green tea, and Mocha coffee'.[7] The want of refinement in Araminta, however, turns out to be a greater obstacle to the consummation of their sentimental friendship, and Angelina returns home chastened, under the care of a female relative who advises her to read *The Female Quixote*. Jane Austen's *Northanger Abbey* (in manuscript form by the 1790s), as the title suggests, pokes fun at the Gothic novels that were all the rage in the closing decade of the century. Since such works were essentially novels of sentiment repackaged to include Gothic architecture and wild natural scenery, the conventions Austen ridicules are more broadly those of her sentimental predecessors. Her heroine, Catherine Morland, is intentionally constructed to undo what Austen saw as the artificial and unnatural virtues of a novel heroine: Catherine is not particularly pretty, she does not excel in the usual feminine accomplishments, such as painting and piano-playing, and she does not write sonnets. But despite her imperfections and her penchant for the writings of Ann Radcliffe, Catherine does have a kind heart and a good nature, and her creator rewards her with that most conventional of romantic endings, marriage to the worthy hero.

Although Cherubina, in Eaton Stannard Barrett's *The Heroine* (1813), is married off happily at the end of the novel, her adventures with fortune-hunters and other characters real and unreal have been extremely prejudicial to her character and dignity. In addition, they have also had serious negative consequences for innocent bystanders: it is with Cherubina's approval that her father is incarcerated in a madhouse, for example. The heroines' names are further symptomatic of the authors' attitudes. While Arabella and Angelina have elegant ones which indicate that the characters are, at least on one level, suited to being heroines, Cherubina has invented her own name, rejecting the unromantic plainness of Dorcas Sheldon; the result is that the reader is reminded of the heroines' absurdity and pretension several times per paragraph, or as often as the names appear.

All the female Quixotes after Arabella share the basic quixotic traits: their excessive reading has skewed their perceptions and expectations of the world. But with the exception of Catherine Morland in *Northanger Abbey*, I believe that these Quixotes are presented as being both more culpable and more vulnerable than Arabella. In general, the effects of their wilful misreadings are messier and more compromising to heroinely dignity. One figure in particular seems to sum up the new danger to the novel-reading Quixote: the lower-class, silver-tongued fortune hunter, who serves as the focus for social and authorial anxieties that were carefully separated in *The Female Quixote*. Class confusion, the self-serving manipulation of the language of romance, and the heroine's own sexual vulnerability are all treated in Lennox's novel, but they do not converge significantly. Edward is a gardener, not a prince — but since he has never tried, by any speech or action, to convince Arabella otherwise, the confusion over rank is all on her side and poses little threat.

Sir George, who does try to manipulate Arabella by speaking in the language of her books, is well and truly upper class himself. And finally, if as some critics have suggested, Arabella is secretly attracted to Edward or others of the suitors she invents, her strict romance code requires her to expect twenty years of courtship before she grants so much as a kiss — so her virtue is never really in danger. In contrast, almost all of the other heroines come very close to marrying a lower-class impostor, whose talent is for romantic speech and whose near-success indicts the heroine by providing evidence of her unruly desires. Polly Honeycombe attempts to run off with the eloquent Mr. Scribble, who turns out not to be 'a gentleman' but rather a mere 'attorney's clerk', nephew to Polly's nurse. Cherubina is taken in by the actor Abraham Grundy who, after he learns that she has ten thousand pounds at her disposal, 'admits' that he is really Lord Altamont Mortimer Montmorenci, and swears to become her protector, later borrowing twenty-five pounds from her to pay his landlady. Even Edgeworth's 'Angelina' fits this pattern, for although the 'suitor' in question is female, she has lured Angelina away from her home by writing her romantic letters about the domestic bliss they will enjoy in a retired country cottage. The lower-class status of the heroine's 'unknown friend' is in a sense the story's punchline: after a prolonged search for the 'aimiable Araminta', Angelina takes one look at the gross, bourbon-swilling 'Miss Hodges', and realizes the error of her ways. In all of these instances, the reading of novels exposes the women to very real dangers from people of a lower class, who correctly read the heroines' improper desires in order to take advantage of them.

Cherubina pays for her transgressions physically, as she is subjected to the kind of 'comic' abuse usually reserved for male Quixotes. Cherubina is mistreated on more than one occasion. Her account of the melee in a milliner's shop is typical: 'I was attempting to rush from the shop, when I found my spangled muslin barbarously seized by the woman, who tore it to pieces in the struggle; and, pulling off the bonnet, gave me a horrid slap in the face'.[8]

However ridiculous Lennox's Arabella may seem at times, it is impossible to imagine her on the receiving end of a slap, or in any kind of proximity to a hog. This is, I think, evidence of her creator's genuine endorsement of Arabella's goals and principles as extracted from her readings, an endorsement wholly lacking in the literature which follows her. Arabella is the only character who, Don Quixote-like, derives significant power from her literary sources, her madness, and her imitative oratory. Later female Quixotes are more unambiguously discredited, if not by physical assault then by the implication that novel-reading makes women immodest, makes them so desperate for male attention that they welcome it even from lower-class men. Catherine Morland in *Northanger Abbey* is in some ways an exception to this rule, but in spite of the affection with which her author treats her, she is lovable despite her reading rather than because of it. *Northanger Abbey* does not abuse its Quixote, but neither does it value her for her literary leanings. In contrast to Arabella, whose uncle thinks that she could have made a great figure in Parliament had she been a man (p. 311), Catherine is not unusually intelligent, and there is no suggestion that her reading provides a consistent, alternate code of behaviour as Arabella's does. Catherine's own simple character — not the rules of romance, as in Lennox's novel — provides the point of view from which the author satirizes the follies of society.

Arabella, then, is the female Quixote closest to Don Quixote, not only in time but also in spirit. Despite her conservative ending, Lennox has taken her heroine seriously, producing a blend of comedy and heroism that resembles the ambiguity of Cervantes's original more closely than anything that follows. After Lennox, the female Quixote becomes a straightforward figure of fun, deployed by her author to suit a much simpler moral and rhetorical agenda. If, as contemporary commentators feared, novel reading might lead women astray, the female Quixote could always be used as a scarecrow to frighten women away from the fertile fields of romance and back onto the straight and narrow path of duty and virtue.

I am grateful to Associated University Presses for permission to reprint material that first appeared in *Echoes and Inscriptions: Comparative Approaches to Early Modern Spanish Literature*, ed. by Barbara Simerka and Christopher Weimer (Lewisburgh, PA: Bucknell University Press, 2000).

Notes to Chapter 14

1. Charlotte Lennox, *The Female Quixote* (Oxford: Oxford University Press, 1989), p. 7. All citations will be to this edition. Scott Paul Gordon observes the ubiquity of the missing mother in the biographies of female Quixotes, commenting that in linking maternal absence to a lack of rational development in the daughter, these narratives 'offer some of the century's boldest affirmations of the importance of mothers and mothering'. See Scott Paul Gordon, *The Practice of Quixotism: Postmodern Theory and Eighteenth-Century Women's Writing* (New York: Palgrave Macmillan, 2006), p. 43, and also Debra Malina, 'Rereading the Patriarchal Text: *The Female Quixote, Northanger Abbey*, and the Trace of the Absent Mother', *Eighteenth-Century Fiction* 8. 2 (1996), 271–92.
2. Miguel de Cervantes Saavedra, *The Adventures of Don Quixote*, trans. by John Michael Cohen (London: Penguin, 1950), p. 82. All citations will be from this edition.
3. Jane Austen, *Persuasion* (New York: Norton, 1995), p. 46.
4. Catherine Craft's 'Reworking Male Models: Aphra Behn's Fair Vow-Breaker, Eliza Haywood's Fantomina, and Charlotte Lennox's Female Quixote', *Modern Language Review*, 86 (1991), 821–38, provides a good account of the operation of Arabella's power. See also Patricia Meyer Spacks, 'The Subtle Sophistry of Desire: Dr. Johnson and the Female Quixote', *MP*, 85 (1988), 532–42 (p. 533), on Arabella's desire for power.
5. George Colman, *Polly Honeycombe, A Dramatick Novel of One Act* (London: T. Beckett and T. Davies, 1760).
6. Lennox herself is of course on one level opposing the realism of her novel to the implausibility of romance. Critics who address the intersections of romance, the novel, and the fictional in Lennox's work include: Laurie Langbauer, *Women and Romance: The Consolations of Gender in the English Novel* (Ithaca, NY: Cornell University Press, 1990), and Deborah Ross, *The Excellence of Falsehood* (Lexington: University of Kentucky Press, 1991).
7. Maria Edgeworth, 'Angelina; or, L'Amie Inconnue', in *Tales and Novels*, vol. 3 (London: Baldwin and Cradock, 1832), p. 23.
8. Eaton Stannard Barrett, *The Heroine* (London: Henry Frowde, 1909), p. 41.

CHAPTER 15

Eliot's Casaubon:
the Quixotic in *Middlemarch*

Chester Mills

A very important contribution to the understanding of *Middlemarch* is found in the epigraph at the beginning of Chapter II, by Miguel de Cervantes Saavedra. It is from this caption that one gets a hint of how reality and illusion will be treated in the book. The characters subsumed under this caption — Dorothea and Casaubon — pivot around the idea of the 'real' and the 'imagined'. However, this idea does not immediately become apparent when one reads the English translation under the epigraph since an important word is left out: 'Lo que veo y columbro, respondió Sancho' [What I see and perceive, responded Sancho]. These sensations are disturbed in Casaubon just as they are disturbed in Don Quixote; and Eliot uses *Middlemarch* and the sensation to criticize a world passed by, just as Cervantes uses *Don Quixote*. Indeed, the quixotic concept of trying to reorder the world according to its earlier medieval and chivalric structure is evinced throughout *Middlemarch*. The epigraph, thus, suggests a relationship between *Don Quixote* and *Middlemarch,* and Casaubon may be considered a quixotic type.

Another implication that George Eliot gives us to suggest a relationship between Casaubon and Don Quixote is the epigraph to Chapter V: 'hard students are commonly troubled with gowts [...] bad eyes [...] and all such diseases as come by over-much sitting: they are most part lean, dry, ill-coloured [...] and all through immoderate pains and extraordinary studies' (p. 31).[1] Certainly, such a description befits both men. Both Casaubon and Don Quixote are about the same age, and Sir James's graphic description of Casaubon ('He is no better than a mummy!', p. 50), as well as Celia's allusion to Casaubon's sallowness, could also be applied to Don Quixote: 'era de complexión recia, seco de carnes, enjuto de rostro, gran madrugador' [he was of a sallow complexion, wizened flesh, lean face, an early riser]. But the most interesting indication of a connection is given by Eliot when James indignantly alludes to Casaubon's legs: 'But look at Casaubon', said Sir James, indignantly. 'He must be fifty, and I don't believe he could ever have been much more than the shadow of a man. Look at his legs!' (p. 50). This reference to Casaubon's legs may simply be another innocuous comment, but to the Spanish-speaking reader, Casaubon's legs take on greater importance than is discussed in the subtle suggestion of Eliot. The word 'Quixote' is an old Spanish word used to indicate the piece of armour that covers the thighs (a *cuisse*), and stems from the Catalan word *cuixot* which means 'thigh'. Then, too, are the many paintings that draw attention to Don Quixote's thighs. One could therefore posit that it was the intention of Eliot in her description of Casaubon to parallel the description of Don Quixote.

Two distinct critical points of view concerning *Don Quixote* have emerged since the eighteenth century. One group of critics has looked at the novel and has considered the protagonist as a hero, as the restorer of traditional values — Byron, Auden, Thomas Mann, and Ortega y Gasset are proponents of this point of view. Don Quixote is seen by this group as an example of modern man antithetic to the role that society has defined for him. In idealistic opposition to the structures of his social environment, Quixote creates a new romantic environment for himself through the strength of his personality, his imagination, and his will.

Another group of critics — Hegel, Heine, Novitsky, Unamuno, etc. — sees Don Quixote as a man with good intentions. But these intentions are questionable since Quixote possesses other character traits that require scrutiny, such as the desire for fame, and the need to substitute and impose an irrelevant idealism from the past onto his present world. The proponents of this view judge the novel in terms of ideal values, and show how the protagonist in *Don Quixote* is out of step with these values. I shall be concerned with this point of view, for if we look at *Don Quixote* from this perspective, we will find distinct similarities between Don Quixote and Casaubon in *Middlemarch*.

Both characters live in a dream world. Both characters try to pattern their lives around a worldview that has long passed. It no longer is: it can no longer be. But although Don Quixote 'escapes' reality and lives the illusion, Casaubon 'lives' the illusion without escaping the reality. Thus, Cervantes portrays Don Quixote as mad, and the knight becomes the subject of ridicule and pity. But 'when we pity him,' says Dr. Johnson, 'we reflect on our own disappointments; and when we laugh, our hearts inform us that he is not more ridiculous than ourselves, except that he tells us what we have only thought'.[2] On the other hand, Eliot portrays Casaubon as no less than a pathetic anachronism 'wandering about the world and trying mentally to construct it as it used to be, in spite of ruin and confusing changes' (p. 13).

Since Casaubon and Don Quixote resort to illusion, we must consider the antecedents to their escape from reality and examine the medium through which each passes. Each character is totally immersed — through books — in the world of illusion. Each struggles — through books — to achieve immortality. The result for Don Quixote is seen in his flight from reality to the world of the knight errant.

On the other hand, the result of Casaubon's attempt to find immortality through books becomes an intensely compulsive behaviour that allows him to take flight from a mundane existence to pursue a futile course. His effort causes much misery, with more evil intentions, and his portrait suggests a sense of tragic waste. As Claude Bissell maintains, 'Casaubon is a study in the pathos of an arid and unimaginative scholarship.'[3] He lacks the ability to determine and recognize the relevance of his work to the time, and to recognize the futility of his endeavours. To Casaubon, the *Key to All Mythologies* is no less a tangible ideal than is the magical helmet of

Mambrino to Don Quixote. For Don Quixote, obtaining such an enchanted helmet would be the culmination of all knightly aspirations; for Casaubon, completing the great work about which all Middlemarch knows, would be the quintessence of his achievement. Thus, both Casaubon and Don Quixote would be immortalized. Don Quixote, the avatar of Lancelot, would have found the Holy Grail; Casaubon would remain forever a scholar. But they are engaged in a study that is irrelevant to the time; that no longer exists. And so, Casaubon and Don Quixote, by using the denominator common to both novels — books — have created a fancy through the world of dreams, and this world of dreams now becomes their reality.

But this world of dreams becomes a reality that leads to total failure, frustration, and death; and that which is left for posterity is only a legend that is 'seca como un esparto, ajena de invención, menguada de estilo, pobre de concetos y falta de toda erudición y doctrina' [dry as grass, far removed from invention, stylistically arid, with no concepts, and lacking in erudition and doctrine] (p. 20).[4] Thus, each person takes refuge in his books. Each person creates his own fanciful flight from reality. In the case of Don Quixote, the plane of reality on which he moves makes him oblivious to the true world. He does not see; he reads. And what he reads tells him that what he sees are giants instead of windmills; an army instead of sheep. Casaubon, on the other hand, develops an obsession, a monomania, which manifests itself in illusions, in dissociations, and in pointless acts. 'He is a scholar', maintains R. T. Jones, 'but a scholar doomed to failure. He gains our admiration and pity here, even while we recognize the fruitlessness of his labours'.[5] However, Casaubon does not deviate too radically from the path of the real world. He, too, does not see. He, too, reads. But his actions and his illusions are expressed through the eyes and emotions of Dorothea. It is through her eyes that we see that 'the large vistas and wide fresh air which she had dreamed of finding in her husband's mind were replaced by anterooms and winding passages which seemed to lead to nowhither' (p. 145). Later in the book, Eliot brings another quixotic bearing to the illusion of Casaubon when we read that Casaubon 'himself was lost among small closets and winding stair, and [...] easily lost sight of any purpose which had prompted him to these labours. With his taper stuck before him he forgot the absence of windows and [...] had become indifferent to the sunlight' (p. 147).

Although one finds certain character traits of Don Quixote in Casaubon, one must be careful not to equate the two personages. Casaubon is far from being the knight errant even though Ladislaw characterizes him as 'crawling a little way after men of the last century' (p. 206). Casaubon does manifest, nevertheless, a quixotic penchant for perfection. However, his mind is not full of ideas, but of hackneyed thought. Beyond these thoughts, Casaubon's mind is empty:

> And Mr. Casaubon had many scruples: he was capable of a severe self-restraint; he was resolute in being a man of honour according to the code; he would be unimpeachable by any recognised opinion. In conduct these ends had been attained; but the difficulty of making his Key to All Mythologies unimpeachable weighed like lead upon his mind; and the pamphlets [...] by which he tested his public and deposited small monumental records of his march, were far from having been seen in all their significance (p. 206).

Where the adventures of Don Quixote interest us, we but suffer the moribund movements of Casaubon throughout the novel. Where, in the case of *Don Quixote* we see Quijano being brought to the realization of the truth and to the acceptance (at his death) of a realistic norm, we experience no such attitude with Casaubon. And although we might, in justice to him, give him credit for his impeccable credentials, we find him becoming more and more morose, more and more introversive, jealous, and vindictive:

> Poor Mr. Casaubon was distrustful of everybody's feeling towards him, especially as a husband. To let anyone suppose that he was jealous would be to admit their (suspected) view of his disadvantages: to let them know that he did not find marriage particularly blissful would be to imply this conversation to their (probably) earlier disapproval. It would be as bad as letting Carp, and Brasenose generally, know how backward he was in organising the matter for his 'Key to all Mythologies'. All through his life Mr. Casaubon had been trying not to admit even to himself the inward sores of self doubt and jealously. [...] But he had forbidden Will to come to Lowick Manor, and he was mentally preparing other measures of frustration' (p. 277).

It is this vindictiveness that causes Casaubon to move on a plane of reality different from that of Quixote.

Karen Horney, in her definition of the vindictive character, maintains that,

> An impelling need for triumph makes this type extremely competitive. As a matter of fact he cannot tolerate anybody who knows or achieves more than he does, wields more power, or in any way questions his superiority. Compulsively, he has to drag his rival down or defeat him. Even if he subordinates himself for the sake of his career, he is scheming for ultimate triumph. Not being tied by feelings of loyalty, he can easily become treacherous. What he actually achieves with his own indefatigable work depends on his gifts. But with all his planning and scheming he will often achieve nothing worthwhile, not only because he is unproductive but because he is too self-destructive.[6]

Certainly this definition typifies Casaubon and not Don Quixote, for as Don Quixote recovers his senses, he confesses that his life as a knight had been but a bad dream (p. 1066). Casaubon, however, calculates that 'there might still be twenty years of achievement before him, which would justify the thirty years of preparation. That prospect was made sweeter by a flavour of vengeance against [...] Carp & Company' (p. 308).

Don Quixote and *Middlemarch* deal with the relationship between the individual and society. Both novels are 'A Study of Provincial Life', and centre on reform. In the world of *Middlemarch*, as well as in the world of *Don Quixote*, change is seen as an intrusion from without. Ladislaw and Lydgate represent these ideals for Middlemarch, and Don Quixote inversely represents the same thing for La Mancha. Don Quixote becomes the anachronism. It would therefore seem that Eliot and Cervantes are criticizing the times in their work. Casaubon and Quixote represent the authors' assault on a past age, and chide the refusal of some to accept change. We do not see change in Don Quixote and in Casaubon. Both remain static in their attempts to understand and maintain the old order. But Eliot in her assault on this old view, shows the reformer, Dorothea, the antithesis to Casaubon, vacillating between the old and the new: 'He was all she had at first imagined him to be: almost everything he had said seemed like a specimen from a mine, or the inscription on the door of a museum which might open on the treasures of past ages' (p. 24) Only at the end of the book does Dorothea separate herself from the established routine of the community and gain autonomy.

Eliot, like Dorothea, also wavers between the old and the new order. She cannot truly condemn Casaubon (or Don Quixote) for what he represents. At the same time, she cannot praise him for what he is not. As Basil Willey suggests: 'From the very outset, however, she showed the instinct — which was deeply imbedded in the consciousness of the century as a whole — to see both sides of any question: to tolerate the ordinary while accepting the new, to retain the core of traditions while mentally criticizing their forms'.[7]

We see this vacillation also operating in Casaubon and Don Quixote. Although they operate on different levels of the fanciful, the escape from reality is the basic factor common to them. Both fail, and both die. Don Quixote, however, is reconciled with reality before he dies: Casaubon is not. His effort seems to have a more evil intent. He remains vindictive till death and causes unhappiness even after his demise. Casaubon's preoccupation with his *Key to All Mythologies* is a futile attempt to gain recognition and immortality. In the final analysis, life is indeed a dream and, as each arrives at death's door, he can be as one with his brother Segismundo.

Notes to Chapter 15

1. References to Eliot's *Middlemarch* are to the Houghton Mifflin edition (Boston, 1956).
2. Samuel Johnson, 'Rambler 2', in *Selected Essays from the Rambler, Adventurer, and Idler,* ed. by W. J. Bate (New Haven, CT: Yale University Press, 1975), p. 6.
3. Claude T. Bissell, 'Social Analysis in the Novels of George Eliot', *Journal of English Literary History,* 18 (1951), 221–39.
4. References to *Don Quixote* are to the Editorial Juventud edition (Barcelona, 1971).
5. R. T. Jones, *George Eliot* (Cambridge: Cambridge University Press, 1970), p. 67.
6. Karen Horney, *Neurosis and Human Growth* (New York: W.W. Norton, 1950), p. 148.
7. Quoted in C. B. Fox, *The Free Spirit* (Oxford: Oxford University Press, 1963), p. 13.

CHAPTER 16

Cervantes as Romantic Hero and Author: Mary Shelley's *Life of Cervantes*

Darcy Donahue

Like other English Romantics, Mary Shelley viewed Cervantes as both a political and literary hero. In her little-known biography of the author of *Don Quixote* (1837) her identification with her subject is obvious. Although she is primarily concerned with a 'history of the heart', which focuses upon the vicissitudes of Cervantes's life, Shelley also examines his works with a writer's eye. The present study will focus upon the relationship between the biographer and her subject as it emerges in this hybrid of life-writing and literary critique. In so doing, it will also examine the possible presence of Cervantes's writing (particularly *Don Quixote*) as subtext in Shelley's own fiction.

Though not the first biography of Cervantes to appear in English (the first was Smollett's), Shelley's *Life* is one of the earliest to have been written by an English citizen. It forms part of a larger work, the three-volume, *Lives of the Most Eminent Literary and Scientific Men of Italy, Spain and Portugal*, commissioned for Dionysius Lardner's *Cabinet Cyclopaedia*, a 133-volume popular encyclopaedia published between 1829 and 1846 aimed at edifying the growing British middle class. Most likely written in the two years leading up to its publication in 1837, *Spanish Lives* was not the author's only concern at this time, 'a period during which she wrote her last novel, *Falkner*, suffered the death of her father, began the "Life of William Godwin", moved back to London from Harrow, and saw her son enter Trinity College'.[1] Nevertheless, it is a work which clearly engaged her intellectually and emotionally, and of all the Spanish writers, it is Cervantes to whom she dedicates most attention.

At the writing of *Lives* Spain had figured in the English national consciousness for over thirty years as a site of constant political upheaval in which England played a continuing and varied role. Like other British radicals, Shelley's father William Godwin and his circle regarded the Spain symbolized by the Constitution of 1812 as a continuation of the forces of freedom set loose in Europe by the French Revolution. Similarly, Ferdinand's betrayal of the Constitution and reinstitution of feudal property rights and the Inquisition was seen as a victory for the political reaction which held sway in Europe after Waterloo.[2] In the Jacobin dichotomy of liberty versus despotism, Cervantes and his famous protagonist came to represent the values of the radical political agenda. According to William Hazlitt, 'if ever the flame of Spanish liberty is destined to break forth, wrapping the tyrant and the tyranny in one consuming blaze, it is owing to Cervantes and his knight of La Mancha, that the spark of generous sentiment and romantic experience from which it must be kindled, has not been quite extinguished'.[3]

Given the highly political milieu in which she was raised it was natural that Mary Shelley would follow Spanish history and politics with the greatest interest. Her admiration for certain aspects of Spanish culture is clear, yet equally evident are biases imposed by culture, religion, and nationality. Thus, in the *Introduction* to *Spanish Lives* she states, 'There is an originality, an independence, an enthusiasm in the Spanish character that distinguishes them from every other people. Despotism and Inquisition, ignorance and superstition, have been unable to level the noble altitude of their souls; and even while the manifestations of genius have been crushed, genius has survived' (p. 9). These comments provide some insight into her approach to the *Lives*. English Protestants of the time looked upon Spain's Catholicism as the primary source of its political and social misfortunes, and Shelley does not differ from her compatriots in this assessment, which is apparent throughout the Spanish biographies. In the view of intellectuals and writers such as Mary and her husband Percy Bysshe Shelley, Spanish history is one of struggle between the forces of oppression (often represented by Catholicism) and the 'natural' heroism and resilience of the Spanish national character, evident in its literary and artistic achievements. The authors Shelley has selected for her volume represent 'the genius that has survived' these evils, 'for her subjects typically embody either Christian virtue or Spanish heroic energy, and both one day, she believes, will find their proper agency in the mental liberation not only of the Hispanic world, but of all nations, into independency'.[4] For Mary Shelley the Romantic rebel, as for her parents' generation of radicals, the greatest representative of these values was Cervantes.

Not surprisingly, there are references to *Don Quixote* throughout Shelley's writing. Her well-studied journals, for example, document the almost daily reading of Cervantes's masterwork by Mary and Percy Shelley between October 7 and November 7 of 1816, a month, as several critics have noted, which was crucial to the writing of *Frankenstein.*[5] More than twenty years before the *Lives*, in *History of a Six Weeks' Tour*, written partly during her elopement with Percy Shelley, Mary made a specific reference to Cervantes's work, stating 'under the shade of trees, we ate our bread and fruit, and drank our wine, thinking of Don Quixote and Sancho'. While this reference need not imply an explicit likening of the Shelleys to the knight and his squire as some critics have inferred, it does suggest a strong presence of Cervantes's protagonists in Shelley's consciousness.[6] On other occasions she does indeed identify her husband explicitly with Cervantes's idealistic hero. During the custody trial for his children in 1817 she wrote to him, 'My sweet Love, You were born to be a don Quixote and if that celebrated personage had ever existed except in the brain of Cervantes I should certainly form a theory of transmigration to prove that you lived in Spain some hundred years before and fought with Windmills.'[7]

In addition to the casual references to *Don Quixote* interspersed throughout her journals and correspondence, there is a strong Cervantine presence in Shelley's fiction. As suggested by her overlapping readings of Cervantes's text and writing of *Frankenstein*, it is possible to argue for *Don Quixote* as a subtext of Shelley's novel, though as Erin Garrett observes, for the most part 'the connection between *Don Quixote* and *Frankenstein* has so far remained unremarked — by either Golden Age Hispanists or English Romanticists'.[8] As proof of the probable impact of these readings upon the composition of Shelley's novel, Garrett cites Charles Robinson's finding that 'one of *Frankenstein*'s most discussed features — the core Safie episode — was inserted into a nearly complete draft of the novel in the weeks immediately following the Shelley's reading of *Don Quixote*'.[9]

It is probable that Mary Shelley was at least partially inspired by the figure of the elderly squire who wilfully recreates himself and his world to reflect the ideals and mores depicted in the chivalric novel. Just as Alonso Quijano, reader of romance, sought to impose his chivalric world upon those around him, so too Victor Frankenstein consciously attempts to control nature, and even usurp its role in his quest for 'the principle of life'. Frankenstein's description of his absolute absorption in his studies of natural science to the exclusion of other intellectual and social pursuits cannot help but call to mind Alonso Quijano's obsession with chivalric novels. Each protagonist becomes deranged through his fixation, and each finally recognizes and rejects his obsession. Don Quixote ultimately fails in his effort to right the world's wrongs, but not without convincing others of his fundamental nobility of purpose. Frankenstein, on the other hand, allows personal ambition to rule his more noble sentiments with far more disastrous results.

Nor is Frankenstein the only character in the novel whose life is dramatically altered by the written word. The Creature is also a reader who believes in the possibility that the fictions he reads can influence his behaviour in the 'real world'. Though he does not, like Don Quixote and Sancho, attempt to fashion himself as a literary character, his relationship to his own creator, Victor Frankenstein, is undoubtedly influenced by his reading of *Paradise Lost*, Plutarch's *Lives* and Goethe's *Werther*. According to W. S. Minot and L. A. Minot, 'Shelley is thus able to offer a critique or interpretation of the texts her reading characters come to enact or embody through the very actions and fates of these characters'. Like Cervantes, Shelley is clearly concerned with fiction as a commentary upon other texts and the reading process, and in both writers intertextuality serves a thematic and a critical function.

In addition to the obvious correspondences between protagonists who single-mindedly create a new life, whether real or imagined, there are also similarities of narrative structure between the Spanish and English works. Both writers distance their stories from a verifiable origin through the creation of multiple levels of narration. *Frankenstein* is framed by the letters of Robert Walton to his sister Margaret Savile, letters that contain the story of Victor Frankenstein. Frankenstein's story in turn is the vehicle for the Creature's revelations and recriminations. Though not nearly as convoluted as the multi-layered narration of the *Quixote*, the final effect is to undermine the veracity of the tale itself by removing it from a single centre of truth. These intertwined narratives also provide various perspectives from which to view the narrated events. As in *Don Quixote*, readers of Shelley's novel find themselves caught between contrasting versions of the narrative verisimilitude. Similarly, both Cervantes and Shelley employ varied genres in telling their stories, and count upon their readers' familiarity with them. While Cervantes's principal narration is a parody of the chivalric romance, he also brings into play numerous other literary forms such as the pastoral, the picaresque, autobiography, and the sentimental romance. His admirer and biographer also displays a variety of narrative styles, including the already mentioned epistolary form and autobiography, embedded within the larger genres of gothic romance and science fiction.

Finally, both Cervantes's and Shelley's novels may be read as social and literary commentaries. At the same time that he purports to parody the chivalric novel as literary genre, Cervantes also subtly critiques the social ideologies and practices of his time, as is apparent, for example, in his treatment of the Duke and Duchess in Part II. Although he does not overtly censure these characters, their self-indulgent entertainment at the expense of Don Quixote reveals them to be representatives of a privileged and idle aristocracy that contributes little to the culture at large. Sancho Panza, the seemingly ignorant peasant, is counterposed to their unmerited privilege in his judicious if short-lived reign as governor of the island of Barataria. Throughout the novel, the primacy of intention and action over lineage is evident, directly contrasting with ideas governing the rigidly hierarchical social structures of the day.[10] Yet Cervantes is always careful to couch his opinion in humour, making it less discernible than Mary Shelley's overt indictment. While their targets are very different, it is clear that Shelley saw potential for criticism in the gothic just as Cervantes saw it in the chivalric, and both authors created literary hybrids combining varied and occasionally contesting discourses as a way of presenting their cultural critique.

Beyond its probable influence on *Frankenstein*, there is evidence that Cervantes's best-known novel may have affected the creation of Shelley's lesser-known works. Mary Shelley clearly equated the name Don Quixote with an idealism that was both ennobling and out of touch with reality, thus entailing both positive and negative potential. She uses his name and that of his imagined ladylove to designate contrasting traits of the characters Ethel Fitzhenry and Fanny Derham in the novel *Lodore*. Both young women are quixotic, Ethel in her idealized vision of herself as Dulcinea and her husband as Don Quixote, and Fanny in her rejection of social convention. The author's own awareness of and identification with Don Quixote is apparent in her correspondence with Charles Ollier, chief literary advisor to the publisher of the novel. After learning that the printer had lost a section of volume three of *Lodore,* and that she would have to rewrite it, she comments wryly, 'You seem to think that you gave me an easy task in rewriting that unlucky MS — quite the contrary...Give my compliments to Mr. Bentley and tell him I am very sorry that like Don Quixote, an Enchanter meddles with my affairs'.[11] Similarly, Shelley avails herself of the associations of the name Quixote to characterize the eponymous protagonist of her final novel, the Byronesque captain John Falkner, whom she describes as being similar in character to Don Quixote. Although he is in many ways diametrically opposed to the lofty-minded *hidalgo*, according to the narrator Falkner 'never heard a story of oppression without forming a scheme to relieve the victim'.[12] Given that Shelley was at work on *Falkner* in the year that the Spanish *Lives* appeared, the Cervantine protagonist would have been a ready literary model upon which to draw for Falkner's redeeming qualities.

It is in the *Life*, however, where Shelley's interest in Cervantes is most explicitly stated, and where her identification with him emerges most clearly. By far the longest of the Spanish *Lives*, it is a highly personalized and even gendered narrative in which Cervantes, in addition to his identity as literary icon, may be a medium for her feelings about her recently deceased father, her late husband, Percy Shelley, and the vagaries of the writer's life. Mary Shelley was certainly shaped by the critical practices and ideologies of her age, and this is evident in her biography. Regardless of whether Cervantes's misfortunes reflect those of Godwin, or even her own, her subject is also in some ways the stereotypical Romantic artist unappreciated by lesser humans.

The opening paragraphs of the *Life* leave no doubt as to the writer's high regard for the Spanish writer and her preoccupation with his emotional and moral response to the adversities he suffered: 'a poor and neglected man — we are anxious, even at this distance of time, to commiserate his misfortunes, and sympathise in his sorrows [...] We desire to learn with what spirit he endured adversity — whether, like his heroic creation, he consoled himself at the worst by the sense of conscious worth and virtuous intention [...] and how far, like his hero, he preserved a serene and undaunted spirit in the midst of blows and derision' (p. 119). The reader is called upon to view Cervantes as unfortunate, the undeserving victim of both historical and social circumstances beyond his control.

In the interior history which is at the core of all her *Lives*, Shelley devotes attention to Cervantes's relationships with family, friends, and critics, but balances it with more traditional historiography. She relies most heavily upon the Spanish biographers Juan Antonio Pellicer (1797) and Vicente de los Ríos (1780), both of whom had contributed material to John Bowle's 1781 edition of *Don Quixote*. Louis Viardot's 1836 biography also figures prominently as a source. The biographer in Shelley seems anxious to provide as much truthful historical data as possible despite the lack of available source materials. She recognizes the inadequacy of the method of piecing together isolated bits of information from varied and limited sources. 'Truth, absolute and unshakeable, ought to be the foundation of our assertions, or we paint a fancy head instead of an individual portrait' (p. 265). Her account of Cervantes's captivity in northern Africa is detailed and draws upon sources from Cervantes's lifetime such as Haedo's *Topografía de Argel*.[13] The author is careful to refer to official documents, frequently citing correspondence, depositions and other verifiable texts, but it is her own commentary which creates the inner or personal history as well as the social history of her subject, and draws the reader in. Although her observations most frequently take the form of an expression of indignation or commiseration at the slings and arrows of Cervantes's fate, they also involve imaginative speculation concerning the events of his life, and reveal the extent to which she related her own life to his.

The reasons for her identification with Cervantes are closely related to his iconic role for English radicals, including her father and husband, but also reflect her identity as a writer, and particularly one, who, like Cervantes, may have perceived herself as underrated. The dual personal and professional affinity is obvious throughout her narration. Thus, while in many cases she translates verbatim the basic events of Cervantes's life from Viardot, Shelley's voice is nevertheless evident in the empathic tone which pervades her biography. For example, in presenting the information about Cervantes's captivity she cannot refrain from commenting upon his character in a highly favourable manner: 'That these details are not fuller we must lament; but, such as they are, they display so much gallantry and magnanimity on Cervantes's part, that they must be read with the greatest pleasure' (p. 127). In this same part of the biography Shelley displays her identification with Cervantes as writer and attributes her own motivations to him as a way of explaining his silence on his captivity experience. She remarks on the frequency with which Cervantes alluded to himself in his works (p. 129). Yet Cervantes's failure to provide a first-person account of his years as a captive becomes a springboard for Shelley's ideas on the nature of autobiographical writing and her own life experience. In her view the imagination is always superior to an unhappy life and she does not doubt that Cervantes shared this belief. Finally, the entire captivity experience becomes the justification for one instance of the author's frequent censure of the social inequity of which she perceived her subject to be a victim (p. 135).

Cervantes's poverty and the system of entrenched social privilege which is its cause is a principal target of his biographer, the product of a radical and even revolutionary political environment. As a way of making his situation understandable to her English readers, Shelley compares it to that of Robert Burns (p. 142). At no point does she admit the possibility of failure on the part of Cervantes, either for his financial difficulties or his apparent inability to make lasting social connections. Rather, the author does not consider Cervantes's personal misfortunes as separate from the evils which beset Spanish society of his day, and class inequity is just one of these. Thus, her discussion of his rather tainted legal history is marked by a decidedly dim view of the processes of the Spanish judicial system. This negative attitude is apparent, for example, in her assessment of the varied charges against him as 'annoyances' (p. 141). Referring to his imprisonment in Seville for failure to account adequately for public funds with which he was entrusted, Shelley concludes, 'In all this, it is evident that no real accusation was levelled against Cervantes, and that it was only the clumsy and arbitrary proceedings of Spanish law that occasioned his imprisonment' (p. 143).

Though she dedicates more attention to his life than his texts, in the final pages of *Life*, Shelley examines his work from the perspective of a fellow author and it is in these pages where, freed from her dependence upon French and Spanish sources, she communicates her own opinions even more freely than in the preceding account of his life. Before doing so, however, she comments extensively upon the seeming disregard in which the Spanish literary and court establishments held Cervantes. After recounting the well-known story of the amazement of a group of French visitors to Madrid at Cervantes's straitened material circumstances, Mary again reveals her anti-aristocratic perspective: 'We cannot help observing that the court and the nobles did not form the whole world. Cervantes had many dear, many well-informed and valued friends, and among these he could forget the carelessness of those who considered all reputation and prosperity to be inclosed within their magic circle' (p. 153). The biographer concludes the life story by extolling the 'equanimity of temperament' (p. 158) which she understands Cervantes to have displayed throughout a life of undeserved hardship.

The critic enters into her analysis of Cervantes's writing almost as an appendix, although her engagement with his works is clear and her critical opinions are clearly stated. She does not consider Cervantes a poet, despite his considerable poetic output. However, she is willing to make an exception for *La Numancia*, finding in it a 'poetry of conception and passion of the highest order' (p. 159). Given her obvious political bias, it is not surprising that this play which eulogizes the heroic last stand of the Numantines against their Roman conquerors would appeal to Shelley's sensibilities. She perceives it as a truly national drama which reflects Spain's intrinsic valour, and comments that it had helped to incite the resistance of the Spanish against the French invaders at the siege of Zaragoza (1808–09). Indeed, this work, in her assessment, embodies 'the grand and the terrible, the pathetic and the deeply tragic' (p. 161) and in its grandeur and scope, aligns Cervantes's genius with that of Shakespeare, certainly the highest encomium which an English critic could bestow.

Not all of the author's critical judgments are so positive, and at times her cultural preconceptions are evident. Thus, in her discussion of *El trato de Argel* [life in Algiers], while acknowledging the autobiographical significance of the play, she cites English abhorrence of the Spanish Inquisition as the basis for a differing reaction between Spanish and English audiences. Shelley expresses the indignation felt by English viewers 'against that nefarious institution' (p. 163). Her position, however, is itself one-sided and nationalistic, since she eschews any mention of the persecution of English Catholics by Elizabethan Protestants during this same period, nor does she allude to the Spanish-English battle for supremacy in global politics. Rather, despite her credentials as a freethinker, she appears to adhere to the stereotypes of Spanish Catholicism that circulated throughout England and Europe.

Regardless of the merits of his plays, and his other prose works, they do not approach his masterwork, an opinion which she states in the following manner: 'From the publication of these works to Don Quixote, what a gap! He would seem to have lived as an unlighted candle — suddenly, a spark touches the wick, and it burst into a flame. *Don Quixote* is perfect in all its parts' (p. 163). Whereas the narrator of *Don Quijote* ridicules the elderly hidalgo's adoption of the chivalric worldview, Shelley regards the impact of reading upon Alonso Quijano as true to life. What some critics might consider her overly Romantic reading of the novel leads Mary Shelley the literary critic to conclude that 'don Quixote is as courageous, noble, princely, and virtuous as the greatest of the men whom he imitates', going so far as to state that, 'Any one suffering from calamities would gladly have recourse to him for help' (p. 163). Despite the work's flawlessness, however, she finds somewhat less to admire in the second part of *Don Quixote* and is particularly unhappy with the figure of the duchess, finding 'the deceptions of this great lady at once vulgar and cruel' (p. 164). Interestingly, for one so inclined to deplore social privilege, Shelley does not recognize Cervantes's probable satiric intent in his unflattering depiction of the Duchess and her husband. Her surprise that a woman of the duchess's social milieu could be either vulgar or cruel appears to contradict her previous anti-class position. The critic does not allow her own commentary to stand as the only encomium for Cervantes's masterpiece, but draws upon the opinions of the 'best men', for support, in this case, none other than William Godwin and Samuel Coleridge, citing the latter's equation of Cervantes and the Bard.

It is evident that Mary Shelley felt a special affinity with Cervantes in 1837 as she wrote his life. Her emphasis upon adversity and suffering is Romantic in sensibility, yet may also reflect the sorrows and devastating loss she had experienced in her own life, including the misfortunes of her father's career. It is undeniable that she also related to the author of the *Quixote* as a writing colleague, albeit removed in time, and according to Garrett, the *Life* may even constitute a 'delayed homage to one of the literary models fundamental to her development as a novelist'.[14] Furthermore, Shelley clearly sees in her subject an embodiment of intrinsically Spanish values that enabled him to overcome his lack of material success and of the acclaim he deserved. In writing the literary *Lives,* she complies with the purpose of the *Cabinet Cyclopaedia* to inspire readers with the best qualities of a nation as represented by its best writers and, in the case of Cervantes, she had no doubts about what these were 'His genius, his imagination, his wit, his natural good spirits and affectionate heart, did, we must hope, stand in lieu of more worldly blessings, and rendered him as internally happy as they have rendered him admirable and praiseworthy to all men to the end of time' (p. 158).

Notes to Chapter 16

1. Lisa Vargo, 'Introduction', in Mary Shelley, *Literary Lives and Other Writings* (London: Pickering and Chatto, 2002), p. xv. Further references to this volume are given after quotations in the text.
2. For an overview of the English radicals' view of Spanish politics from Napoleon's installation of his brother, Joseph Bonaparte, on the Spanish throne in 1808 to the Spanish Revolution of 1820, see Jean Moskal, 'To Speak in Sanchean Phrase', in *Mary Shelley in Her Times*, ed. by Betty Bennett and Stuart Curran (Baltimore, MD: Johns Hopkins University Press, 2000), pp. 23–28.
3. Moskal, 'To Speak in Sanchean Phrase', p. 27.
4. Vargo, 'Introduction', p. xix.
5. According to Erin Garrett, 'Recycling Zoraida: The Muslim Heroine in Mary Shelley's *Frankenstein*', *Cervantes*, 20. 1 (2000), 133–56: 'Mary Shelley had begun composing her most famous work in June of 1816 and would continue to work on it for the next eleven months. The journal entries for October to November of 1816 fall almost exactly one third of the way through the completion of *Frankenstein*' (p. 136).
6. Moskal in 'To Speak in Sanchean Phrase' (p. 19) interprets this brief reference to Don Quixote and Sancho Panza as an explicit identification by Mary Shelley of Percy Shelley with the idealistic protagonist and herself with Sancho.
7. *The Letters of Mary Wollstonecraft Shelley*, ed. by Paula Feldman and Diana Scott-Kivert (Baltimore, MD: Johns Hopkins University Press, 1980–88), p. 27.
8. Garrett, 'Recycling Zoraida: The Muslim Heroine in Mary Shelley's *Frankenstein*', p. 134.
9. Moskal in 'To Speak in Sanchean Phrase' (p. 19) interprets this brief reference to Don Quixote and Sancho Panza as an explicit identification by Mary Shelley of Percy Shelley with the idealistic protagonist and herself with Sancho.

10. For a recent and brief overview of the social and political situation of Cervantes's Spain, see B. W. Ife, 'The Historical and Social Context', in *The Cambridge Companion to Cervantes,* ed. by Anthony J. Cascardi (Cambridge: Cambridge University Press, 2002), pp. 11–30, and John Lynch, *Los Austrias* (Barcelona: Crítica, 2007).

11. *The Letters of Mary Wollstonecraft Shelley*, p. 206.

12. Mary Shelley, *Falkner: A Novel* (London: Saunders and Otley, 1837), p. 130.

13. Although Shelley attributes the work to Diego de Haedo, it was in fact written by Antonio de Sosa, a Portuguese cleric who was a captive in Algiers at the same time as Cervantes. After being released from captivity in 1581, Sosa gave the manuscript to Diego de Haedo, Inquisitor and Archbishop of Palermo. The Archbishop passed Sosa's unfinished writings on captivity to his nephew of the same name, who edited and published the manuscript in 1611.

14. Garrett, 'Recycling Zoraida', p. 139.

CHAPTER 17

Dickens, Cervantes and the Pick-Pocketing of an Image

Pamela H. Long

When an author wanders into an illustrator's shop and idly fingers the galley proofs of another author's soon-to-be-published translations, and converts the characters in those proofs into his own literary characters, we might have an incident of (innocent) book-snatching. In Dickens's *Oliver Twist*, Oliver's epiphany regarding the relationship between the pocket handkerchiefs and the jewels in Fagin's den and the thievery on the street occurs as the Artful Dodger and Charley Bates slip their fingers into Mr. Brownlow's pocket and relieve him of a silk handkerchief. Oliver, watching from across the street, is shocked and terrified, and takes to his heels (pp. 56–60).[1]

It is not insignificant that this moment occurs at a bookstall, where Oliver's future philosopher–benefactor Brownlow is lost in a quixotic moment of book-lust, unaware of the picaresque characters swarming around him. Later, at magistrate Fang's court, as Oliver is being accused of the crime of picking Brownlow's pocket, Brownlow himself is found to have a purloined volume still in his hand. The bookseller refuses to press charges on Brownlow, realizing that the confusion of the moment has caused his customer to hold onto the book absent-mindedly (p. 66). Dickens's book-snatching, however, may not be quite as guileless as Brownlow's. The parallels of characters, settings, linguistic traits and other narrative elements from Cervantes's *Rinconete and Cortadillo* suggest that the English author was more than slightly aware of the petty larceny he was engaged in.

Dickens's father's library contained a volume of *Don Quixote*. Dickens himself admitted to having based his character Mr. Pickwick almost directly on the Manchegan knight. Furthermore, while Dickens was finishing *The Pickwick Papers*, he was already at work on *Oliver Twist*.[2] However, it is not within the bounds of this essay to attempt what other scholars have more thoroughly done: to draw parallels between Quixote and Pickwick.

Although Dickens and his biographer Forster denied that George Cruikshank's illustrations influenced the development of the characters of *Oliver Twist*,[3] it is clear that the artist's sketches of the criminal underworld pre-existed Dickens's novel by more than a decade.[4] These Cruikshank pencil drawings, found by Vogler in the Victoria and Albert Museum Print Room, probably date from 1819. Vogler believes that these drawings, which depict criminals such as prostitutes, housebreakers, thieves, etc., may have been the sources of Sikes, Nancy, and the other rogues and prostitutes in the illustrations Cruikshank later made for the Dickens novel. Whether Dickens had access to those early drawings is not certain.

And yet it is the triangular relationship of writer and illustrator to the works of Cervantes that continues to interest us: Cruikshank himself had illustrated the Smollett translation of *Don Quixote*, which appeared in 1833, and Dickens first became aware of Cruikshank's work through this translation.[5] In fact, the translator of Cervantes's *Exemplary Novels*, Thomas Roscoe, had written the 'Memoir of the Author' for this edition, and this may have been a volume suggested to Dickens by the illustrator. Cruikshank argued throughout his life that the characters in *Oliver Twist* were derived from his engravings, and it is possible that Dickens's interest in Cervantes was aroused or reawakened by the illustrator's work on *Don Quixote*.

What seems clear, however, is that Dickens had access to a new version of Cervantes's *Exemplary Novels* recently translated by Thomas Roscoe, under the title *The Spanish Novelists: A Series of Tales from the Earliest Period to the Close of the Seventeenth Century*. This compilation of novels was published in 1832 by Richard Bentley, the same publisher of the *Bentley's Miscellany* that carried *Oliver Twist* in serial form with three interruptions between February 1837 and March 1839. Although it is impossible to verify Dickens's direct familiarity with *Rinconete and Cortadillo* in the Roscoe translation, there are many striking coincidences between the Spanish novel and *Oliver Twist*: the lugubrious yet comic atmosphere of the school of thieves; the presence of a fraternity of pickpockets; an initiation through language and renaming; the pocket-handkerchief game; and several parallel characters, such as Monipodio and Fagin, women of ill repute, and particularly the correspondence between Rinconete and Cortadillo with Charley Bates and the Artful Dodger.

Like the innocent Oliver, the already corrupt delinquents Rincón and Cortado enter the world of thieves through the graces of an urchin who guides them to the house of the mentor of thieves. In the case of Oliver, this streetwise guide is Jack Dawkins, known as the Artful Dodger (p. 48–50); for Rincón and Cortado, it is Ganchoso, the 'Hook' (p. 257). Dodger leads Oliver to the den of Fagin just as Ganchoso guides Rincón and Cortado to the patio of Monipodio. In both accounts, the innocents are approached by the guides who speak glowingly of 'a 'spectable old genelman' (p. 48): Ganchoso refers to Monipodio as 'the most exemplary man of our profession' (p. 259). Just as Oliver 'secretly resolved to cultivate the good opinion of the old gentleman as quickly as possible' (p. 49), Rincón urges Ganchoso to step up his pace, as he is eager to meet 'the worthy cavalier' (p. 258), 'our respectable friend Monipodio, of whose virtues you have said so much' (p. 261). Rincón and Cortado are already petty thieves and cutpurses before they meet Ganchoso, but their credulous reaction to the praises Ganchoso heaps upon Monipodio anticipates Oliver's truly ingenuous interest in the 'virtuous' gentleman described by Dodger: '"Sir", replied the guide, "I am no theologian, and therefore cannot argue on the subject; but this I know, that everybody ought to praise God in the vocation to which Providence has been pleased to call him; and the more so as our master Monipodio has expressly ordered it". "Doubtless that gentleman must be of a very religious turn", said Rincón, "since he makes his thieves praise God"' (p. 259).

A comparison of the Dickens description with that of the Roscoe translation shows two shabby houses on the verge of collapse. In both houses, the descriptions centre on cheap vessels and furniture: 'The walls and ceiling of the room were perfectly black, with age and dirt. There was a deal table before the fire: upon which were a candle, stuck in a ginger-beer bottle: two or three pewter pots: a loaf and butter: and a plate' in *Oliver Twist* (p. 50); 'They entered a small courtyard, paved with fanciful brickwork, of a bright red colour: on one side was a bench, with three legs; and on the other a broken jar, placed on a stand not in a much better condition. In another was a rush mat, and in the middle was a space for flowers' in *Rinconete and Cortadillo* (p. 261). The Roscoe translation, which omits much of the original, lists the denizens of Monipodio's den: two young men dressed as students, two more cutpurses, a blind man, two elderly people, an old woman and two rogues (p. 262). This multifarious group is termed a 'fraternity' in the Roscoe book, from 'cofradía' in the original; this term carries the double sense of a group of persons of similar purposes, especially religious pursuits or trade guilds, and a gathering of thieves. As Rincón and Cortado are brought into the patio they meet with two other thieves, who inquire 'whether they belonged to the fraternity? Rincón answered in the affirmative, making great demonstration of respect, which the formidable appearance of the querists seemed to demand' (p. 262). Monipodio then explains to them the nature of the association in terms of a religious confraternity (pp. 265–67).

In spite of the overtones of satire aimed at the religious aspects of the trade guilds, it is very likely that Dickens, and Roscoe for that matter, would have missed, or ignored, the allusions played out in the Cervantine den of thieves. These elements do not figure prominently in the Roscoe translation, and do not appear at all in the Dickens novel. Fagin, as well, considers his little cadre of thieves to be a very intimate community of goodwill: '"In a little community like ours, my dear", said the Jew, who felt it necessary to qualify this position, "we have a general number one; that is, you can't consider yourself as number one, without considering me too as the same, and all the other young people"' (p. 275).

In both novels the use of language distinguishes between the criminal, who is covering up things, and the innocent who is discovering things, between the deceiver and the deceived. All new members must pass through an initiation based upon language. The presence of underworld argot is so ubiquitous in the Dickens novel that much dialogue is contrived to explain the terminology to Oliver and the reader. In the first encounter between Oliver and Dodger, the latter must explain the term 'beak' (p. 48) to Oliver not only so that they can communicate with each other, but also so that Oliver may begin to comprehend the nature of the enterprise in which they are engaged. In Cervantes's novel, Ganchoso, the Dodger figure, explains the language of thieves to Rincón and Cortado: 'But come along, and on the road I will explain to you a little of our vocabulary, which it will be necessary for you to know' (p. 259). During this walk, which was not very short, their new acquaintance instructed them in the language of the craft, very much to the edification of the novice.

Much like the narrator of *Don Quixote* who eventually imitates Don Quixote's chivalric tone, the narrator in Dickens's novel mimics Fagin's artificially bourgeois discourse, in the chapter titles, which, according to Colby, at once conceal and divulge Dickens's critique of both the Old and the New Poor Laws. In ambiguously ironic chapter titles such as 'How Oliver passed his Time in the improving Society of his reputable Friends', Dickens is giving the reader a sensation of drawing aside the artistic curtain, a sort of peek behind Maese Pedro's puppet theatre. What Dickens had essentially learned from the exemplary novel, then, was that linguistic foppery could be used to comic effect — all men are criminals, fops or angels, depending on the author's (or puppeteer's) choice, and upon the sartorial or lexical elements he chooses to adorn them with.

In both Dickens's and Cervantes's novels, members of the criminal 'fraternities' undergo name changes as part of the initiation into the world of thievery. Just as Jack Dawkins is known as 'The Artful Dodger', and the mole Noah Claypole is rebaptized 'Morris Bolter', Rincón and Cortado must be renamed with diminutives: 'Rinconete' and 'Cortadillo' (p. 264).

Another more comical element in which both novels coincide is the picking of pocket-handkerchiefs. For Fagin, it is the quintessential pedagogical device in the training of pickpockets. Fagin's boys routinely attract the attention of a gentleman while others rob him of the handkerchief. In the same way, Cortado distracts the sacristan while he steals his belongings:

> Saying this, he drew from his pocket a handkerchief to wipe the perspiration from his countenance; a moment not lost on Cortado, who immediately seemed to take a more vivid interest in the poor man's loss, and suggested several expedients for its recovery. The advice of Cortado was given in so vague a manner, that the sacristan was tempted to ask a repetition; during which, Cortado, taking advantage of the sacristan's anxiety, contrived to beguile him of his handkerchief, when, with many expressions of condolence, he took his leave, recommending him to use all diligence in the recovery of his property; and then returned to Rincón (pp. 256–57).

An important comparison between the works, and the one which most strongly suggests Dickens's familiarity with the Spanish novel, is the remarkable coincidence between the descriptions of Fagin and Monipodio. The similarities between the two masters of rogue academies are most striking in their physical attributes. Fagin 'was a very old shriveled Jew, whose villainous-looking and repulsive face was obscured by a quantity of matted red hair. He was dressed in a greasy flannel gown, with his throat bare' (p. 50). Monipodio is described as 'about forty-five years of age, tall of stature, his countenance of a sullen hue, with sunken eyes, eyebrows joined in the centre, and a black bushy beard. He was dressed in a shirt and covered with a huge cloak reaching to his feet, on which were [*sic*] a pair of old shoes down at the heels [...] In short, the appearance of this gentleman, whose reputation had been so strenuously supported, was anything but favourable, he being, unfortunately, one of the most ill-looking, misshapen barbarians in the world' (p. 263). The details vary only in their morphologies of the Semite bogeyman — for the Englishman, the crouching, avaricious Jew; for the Spaniard, the menacing Moor. The effect of the appearance of this master of rogues is a tremendous shock to the expectations of the initiates. However, Rincón and Cortado do not show any signs of disillusionment, as the reader expects, nor does Oliver. Oliver's anticipation is even more poignant, as he is a true innocent at large, in contrast to Rincón and Cortado, already accomplished delinquents. Both novels demonstrate a comic level of etiquette and decorum among low-lifes, for example in elements of ironic courtesy in the greetings of Fagin and Monipodio. When Oliver is first presented to Fagin we are told: 'The Jew grinned; and, making a low obeisance to Oliver, took him by the hand; and hoped he should have the honour of his intimate acquaintance' (p. 50). In their first interview with Monipodio, Rincón and Cortado are treated as honoured guests, as the master of thieves ceremoniously asks their professions, the names of their parents, and their origins (pp. 264–65).

There exist, as well, great differences between *Oliver Twist* and *Rinconete and Cortadillo*, which need to be explored. These variations speak as much to the manner in which the Cervantes novel was translated as they do to the differences in the socio-historical milieu into which they were born, as well as the basic differences between the two novelists themselves. Monipodio's den of thieves can be construed as a carnival mirror image of the Spanish monarchy of the seventeenth century. The den of thieves was a closed world sufficient unto itself: the mock civility of the thieves, their cock-eyed system of justice, their code of honour, their trade specializations, their superficial religious ritualism are models of the world in which Cervantes found himself creating the novel. The 'misdeeds' of the Monipodio's associates in *Riconete y Cortadillo* are not heinous crimes worthy of hanging, such as those we see in Oliver Twist, but rather acts of religious hypocrisy, minor theft and pick-pocketing. Dickens makes another comment in his prologue which needs to be reconsidered. In a sentence in the prologue to the 1841 edition that many have thought referred exclusively to *Don Quixote*, he writes: 'Cervantes laughed Spain's chivalry away, by showing Spain its impossible and wild absurdity. It was my attempt, in my humble and far-distant sphere, to dim the false glitter surrounding something which really did exist, by shewing it in its unattractive and repulsive truth' (p. xxvii). This 'impossible and wild absurdity' applies as well to the inverse monarchy of Rinconete and Cortadillo as it does to the Knight of the Sad Countenance. Whereas Cervantes employs satire in his novels to achieve social comment, Dickens's irony casts a shadow of pathos over his protagonist.

This is not the last parallel to be drawn between the English and Spanish novelists. Cervantes had defended himself in the prologue of the *Novelas ejemplares* against (as yet) unspoken charges of plagiarism. Just as Dickens defended himself against Cruikshank's claims of paternity over the Twist characters, so Cervantes self-justified the authorship of his own novellas. The reader, agape like Oliver in the midst of the street, may descry another type of sleight of hand: Dickens may well guilelessly defend himself against the charges of pinching Cruikshank's characters because indeed he hadn't. It was Cervantes's pocket he had picked.

Notes to Chapter 17

1. All references to *Oliver Twist* will refer to Charles Dickens, *Oliver Twist* (Oxford: Clarendon Press, 1966). All references to Roscoe's translation of *Rinconete and Cortadillo* refer to T. Roscoe, *The Spanish Novelists: A Series of Tales, from the Earliest Period to the Close of the Seventeenth Century. Translated from the Originals, with Critical and Biographical Notices* (London: Richard Bentley, 1832).
2. J. Butt and. K. Tolletson, *Dickens at Work* (London: Methuen, 1957), p. 14.
3. J. Forster, *The Life of Charles Dickens* (Philadelphia: Lippincott, 1889), p. 347–48.
4. R. A. Vogler, *The Graphic Works of George Cruikshank* (New York: Dover, 1979), p. 74–77.
5. Miguel de Cervantes Saavedra, *The History and Adventures of the Renowned Don Quixote, translated from the Spanish by T. Smollett, to which is prefixed a memoir of the author, by Thomas Roscoe. Illustrated by George Cruikshank*, 3 vols (London: Effingham Wilson, et al., 1833).

CHAPTER 18

Robin Chapman's *The Duchess's Diary* and the Other Side of Imitation

Edward H. Friedman

It is fitting that a novel such as *Don Quixote*, which moves literature forward by both venerating and critiquing the texts of the past, should itself become the basis for later creation. The downside of this argument might be, of course, a summoning of the spurious sequel to Part I of *Don Quixote*, by the pseudonymous Alonso Fernández de Avellaneda, who rages against the author for daring to disparage the dramatic formula and the commercial success of Lope de Vega in Chapter 48 of the 1605 *Quixote*. This intrusion into Cervantes's life and art was, at the same time, a curse and a blessing: a nightmare for the writer and a benefit for the 'real' Part II. The facetious and satirical 'true history' now becomes the true history of Don Quixote, as Cervantes aligns himself, whether grudgingly or not, with the Arab historian Cide Hamete Benengeli. The protagonist, rendered passive by the metatheatrics of Sansón Carrasco and the duke and duchess, has a new enemy to combat. Avellaneda makes Cervantes's *Don Quixote* more intricate, more self-referential, and more persuasive in erasing the lines between history and poetry, reality and fiction.

Robin Chapman's *The Duchess's Diary* (1980)[1] is a good-spirited supplement to the quixotic canon, written (by the duchess and by Chapman) not so much to ruffle feathers as to fill in gaps. Interestingly, the enterprise has an analogue in the pastoral episode of Marcela and Grisóstomo (*Don Quixote* Part I, Chapters 12–14). The friends of the lovesick gentleman-turned-shepherd blame his beloved Marcela for his death. They depict her as pitiless and unfeeling, a torturer of men. The reader is predisposed to despise her, but Marcela delivers a discourse in which she eloquently justifies her stance. She cannot help the fact that her beauty attracts admirers, but she has done nothing to encourage them. She feels that she is entitled to trust her instincts and to adhere to her own will, and she savours the solitude of the countryside. She adds to the equation a new perspective that is at once a feminist rewriting of the pastoral[2] and a testament to point of view and subjectivity. Marcela expands and helps to clarify the story. So does the duchess, as cast, or ventriloquized, by Chapman, who gives the reader another side of the story and a metacommentary on *Don Quixote*.

The duke and duchess figure prominently in the 1615 *Quixote*. As readers of Part I and as idle aristocrats, they are able to devote time and effort to entertaining Don

Quixote and Sancho Panza in their castle, which is to say that they use the knight errant and his squire for their private entertainment. They have the resources — intellectual and economic — to make a spectacle, as it were, of their guests. From their reading, they understand Don Quixote's delusions and illusions, and from Sancho they learn of the adventure of the Cave of Montesinos and the knight's chivalry-inflected account, which also brings in the 'enchanted' Dulcinea, who is, at least initially, purely a figment of Sancho's imagination. The duke and duchess take these plot elements and transform them into their own dramatic scenarios, within their court and on the island of Barataria that they construct for the governorship of Sancho Panza. The duke is portrayed as heartless and callous, but it is the duchess who more readily strikes a chord — a negative chord, to be sure — with readers. The physical and emotional well-being of the knight and squire is of little concern to her. She is insensitive to the malady of Don Quixote; any act is justified as long as it causes her amusement. Her sense of humour is perverse, and her cruelty seems to know no limits. She is ingenious and a skilled rhetorician. She aims to make Sancho concede that perchance the enchantment of Dulcinea really is the work of an enchanter who has brought the squire into his scheme. She is willing to go on the attack, armed in one instance with cats and bells (II, 46). Through the duke and duchess, who occupy a significant portion of Part II, Cervantes emphasizes a key aspect of reader-response and intensifies the narrative self-consciousness that makes Part I, as opposed to the romances of chivalry, the primary intertext of Part II.

On one level, the duke and duchess pay homage to Don Quixote by emulating his modus operandi. They 'stage' life as if it were chivalric romance. They incorporate those around them in a fictional game that they claim to represent the truth. They build from an existing model and go to extreme lengths to substantiate their argument. Their theatre — their metatheatre — is far more elaborate than the knight's, although it could be maintained that his stage is the world at large. They assemble a cast of thousands, and, as their progenitor, Cervantes the failed playwright produces countless dramas and dramas-within-dramas in which Don Quixote and Sancho Panza are actors at the service, and at the mercy, of scripts conceived by their hosts. The creative spirit of Don Quixote is dimmed to a degree in Part II, as the surprise, or *admiratio*, that had greeted him in the past cedes to the fame, the celebrity status, that the published chronicle of his exploits has brought him. He is a known quantity, to his delight and to his detriment. Early in Part II, Sancho usurps some of that ground by enchanting Dulcinea through an ingenious example of role reversal. Don Quixote is upstaged by the success of the book and by a squire who has learned from experience that invisible enchanters can come to the rescue of those in search of explanations. The duke and duchess celebrate the literary and historical triumph of Don Quixote while undermining his individual agency, his inventiveness, his authorial and directorial force. They are, in a manner of speaking, like him, readers gone mad, as the grave ecclesiastic in their employ chastises them on more than one occasion. They play into, and reshape, the allegories of reading and writing introduced and distilled in Part I. Cervantes appears to examine the implications of rank and class within the context of leisure reading. The impact of the printing press is palpable throughout *Don Quixote*, and the duke and duchess offer variations on the theme, as informed by social hierarchies and by shifts in cultural paradigms.

In *Don Quixote*, the reader sees very little of the background (and back-stories) and the inner lives of the duke and duchess. There are brief allusions to their past in the recitations of the ladies-in-waiting who are actresses in their metadramas, but the nobleman and noblewoman seem to be devised to intervene in the ongoing and ever more outrageous fictions. They are sovereigns as puppeteers, with their court as an impromptu theatre and their famous visitors as jesters. They have little graciousness and little respect for their fellow human beings. Don Quixote arrives at their palatial estate with a false sense of security, buoyed by the belief that, for the first time since he has sallied forth, he will be regarded directly and unequivocally as a knight errant (II, 31). He does not have to justify his mission, and he thinks that this is a good thing, but the duke and duchess strive to relegate him to the margins of artistry as they assume his former role. If the knight and the squire are mocked, beaten, and humiliated, that is no problem. The show must go on, and burlesque follies are crucial components of the new vision. In the sequences of this section of the narrative, Don Quixote and Sancho Panza manage to hold their own, the first as a faithful defender of Dulcinea del Toboso and as a sage counsel to the governor-to-be, and the second as a civil servant with estimable common sense. While ultimately thwarted in their heroic and administrative endeavours, respectively, they maintain their dignity, and, if a bit paradoxically, their centrality in the comprehensive scheme. Nonetheless, the ducal pair are formidable foes and strong symbols, a distinct brand of antagonist for the knight errant and purveyors of a different angle on the exploration of reading. For better or worse, they become enchanters, geared to reposition Don Quixote in his own history and thus to rewrite history. They epitomize, through a strong dose of irony, the commanding presence of the reader, who is by no means idle.

One cannot fail to notice a detail conveyed by Doña Rodríguez in a conversation with Don Quixote in Chapter 48 of Part II. The duchess may seem to be radiant, with 'cheeks of milk and carmine' and in the best of health, but, as the lady expounds, all that glitters is not gold, for 'your grace should know that for this she can thank God, first of all, and then the two issues she has on her legs, which drain the bad humors that the doctors say fill her body' (p. 771).[3] In Chapter 50, 'phantoms' invade the room to exact revenge for the audacious gossip, beating the duenna and pinching and scratching Don Quixote. Doña Rodríguez and the narrator reveal embarrassing intimacies that disrupt the image of natural beauty projected by the duchess, and she is mortified. The reader may view this as a dose of poetic justice, but the duchess clearly is not amused. If the perceived affront to Lope de Vega motivates Avellaneda to write a continuation, the insult to the duchess may be the pretext for *The Duchess's Diary*. Though hardly complimentary, the description of the duchess's incisions — what goes on under her skirt — hints of an inner self, a 'real' person to counter the courtly deceiver, the manipulative theatrical engineer, the wealthy lady with too much time on her hands. Chapman develops the duchess's psyche, thereby transferring her from a narrative (and metanarrative) personage into something on the order of a flesh-and-blood woman. In a sense, he finds her humanity; he restores the soul that arguably is lacking in Cervantes's and Cide Hamete's account. And, as in all cases of refashioning, writing becomes a function of reading, so that Chapman and his protagonist are interpreters and critics of *Don Quixote*.

In the spirit of Cervantes, Chapman includes a preface that explains that the narrative persona — more editor than writer — has found the manuscript of the diary of Doña María Isabel Echauri y Pradillo, Duchess of Caparroso, who records events that took place during the early months of 1616. She is not the fictionalized character, but the woman on whom the character was based. She and her husband, the duke Don Jerónimo, were hosts to Miguel de Cervantes during the summer of 1608, following the enormous success of Part I of *Don Quixote*. She became attached to him and was shocked by what she considered to be the gross misrepresentation of her double in Part II. The speaker in the preface ends with the comment, 'Then as now authors are not to be entirely trusted; our simplicities become their complexities' (p. 7).[4] It cannot be lost on the reader that Chapman recreates the conventions of the found manuscript and the multi-layered and potentially dangerous act of translation, which involves mediation that can serve or defer the truth. Possibly guided by the feminine variations of the picaresque, with men fabricating the voices of women, Chapman crafts a female character and voice. He enters the frame of *Don Quixote*, yet widens it to match the historical Cervantes with the Duchess of Caparroso. Not unlike the scheme of *Don Quixote*, *The Duchess's Diary* is revisionist fiction posing as revisionist history. Chapman takes an unlikeable and unsympathetic figure, a spoiled member of the aristocracy, and demonstrates that she has feelings, that she bleeds when wounded. He notes Cervantes's preoccupation with the status of women in society, as manifested in *Don Quixote*, the *Exemplary Novels*, and other works, and he adds the duchess to the list of damsels (or *damas*) in distress. He elides her villainy and gives her a series of trials and a fortitude that eludes her alter ego.

The translated segment of the diary begins with an entry in which Cervantes ('our guest') is on the duchess's mind. Her neighbours have read Part II of *Don Quixote* and have been engrossed in it. Aware that they are privy to her 'secret condition' and to her friendship with the author, the duchess lifts her skirts before the local gentry, who recall her amateur theatricals based on the novel. She cries, '[Y]ou don't understand, the author divided himself in two but cut me into little bits, we must distinguish between truth and fiction' (pp. 10–11). She cannot believe that Cervantes, who praised her as his inspiration eight years before, has betrayed her and has made her an object of ridicule; he is an amalgam of charm and treachery. Her private life is, in essence and in corrupted form, in the public domain. The duchess addresses her confrontation with the book, with pleasure in the early parts being overshadowed by the reaction to the fictional duchess. She had hoped that the author would dedicate his book to her, and she certainly had not expected this literary treason. Her recollections indicate that she became attached to him and that she hung onto his every word. Despite the insult, she speaks of him with warmth, whereas she consistently refers to the duke as 'my husband in name only', a man she married for his social position as a sacrifice for her parents;

he is an uncouth bully who has behaved miserably toward her. Her 'enchanter', in contrast, 'was scrupulously clean and never seemed to perspire. Inside him was bounce. It appeared that the world was still brand new to him, he could look at it as if it has never happened before, so if you were with him you started to see it like that, too. I've never been so happy as when I saw the world again through his eyes' (pp. 26–27). With the duke, she can have style; with Cervantes, substance. She was not fascinated nearly so much by literature and art as by him, a man who loved to discuss the Battle of Lepanto but was reticent to recount his years of captivity. He was calm, patient, engaged, and engaging, modest and unassuming but not without confidence in his skills as a writer. He whets her critical appetite: 'You always talk in opposites, I said, everything is a paradox. I think it's an easy way of sounding clever, don't you? No reply. The hint of a shrug in his shoulders. Silence. I'd wanted to feel victorious, but I didn't' (p. 32).

The priest who became the 'grave ecclesiastic' has died, and in his place is a chaplain dedicated to the reformation of the duchess. In alliance with the duke, he plans to have her join a barefoot sisterhood for wayward gentlewomen. The lady's thoughts are simultaneously on resistance and memory, seeking to avoid a spiritual imprisonment and remembering her encounters with an author whom she rarely identifies by name. On the one hand, she is throwing tantrums. On the other, she reminisces about how the writer changed her perception of the world and her understanding of art. Life imitates art, to a degree, when the duchess plays the role of Dulcinea in a masque that the author would attend and critique favourably, with special appreciation for her performance. The juxtaposition is telling, for the duchess is dramatizing her predicament. She is the lead actress in a melodrama that she would convey, perhaps correctly, as tragedy. He becomes a reviewer, and he laments that he is one of the least successful dramatists in Spain. The duchess concludes that this is because '[h]e is not a master of the obvious cleverly redecorated. For him everything must be qualified by contradictions which successively undermine the reader's certainty, even of what he's reading. It is a slowly dawning pleasure and mystery, quite the opposite of the quick duellings of drama' (p. 53). She adds, slyly, 'I mean, of course, it is a pleasure provided you do not find yourself portrayed as sinking in the amusing quagmire of his world' (p. 53). The diary treats the producer, the performer, the consumer, the critic, and the metacritic of drama, as backdrop for the duchess's 'real-life' dilemma, and to save herself she must resort to metatheatrical strategies. It is noteworthy that she plays Dulcinea, an absence in the novel, except when enchanted by Sancho Panza and when making guest appearances in the Cave of Montesinos and, to be sure, in theatricals at the ducal palace.

The author mentions his work-in-progress, revealing that 'Don Quixote has just defeated another knight known as the Knight of the Mirrors. He is the complete hero now, he is successful in everything he does because he no longer quite believes in what he does' (pp. 57–58). The duchess makes him promise that he will not convert the protagonist into a cynic, and he agrees, but discloses that 'as the world honours him for what he was so he begins to doubt what he is' (p. 58). In a request that will prove to be ironic, she urges the writer not to divulge more of the story, since she wishes to be surprised. The two share thoughts and read together, relishing books and conceptual pursuits, and the duchess finds herself 'enchanted' by her admirer, who even devises subtle ways of protecting the duchess against the ill will of her husband. In the meantime, she has to fight off the duke's accomplices, the foremost among them a doctor who opens the sutures in her leg to guard against hysteria. She confides in the writer, narrating her family history, tainted by the duke's three illegitimate children, and trusting him enough to expose the wounds inflicted by the surgeon. The author, in turn, opens his heart to her by speaking of his seven months in jail in Seville for bookkeeping errors during his tenure as a tax collector, with emphasis on the judge who revelled in the power of his position — and in the infliction of pain — as he sentenced the guilty party. This leads the duchess to cite a man detested by her and the writer, the late Father Gattinara, the prototype of the grave ecclesiastic, who rates *Don Quixote* as no better than the books that it proposes to mock and who mercilessly scorns its author. This allows Chapman to write a wise, witty, and balanced defence, in the first person, for Cervantes (pp. 76–77).

As narrator and critic, the duchess mixes her dismay at her characterization in Part II with remarks on the book itself. The duke has submitted that the second part is inferior to the first, calling the continuation 'wretched' and claiming that 'if you ask me, the author has written himself out' (p. 82). The duchess is unconvinced: 'Even I could see that that wasn't true. The sequel was far better, deeper and darker, which was why it hurt me to be seen as part of it, to be shown as the guiding spirit, the smiling torturer of his heroes whom the reader has learnt to love so much'; her 'other' is nothing but 'a beautiful shell concealing heart-constricting poison, an alabaster Diana with venomed arrows' (p. 82). Chapman reading (and writing) the duchess reading Cervantes is a tour-de-force of self-referentiality, one that captures the tone and the literary macrocosm of *Don Quixote*. In *The Duchess's Diary*, he amplifies the base by affording the lady the opportunity to deal with Cervantes's offensive delineation when, to her credit, she accentuates the brilliance and profundity of the second part. This is a new take on poetic licence and on the interplay of history and fiction that initiates and remains at the centre of the two parts of *Don Quixote*.

The duchess resumes the story of her abuse. She has been placed with holy women and dressed in sackcloth, her head shaven. She makes up and recites again and again a prayer: 'please let me see everything as he does' (p. 84). The nuns have respected her, but she is eager to escape the convent, and she manages to do so with the aid of her faithful servant Juana. There is a thirteen-day gap in the diary to mark the episode. She is caught and institutionalized once more, and her husband will have nothing to do with her; he says that she is dead to him. Resigned and tranquil, she contemplates details of the theatrical piece constructed around the wooden horse, Clavileño. She relates that in the collaboration with her guest, she lets slip the words 'I love you', to which he replies with tenderness and tact (pp. 88–89). Theirs is an intimate friendship, a respite from the hardships and coldness of the world. When he takes his leave, she writes to him, but he soon ceases to respond. Eventually she returns to her deserted home, and as she consults the book in which she appears, her anger has been tempered: 'Each time I see the duchess mentioned my determination increases but I no longer feel desolated or outraged. My indignation is strong and coherent now' (p. 101). She writes of a precarious situation on her way home in which she was saved by a man who evokes Juan Palomeque, the innkeeper in *Don Quixote* who endorses fiction over history (I, 32). Here, she deems herself a real damsel in distress, rescued by a middle-aged man dressed not in armour but in an apron. His bold action restores her trust in human decency and bears out Cervantes's judgment, which she had doubted, 'that this world is good, is kind, at its worst is farcical' (p. 107). The duchess resolves to reconnect with the author, who 'must, in all honour, tell me the truth. He must give me myself back' (p. 108). In Tarazona, she takes refuge in the house of an elderly priest who, fortunately for her, has not read *Don Quixote*. Reproducing a conversation with a local gentleman, Don Rufo de Paz, she somewhat reluctantly names Cervantes for the first time, given that 'I was never going to add to his fame' (p. 111). Accompanied by the inexperienced Don Rufo, she continues her journey, only to be attacked by Morisco highwaymen, who kill the young man. She is so upset by the circumstances that she is reduced to employ a distancing device, narrating a good part of the story in the third person. Saved by one of Don Rufo's outriders and escaping further peril, she finally enters Alcalá de Henares, where the people are conspicuously proud of their native son. She is close to her destination: Madrid. She will track down the man she names 'Miguel de Serpientes' (p. 112).

The duchess imagines a conversation with the author, in which she makes light of her disappointment in him, thus underplaying her role. She admits that when she has reread the chapters in which she appears, '[t]hey are not quite as shocking as I remember them but this time I have been impressed by the poverty of his imagination', and, on surveying the palace scenes, she adds, 'How dare he batten on reality so?' (p. 122). She makes the terse statement, 'I saw him yesterday. He was dressed as a Franciscan' (p. 122), yet when she reaches his house, he is dead. She is still obsessed by the question of why he put 'that small, private detail' in the book, but now she is ready to forgive him, and to suggest that 'I had already answered it for myself somewhere' (p. 123). She has come to the end of a process and achieves a peace of sorts, recognizing that 'when you meet someone dead you don't meet him but yourself' (p. 124). In her final entry, she makes the point that 'if anyone does ask my opinion of Miguel de Cervantes I shall say that when I knew him he was human to a fault' (p. 126). The editor appends an epilogue that refers to two documents regarding the duchess: one with reference to a robbery that took place in Madrid in May of 1616 and the other a memorial tablet from Puerto Rico dated 29 June 1645. On the first count, she was acquitted for the theft of a pair of shoes. On the second, it seems feasible that she travelled to the West Indies to join her brothers and that she remarried and had children. She was fifty-nine years old.

In *The Duchess's Diary*, Robin Chapman concentrates on *lacunae* and on the act (and art) of writing as rewriting. Like Jorge Luis Borges and a bright array of literati, he follows Cervantes's lemma of creative alchemy, through which the past is absorbed and recreated in the present while positioning itself in the future. The narrative is certainly ingenious, but it is more than merely a skilful complement.

Chapman takes advantage of the dialectics of history and poetry that helps to transport *Don Quixote* into new realms. The 'historical' duchess interacts with the historical author, who writes her into his text. She charges that he misrepresents — *misreads* — her, and her diary is a play of perspectives that befits Cervantes himself. She is an abused and beleaguered wife, subject to the protocols and injustices that affect the women of the period. Miguel de Cervantes challenges her intellect and animates her spirit, and then he lets her down by fictionalizing her as a shallow and silly despot, who makes fun of and inflicts pain on the mad knight and his gullible squire. In the course of composing the diary, she becomes a writer, a thinker, and a social and literary critic. She sets forth a persona to rival Cervantes's duchess, and she broadens the biography of the author, giving him a more defined personality. He is quick, comforting, genteel, and elusive. He prefers not to speak of his time in Algiers or of his marriage. He opposes the duke's aggressive style and his mistreatment of the duchess. He talks about life, literature, and his own works. He is a spectator at his hostess's theatrical performance and a driving force in the drama of her existence. All this establishes what may be labelled a series of *mise-en-abyme* effects that take their lead from *Don Quixote*. Cervantes and the duchess cross paths in a system of parallel universes. Each has a mystifying impact on the other, as reified first in a novel that pretends to be a chronicle and then in a novel that pretends to be a diary. Both history and reality are so near and yet so far.

It is clear that the authors of *The Duchess's Diary* — the real and the fictional authors — are meticulous readers of *Don Quixote*. They share a sense of humour and a sense of irony. The particular variety of revisionism serves a higher cause, a cause that goes beyond making the reader more tolerant of the duchess and beyond artistic freedom, as well. In a unique manner, Chapman replicates Cervantes's dialogue with literature, as a mirror to reality and as an end in itself. The cross of history and metafiction would seem to be incongruous, but *Don Quixote* proves that this is not so. It could be argued that Cervantes is advocating that realism is but one approach to reality and that when one investigates the structure and construction of literature, it is possible to gain insights that go far beyond aesthetics.[5] Chapman devises a fiction in which the historical Cervantes enters an imagined world, as happens in the prologue to Part I of *Don Quixote*. By 'historicizing' the duchess of Part II, Chapman works backwards. His Cervantes stands in the middle, not only as a 'real' character in a work of fiction, but as an actor and speaker whose conduct and words are supplied from without, that is, whose 'gaps' are filled in by a second author. The duchess's strong will and centrality as diarist make her the protagonist of the story. Two men frame her in what resembles a triptych. Cervantes is subtly drawn, strong and elliptical, exemplary yet flawed, in short, human. Captivated by him, the duchess tries to penetrate the enigmas of his life and of his psyche. The openness in this respect seems quite consistent with the 'true history' of Don Miguel. The portrayal of the duke Don Jerónimo is by no means subtle. He is monstrous in form and substance, an ogre whose villainy far exceeds the scope of his intervention in Part II. His presence in *The Duchess's Diary* gives Chapman the chance to scrutinize the conditions under which women, and notably married women, were forced to operate in early modern Spain, from a (man-made, to be sure) woman's perspective. Chapman enters a narrative territory inhabited by the likes of Francisco Delicado, Alonso Jerónimo de Salas Barbadillo, and Alonso de Castillo Solórzano — inventors of *pícaras* — but he executes his task with an air of generosity and sympathy that his predecessors did not choose to highlight.

Learning from the greatest master, Chapman plays with perspective in order to elevate fiction, which is to elevate subjectivity, in a double sense. Aristotle equates history with objectivity, as distinguished from the subjectivity of poetry. In *Don Quixote*, Cervantes rejects the distinction by exploiting the mediating factors that inform historiography and the very act of perception. He becomes the advocate, and the genius, of the relative and its corollary, relative truth. If in *The Duchess's Diary* Chapman inverts some of the premises of *Don Quixote*, he is precisely in line with the message systems of Cervantes's novel. A fundamental message, and motif, is the inseparability of fact and fiction, existence and artistry, observation and expression, and so forth. Cervantes turns life into art and Chapman turns art into life, but neither category remains stable, and that is the idea. More about Cervantes than Don Quixote, *The Duchess's Diary* nonetheless could be classified as a quixotic novel. Chapman reveres Cervantes, literature, and the limitless potential of the intertext. His duchess, seen first in *Don Quixote* as a huntress, undertakes a personal quest for the truth, and her creator and editor inflects the venture with wit, irony, passion, compassion, and social conscience. By virtue of multiple deployments of distance, the result is studiedly and logically anachronistic, which is not only appropriate but desirable. *Don Quixote* invites the reader to evaluate and re-evaluate, to configure and reconfigure, and to acknowledge strings — and legs — being pulled. *The Duchess's Diary* does likewise, on its own terms and with its own combination of voices.

Notes to Chapter 18

1. Robin Chapman, *The Duchess's Diary* (London and Boston: Faber and Faber, 1985). The novel was reissued, with revisions, in 1985. Chapman (b. London) has credits as a novelist, playwright, screenwriter, and actor. *The Duchess's Diary* is the first of a trilogy based on *Don Quixote*. The other novels are *Sancho's Golden Age* (Oxford: David Brown, 2004) and *Pasamonte's Life* (Oxford: Aris & Phillips, 2005). I have written on the intertextual ties of *The Duchess's Diary* to *Don Quixote* and on critical treatment of the duchess in 'Voices Within: Robin Chapman's *The Duchess's Diary* and the Intertextual Conundrum of *Don Quixote*', *Romance Languages Annual*, 2 (1991), 400–05. For a recent study of the duchess and women's reading practices, see José María Paz Gago, 'La noble lectora: Las lecturas caballerescas de la duquesa', *Edad de Oro*, 26 (2007), 175–83.
2. See Yvonne Jehenson, 'The Pastoral Episode in Cervantes' *Don Quijote*: Marcela Once Again', *Cervantes*, 10. 2 (1990), 15–35.
3. References to *Don Quixote* are taken from Miguel de Cervantes, *Don Quixote*, trans. by Edith Grossman, introduction by Harold Bloom (New York: Ecco, 2003).
4. All quotations from *The Duchess's Diary* will refer to the 1985 edition, and page numbers will be indicated in parentheses.
5. This is a central thesis of my study *Cervantes in the Middle: Realism and Reality in the Spanish Novel from 'Lazarillo de Tormes' to 'Niebla'* (Newark, DE: Juan de la Cuesta, 2006).

PART IV

CERVANTES AND THE BRITISH THEATRE

CHAPTER 19

Cervantes on the Jacobean Stage

Trudi L. Darby and Alexander Samson

In his address to his patron, Pedro Fernández de Castro, conde de Lemos, in the dedication to the *Segunda parte del ingenioso cavallero Don Quixote de la Mancha* (1615), Cervantes took a swipe at the vastly inferior apocryphal second part of Avellaneda and revealed that his sequel was most eagerly desired not in fact by his protector but from as far away as China:

> the person who has shown the deepest interest (in Part II) has been the great Emperor of China, who, not more than a month ago, sent an emissary with a letter for me in the Chinese language, asking, or I should say begging, me to send the knight to him, because he wanted to establish a college in which the Castilian language would be read, and the book he wanted the students to read was the history of Don Quixote. He further said that he wanted me to be the rector of the college.[1]

His tongue-in-cheek claim to have been invited by Chinese envoys to found and head a school of Quixotic studies, pointed to the emerging phenomenon of literary fame and a multilingual vernacular culture in early modern Europe in which texts were prized as both cultural goods and simultaneously language learning tools. In his 'Aprobación' Francisco Márquez Torres, a chaplain of Bernardo de Sandoval y Rojas, cardinal Archbishop of Toledo and great uncle of the Duke of Lerma,[2] recorded how Cervantes's work had been appreciated in France, Italy, Germany and Flanders (p. 612). An ironic recognition of the globalization of literature and the myriad paths of its reception (generic, linguistic and cross-cultural) by the author was underlined by Torres in an anecdote about the reaction to mention of Cervantes's name amongst the train of French gentlemen accompanying the Valois ambassador, Noël Brûlart de Sillery, in Madrid to negotiate the double Habsburg–Valois marriages of 1615:[3]

> a number of the French gentlemen accompanying the ambassador, as courteous as discerning and lovers of good writing, approached me and other chaplains of the Cardinal my master, desirous to know which the mostly highly-prized witty books on the market were, and mentioning that I happened to be censoring at that moment this book, scarcely had they heard the name of Miguel de Cervantes, than they began to all talk at once, extolling the esteem in which his works were held in France and neighbouring states, the *Galatea*, which one of them knew the first part of almost off by heart, and the *Novels*.

Their praise was such that I offered to take them to visit the author which they corresponded with a thousand demonstrations of their lively desire to do so. They asked in detail about his age, profession, quality and quantity. I found myself obliged to report that he was an old soldier, a gentleman but poor, to which one of them replied in formal terms: 'How is it that Spain does not make such a man rich, supported from public funds?' Another one of them arrived and with this witty thought said: 'If necessity keeps him writing, then may it please God that he never know abundance so that with his works, although he is poor, he enriches all the world.'[4]

Although fame evidently did not yet translate (to the surprise of at least one member of the French embassy) into substantial advances and personal wealth, it meant at least that his cultural influence was palpable even in his own lifetime. The slow emergence of the figure of the author can be illustrated by comparing Cervantes with his great rival Lope de Vega, who remained practically unknown in England except for an anonymous and unattributed translation of his 1604 prose romance *El peregrino en su patria* as *The Pilgrim* (1621), perhaps by the Oxford lawyer William Dutton. A reissue of this translation, coinciding with the Prince of Wales's journey to Madrid in 1623, informed the reader that he was 'accompted in his owne Countrey one of the choysest Spirits'.[5] Although his literary celebrity was a factor underlying the translation, Lope's name still did not appear anywhere on the text and the translator similarly remained anonymous. Fletcher wrote a play based on it, performed by the King's Men at court on 1 January 1621–22.[6] In the same way that dynastic marriages produced multilingual rulers and empires, the paths of literary fashion, along which fiction was disseminated in early modern Europe, followed contours of political engagement, and the fictions were shaped and distorted in turn by the ideological landscapes over which they travelled. It has been argued that a book's ability to move across cultural and linguistic frontiers, influencing beyond merely national traditions, its translatability, is the key to its importance and value.[7] Cervantes's stories were taken up after their publication both within Spain and beyond. At least twenty adaptations of his works appeared in Spain before 1680, including adaptations of two of the *Novelas ejemplares* (1613) by his rival Lope, as plots for his plays *La ilustre fregona* (*Parte XXIV*, 1641) and *El mayor imposible* (*Parte XXV*, 1647 based on 'El celoso extremeño'). The French translation of the *Novelas ejemplares* came out within a year of their publication in Spain,[8] and there were a further eight editions of this French translation before 1700. The popularity of Cervantine material in France can be gauged equally from there being no fewer than twenty-three stage adaptations of his work during the same period.[9]

What the censor, Francisco Márquez Torres's list of countries ignored or was indifferent to, was the vogue for Cervantine prose fiction, its translation and eager consumption by English-speaking audiences. The evidence of Beaumont's *Knight of the Burning Pestle* (c.1607) demonstrates just how early the Cervantine counter-romance (Part I was published 1605) began to influence the Jacobean stage.[10] The printer Walter Burre commented on the failure of the play on stage owing to its audience's failure to read 'the privie marke of irony about it'.[11] By 1621, however, the influence of Cervantes's ironic refashioning of romance was apparent in the first published romance by a woman in England, Mary Wroth's *The Countess of*

Montgomery's Urania (1621). The Sidney circle had been interested in Spanish romance from the early 1580s. Philip Sidney's *Arcadia*, for example, displayed the influence of Bartholomew Yong's manuscript translation of Jorge de Montemayor's *Diana* from 1582–83.[12] When it was eventually published, it bore a dedication to the supposed original of Stella in Sidney's *Astrophil and Stella*, Penelope Rich (at one time proposed as a possible bride for him), who had been brought up at Ashby-de-la-Zouche by Sidney's aunt Katherine, Countess of Huntingdon. This was the seat of the Hastings family. Fletcher's collaborator and bedfellow, Francis Beaumont, was a cousin of the fifth Earl of Huntingdon, Henry Hastings. Yong had been in Spain in 1578 with his stepbrother Richard Parker, where he had met Jane Dormer, duchess of Feria, a first cousin of Sidney's father and member of Mary I's household in 1554 when Philip II and his court had travelled to reside in London. Philip Sidney was named after the uncrowned king of England, Philip II, who was his godfather.[13]

The *Diana* Yong translated was mined for the main plot of Shakespeare's *The Two Gentlemen of Verona*, probably in the early 1590s, i.e. before its publication. This provides yet another link between Shakespeare and the culturally Hispanophile group associated with John Fletcher and the Hastings, and so in turn the translators Leonard Digges and James Mabbe, both resident in Spain in 1611–14 and contributors of prefatory material to the First Folio in 1623. Mary Wroth's work betrayed its immersion in Iberian romances from *Amadis de Gaula* and the *Palmerin of England* to *The Mirror of Knighthood*, translated by Margaret Tyler in 1578. The four volumes of *Amadis* translated by Anthony Munday and published 1618–19 were dedicated to Philip Herbert, husband of Wroth's close friend Susan, Countess of Montgomery.[14] Susan and her husband were also the dedicatees of Thomas Milles translation of Pedro de Mexía's *Silva de varia lección* in 1619.[15] Wroth was having an adulterous affair with her cousin, William Herbert, Earl of Pembroke, one of the dedicatees of Leonard Digges's *Gerardo the Unfortunate Spaniard* (1622), the source of Middleton and Rowley's *The Changeling* and Fletcher and Massinger's *The Spanish Curate* both performed in that same year.[16] All of these families, the Sidneys, Hastings and Herberts were linked by marriage and the fostering of the others' children and charges. Mary Sidney, sister of Philip, had married into the Herbert family in 1577, while the Hastings, Earls of Huntingdon had given one of their charges, the Earl of Rutland's sister to the Herberts.[17] These three families displayed an interest in Spanish culture over several generations. The argument that *Don Quixote* sounded the death knell of romance, given that after its publication no new work of chivalric romance was produced in Spain, neglects the durability of literary forms transported and transposed to foreign cultures, where they were both ironized and redeployed.

During the interregnum following the Civil War the court of Charles II had resided in the Spanish Netherlands between 1656 and 1660, with a visit to Spain itself in 1659, as well as to Paris, where they had witnessed the vogue for Spanish drama then sweeping the Low Countries and France. This exposure to Hispanic theatrical traditions in Paris and Brussels meant that after the Restoration a number of plays based on Spanish originals were staged in London. Samuel Pepys, who knew Spanish and Portuguese and was an avid collector of Spanish books, commented on Sir Samuel Tuke's *The Adventures of Five Hours*, an adaptation of *Los empeños de seis horas* by Antonio Coello (although then thought to be by Calderón), that it was: 'the best, for the variety, and the most excellent continuance of the plot to the very end'.[18] This play was co-authored by the Earl of Bristol, George Digby, who was born in Madrid and also penned three adaptations of Calderón including *Elvira; or, The Worst Not Always True* an adaptation of *No siempre lo peor es cierto* and two other plays which have not survived. These plays were read for plot, the complaint often heard in both France and England about the *comedia* being that they had too much plot. The character Wildblood claimed in the play *An Evening's Love; or, The Mock Astrologer* based partly on Calderón's *El astrólogo fingido* in 1668, 'I hate your Spanish honour ever since it spoiled our English plays'.[19] Four years earlier Dryden had written *The Rival Ladies* (1664) derived from Cervantes's 'Las dos doncellas'. His play *The Indian Emperour* was taken from Calderón's *El príncipe constante*. Sir Richard Fanshawe, after graduating from Cambridge, spent a year in France and then went to Spain for two years, after which he was given a job in the service of the English ambassador where he remained for another three years until his return to England in 1638. In 1653, Fanshawe completed translations of Camões's *Os Lusiadas* and Antonio Hurtado de Mendoza's *Querer por solo querer* and his dramatic entertainment *Fiestas de Aranjuez*.[20]

Despite a concerted and intense interest in the *comedia* and 'Spanish plots' after the Restoration, critics have argued that it was unimportant before this date, with only four plays from the Jacobean and Caroline periods demonstrating a direct influence. The earliest assessment by Martin Hume in his 1905 *Spanish Influence on English Literature* exaggerated the *comedia*'s influence, suggesting 'the plots were almost as frequently taken from Spanish and from Italian sources' and that Fletcher 'was a good Spanish scholar'.[21] A corrective published by Rudolph Schevill a year later identified only three plays derived from *comedias*: the anonymous *Love's Cure; or, The Martial Maid* printed in the Beaumont and Fletcher folio of 1647, based on Guillén de Castro's *La fuerza de la costumbre*,[22] and two works by James Shirley *The Young Admiral* (1633) based on Lope's *Don Lope de Cardona* and *The Opportunity* (1634) from Tirso's *El castigo del penséque*.[23] Another play from before the Restoration with a dramatic Spanish source was Massinger's *The Renegado* (1624), which drew on Cervantes's *Los baños de Argel* published in 1615 in his *Ocho comedias y ocho entremeses*. The alleged indifference to Spanish drama in the early seventeenth century, in contrast to the fascination with prose fiction and history, rests on the mistaken assumption that Fletcher, his circle and others could only access Spanish material in the original with difficulty. The Earl of Nottingham's embassy to Valladolid to conclude the Treaty of London in 1605 had been treated to a performance of Lope de Vega's *El caballero de Illescas*, while a performance at court for Charles I by the company of Juan Navarro Oliver in 1635, presumably in Castilian, underlines the level of interest in this national theatre and assumed a degree of familiarity in its courtly audience with the Spanish language.[24] At least three of Fletcher's own plays were derived in whole or part from material only available to him as far as we know in Spanish, including two *comedias*: *The Island Princess* (1619–21), based on Bartolomé Leonardo de Argensola's prose history *Conquista de las Islas Molucas* (1609); the plot of *Rule a Wife Have a Wife* (1624), which was taken from Alonso Jerónimo de Salas Barbadillo's *El sagaz Estacio, el marido examinado* (1620);[25] and, with some reservations about its attribution to him, *Love's Cure or The Martial Maid*, derived from Guillén de Castro's *La fuerza de la costumbre*, not published until 1625, but perhaps written by 1610. Most critics suggest that the text published in the Beaumont and Fletcher folio was a Massinger revision of a script initiated before 1613.[26] This raises interesting questions about how they were able to get hold of a play, unpublished in their lifetimes. Arguments that Fletcher's *The Loyal Subject* (1618) was an adaptation of Lope's *El gran duque de Moscovia* (1617), and that *The Prophetess* (1622) and Massinger's *The Roman Actor* (1626) both derived from Lope's *Lo fingido verdadero* (1621), have been rebutted on the grounds that the resemblances are isolated and plays concerns too divergent in theme and tone.[27] In addition, a suggestion that another Lope play, *El valor de Malta* (1596–1604?), could not have influenced the joint work by Philip Massinger, John Fletcher and Nathaniel Field, *The Knight of Malta* (1616–18), because it remained unpublished during Lope's lifetime, needs to be seen in the light of evidence that these playwrights were able to access *comedias*, whether as manuscript copies or *sueltas* (i.e. early printed editions of single plays) now lost.[28] It has also been suggested that *The Fair Maid of the Inn* (1625–26) was based not on the Cervantes short story but a stage version sometimes attributed to Lope de Vega.[29]

Definitive evidence of Fletcher being able to read Spanish, however, comes from *The Island Princess*. Detailed textual comparison uncovers clear borrowing from Argensola's Castilian *Conquista de las Islas Molucas*, rather than the French version by Sieur de Bellan's *Histoire mémorable de Dias espagnol et de Quixaire Princesse des Moluques* appended to the French translation of the *Exemplary Novels*.[30] Revealing of his *modus operandi* then, Fletcher's awareness of the story through the French translation of the *Novelas ejemplares*, published in 1615, had led him to obtain a copy of the original Spanish prose history. Fletcher also worked directly from the Spanish texts on *The Chances*, *Rule a Wife and Have a Wife* and *The Fair Maid of the Inn*.[31] A detailed comparison of *The Custom of the Country* (1620) with the corresponding passages in *Persiles y Sigismunda* similarly reveals echoes and parallels too striking to be mere coincidence.[32] The argument about whether Fletcher read Spanish or not needs to be situated clearly in the context of a multilingual vernacular culture, in which writers worked on multiple versions of texts or parallel texts and from familiar to unfamiliar languages. It is clear that Fletcher worked sometimes directly from Spanish originals, at other times from French translations, and sometimes from both simultaneously whether mediated by others or not. Regardless of whether associates, such as Leonard Digges or James Mabbe, provided him with manuscript translations that have not survived, plot summaries, read or discussed stories with him, Fletcher's encounter with Spanish material was definitively in the original in a significant number of cases from *El sagaz Estacio* to *La fuerza de la costumbre*. E. M. Wilson concluded that it is 'simpler to believe that he read Spanish with some fluency than to postulate undiscovered translations or to invent unwanted collaborators'.[33] The only logical conclusion on the basis of the available evidence is that Fletcher did read Spanish and could work with Castilian texts. Although Wilson dismissed the extent of his cultural borrowing from Spanish, this feature of his plays from Spanish sources, needs to be seen as much in the context of its reception as its origin; in other words how the insertion of Spanish phrases was expected to play with audiences. More interesting questions about Fletcher's engagement with Spanish sources surround how he knew what to look for, why he chose the material he used and how he acquired that material in the first place. Although the Argensola novel had been published in 1609, Guillén de Castro's was unavailable in print until after Fletcher's death. An awareness of the literary scene in Spain even before the Prince of Wales' visit in 1623 and his use of plays apparently unpublished even in Spanish underline the extent of his connections with the international book trade, diplomats, politicians and spies.[34]

Although Fletcher's collaborative form of authorship makes generalization difficult, in a canon of around fifty-four plays more than a quarter were from Spanish prose fiction originals.[35] Of the total of seventeen plays with recognized Spanish sources, the majority came from Cervantes, thirteen of this total.[36] Despite his cultural Hispanophilia and profound debt to Cervantes, his political views reflected a strongly Protestant background. When in *The Fair Maid of the Inn* Forobosco proposes to conjure the devil in high Dutch, the clown retorts: 'no, *Spanish*, that roares best; and will appeare more dreadfull' (II.ii. ll. 118–19: x, 586).[37] Later in the play, picking up on the stereotype common in England by this time about the scarcity of meat in Spain,[38] Forobosco suggests to a muleteer that to make his fortune he need do no more than travel to Madrid with an ox 'roste him whole, with a pudding in's belly; that would the eight wonder of the world in those parts I assure you' for it would 'Goe beyond all their garlike olla Podrithoes, though you sod one in Garguentuas cauldron, bring in more mony, then all the monsters of Affrick' (IV.iii.177–78 and 180–82: x, 619). Fletcher's grandfather had been a friend of the martyrologist John Foxe, while his father had witnessed the execution of Mary, Queen of Scots, and eventually become Bishop of London. Fletcher's patrons, the Hastings family, Earls of Huntingdon, based at Ashby-de-la-Zouch in Leicestershire, had probably been introduced to him by his collaborator Francis Beaumont, who had lived near the family seat as a child and was a first cousin of Henry, the Fifth Earl, a similar age and had attended Oxford and the Inns of Court at the same time.[39] The fact that Henry's great uncle, the Third Earl, had been briefly a custodian of Mary, Queen of Scots, during the same period in which Fletcher's grandfather had acted as her chaplain may have provided an additional connection to smooth the playwright's passage into their protection. Writing to his patron Elizabeth, the Countess of Huntingdon, probably in 1620, perhaps against the background of the flight of James I and VI's daughter Elizabeth and the Elector Palatine, Frederick V, from Prague, Fletcher wrote witheringly of the masque, courtly extravagance and mused about: 'whether ytt be true / wee shall have warrs wth Spaine: (I wolde wee might)'.[40] Cervantine ambivalence to Spanish imperial and colonial aspirations, counter-epic discourse in his work and the critique of transparency in relation to identity produced by Spain's hegemonic response to the '*converso* problem', his awareness of cultural hybridity,[41] probably found a counterpart in Fletcher's political hostility to Spain, opposition to the royal policy of rapprochement, anxieties about the colonial process and exploration of political alternatives to Jacobean absolutism.

Social network analysis such as that suggestively carried out by Trudi Darby in her chapter on Rowley, can shed useful light on the provenance of material, as well as the connections between the printers, noble patrons, translators, literati, travellers, merchants and intelligencers through whose hands cultural goods passed. The religiously ambivalent figure of Anthony Munday is an interesting case in point, pivotal in linking many of the figures discussed here, from dramatists, some of whom collaborated with each other, to noble patrons exercised with Spanish material, printers and publishers. In 1602 Munday was linked with the dramatists Thomas Dekker and John Webster, through their contribution of verses to the preliminaries of his translation of the third part of *Palmerin of England*; the latter writing 'translation is a traffique of high price: / It brings all learning in one paradise'.[42] Webster later contributed to Fletcher's *The Fair Maid of the Inn*, derived from 'La ilustre fregona', while Dekker was involved in *The Spanish Gipsy* based on 'La fuerza de la sangre' and 'La gitanilla'.[43] Later two of Munday's translations of *Amadís* were dedicated, as we have seen, to Philip Herbert, Earl of Montgomery. Philip and his wife Susan (née Vere) were also the recipients in 1619 of Thomas Milles's translations compiled in his *Treasury of auncient and moderne times*, previously dedicated to Thomas Brudenell in 1613, a miscellany that included work by Pedro de Mexía as well as French and Italian authors.[44] Philip and his brother William, Earl of Pembroke, were similarly the dedicatees of Leonard Digges' translation *Gerardo the Unfortunate Spaniard* (1622), a source of at least two more plays as we have seen. Fletcher's collaborator, Philip Massinger's father had been general agent to the Earls of Pembroke and the dedication in 1624 of *The Bondman* to Philip Herbert may have been the reason for a pension that he and then his widow received from the family.[45] He also dedicated a play to Katherine, sister of Fletcher's patron the Earl of Huntingdon, the wife of Philip Lord Stanhope, dedicatee of the anonymous translation of Cervantes's *The Travels of Persiles and Sigismunda* in 1619. *The Rogue* also of 1622, a translation by James Mabbe of Mateo Alemán's picaresque novel *Guzmán de Alfarache*, contained dedicatory material from both Leonard Digges and Ben Jonson, as well as Fletcher. Beaumont and Fletcher had penned dedicatory verses for Jonson's *Volpone* as early as 1607. Digges and Mabbe, as we have seen, both provided material for the First Folio of Shakespeare in 1623, as did Jonson, who had received money from William Herbert, following the dedication of *Sejanus* to him. All of these figures were engaged by Spanish cultural goods and yet associated with the anti-Spanish faction at court. Pembroke, for example, whose famous uncle, the poet Philip Sidney, had died fighting Habsburg forces, invested in a number of English colonial ventures designed to challenge Spanish imperial hegemony. He was the second-biggest shareholder in the Virginia Company and put money into the Guiana Company, the Somers Islands Company, the project to discover the Northwest Passage and the East India Company. He was a powerful opponent of the Spanish match. The social network studied here exemplifies an engagement with Spain, produced by militantly Protestant, anti-Spanish and anti-Catholic hostility. Nevertheless, religious affiliations were often subordinated by this group to other loyalties, including aesthetic and local ones. The Beaumont family, for example, had several recusant members and when the Earls of Essex and Southampton (who had Catholic family connections) sailed to raid Cadiz they took Spanish translations with them on their voyage to practise their language in idle moments.[46]

In the verses Fletcher contributed to James Mabbe's translation of *Guzmán de Alfarache*, he praised the text for it 'by strange / Bifronted posture, Ill, to good, doth change',[47] a statement of the playwright's theory of satire as a force for moral improvement, working through irony, at the heart of his 'politics of unease'.[48] Gordon McMullan argues that 'this "Bifronted posture" or doubleness is a key feature of Fletcher's work, from his habitual practice of collaboration to the characteristic mixed genre of his plays, tragicomedy'.[49] The Spanish *comedia* was of course characterized by its generic hybridity, combining tragic and comic elements. What drew Fletcher to Cervantes was the 'self-consciousness and anti-romance' found in his stories, a 'correlative of his own generic experiments' and while he and his collaborators have been unjustly dismissed as writers of 'overblown and uncritical "romantic tragicomedy"' these same 'romance elements are simultaneously utilized and ironized'.[50] These comments brilliantly encapsulate the attraction of some of the prose fiction and plot elements derived from Cervantes. While *Don Quixote* seems to have had an indirect and diffuse impact on a number of different works from Beaumont's *Knight of the Burning Pestle*, George Wilkins' *The Miseries of Infant Marriage* and Thomas Middleton's *The Five Gallants* (all 1607), it was the interpolated narrative of 'El curioso impertinente', a novella of adultery, that had the greatest direct hold, inspiring Beaumont and Fletcher's *The Coxcomb* (1609), Middleton's *The Second Maiden's Tragedy* (1611), Nathan Field's *Amends for Ladies* (1611),[51] and the subplot of the lost *Cardenio* (1613) one of the three Shakespeare and Fletcher collaborations.[52] Nicolas Baudoin's very early 1608 translation of 'El curioso impertinente', *Le Curieux Impertinent* may partially explain why this particular interpolated narrative proved so popular in England, inspiring at least four plays by 1613. The 1607 Brussels edition of *Don Quixote* Part I may similarly be the one Shelton translated, and underlie the introduction of Don Quijote to an English-speaking audience. The arrival of the Earl of Nottingham's entourage in Spain in 1605, to put an end to thirty years of hostilities, coincided with the publication of Cervantes's masterpiece. While his train visited the capital, at that time Valladolid, a permanent embassy was soon established in Madrid on the court's return there the following year. Other material taking inspiration from *Don Quixote* — such as the culinary disappointments of Castruchio in Act V of *The Double Marriage* (*c*.1621), written with Massinger (which drew inspiration from Sancho's disenchantment with the way his status interfered with a good meal in *Don Quixote* Part II), or the Sanchoesque Geta in *The Prophetess*, also a Fletcher and Massinger collaboration — merely cannibalised or pirated the text for comic and satirical ideas. Although amongst the *Exemplary Novels*, there were those that traduced and made ironic use of romance, particularly *La señora Cornelia* and *La ilustre fregona*, others like *El casamiento engañoso* and *Las dos doncellas* appealed for verisimilitude and their affiliation with stories like the real-life murder in Alicante that underlay *The Changeling*. *Las dos doncellas* lent itself to dramatization particularly because of the place cross-dressing played, a staple of the early modern stage in England and Spain.

When reading for plots, how did early modern English playwrights pirate, adapt, and transform the stories they encountered and to what extent was this due to the exigencies of the representable, verisimilitude, the acting company, conditions of performance, or moral and social mores of Jacobean England? An examination of the use made of one of the inset narratives from *Don Quixote* will offer some answers. Cervantes's *Don Quixote* was first published in Madrid in 1605 and, although John Shelton's translation into English was not published until 1612, the influence of the novel was being felt on the English stage by 1610 at the latest, and possibly earlier. The English would soon come to think of Don Quijote as the archetypal knight errant and indeed, a play by Francis Beaumont, published in 1613, but possibly written as early as 1607, is thought to be an early skit on Cervantes's hero: 'My beloved Squire, and *George* my Dwarfe,' says Rafe an apprentice Grocer in an echo of Quixote's instructions to Sancho Panza, 'I charge you that from hence-forth you never call me by any other name, but the *Right Courteous and Valiant Knight of the burning Pestle*, and that you never call any female by the name of a woman or wench, but faire Ladie, if she have her desires, if not distressed Damsell; that you call all Forrests and Heaths Desarts, and all horses Palfries.'[53] Yet the most influential aspect of the *Quixote* was initially not the escapades of Quixote and his squire, as it would be in the eighteenth century, but one of *Don Quixote's* inset narratives: *El curioso impertinente*. Its particular influence may be due in part to the fact that it was translated into French by Nicolas Baudoin as a self-contained work and published in 1608 in parallel text as *Le Curieux Impertinent. El Curioso Impertinente*.[54] The discussion that follows examines the effect that the *curioso* had on two plays written between 1610 and 1612, before Shelton's translation of the first part of *Don Quixote* became widely available: *The Lady's Tragedy* by Thomas Middleton and *The Coxcomb* by Francis Beaumont and John Fletcher.[55] *The Coxcomb* demonstrates how a broad scenario established by Cervantes in the *curioso* could be used by playwrights to develop in a completely different direction from the storyline in the prose fiction; *The Lady's Tragedy*, on the other hand, is an example of a dramatist thoroughly absorbing Cervantes's prose fiction and turning a lengthy narrative into a tightly-plotted and concise drama.[56]

What attracted playwrights to Cervantes, and in particular to *El curioso impertinente?* Above all, all playwrights need material to dramatize: they need a plot and they need characters. The *curioso* offered these in abundance. The story is set in Florence and concerns Anselmo and Lotario, who are such close friends that they are always known as 'the two friends', and Anselmo's wife, Camila. Anselmo develops a pathological desire to know whether or not Camila is chaste and asks Lotario to test her by attempting to seduce her into adultery. Lotario refuses at first, then reluctantly humours Anselmo, who spies on one instance of Lotario's wooing. In due course Lotario and Camila do indeed commit adultery but, with the aid of Camila's maid, Leonela, they trick Anselmo into believing that Lotario has failed to seduce her by staging a scene on which they know he will spy. Some time later, however, Leonela (who herself has a lover) betrays her mistress and Anselmo dies of a broken heart, forgiving Camila on his deathbed. Lotario dies in battle, and Camila becomes a nun. The narrative, then, offers a strong central relationship between the three main characters; potential for compelling stage dialogue as Anselmo persuades

Lotario to woo Camila; striking staging effects when Anselmo spies on the other characters; dramatic irony in the situation Anselmo has set up, of his best friend attempting to cuckold him at his own request; and the tragically absurd character of the man who destroys his own happiness and that of those around him through a foolish obsession.

In *The Coxcomb*, Beaumont and Fletcher take just one element of Cervantes's narrative for their play: the man who is *impertinente*, that is, acting inappropriately, is Antonio, who is the coxcomb of the title, but he has none of Anselmo's jealous curiosity. The initial action that sets the context for the play is Antonio's return from travel abroad with his friend Mercury. He is so fond of Mercury, and so determined to be a good friend, that he insists that Mercury stay with him, even though Mercury tries to excuse himself: 'give me leave / To take mine owne wayes now; and I shall often / With willingnesse come to visit you'.[57] When he realizes that Mercury is in love with his own wife, Maria, he goes out of his way to throw them together and give them the opportunity to consummate an affair, although Maria sees through her husband's foolish tricks. Cervantes's influence here, then, is in the initial concept of the close friends. In the Cervantes *novela*, in the early days of Anselmo's marriage to Camila, Lotario tries to excuse himself from visiting them too frequently on the grounds that it is not seemly to visit newly-weds too often: 'for it seemed to him — as it reasonably would seem to all discerning people — that one should not visit or linger at the houses of married friends as if both were single; although good and true friendship cannot and should not be suspect for any reason, the honor of the married man is so delicate that it apparently can be offended even by his own brothers, let alone his friends' (Part I, Chapter XXXIII).[58] The reluctance of the friend — in *The Coxcomb*, this is Mercury — to stay with the married couple is, then, reflected in the Beaumont and Fletcher play, but once the initial characterizations have been established, and the motif of the husband behaving inappropriately has been drawn up, Beaumont and Fletcher's play goes in a diametrically opposite direction to Cervantes's prose fiction. Mercury, like Lotario, tries to act honourably until his friend makes it impossible for him to do so, and Maria, like Camila, is much smarter than her husband; but whereas Anselmo is a jealous husband, Antonio deliberately seeks to make himself a cuckold. What the playwrights have borrowed is the broad concept of a man who foolishly acts against his own best interests but they have located it in the genre of the city comedy, based in contemporary London and without the emotional depth of Cervantes's story. Yet, superficial as the connections between the *curioso* and *The Coxcomb* may seem, in 1610 *The Alchemist* by Ben Jonson referred to 'a Don Quixote. Or a Knight o'the curious coxcomb'.[59] It is a strange phrase, and only really intelligible by assuming that Jonson, a fellow playwright and part of the same *coterie* as Beaumont and Fletcher, was recognizing a link between Cervantes's work and *The Coxcomb*.

The Lady's Tragedy, which was licensed for performance by the King's Men (Shakespeare's company) on 31 October 1611, is much closer to *El curioso impertinente* in plot, characterization and mood. The cast is similar to Cervantes's: Anselmus, the husband, his Wife (she is never given a name, a trait quite common in Middletonian drama), Votarius the friend, Leonella the maid and her lover, who unlike his

Cervantine counterpart does have a name, Bellarius. Middleton dispenses with the 'back story' of the two friends. The context instead is a palace revolution in an unnamed country, in which Anselmus's brother Govianus has been deposed. (The main plot of the play centres on the chastity of Govianus's betrothed, The Lady, who kills herself rather than submit to the usurper who wishes to marry her.) Votarius, like Lotario, tries to excuse himself from Anselmus's trial of the Wife and uses the same metaphor of trying to test a diamond to destruction:

> Must a man needs, in having a rich diamond,
> Put it between a hammer and an anvil
> And not believing the true worth and value,
> Break it in pieces to find out the goodness,
> And, in the finding, lose it? (1.2.53–57)

Cervantes had used this image in the course of a protracted debate between Anselmo and Lotario, in which Lotario tries to dissuade Anselmo from his obsession, and Cervantes uses the image more logically: '(if) the stone withstood so foolish a test, it would not, for that reason, gain in value or fame, but if it shattered, which is possible wouldn't everything be lost?'[60] Cervantes makes the assumption that a true diamond will not shatter under the hammer; Middleton says that it will be broken in pieces. Did he not understand mineralogy, or does he give a clue here that the pure diamond (the Wife) will indeed prove to be glass and break?[61] Middleton does not linger overly long on the debate between Votarius and Anselmus, whereas for Cervantes, this dialogue is one of the most sustained episodes in the story.

Cervantes is able to take time to explore his characters' motivations and inner thoughts; *El curioso impertinente* is a lengthy interpolation in Part 1 of *Don Quixote* consisting of 16,534 words and taking up all of chapters XXXIII, XXXIV and the second half of chapter XXXV. Nearly a quarter of the story (4,180 words) is taken up with the debate between Anselmo and Lotario about whether Camila should be tested.[62] Middleton, on the other hand, is writing a subplot in a play that it is any case time-limited; he dramatizes the entire narrative in four scenes, a total of 981 lines.[63] He has to move more quickly than Cervantes, and so Votarius makes his first attempt on the Wife's virtue in the same scene (1.2) in which Anselmus initially approaches him. A distinctive feature of *El curioso impertinente* is Anselmo's voyeurism: he watches one of Lotario's conversations with Camila at the beginning of the trial of her honour, and once she has fallen, she and Lotario hoodwink him by setting up a scene on which they know he will spy. Middleton takes over this plot-device, but whereas Anselmo spies on Lotario and Camila on the first occasion because he is not convinced that Lotario has indeed been attempting the seduction, Middleton's Anselmus spies on Votarius and the Wife simply because he feels like it: 'I love to have such things at the first hand!' (1.2.71). Like Lotario, Votarius initially does not want to seduce the Wife but Anselmus, having overheard the conversation in which nothing much has happened in the way of seduction, forces him to vow to make more effort and stages his absence from the house to give Votarius more scope. Here again Middleton follows Cervantes closely, as he does in the Wife's final yielding. Like Lotario, Votarius sees a mysterious man in the house in the early morning, assumes that he has himself been betrayed by his new love, and tells the husband that his wife is, after all, not chaste. In Cervantes's story, the mysterious man is merely the lover of Camila's maid, Leonela, whom the maid has introduced into the house; Middleton adds an extra twist and makes the man not only Leonella's lover Bellarius but also Votarius's sworn enemy. This will be important in the denouement.

The major divergences come in the endings that Cervantes and Middleton contrive for their stories, and again, the differences are due to the practical constraints of what can be fitted into a theatrical script. Cervantes's Camila at first stages a scene, on which she knows Anselmo is spying and in which she seemingly defends her virtue by fighting off an approach from Lotario and stabbing herself, with a flesh wound. Anselmo is convinced of her chastity and the wife, lover and cuckolded husband continue happily for some time until Leonela, worried about a threat to her own lover, betrays her mistress and brings down the house of cards. Middleton has to compress the action, and so makes the Wife's staged attack on her lover Votarius the climactic moment. The Wife has instructed Leonella to warn Votarius to wear 'privy armour' (4.1.112) but, since he and Votarius are enemies, Bellarius persuades Leonella not to deliver the message. Instead, she and Bellarius set up the scene with a poisoned sword with which the Wife will unwittingly attack Votarius. The scene ends in carnage, with Votarius killed accidentally by the Wife and the Wife engineering her own suicide by running between Bellarius and Anselmus as they fight, spearing herself on both of their swords. It seems that Anselmus is dead and his brother Govanius, wandering in from the main plot to ask for his advice, finds apparently only Bellarius still alive but nearing his end. Bellarius tells Govanius the truth as he dies; Anselmus revives for long enough to curse the Wife: 'O thou beguiler of man's easy trust, / "The serpent's wisdom is in women's lust!"' (5.1.178–79). When the Wife had died, Anselmus had thought her innocent and had killed Leonella for traducing her mistress; now he knows that he has been deceived all along. These final lines of Anselmus were an afterthought by the dramatist, written into the script after the main dialogue was completed,[64] and provide a coda analogous to the delayed tragic ending of *El curioso impertinente* which is separated from the rest of the *novela* by the first half of Chapter XXXV (Chapters XXXIII and XXXIV carry the main body of the story continuously up to the point that Anselmo erroneously accepts that Camila is chaste).

Of necessity, then, Middleton the playwright had to be more concerned with structure and tight plotting than did Cervantes the novelist. Cervantes's narrator could get inside the minds of his characters and tell his readers what they were thinking; Middleton had to rely on dialogue and soliloquy. Cervantes can allow events to unfold slowly and even tease the reader by reverting to the main narrative of the *Quixote* for the first half of Chapter XXXV; Middleton has to wrap up the events by the time Govianus comes in from the main plot, the timescale of which acts as a gear that drives the timing of the subplot.

So, to return to our opening question, what attracted Middleton to Cervantes's story? At the purely technical level, *El curioso impertinente* offered him a neat structure with a small cast of characters that would transfer well to the stage. Further, though, it had dramatic ironies that Middleton would have appreciated, such as the fact that the friend is trapped in a double bind: if he keeps his word to the husband and attempts to seduce the wife, then he is implicitly betraying him, but if he fools the husband by not attempting the wife, then he is breaking his word. The significance of this for Middleton is indicated by the importance that Anselmus gives to Votarius's vow that he will not repeat his first, feigned, attempt at seduction and will now do what Anselmus asks of him: 'For thy vow's sake, I pardon thee. / Thy oath is now sufficient watch itself / Over thy actions. I discharge my jealousy' (1.2.144–46). It may even have been this crux in the moral dilemma of the play that led Middleton to change the L of Lotario into the V of Votarius and create a name associated with the Latin word for a vow. The characters' names themselves give us a clue into Middleton's thinking: most of the names in the play, especially in the main plot, represent types, so that 'Wife' is more typical of this world than 'Anselmus'. Where he has invented a name — Bellarius — it is another word suggesting a characteristic, in this case 'belligerent'. The names that suggest people, rather than characters, are the ones borrowed from Cervantes.

The strongest influence from Cervantes, though, and the one that made *El curioso impertinente* so valuable to Middleton, was the interest in voyeurism. There are numerous tales of husbands testing their wives' chastity, and Middleton himself, a decade later, would use one in the scenes he wrote for *The Changeling*, one of his most successful plays. But Anselmo/Anselmus goes further in his need actually to see and hear the seduction of his wife, with an obsession that amounts to perversion.[65] Sexuality in its manifold forms was a theme that interested Middleton throughout his career as a playwright. Gary Taylor writes that, 'Middleton sexed language, and languaged sex, more comprehensively and creatively than any other writer in English'.[66] Cervantes offered stories that could be plotted into the structure of a play, and he gave characters with emotional affect that an actor could bring to life; these would be some of the factors that would draw John Fletcher back to him time and time again as he went on to become one of the major playwrights of the Jacobean age.[67] But what Middleton in particular had the genius to see was the intellectual complexity and moral irony of his work, and this was what made it so influential on the English stage.

It was a happy coincidence that Cervantes was at the peak of his powers at a time when conditions were ripe for his work to become known in English intellectual circles. Philip III and James I had signed the Treaty of London in 1604, ending the Anglo–Spanish war that had hung over the reigns of Philip II and Queen Elizabeth, and throughout his reign (1603–25) James I was an enthusiastic peacemaker, actively seeking rapprochement with Spain. This policy was most noticeable in his desire to marry the heir to the thrones of England, Scotland and Ireland, Prince Charles, to a Spanish Infanta, and negotiations around the 'Spanish Match' were an important force in James's court during the last decade of his reign.[68] The concerns of the court were reflected in cultural production, for example in the number of translations from Spanish that were published and the number of plays with Spanish themes that were staged.[69] This trend reached its peak in 1623, when Charles visited Madrid and his return in October, without a Spanish bride, was greeted with bonfires in the street and a performance at court a month later of *The Spanish Gipsy*, another play deriving from Cervantes in which Middleton had a hand. However, this 'Golden Age' in Anglo–Spanish literary relations was relatively brief and did not survive James I's death. By 1627 Charles I and Philip IV were at war. Although Cervantes did not disappear from the English literary scene (James Mabbe published a translation of six of the *Exemplary Novels* as late as 1640 and John Dryden took a keen interest in Cervantes in the Restoration period), the intensity of interest that had marked the Jacobean period would not be revived until the eighteenth century adopted *Don Quixote* as a major influence on the novel in English.

Notes to Chapter 19

1. The English is from Miguel de Cervantes, *Don Quixote: A New Translation by Edith Grossman* (London: Secker and Warburg, 2004), p. 453. All further references are to this edition.

2. On this figure see Elias Rivers, 'On the Prefatory Pages of Don Quixote Part II', *Modern Language Notes*, 75 (1960), 214–21.

3. The marriage itself was of course a spur to the cross-fertilization apparent in the influence of Cervantes and others in France in the seventeenth century.

4. Our translation: 'muchos caualleros francesses de los que vinieron acompañando al embaxador, tan corteses como entendidos y amigos de buenas letras, se llegaron a mi y a otros capellanes del cardenal mi señor, desseosos de saber que libros de ingenio andauan mas validos, y tocando a caso en este que yo estaua censurando, apenas oyeron el nombre de Miguel de Ceruantes, quando se començaron a hazer lenguas, encareciendo la estimacion en que assi en Francia como en los reynos sus confinantes, se tenian sus obras, la *Galatea*, que alguno dellos tiene casi de memoria la primera parte desta, y las *Nouelas*. Fueron tantos sus encare(ci)mientos, que me ofreci lleuarles que viessen el autor dellas, que estimaron con mil demostraciones de viuos desseos. Preguntaronme muy por menor su edad, su profession, calidad y cantidad. Halleme obligado a dezir que era viejo, soldado, hidalgo y pobre, a que vno respondio estas formales palabras: "Pues ¿a tal hombre no le tiene España muy rico y sustentado del erario publico?» Acudio otro de aquellos caualleros con este pensamiento y con mucha agudeza, y dixo: «Si necessidad le ha de obligar a escriuir, plega a Dios que nunca tenga abundancia para que con sus obras, siendo el pobre, haga (next page) rico a todo el mundo"' (pp. 612–13).

5. Lope de Vega Carpio, *The Pilgrime of Casteele*, 2nd edn (London: Edward Allde and John Norton for Thomas Dewe, 1623), sig. A2ʳ. On the issue of the emergent figure of the writer in Spain, see Donald Gilbert-Santamaría, *Writers on the Market: Consuming Literature in early Seventeenth-century Spain* (Lewisburg, PA: Bucknell University Press, 2005).

6. G. E. Bentley, *The Jacobean and Caroline Stage*, 7 vols (Oxford: Clarendon Press, 1941–68), I, 113. There is unfortunately no date on Norton's first edition of a translation from 1621. The coincidence of dates seems unlikely to be fortuitous. P. E. Russell, *A Catalogue of Hispanic Manuscripts and Books before 1700 from the Bodleian Library and Oxford College Libraries* (Oxford: Dolphin Book Co., 1962), p. 26. Also the discussion of it in Dale Randall, *The Golden Tapestry: A Critical Survey of Non-chivalric Spanish Fiction in English Translation (1543–1657)* (Durham, NC: Duke University Press, 1963), pp. 102–12.

7. Susan Sontag, 'The World as India: Translation as a Passport within the Community of Literature', *Times Literary Supplement*, 13 June 2002, pp. 13–15.

8. The version by François de Rosset and Vital d'Audiguier (translator of *El peregrino en su patria* into French) with additional story by Sieur de Bellan.

9. Esther Crooks, *The Influence of Cervantes in France in the Seventeenth Century* (Baltimore, MD: Johns Hopkins University Press, 1931), George Hainsworth, *Les 'Novelas ejemplares' de Cervantes en France au XVIIe siècle* (thesis, Paris, 1933), José Manuel Losada Goya, *Bibliographie critique de la littérature espagnole en France au XVIIe siècle: présence et influence* (Geneva: Droz, 1999) and Guiomar Hautcoeur Pérez-Espejo, *Parentés franco-espagnoles au XVIIe siècle: Poétique de la nouvelle de Cervantes á Challe* (Paris: Honoré Champion, 2005).

10. See Trudi Darby's discussion of the play in this volume.

11. Gordon McMullan, *The Politics of Unease in the Plays of John Fletcher* (Amherst: University of Massachusetts Press, 1994), p. 261. Burre later published a translation of the Protestant convert Juan Nicholas Sacharles's *The Reformed Spaniard* (London: Walter Burre, 1621).

12. Philip Sidney was the dedicatee of *A Compendious Treatise entitled De re militari* (London: Thomas East, 1582) by Luis Gutiérrez de la Vega, translated by Nicholas Lichfield.

13. Among Yong's books are annotated copies of Geronymo Gudiel's *Compendio de algunas historias de España* (Alcalá, 1577) BL 593.g.4 and Juan Boscán Almogáver, *Las obras* (Antwerp, 1551?) BL C.46.a.23.

14. On this text see Helen Hackett, *Women and Romance Fiction in the English Renaissance* (Cambridge: Cambridge University Press, 2000), pp. 163–74.

15. See below.

16. Middleton had been a dedicatee of the intelligencer Lewis Owen's *The Key of the Spanish Tongue* (London: Thomas Creede for W. Welby, 1605), as one of the 'speciall fauourers, as of all schollers & learned men: so also of such as trauell in this kinde, for the knowledge of *exotique* Languages', sig. A2^r.

17. Patricia Fumerton, 'Exchanging Gifts: The Elizabethan Currency of Children and Poetry', *ELH*, 53 (1986), 241–78 (p. 247).

18. John Loftis, 'La comedia española en la Inglaterra del siglo XVII', in *La comedia española y el teatro europeo del siglo XVII*, ed. by Henry Sullivan, Raúl A. Galoppe and Mahlon Stoutz (London: Tamesis, 1999), pp. 101–19 (p. 111).

19. Cited in Loftis, 'La comedia española en la Inglaterra del siglo XVII', p. 112.

20. See John Loftis, *The Spanish Plays of Neoclassical England* (London: Yale University Press, 1973), pp. 31–59 (p. 48) and Ángel García Gómez, 'Sir Richard Fanshawe y Querer por sólo querer de Antonio Hurtado de Mendoza: El cómo y porqué de una traducción' in *La comedia española y el teatro europeo del siglo XVII*, pp. 120–42.

21. Martin Hume, *Spanish Influence on English Literature* (London: Eveleigh Nash, 1905), Chapter IX 'The Spanish Theatre and the English Dramatists', pp. 246–79 (pp. 276 and 279).

22. See Martin Erickson, 'A Review of Scholarship Dealing with the Problem of a Spanish Source for *Love's Cure*', in *Studies in Comparative Literature*, ed. by Waldo McNeir (Baton Rouge: Louisiana Sate University Press, 1962), pp. 102–19.

23. Rudolph Schevill, 'On the Influence of Spanish Literature upon English in the Early 17th Century', *Romanische Forshungen*, 20 (1905/06), 604–34.

24. Loftis, *The Spanish Plays*, p. 27.

25. On Salas Barbadillo's *El sagaz Estacio* as a source of *Rule a Wife Have a Wife* see E. M. Wilson, '*Rule a Wife Have a Wife* and *El sagaz Estacio*', *Review of English Studies*, 24 (1948), 189–94.

26. According to Bentley, *The Jacobean and Caroline Stage*, III, 363–66 and Cyrus Hoy, 'The shares of Fletcher and his collaborators in the Beaumont and Fletcher canon', *Studies in Bibliography*, 6 (1961), 45–67 (pp.48–56). See also Loftis, *Renaissance Drama in England & Spain*, pp. 252–56.

27. Arguments for this attribution are made by O. M. Villarejo, 'Shakespeare's Romeo and Juliet: Its Spanish Source', *Shakespeare Survey*, 20 (1967), 95–105 (p. 103, note 2). The argument is rebutted by Loftis, *Renaissance Drama in England & Spain*, pp. 244–46, from a version in Ervin Brody, *The Demetrius Legend and its Literary Treatment in the Age of the Baroque* (Rutherford, NJ: Fairleigh Dickinson University Press, 1972).

28. This play, whose attribution to Lope has been questioned, is reproduced from Biblioteca Nacional Madrid Ms 15013 in Marcelino Menéndez Pelayo (ed.), *Biblioteca de Autories Españoles. Obras de Lope de Vega* (Madrid: Ediciones Atlas, 1969), vol. 27, pp. 179–226.

29. See García Gómez, 'Sir Richard Fanshawe y Querer por sólo querer de Antonio Hurtado de Mendoza', p. 126 and Bentley, *The Jacobean and Caroline Stage*, III, 339. On the authorship of the play see Marco Presotto, 'La tradición textual de "La ilustre fregona" atribuida a Lope de Vega', *Criticón*, 89 (2003), 697–708.

30. See John Loftis, *Renaissance Drama in England and Spain: Topical Allusions and History Plays* (Princeton, NJ: Princeton University Press, 1987), p. 239.

31. See E. M. Wislon, 'Did John Fletcher Read Spanish?', *Philological Quarterly*, 27 (1948), 187–90; 'Cervantes and English Literature of the Seventeenth Century', *Bulletin Hispanique*, 50 (1948), 27–52 and '*Rule a Wife and Have a Wife* and *El sagaz Estacio*', *Review of English Studies*, 24 (1948),

189–94. See Loftis, *The Spanish Plays of Neoclassical England*, p. 26, *Renaissance Drama in England & Spain*, pp. 240–41, and William Appleton, *Beaumont and Fletcher: A Critical Study* (London: George Allen & Unwin Ltd., 1956), pp. 72–74.

32. See Alejandro Ramírez, 'Cervantes y Fletcher: el Persiles y The Custom of the Country', in *Homenaje a Sherman H. Eoff* (Madrid: Castlia, 1970), pp. 203–20.

33. Ramírez, p. 190.

34. There are many unanswered questions surrounding these issues: where did the manuscripts come from and how did he or the culturally Hispanophile circle around him gain access to original, contemporary manuscripts from the repertoires of Madrid's *corrales* and acting companies?

35. Leaving aside his use of Lope de Vega's *El peregrino en su patria* in *The Pilgrim*, Gonzalo de Céspedes y Meneses's *El Español Gerardo* for *The Spanish Curate*, de Argensola's novella, source of *The Island Princess*, and Guillén de Castro for *Love's Cure; or, The Martial Maid*, Fletcher's main source, Cervantes, saw him draw on: *Don Quixote* for *The Coxcomb*, *Cardenio* (now lost), *The Double Marriage*, *The Wild Goose Chase*, *The Prophetess* and *The Noble Gentleman*; *Persiles y Sigismunda* (as well as Salas Barbadillo) for *The Custom of the Country*; and the *Novelas ejemplares* for *Love's Pilgrimage* ('Las dos doncellas'), *The Chances* ('La señora Cornelia'), *The Queen of Corinth* ('La fuerza de la sangre'), *A Very Woman* ('El amante liberal'), *Beggars' Bush* ('La gitanilla'), *Rule a Wife and Have a Wife* ('El casamiento engañoso') and *The Fair Maid of the Inn* ('La ilustre fregona'). On *The Custom of the Country* see chapter on the influence of *Persiles y Sigismunda* by Clark Colahan and on *Cardenio* see Stelio Cro's piece in this volume. On the rest see below.

36. On these figures see above all Gordon McMullan, *The Politics of Unease in the Plays of John Fletcher* (Amherst: University of Massachusetts Press, 1994), p. 259 and his entry on Fletcher in *DNB*, and Bentley, *The Jacobean and Caroline Stage*, III, 305–433. Slightly different figures are given in R. Patricia Grant's 'Cervantes' *El casamiento engañoso* and Fletcher's *Rule a Wife and Have a Wife*', *Hispanic Review* 12 (1944), 330–38 (pp. 332–33), where only ten come from Cervantes and it is suggested that six more than the total figure of seventeen may be drawn from Spanish material. See on this James Fitzmaurice-Kelly, *Relations Between Spanish and English Literature* (Liverpool: Liverpool University Press, 1910), p. 22.

37. All references to the plays are taken from Fredson Bowers' edition of *The Dramatic Works in the Beaumont and Fletcher Canon*, 10 vols (Cambridge: Cambridge University Press, 1966–96); volume and page numbers will be given in the text.

38. On the image of Spain in England in this period see Jocelyn N. Hillgarth, *The Mirror of Spain, 1500–1700: The Formation of a Myth* (Ann Arbor: University of Michigan Press, 2000).

39. McMullan, *The Politics of Unease*, pp. 14–18.

40. McMullan, p. 18.

41. On these aspects of Cervantes work see Babara Simerka, *Discourses of Empire: Counter-epic Literature in Early Modern Spain* (Pennsylvania: Penn State Studies in Romance Literature, 2003) and Barbara Fuchs, *Passing for Spain: Cervantes and the Fictions of Identity* (Urbana: University of Illinois Press, 2003).

42. Francisco de Morales, *The Third and last part of Palmerin of England*, trans. by Anthony Munday (London: I. R. for William Leake, 1602), sig. A4[r].

43. *Blurt, Master Constable* (1602) which echoes *Lazarillo de Tormes* has been attributed to Dekker.

44. Pedro de Mexía and Francesco Sansonvino, *Treasury of auncient and moderne times*, trans. by Thomas Milles (London: William Jaggard, 1619).

45. The depth of Massinger's immersion in Spanish culture can also be seen from references in *The Unnatural Combat* (1624–25) (II.ii.13) to 'old Caranza' and again in *The Guardian* (1633) (III.iii.50) 'I have often read Caranza'. See Pedro Javier Romero Cambra, 'Massinger and Carranza: A Note on Fencing and Point of Honour in Sixteenth- and Seventeenth-Century Drama', *Notes and Queries*, 54 (2007), pp. 392–93. He clearly read Spanish, although probably, like Fletcher, he also made use of translations.

46. McMullan, *The Politics of Unease*, pp. 25 and 258.

47. Mateo Alemán, *The Rogue*, trans. by James Mabbe (London: printed for Edward Blount, 1622), sig. A4[r].

48. McMullan, *The Politics of Unease*, p. 257.

49. McMullan, *The Politics of Unease*, p. 259.

50. McMullan, *The Politics of Unease*, p. 260.

51. See William Peery, 'The Curious Impertinent in *Amends for Ladies*', *Hispanic Review*, 4 (1946), 344–53, and Sandra Clark, *The plays of Beaumont and Fletcher* (Hemel Hempstead: Harvester, 1994), p. 131.

52. See Gamaliel Bradford, 'The History of *Cardenio* by Mr. Fletcher and Shakespeare', *Modern Language Notes*, 25 (1910), 51–56; John Freehafer, '*Cardenio* by Shakespeare and Fletcher', *PMLA*, 84 (1969), 501–13, and the chapter by Stelio Cro in this volume.

53. Francis Beaumont, *The Knight of the Burning Pestle* ed. by Cyrus Hoy, I. I. 261–66 in *The Dramatic Works in the Beaumont and Fletcher Canon*, ed. by Fredson Bowers, 10 vols (Cambridge: Cambridge University Press, 1966–96), I, 22–23.

54. See *The Second Maiden's Tragedy*, ed. by Anne Lancashire (Manchester and Baltimore: Manchester University Press and Johns Hopkins Press, 1978).

55. For discussion of *The Coxcomb*, *The Second Maiden's Tragedy* and *Amends for Ladies* by Nathan Field see Sandra Clark, 'Cervantes' "The Curious Impertinent" in Some Jacobean Plays', *Bulletin of Hispanic Studies*, 79 (2002), 477–89.

56. The definitive edition is *The Lady's Tragedy*, ed. by Julia Briggs, in *Thomas Middleton: The Collected Works*, ed. by Gary Taylor and John Lavagnino (Oxford: Clarendon Press, 2007), pp. 833–906. There was no contemporary edition of *The Lady's Tragedy*, which survived in a manuscript now in the British Library (BL Lansdowne 807). The manuscript gives neither title nor author's name. In recent years the play has variously been edited as *The Second Maiden's Tragedy* (by Anne Lancashire for Clarendon Press in 1978) and *The Maiden's Tragedy* (by Martin Wiggins in a 1998 anthology for Oxford World's Classics, *Four Jacobean Sex Tragedies*).

57. Francis Beaumont and John Fletcher, *The Coxcomb*, ed. by Irby J. Cauthen Jr, I. I. 41–43 in *Dramatic Works in the Beaumont and Fletcher Canon*, I, 263–346.

58. *Don Quixote: A New Translation*, 273.

59. *The Alchemist* IV. 7. 39, quoted by Cauthen, *The Coxcomb*, p. 265.

60. *Don Quixote*, trans. by Grossman, p. 279.

61. Cf. the Wife's speech at V. I. 80–82 for an explicit comparison of the Wife and the Lady: 'I'll imitate my noble sister's [i.e. the Lady's] fate / Late mistress to the worthy Govianus, / And cast away my life as she did hers'.

62. I am grateful to B. W. Ife for these figures.

63. See Taylor and Lavagnino, *Middleton Collected Works*, p. 906, for the number of lines in each role.

64. *The Lady's Tragedy*, pp. 619–20.

65. For a comprehensive review of the sources of *El curioso impertinente*, see B. W. Ife, 'Cervantes, Herodotus and the Eternal Triangle: Another Look at the Sources of *El curioso impertinente*', *Bulletin of Hispanic Studies*, 82 (2005), 671–81.

66. Taylor, *Middleton Collected Works*, p. 25.

67. See Alexander Samson's chapter in this volume.

68. For detailed analysis of the cultural politics of this period, see Glyn Redworth, *The Prince and the Infanta: The Cultural Politics of the Spanish Match* (New Haven and London: Yale University Press, 2003) and *The Spanish Match: Prince Charles's Journey to Madrid, 1623*, ed. by Alexander Samson (Aldershot: Ashgate, 2006).

69. Data on book production are available online in the database compiled by Alan Paterson and Alexander Samson hosted at <http://www.ems.kcl.ac.uk/content/proj/anglo/tldb/index.html>.

CHAPTER 20

'Last thought upon a windmill'?: Cervantes and Fletcher

Alexander Samson

Of all the seventeenth-century playwrights who turned to Cervantes for inspiration, it is John Fletcher whose work shows the strongest influence from the Spanish writer.[1] Both in plays for which he was sole author and plays in which he was a collaborator, Fletcher turned time and again to Cervantean prose fiction for plots, characters and situations. Shakespeare's successor as regular playwright for the King's Men, Fletcher's work was performed both at Court and in the public playhouses and was published in a prestigious Folio edition in 1647, thus ensuring that his reputation was maintained while the theatres were closed during the time of the Civil War and Commonwealth (1642–60) and that, at the Restoration, Fletcher's plays returned to the newly re-opened stages. This essay looks at the nature and significance of the Cervantean influence on the Fletcher canon.

In using Cervantean material, Fletcher's reading of the *Novelas ejamplares* of 1613 was the most fruitful. The earliest adaptation from the *Novelas ejemplares* was probably Beaumont and Fletcher's *Love's Pilgrimmage* (1615) from *Las dos doncellas*, the story of two women in love with and abandoned by the same man, Mark-Antonio. The prologue to the play echoed Cervantes's claim for the novelty of his stories 'I am the first to write novellas in the Castilian tongue [...] these are my own stories, not imitations, nor stolen',[2] asserting that 'New / I am sure it is' (Prologue, ll. 9–10: II, 575).[3] The plots of play and short story mirror each other closely, with verbal echoes notably in evidence at key dramatic moments whose visual and dramatic quality lent them to the stage, as when Philippo remains silent after his sister has unburdened herself to him, leading her to assume her story has sent him to sleep.[4] In the dialogue between the two cross-dressed protagonists, when Leocadia reveals her identity to Theodosia and in a fit of jealousy insults and threatens to kill her love rival, standing before her at that very moment masquerading as her protector Theodoro, the anxiousness of the latter in Cervantes to find out if she has actually slept with Mark-Anthony is comically exaggerated and made even more explicit in Beaumont and Fletcher's rendering:

> And so, when that happiest of nights arrived what did he do? Did he come
> by chance? Did you enjoy him? Did he again confirm the agreement? Was he
> pleased having got from you what you say was his? Did your father find out and
> in what did such honest and wise beginnings result?[5]

> *Theodosia.*   And when the night came, came he, kept he touch with ye?
>   Be not so shamefast; had ye both your wishes?
>   Tell me, and tell me true, did he injoy ye,
>   Were ye in one anothers arms, abed? the Contract
>   Confirm'd in ful joys there? did he lie with ye?
>   Answer to that; ha? did your father know this.
>   (III.ii. ll. 95–100: II, 624)

In general, Fletcher downplays the murderous violence of Leocadia's feelings to be found in Cervantes, the repeated threats to murder her rival, and introduces instead a series of comic insults to her honour and chastity, underlining light-heartedly the tension in Theodosia between her assumed and true identity:

> — How is Teodosia to blame — Teodoro asked — when she was probably deceived as well by Mark Anthony in the same way that you have been Lady? — How can that be — Leocadia replied — when he carried her off with him? What deception can there be between people who love each other when they are together, none of course, they are happy, since they are together, as they now are, as they say, as if they were in the remotest, burning deserts of Libya or alone in frozen Scythia. She enjoys him, no doubt, wherever they are, and she alone must pay for what I have suffered up until the moment I find her.[6]

> *Theodosia.*   Who can say
>   But she may be forsaken too? he that once wanders
>   From such a perfect sweetness, as you promise,
>   Has he not still the same rule to deceive?
> *Leocadia.*   No, no they are together, love together,
>   Past all deceit of that side; sleep together,
>   Live, and delight together, and such deceit
>   Give me in a wild desert.
>   (III.ii. ll. 151–58: II, 626).

Beaumont and Fletcher misread the image of the lovers' successful flight together or passion transporting them to unreachable distances, understanding the image of Libya and Scythia in Cervantes instead in self-pitying or indirectly threatening terms.[7] As their conversation draws to a close Theodosia/Theodoro attempts to draw her love rival's attention to her excessive passion and perhaps shield herself from further insult:

> Since as I can see the passion you feel does not allow you a more apt discourse, I see that now is not a time when you will listen to salutary advice.[8]

> *Theodosia.*   For I perceive your anger voyd of councel,
>   Which I could wish more temperate
>   (III.ii. ll. 196–97: II, 627)

While there are very close verbal echoes as here, the major difference between the two versions of the story lies in the insertion of a series of comic scenes and the increased importance of the fathers' disagreement. The anger of Alphonso, father of Philippo and Theodosia, is sharpened, and Leonardo, father of Mark-Antonio joins the two maidens and brother in seeking his son in Barcelona. The civil unrest and shelling of Barcelona in Cervantes's short story is made the fault of the impetuous

Mark-Antonio's desire to see the face of the governor's wife in Beaumont and Fletcher, despite his earlier tirade against love and women in conversation with his general Rodrigo. This speech contains a cryptic reference to *Don Quixote* as Mark-Antonio describes how he has cured himself of love according to the example of the greatest of love melancholics, 'the fit held til midnight' but by reciting certain charms 'and they are all one; / Last thought upon a windmill, and so slept, / And was well ever after' (II.iii. ll. 108, 113–15: II, 616). The riot scenes turn on a cultural difference alluded to frequently in accounts of Spain, the custom of women going veiled: 'To draw that curtain here, though she were mean, / Is mortall' (IV.i. ll. 25–26: II, 639) Mark-Antonio is warned. The veil plays a crucial role as well in the subplot based on 'El casamiento engañoso' of *Rule a Wife and Have a Wife*, as an erotic enticement to discover what the lady with the fair white hand looks like. The governor's wife later plays a critical role in reconciling the choleric Alphonso and Sancho, fathers of the wronged Theodosia and Leocadia.

Further topical allusions are made in the name of the *gracioso* (comic character) Don Incubo de Hambre, and his constant allusions to the poverty and scarcity of food, an example where linguistic borrowing is not merely mangled pastiche. Wilson suggested that the nature of such calques provided evidence to suggest that Fletcher had no more than a reading knowledge of Spanish.[9] The character Lázaro, who tries to cheat Philippo out of his oats, is another literary stereotype drawn from a text framed by its first translator as a 'true discription of the nature & disposition of sundrie Spaniards',[10] and provides a comic relief that relies on the audience's acquaintance with the picaresque as a genre as well as its association with national types. Linguistic borrowing from Spanish abounds in the inserted comic scenes in the play from the series of jokes of Incubo in the first scene using the Spanish 'cuerpo' that has parallels with passages in Ben Jonson's *The New Inn* (1629), to semantic areas such as money, food, clothing and honorifics: 'Ducket', 'Marvedis' (I.i. ll. 108 and 148: II, 579 and 581), 'Sardina', 'cardonado'd',[11] 'olyffs', (I.i. ll. 131, 134 and 149: II, 580–81), 'paramentos' (I.i. l. 34: p. 2.577), 'Dons with duckets' (II.iv. l. 69: II, 620) and 'Constables son' (I.i. l. 168: II, 582). In this play, there are references to the fencing theorist, Jerónimo Sánchez Carranza, whose theoretical treatise was alluded to by Quevedo in *El Buscón* and was clearly widely known in England at this time: the choleric, lame Don Sanchio, Leocadia's father, asks 'Hast thou ever read Caranza? / Understandst thou honour, Noble Governour?' and then alludes to him twice more, 'Have you read Caranza Lady? / *Eugenia*. If you mean him that writ upon the duell, / He was my kinsman' (V.iv. ll. 202–03 and vi. ll. 62–64: II, 666 and 669).[12] In general the transformation of Cervantes's story involved exploiting its possibilities for dramatic irony and confusion of identities, introducing comic material, including a series of anti-Spanish jibes, and minimizing female agency, in particular that of Leocadia. It also foregrounds female beauty and misogyny through the plot device of the governor's wife provoking and resolving the rioting.

The next play based on Cervantes was probably *The Chances* (1613–25), this time exclusively the work of Fletcher and taken from the novella *La señora Cornelia*. Framed, although not by Fletcher, as a play eschewing 'strange turns and windings in the plot, / Objects of state' (Prologue ll. 13–14: IV, 625), it again follows the original closely, with the main change being to the characters of the two protagonists Don John and Frederick. Pious, chaste and even angelic in Cervantes, on the one hand, although these identifications have been complicated in recent readings of the story that uncover ambivalence in the Italian responses to the *español*,[13] they are transformed into Plautine *miles gloriosus*, 'wenching soldiers, / That know no other paradise but plackets' (I.i. ll. 5–6: IV, 551), as their servant Peter asserts at the outset; plackets being a slit in women's skirts and crudely explicit sexual euphemism.[14] Diana de Armas Wilson has used privateering as a metaphor to unpack the literary relationship between Cervantes and Fletcher in this play, noting the way in which the playwright has excised the maternal from Cervantes's text. Touching scenes of breastfeeding, the thematic consideration of childbirth and care, are replaced in the Jacobean version by scenes of a variety of sexual *pecadillos*; a tenor typified in John's reactions to the child as 'A lump got out of laziness', 'A lump of lewdness' (I.v. l. 11, II.i. l. 69: IV, 558 and 572), his disappointed response to the arrest of the bawd, the other Constantia 'A stout whore! / I love such stirring ware. — Pox o' this business! / A man must hunt out morsels for another, / And starve himself!' (IV.iii. ll. 136–39: IV, 614) and the play's obsessive concern with venereal disease 'I shall have further knowledge from a surgeon's, / Where he lies moor'd to mend his leaks' (I.vi. ll. 3–4: IV, 559). The whoring soldiers' drunk landlady, Gillian, rather than convincing the ironically named heroine Constantia (Cornelia in the original) to flee out of fear of her brother's bloody vengeance, warns her against the unrestrained lust of the two friends. There is, though, a hint in the novella at Fletcher's preferred explanation, when at the end of her speech the landlady suggests 'perhaps they will be Galicians where you are concerned',[15] an allusion to the commonplace of Galician brutishness, also invoked by the lustful serving maids in 'La ilustre fregona'. The confusion in the Cervantine original of Cornelia with a house servant's '*pícara* of those lost to the world',[16] gives way to a brothel scene in which Francisco, a musician and servant of Antonio, kinsman of Constantia and her brother Petruchio, has stolen away along with his goods and mistress a bawd, also named Constantia. The priest, the Duke's friend, who shelters Cornelia and the landlady in Cervantes, gives way to a conjurer and magician, Peter Vecchio, who is used by Fletcher as a vehicle to poke fun at religious non-conformists as John suggests his power to raise and compel devils may derive from making them 'eat a bawling Puritan / Whose sanctified zeal shall rumble like an earthquake' (V.ii. ll. 6–7: IV, 616). These conjuring scenes seem calculated to make fun of the whole idea of magic, as a theatrical trick and imposture. Again the text is lightly scattered with cultural borrowings from Spanish from John's 'basta' and 'Oh, de Dios!', to the mangled 'Alligant' for Alicante and 'bilbo' a synecdoche for swords made in Bilbao (II.ii. l. 36, II.iii. l. 17, I.viii. l. 10, V.ii. l. 16: IV, 576, 578, 562 and 616). A debt offset by the invocation of the xenophobic commonplace of Spanish lust, already suggested by the main characters but made explicit by Gillian: 'They are Spaniards, lady, jennets of high mettle, / Things that will thrash the devil or his dam [...] Twenty a night is nothing' (III.iii. ll. 23–25, 38: IV, 595–96). Nevertheless, the play's sexual politics do not straightforwardly overlay political relations, despite such references to contemporary prejudice. The invocation of honour in the plot may constitute a more subtle response to national stereotypes as well as the Spanish honour plot typical of the *comedia*, decried by Wildblood in Dryden's Restoration play *An Evening's Love; or, The Mock Astrologer* (1668), with the governor of Bologna Petruchio agonizing that 'I wish it with my soul, so much I tremble / To offend the sacred image of my Maker — / My sword could only kill his crimes! No, 'tis honour, / Honour, my noble friends, that idol honour / That all the world now worships, not Petruchio, / Must do this justice' (I.ii. ll. 26–31: IV, 554–55). This contrasts sharply and ironically with John's tirade against his friend's introduction of him as a 'honest morall man', which culminates with his insult 'Hang up your eunuch honour!' (II.iii. ll. 84 and 96: IV, 581). A striking feature of Cervantine plots is their resistance to the outcomes commonly found in honour plays, whether ending happily in marriage or unhappily in tragedy and death. Their complication of revenge through a form of Christian humanism brings them again and again to forgiveness, regardless of the moral stature of those who overcome their attachment to traditional models of honour.

The Custom of the Country (c.1619–20) and its relationship with its source in two episodes in *Persiles y Sigismunda* is discussed elsewhere in this volume and has had more written about it than perhaps any other of the Spanish-derived stories. Fletcher and Massinger's play 'transferred the action from an ethnographically exotic to a recognizably contemporary society' and transformed the marriage rite into an example of *droit de seigneur* or *ius primae noctis*, an adaptation that can be attributed to two factors: firstly the exigencies of stagecraft and limited number of players in acting troupes and secondly the fact that while Cervantes' resituation of a ritual allegedly practised in Inca civilization in a tribal, barbarian northern Europe stretched the bounds of verisimilitude, the dramatists situation of something similar in southern Europe would have been definitively *incredible*.[17] Female agency is again downplayed with Zenocia being a less assertive woman than her prototype, Transila, her escape is effected with the two men, bow and arrow replacing the spear thrust into the guts of the first to attempt to 'gather flowers in that garden where her husband onely should have entrance'.[18] It has been argued that Cervantes presented the custom as 'a shameful and barbarous outrage', whereas Fletcher and Massinger exploited its titillating potential, with Rutilio describing the custom early on in the play as 'admirable rare]...] Would I were the next heir' (I.i. ll. 34 and 39: VIII, 646).[19] Dryden wrote: 'There is more bawdry in one play of Fletcher's, called *The Custom of the Country*, than in all ours together'.[20] The notion that Fletcher's transformation of episodes from Cervantes's romance epic involved pornographic additions has persisted until recently in criticism of the play, but is now contested. Celia Weller and Clark Colahan, for example, assert that 'Fletcher's play is not pornographic or obscene',[21] but on the contrary shares with Cervantes a vision of life as a pilgrimage through violence and adversity. Clusters of images are taken over into the play of barbarism, bestiality, the movement from darkness to light, from hate to love, the black of mourning to the white of marriage. Both fictions develop their protagonists into more 'complete persons' and make them ready 'for the higher kind of marriage proposed by Christian Humanists',[22] using similar techniques, unifying imagery, symbols of aggressive passions are counterbalanced by others of moral restraint and love, and sexual role-reversal. Although it is only Rutilio's name that has been appropriated from the *Persiles*, both Rutilios are identical *exemplae*, cautionary tales of lust symmetrically tamed and punished; Fletcher's male brothel and gigolo's complaint 'how my hams shrink under me [...] I feare nothing now, no earthly thing / But these unsatified Men-leeches' (IV.v. ll. 2 and 18: VIII, 712) equating with Cervantes's witch/she-wolf, who after rescuing the Italian dancing master from prison for his seduction of a young pupil is stabbed as she in turn attempts to seduce him, an incident that eventually leads him to become an anchorite. The process of de-exoticization at work in the adaptation of Cervantes for the stage is counterpointed by the peppering of the text with exoticizing hints at its Spanish origin rather than its Italian setting, from Hyppolita's call for her 'Caroch'[23] to the picaresque 'Bravo' introduced in a stage direction and reference to the 'Strappado', which although originally an Italian or French word has a pseudo-Spanish ending '–ado' and was introduced into English by John Frampton, in his account of his torture by the Spanish Inquisition (III.iv. l. 55 and IV.ii. l. 7: VIII, 692 and 699).[24]

Rule a Wife Have a Wife (1624), one of Fletcher's most enduring successes as a dramatist, brought together the shortest novella in Cervantes's collection 'El casamiento engañoso' with a plot taken from Salas Barbadillo's *El sagaz Estacio, marido examinado* published in 1620 (evidence of Fletcher's knowledge of Spanish, since there is no known translation from the period).[25] The play lingered on visual details, synecdoches invested with erotic promise, central to the seduction of Perez, such as the fair hand 'Shee had a hand would stirre a holy Hermite' (I.i. l. 116: VI, 507) and veil, echoing closely imagery in the Cervantine prose.[26] The two plots mirror each other with Leon getting the better of the sexually rapacious Margarita, a taming of the shrew, and Estifania besting Perez, exemplifying the trickster tricked. This is the most overtly political of Fletcher's adaptations with its context of Spanish campaigns in the Low Countries, allusion to the problems of colonialism in Leon's promise to visit Margarita's estates in the Indies 'Thither weele goe, and view a while those clymats, / Visit your Factors there, that may betray ye' (IV.iii. ll. 200–01: VI, 561) and its framing in the prologue, which makes a direct appeal to the audience's indulgence in the immediate aftermath of Prince Charles's joyous return from Spain the previous year without the Infanta: 'this day w'are Spaniards all againe, / The story of our Play, and our Sceane Spaine: / The errors too, doe not for this cause hate, / Now we present their wit and not their state' (Prologue, ll. 5–8: VI, 502). The lack of an ending in *El casamiento engañoso*, for Cervantes principally a frame narrative in which the Alférez contracts venereal disease, enters a hospital to sweat it out and overhears the culminating tale of this collection 'El coloquio de los perros', is ironed out by Fletcher through Estifania being found by Perez, who has vowed to kill her, and their reconciliation through his involvement as an accomplice in her cozening of the clown, Cacafogo, out of his thousand ducats in exchange for the Captain's fake jewels. Along with the obvious scatological joke and allusion to the ship captured by Sir Francis Drake on his circumnavigation, the Cacafuego, and the usual smattering of cultural borrowings from Spanish, there are also references to Spanish involvement in North Africa and to one of the most frequently republished English translations of a Spanish prose romance, *Palmerín de Inglaterra*.[27] Estifania asks Perez (Campuzano in the original, although this name is employed in the text as the name of a relation of Clara, Captain of Carbines) 'Did not you win this at Goletta Captine, / Or took it in the field from some brave *Bashaw*' (IV.i. ll. 82–83: VI, 550). In the following scene, Cacafogo refers to Leon's defence of his wife's honour before the duke, labelling him 'The next Sir *Palmerin*' (IV.i l. 129: VI, 551) — a text of which, in its various incarnations, there were thirteen editions in English between 1588 and 1639, all translated by Anthony Munday. The first translation, published in the year of the Armada, was dedicated to the Earl of Oxford, Edward de Vere, whose daughter Susan was married to the Earl of Montgomery, who would later be one of the two dedicatees of the First Folio and who was the brother of Fletcher's patron. The 1602 edition of the third part of *Palmerin of England* contained dedicatory poems from two other playwrights, Dekker and Webster.

Although according to Cyrus Hoy, Fletcher was only responsible for a small part of *The Fair Maid of the Inn* (1625), most of the play being written by a team consisting of Webster, Massinger and Ford, given his predilection for the *Novelas ejemplares*, the idea and inspiration for central plot elements were almost certainly Fletcherian. (Massinger had already worked on Cervantine material, basing elements of his play *The Renegado* on Cervantes's play *Los baños de Argel*.) Based on *La ilustre fregona*,[28] there are significant divergences from the original. The picaresque frame story is excised completely, as is the noble Tomás de Avendaño's serving at the inn and his friend Diego de Carriazo's becoming a waterseller. This social transgression lies at the heart of the Cervantine story and informs its subversiveness, whereas in the play, the aristocratic Caesario who frequents the inn equates in this respect with the hapless Don Pedro, the corregidor's son. The idea of noblemen taking on the lowly occupations and personae did not have an obvious corollary in Jacobean England, although social transgression in the choice of erotic object was common. Whereas Tomás chooses to take on his lowly station, the revelation that Caesario is a changeling is forced on him. The duel between the friends Caesario and Mentivole sets their families, natives of the city, against each other, and he is disavowed by his mother, as it turns out falsely, in order to protect him from his enemy's hate. While the lustful Galician serving wenches are absent from the Jacobean drama, the Duke offers Caesario, following the revelation that he is base-born, marriage to the woman he had previously believed was his mother as a way to repair his fortunes. Knockabout comedy in the inn involving Forobosco the cheating mountebank and the Clown's fake possession strongly recall the fifth Tratado of *Lazarillo de Tormes* and the bullseller's staged exorcism of the bailiff.[29] Costanza in Cervantes is the product of Diego de Carriazo's father's rape of a 'señora principal' (great lady), whose servant he might have been, as opposed to the lost child of Baptista. While Tomás de Avendaño's sister in the novella is a mere afterthought to complete the three marriages at the resolution of the plot, in contrast Clarissa plays a significant role in the play in the context of the family feud and reappearance of Juliana, Baptista's wife at the denouement. The change of fortunes, exploration of the theme of love and social transgression, is a levelling down and then up, Bianca and

Caesario are made equal in baseness and then nobility with the return of Baptista's wife and Bianca's mother Juliana. The treatment of class is much more conservative on the stage than in the novellas and differences are again apparent in the treatment of gender. Forthright female sexuality and rape are replaced in the play by the spectre of incest, shipwreck, and the romance of exile.

With such a broad and disparate range of material as that which has been discussed in the foregoing pages it is difficult to generalize. Cervantes's stories lent themselves to immediate adaptation and translation, and particularly to their use as plots for the stage, both in England and France. Fletcher derived imaginative geographies from Cervantine short stories, which he tied in to a literary landscape sufficiently well known to function as a source of humour for at least some of his audience. One of the problems with tracing the dissemination of material is that translations often remained unpublished for very long periods of time. A manuscript copy of James Mabbe's translation of *Celestina* dated tentatively to 1598 was only published as *The Spanish Bawd, represented in Celestina* in 1631.[30] When his translation of the *Novelas ejemplares* was published in 1640, three of the six he omitted had already been used as the basis for Fletcherian plots, i.e. *La gitanilla*, *La ilustre fregona* and *El casamiento engañoso*. Earlier scholars have tended to look for direct, sustained parallels, while many of the examples studied here suggest that more diffuse ways of thinking about sources need to be employed; from the way Rutilio's name may have suggested a comic subplot in *The Custom of the County* to the presence of literary allusions in *Rule a Wife and Have a Wife* and *Love's Pilgrimage*, and the combination of multiple plots from different writers in one play or the inclusions of episodes from other texts.

Another problem has been a failure to understand the multilingual nature of vernacular culture in early modern Europe and practices of working on multiple polyglot versions of given texts. Much more work on Anglo–Spanish cultural exchange and relations remains to be done; nevertheless, the cursory social network analysis carried out in this volume has perhaps partially uncovered one particular node, where passion and fashion led to a significant transmission and dissemination of Spanish material in the original and in translation. This particular hub of activity and engagement is distinguished by being politically anti-Spanish,[31] drawn specifically perhaps to the oppositional politics of Cervantes's work, its resistance of utopian idealism, nuanced relationship with the Habsburg monarchy and official royal policy, explored in stories from the margins, rooted and originating in provincial or rural settings before taking in the wider world from such oblique perspectives. It may be a corollary of the opposition to the corruption and excesses of court life, the idealization of political alternatives through an engagement with provincial, country life to be found in the work of Fletcher and the circles of patronage in which he moved, expressed through an ironic engagement with pastoral and romance. The dismissal of linguistic influence as mere travesty has also been too facile: names, Spanish words, calques and cultural borrowings need to be closely related back to available Spanish language learning materials, their political and historical contexts as well as illuminating what playwrights took for granted by way of cultural reference points. The example of *The Island Princess*, which helps us to be certain that Fletcher had a Spanish text in front of him, refers to native princes taking 'as much delight in a Baratto, / A little scurvy boat to row her' (I.i. l. 19: v, 553), an obscure term found in Minsheu's *Dictionary*,[32] but not with this sense. When reading for plots, how did early modern English playwrights pirate, adapt, and transform the stories they encountered, and to what extent was this due to the exigencies of the representable, verisimilitude, the acting company, conditions of performance, moral and social mores of Jacobean England? In the case of Fletcher, a process of de-exoticization, different concerns in relation to gender and sexuality, as well as common themes, from a serious interest in comedy as a vehicle of reform to the critique of colonial aspiration, transvestism, inversion of social hierarchies and sexual roles, anti-romance, and generic hybridity, all shaped the way he worked on Cervantine material. Fletcher's modus operandi as a playwright, most commonly working in tandem with one or more other writers, his shared compositional mode, may have marked the way he used his influences and inspirations as well. It is probably also a major reason why his reputation has not prospered in the post-Romantic era, when originality has been prized as a sign of genius, in the same way as other writers, whose works were 'their own'. Perhaps the successful appeal by the National Portrait Gallery[33] and the purchase of the only surviving likeness from his lifetime, dated tentatively to 1620, will herald a new era in the appreciation of John Fletcher; and in that new story, the critical role played by Cervantes in the development of English Renaissance drama in the early seventeenth century will similarly gain the recognition it deserves, fostering an awareness of England's huge cultural debt to Spain and its foremost men of letters. If it is true that Fletcher's generic experiments influenced subsequent generations of dramatists, then the story of the Cervantine plot as the substrata of Restoration drama remains to be told.

Notes to Chapter 20

1. See Samson and Darby's chapter in this volume for more on the context of Fletcher's use of Cervantes.
2. 'soy el primero que he novelado en lengua castellana [...] éstas son mías propias, no imitadas ni hurtadas', Miguel de Cervantes, *Novelas ejemplares*, ed. by Harry Sieber, 2 vols (Madrid: Cátedra, 1980), I, 52. Translations are my own unless otherwise indicated.
3. All references to the plays are taken from Fredson Bowers' edition of *The Dramatic Works in the Beaumont and Fletcher Canon*, 10 vols (Cambridge: Cambridge University Press, 1966–96).
4. Compare *Novelas ejemplares*, II, 208 with I. ii. ll. 111–15: II, 595.
5. 'Y bien, así como llegó esa felicísima noche, ¿qué hizo? ¿Entró por dicha? ¿Gozáste(i)sle? ¿Confirmó de nuevo la cédula? ¿Quedó contento en haber alcanzado de vos lo que decís que era suyo? ¿Súpolo vuestro padre o en qué pararon tan honestos y sabios principios?', *Novelas ejemplares*, II, 218.
6. '- ¿Pues qué culpa tiene Teodosia -dijo Teodoro-, si ella quizá también fue engañada de Marco Antonio, como vos, señora Leocadia, lo habéis sido? -¿Puede ser eso así -dijo Leocadia-, si se la llevó consigo? Y estando juntos los que bien se quieren, ¿qué engaño puede haber? Ninguno por cierto; ellos están contentos, pues están juntos, ora estén, como suele decirse, en los remotos y abrasados desiertos de Libia o en los solos y apartados de la helada (E)scitia. Ella le goza, sin duda, sea donde fuere, y ella sola ha de pagar lo que he sentido hasta que le halle', ibid, pp. 219–20.
7. A comparison with François de Rosset and Vital d'Audiguier's translation does not help explain this misreading: 'Aucune certainement, ils sont contens, puis qu'ils sont ensembles, fussent ils aux plus reculez & embrassez deserts de l'Afrique, ou aux plus solitaires & escartez de la froide

Scythie. Elle le possede sans doute, en quelque part qu'elle soit; Et elle suele payera la paine que ie sentiray iusqu'a tant que ie le treuve', *Les nouvelles de Migue Cervantes Saavedra. Ou sont contenues plusieurs rares advantures et memorables exemples d'Amour, de Fidelité, de Force de Sang, de Ialousie, de mauvaise habitude, de charmes, & d'autres accidens non moins estranges que vertitable...*, 2nd edn (Paris: Jean Riches, 1620), sig. Ffiiii^r, p. 79.

8. 'así como veo que la pasión que sentís no os deja hacer más acertados discursos, veo que no estáis en tiempo de admitir consejos saludables', *Novelas ejemplares*, II, 220.

9. Wilson, 'Did John Fletcher Read Spanish?', *Philological Quarterly*, 27 (1948), 187–90 (p. 187).

10. David Rowlands (trans.), *The Life of Lazarillo de Tormes* (London: Abell Jeffes, 1586; repr. Warminster: Aris and Phillips, 2000), pp. 47–48.

11. See John Minsheu, *A dictionarie in Spanish and English* (London: Edmund Bollifant, 1599), 'Carbonada', fol. 58.

12. Jerónimo de Carranza, *Libro de Hieronimo de Caranca, natvral de Sevilla, que trata de la philosophia de las armas y de su destreza y de la aggression y defension christiana* (Sanlucar de Barrameda: 1582). See Massinger's reference to the same figure in this volume (Chapter 19, note 45), and Francisco de Quevedo, *El Buscón*, ed. by Domingo Ynduráin (Madrid: Cátedra, 1996), p. 173.

13. See for example Eric Kartchner, *Unhappily Ever After: Deceptive Idealism in Cervantes' Marriage Tales* (Newark, Delaware: Juan de la Cuesta, 2005), pp. 101–12. I would like to thank Barbara Fuchs for drawing my attention to this, see also her forthoming 'Italia la pluma: Ironía e imperio en las *Novelas ejemplares*'.

14. Diana de Armas Wilson, 'Of Piracy and Plackets: Cervantes' La señora Cornelia and Fletcher's The Chances' in *Cervantes for the 21st Century / Cervantes para el siglo XXI: Studies in Honor of Edward Dudley*, ed. by Francisco La Rubia Prado (Newark, DE: Juan de la Cuesta, 2000), pp. 49–60.

15. 'quizá para consigo serán gallegos', *Novelas ejemplares*, II, 263.

16. 'pícara de las perdidas del mundo', ibid, p. 270.

17. Trudi Darby, 'Resistance to Rape in *Persiles y Sigismunda* and *The Custom of the Country*', *The Modern Language Review*, 90 (1995), 273–84 (p. 281). See also discussion in Diana de Armas Wilson's *Allegories of Love: Persiles y Sigismunda* (Princeton, NJ: Princeton University Press, 1991), pp. 198–99 and 200–22, and 'Contesting the Custom of the Country: Cervantes and Fletcher', in *From Dante to García Márquez: Studies in Romance Literatures and Linguistics*, ed. by Gene H. Bell-Villada, Antonio Giménez and George Pistorius (Williamstown, MA: Williams College, 1987), pp. 60–75.

18. Diana de Armas Wilson, 'Contesting the Custom of the Country: Cervantes and Fletcher', pp. 280 and 283.

19. W. D. Howarth, 'Cervantes and Fletcher: A Theme with Variations', *The Modern Language Review*, 56 (1961), 563–66 (p. 565).

20. Cited by Alejandro Ramírez, 'Cervantes y Fletcher: El Persiles y The Custom of the Country', in *Homenaje a Sherman H. Eoff* (Madrid: Castalia, 1970), pp. 203–20 (p. 204).

21. Celia Weller and Clark Colahan, 'Cervantine Imagery and Sex-Role Reversal in Fletcher and Massinger's The Custom of the Country', *Cervantes: Bulletin of the Cervantes Society of America*, 5 (1985), 27–43 (p. 29).

22. Weller and Colahan, p. 30.

23. The earliest known use of the term, according to the *OED*, is in the first Spanish–English dictionary, Richard Percyvall's *Bibliotheca Hispanica Containing a Grammar; with a Dictionarie in Spanish, English, and Latine* (London: John Jackson for Richard Watkins, 1591).

24. See *OED* and John Strype's *Annals of the Reformation and Establishment of Religion*, 2nd edn, 4 vols (London: Thomas Edlin, 1729–31), I, 239–45 (p. 243). Frampton was the translator of Nicolas Monardes, *Ioyfull Newes out of the newe founde worlde, wherein is declared the rare and singuler vertues of diuerse and sundrie Hearbes, Trees, Oyles, Plantes, and Stones, with their applications* (London: William Norton, 1577).

25. See the analysis of this plot by Barbara Fuchs in her forthcoming article 'Beyond the Missing Cardenio: Anglo–Spanish Relations in Early Modern Drama', *Journal of Medieval and Early Modern Studies*, special issue ed. by Marina Brownlee. I would like to thank her for allowing me to see this unpublished article.

26. See R. Patricia Grant's 'Cervantes' *El casamiento engañoso* and Fletcher's *Rule a Wife and Have a Wife*', p. 334 and the analysis of the close verbal parallels between the play and its source that follows.

27. The name Cacafugo recurs in *The Fair Maid of the Inn*, 'she will be ravisht before our faces, by rascalls and cacafugo's (wife) cacafugo's' (III.i. ll. 5–6: x, 521).

28. Although it has been argued it is from Lope's play see Ángel García Gómez, 'Sir Richard Fanshawe y *Querer por sólo querer* de Antonio Hurtado de Mendoza: El cómo y porqué de una traducción' in *La comedia española y el teatro europeo del siglo XVII*, ed. by Henry Sullivan, Raúl Galoppe and Mahlon Stoutz (London: Tamesis, 1999), pp. 120–42 (p. 126).

29. See IV.ii: x, 614–24.

30. My thanks to Anne Gill for drawing this to my attention, see her '"A kynde of Woman-beast": the invention of the female bawd in Jacobean theatre and culture' (unpublished doctoral dissertation, University of London, 2007), pp. 136–37.

31. For more details on this see the introductory chapter to this section.

32. John Minsheu, *A dictionarie in Spanish and English* (London: Edmund Bollifant, 1599), 'Baratto', fol. 43.

33. <http://www.npg.org.uk/live/prjohnfletcher.asp> [accessed 4 March 2008].

CHAPTER 21

The Utopian in Cervantes and Shakespeare

Stelio Cro

In *Don Quixote*, we have several manuscripts, the suggestion of several authors, a bilingual translator and a series of novels within the novel, all these elements contributing to create a universe of fiction vertically and horizontally traversed by the constant shift between appearance and reality. This procedure was underlined by the structure of the play within the play, framing most of the episodes. This systematic calling into question of our senses and our judgment is compensated for by the author's profound Christian faith, which becomes an anchor of salvation facing the impending decadence of Spain. With the defeat of the Armada, this crisis became palpable. Whereas Catholic Spain is sensing the beginning of the end, Elizabethan England experiences with the victory over the invading force a new sense of national pride, well expressed in Shakespeare's dramas. And, although in several of his plays Shakespeare shared with Cervantes the play within the play, the similarity of structure and even of certain characters and situations do not imply a similarity of purpose. Behind the play and within the play of *Don Quixote* we perceive the nostalgia for a vanishing world, the idealistic world of Don Quixote, an admirable fool who redeems himself by dying a very Christian death. Conversely, Hamlet finds human justice thanks to the 'Mousetrap' to indict the murderer of his father, while Prospero learns how to control nature and shows his human generosity by pardoning his enemies — but not without placing a heavy toll on their future, by having Ferdinand marry his daughter Miranda. The sense of triumph and expansion of England after the defeat of the Armada in 1588 has in Shakespeare's dramas its most accurate psychological reaffirmation of human success.

These two diverging tendencies in Cervantes and Shakespeare have in common sources and treatments. For my discussion I will compare the episode of the 'island' of *Barataria* with Shakespeare's *Tempest*. With the death of Queen Elizabeth in 1603, English drama loses some of its nationalistic accent, but keeps that sense of overwhelming accomplishment, personified by the trajectory of Prospero. First an outcast with his infant daughter on a remote island, probably in the Caribbean, he acquires the art of make believe and, like an inventive Machiavellian producer, traps his enemies in his scenario in order to force a sense of repentance dictated, not by a religious impulse, but by a sense of their inevitable defeat and Prospero's victory.

The utopian dimension of *Barataria* begins with Don Quixote offering his advice to Sancho, in view of Sancho's imminent nomination as governor. On the writing of prose fiction, it is affirmed in *Don Quixote* that, 'the more truthful it appears, the better it is as fiction, and the more probable and possible it is, the more it captivates' (p. 478).[1] When he wrote *Persiles*, Cervantes imagined a foreign and distant land, a northern landscape with American overtones, describing shipwrecks, natives rich in pearls and precious metals, and a pristine environment.

Shakespeare's *Tempest* offered some of these topics. To begin with, it is the only drama in which Shakespeare has chosen an island as the scene of the action. The second point is that there are multiple scenarios, easily fitted into a continuous play within the play. This scenario resembles a set of Chinese boxes, of which the main one includes the spectators; this, in turn, includes the characters; and this last one opens inward from the audience to the scenario seen by Prospero's guests and prisoners; and finally, in the innermost box, to Prospero, the main character, who calls himself the author: 'graves at my command / Have wak'd their sleepers, op'd, and let them forth / By my so potent art'.[2] In the 'Epilogue', Prospero, now again the character without magical powers, invites the audience to be the author by simply applauding and thus freeing him from the exile of the island: 'Let me not, / Since I have my dukedom got / And pardon'd the deceiver, dwell / In this bare island by your spell; / But release me from my bands / With the help of your good hands' (v. 1. 323). This resembles the structure of Cervantes's work, especially *Don Quixote*, in which the author repeatedly invites the reader to join him in condemning the kind of literature that makes Don Quixote an ageless hero.

The first scene of *The Tempest* occurs on a ship, in the midst of a storm. The crew is trying to avoid a shipwreck because the vessel is perilously being pushed by the swells towards the rocks. But all is in vain. The crew and the passengers realize the imminent destruction of the ship.

In Scene 2, Miranda, witnessing from the shore the shipwreck, is profoundly distraught and wishes that she could help the people on board. Prospero, her father, reassures her that 'there is no harm done' (I, 2, 16–19) and, in order to explain his actions, he disrobes his 'magic garment' (I, 2, 24). From this moment the audience sees a play within the play, because Prospero treats Miranda as part of the audience, thus suggesting the identification of Prospero with the author himself. To begin with, Prospero says, the shipwreck is fiction: 'the wreck, which touch'd / The very virtue of compassion in thee, / I have with such provision in mine art / So safely order'd, that there is no soul — / No, not so much perdition as an hair, / Betid to any creature in the vessel / Which thou heard'st cry, which thou saw'st sink. Sit down; / For thou must now know further' (I, 2, 26). By telling his daughter Miranda to sit down and listen, the author is engaging the audience. The story he tells really is the traditional prologue of the play, transformed by Shakespeare into a live action in the play. This is also the opening scene of the play within the play that will go on to the very end, when the scenario conjured by Prospero's art will recede in order for the plot to bring justice and redress wrongs among the real characters behind the masks. Miranda's answer brings her back into the fiction, the curtain separating reality and fiction once more hidden, so that the artifice of the play to unfold: 'You have often / Begun to tell me what I am, but stopp'd, / And left me to a bootless inquisition, / Concluding, 'Stay; not yet'' (I, 2, 32). Prospero inquires of Miranda's memories, whether she remembers how she arrived on the island. But all she remembers is being looked after by several chambermaids. Prospero informs her that they have been on the island for twelve years and that he was 'the Duke of Milan and / A prince of power' (I, 2, 54). His brother Antonio carried out his treacherous plan of usurping Prospero's dukedom while he, Prospero, neglected his public office in order to pursue knowledge: 'The government I cast upon my brother, / And to my state grew stranger, being transported / And rapt in secret studies' (I, 2, 75). The metamorphosis of Antonio, from submissive helper to open and cruel usurper, is told by Prospero as a tale of a Machiavellian hero who is learning the tricks of power and plans the treason of his brother, gradually achieving his goal with perfidiousness and audacity. He gradually corrupts the court and grows in influence with the help of Alonso, King of Naples and the political rival of Prospero. The gradual crescendo of the treason is punctuated by several pauses, overtly designed to ensure Miranda's attention, but aiming at capturing the interest of the audience (I, 2, 78, 87, 106). The Machiavellian doctrine of simulation, a key virtue to achieve and conserve power for the Florentine historian, rises to a dramatic format in the play. In Machiavelli's *Prince*, the dramatic role of the protagonist is implied, but in the *Tempest* it is fully displayed with Prospero's account of Antonio's treacherous plan. Even the language of the scene reveals the implied referential structure supporting the drama of political trickery:

> To have no screen between this part he play'd
> And him he play'd it for, he needs will be
> Absolute Milan. Me, poor man, — my library
> Was dukedom large enough: of temporal royalties
> He thinks me now incapable; confederates, —
> So dry he was for sway, — wi' the King of Naples
> To give him annual tribute, do him homage:
> Subject his coronet to his crown, and bend
> the dukedom, yet unbow'd, — alas, poor Milan! —
> to most ignoble stooping' (I, 2, 107).

Both *Barataria* and the *Tempest* are conceived as islands, but whereas the first is a parody, with Sancho, the new governor, arriving at his island in a carriage, without ever crossing a puddle, the second is an actual island, located somewhere in the Caribbean.[3] Early in the play, Ariel tells Prospero how and where he has led the ship during the storm, with the rest of the fleet scattered on the ocean and too distant from King Alonso's ship to realize that they were saved (I, 2, 224–37).

The *Tempest* was inspired by the same collective unconscious that had inspired Cervantes: the fabulous islands discovered by Columbus, the Spanish conquistadors and the English explorers and conquerors of wide regions in North America. On the record, The *Tempest* was inspired by the English ships that had been dispatched to Virginia in 1609. The leading vessel, with the Lieutenant Governor of Virginia and Admiral Sir George Somers, was wrecked near the Bermudas. The crew was saved, and they brought on shore essential supplies that helped them to survive on the island for nine months. Then, directed by Somers, the sailors built two boats with which the crew sailed towards Virginia, where they landed in May 1610. The news of their odyssey reached London in September. Up to five different accounts were published of this extraordinary adventure. According to Quincy Adams, 'Shakespeare may have read several of these, including Jourdain's narrative entitled *A Discovery of the Bermuda, Otherwise Called The Isle of Devils*; and he seems also to have had access to a confidential letter written by William Strachey, Secretary for the Council in Virginia, to "an Excellent Lady" in England, July 15, 1610, which remained unpublished until 1625'.[4]

In *Don Quixote* and in *The Tempest* the island functions as a laboratory of applied humanism. The dramatic devices present in both works provide a more entertaining venue for the moral content of the work. Both protagonists, Prospero and Don Quixote, have a passion for books. In the first chapter of *Don Quixote* of 1605, we read: 'You must know that the above-mentioned gentleman in his leisure moments (which was most of the year) gave himself up with so much delight and gusto to reading books of chivalry that he almost entirely neglected the exercise of the chase and even the management of his domestic affairs. Indeed his craze for this kind of literature became so extravagant that he sold many acres of arable land to purchase books of knight errantry, and he carried off to his house as many as he could possibly find' (p. 57).

And in *The Tempest*, Prospero tells his daughter Miranda:

> I pray thee, mark me.
> I, thus neglecting worldly ends, all dedicated
> To closeness and the bettering of my mind
> With that, which, but by being so retir'd,
> O'erpriz'd all popular rate, in my false brother
> Awak'd an evil nature; and my trust,
> Like a good parent, did beget of him
> A falsehood in its contrary as great
> As my trust was; which had, indeed no limit,
> A confidence sans bound. He begin thus lorded,
> Not only with what my revenue yielded,
> But what my power might else exact, — like one,
> Who having, into truth, by telling of it,
> Made such a sinner of his memory,
> To credit his own lie, — he did believe
> He was indeed the duke (I, 2, 88).

In both works the main characters are swept away by an obsession for knowledge to such an extent that both lose control of their own lives, finances and responsibilities: Don Quixote of his household and Prospero of his role as a head of state. That loss of control has immediate consequences for both: Don Quixote turns mad and is made the object of ridicule, unable to recover his reason until he is on his deathbed; Prospero, by losing his dukedom, will spend twelve years in forced exile.

Both works are concerned with literature and with didacticism: for Prospero a long and laborious search for freedom from enforced solitude for himself and his daughter Miranda; for Don Quixote, a series of misadventures in which he displays great courage and even surprising acumen in judging people and situations, but one that will end only with his death. The difference is that, whereas the trial of Prospero is ending at the beginning of the play, that of Don Quixote is beginning.

To the topic of the island one must inevitably associate the broader topics encompassed in the new humanism, due to the influence of More's *Utopia* in Shakespeare's *Tempest* and in Cervantes's *Barataria*. There are common cultural references to the northern humanism which must have been shared by Shakespeare and Cervantes and consisted of a shared acquaintance with More's *Utopia*, Erasmus's *Adages* and *Ciceronianus* and Luis Vives's theory on education, as it is contained in works such as *De disciplinis* and *De instrumento probabilitatis*.[5] Furthermore, travel literature, most of which originated in Spain, was popular throughout the sixteenth century in Europe, including England. The many Spanish books translated and published, or circulated, in England, especially in the second half of the sixteenth century, include the translation of the *De Orbe Novo* by Richard Eden in 1555 and, in 1598, the Latin translation and illustration of Las Casas' *Brevísima relación* by Theodore de Bry.[6]

These editions confirm the great interest in the Discoveries among European readers, in particular among the humanists of Northern Europe. The news reached Europe at a time of deep religious and political crisis which resulted in a profound metamorphosis in European culture. In this change we must include the leadership of Lorenzo Valla (1407–57), his struggle against the predominance of Aristotle in the European universities, his desire to renew Classical studies in the first half of the fifteenth-century, his influence on Erasmus, More and Vives, his ideal disciples, the humanists of the next generation, who are among the leaders of Northern European humanism, which stood for change.

Both *The Tempest* and *Barataria* identify a process of education which rejects bookish humanism, a process made evident in both the governorship of Sancho and the spontaneous love between Ferdinand and Miranda. Neither episode betrays the medieval, dogmatic culture which sealed Spain's decadence.[7]

The iron age, coinciding with the period of the discovery, was the reason why More wrote *Utopia*. It was a time of discovery but also a time of crisis. Shakespeare contributed to the draft of *Sir Thomas More*, co-authored with Fletcher, apparently because in the original draft there were political overtones that needed to be eliminated. The great humanist, sent to the gallows by Henry VIII and sanctified as a martyr by the Catholic Church, must have been a favourite topic for English intellectuals. After the discovery of the New World, the Old was uneasy about it. There were colonial, religious, economic and political rivalries. Within two decades of Columbus's discovery, the unity of Christendom was about to be broken. More was a witness and a victim of the institutional and religious crisis provoked by Henry VIII. *Utopia* was a revolutionary book: it challenged major tenets of western thought, above all in the economic, social, political and religious organization. To begin with, it described an alternative society. As we will see, even the identification of its location offers the author the opportunity to make an allusion to the New World, presenting the important question of discovery. In More's work, Vespucci's Portuguese pilot, Raphael Hythlodaeus, is more like Ulysses or Plato, a philosopher–traveller who is well aware of new lands and nations, new customs and laws. At a time when European powers were striving for supremacy, More is criticizing the politics of several Christian princes, projecting instead the concept of a united Christendom. This concept of Christendom acquires in *Utopia* a new geopolitical meaning, used to underline an ideal unity, a New Christian World.

In a letter written to Guillaume Budé and placed at the beginning of *Utopia*, Peter Giles shared his interest in the location of the island of Utopia.[8] This concern is perhaps a metaphor for the location of America and, more generally, the difficulty of finding the truth, of achieving knowledge, a fundamental topic of humanism. *Utopia* contains a theory of education that differs dramatically from the pedagogical tradition of the time. For instance, the explorer, Raphael, describes a nation where polyphonic music was an appreciated art, commonly known and popular with Utopians, contrary to Plato's *Republic*, in which Socrates excludes all musical instruments, except the martial monotonic trumpets and drums. In Utopia the queen of the arts is medicine, contrary to the low esteem in which physicians were held in the *Republic* and, after the example of Petrarch's *Contra Medicum*, among the European humanists. More was well ahead of his times. Whereas his contemporaries were satisfied with the imitation of the ancient, he belonged to a very select group of thinkers. One of them was Juan Luis Vives who, in his dialogue *De disciplinis*, argued that it was difficult to achieve absolute certitude, a point he elaborated in another treatise, *De instrumento probabilitatis*. In this work, after stating that nature is far from being exhausted and reserves further truths that will be discovered by future generations, Vives mentions as proof of his thesis the discovery and conquest of the New World.[9]

Well acquainted with the life of Thomas More, Shakespeare wanted to restore the irony of the original and to contrast it with Don Quixote's poetic evocation of the Golden Age in his dialogue with the goatherds, a point of view that is also found in *Barataria*. Machiavellian reason of state abounds in *The Tempest*. Even Prospero is not exempt from its tainting, when he pretends to treat Ferdinand as a spy and a traitor, in order to make his engagement to Miranda more valuable, by having Ferdinand struggle for it (I, 2, 446–53).

Both Cervantes and Shakespeare lived through momentous events in their countries. In *Don Quixote*, Cervantes opted for a more idealistic philosophy, looking backwards and treasuring tradition for future generations. In *Vida de Don Quijote y Sancho*, Miguel de Unamuno underlined the historical, autobiographical nature of so many pages in *Don Quixote*. Frye also believes that in *The Tempest* the character of Prospero 'has characteristics that seem to suggest some self-identification with Shakespeare'.[10] There is some resistance to this idea by Schoenbaum, who blamed the nineteenth century for such a view.[11] However, even before Schoenbaum and Frye, it was Borges who resuscitated it, in his beautiful poem in prose, 'Everything and Nothing': '[Shakespeare] antes o después de morir, se supo frente a Dios y le dijo: "yo, que tantos hombres he sido en vano, quiero ser uno y yo". La voz de Dios le contestó desde un torbellino: "Yo tampoco soy; yo soñé el mundo como tú soñaste tu obra, mi Shakespeare, y entre las formas de mi sueño estás tú, que como yo eres muchos y nadie"' [Before or after dying, Shakespeare spoke with God and he said: 'After having been so many different characters, I want to be only one and myself'. The Lord's voice answered him from a whirlwind: 'Neither am I, my Shakespeare. I dreamed the world like you dreamed your work and you are one of my dreams because, like me, you are everything and nothing'].[12]

The Tempest bears an irresistible allusion to a great dramatist hanging up his cloak, as Prospero does when he reveals to his daughter Miranda the truth of their exile on the island (I, 2, 22–25); he then puts on the cloak again in order to unmask his enemies, an essential element of the play within the play. Significantly, the act of disrobing and donning the 'magic garment' is accompanied by connotative words, like 'Lie there, my art' (I, 2, 23) and 'Now I arise' (I, 2, 169). The interaction of appearance and reality generated by Prospero is punctuated by the physical presence of the 'magic garment' (I, 2, 24). When, towards the end of the play, he abandons forever the magic garment and puts on his old garments as Duke of Milan, he might resemble Alonso Quijano el Bueno renouncing his library of knights, giants and enchanters. He speaks to God, who undoubtedly dreamed him, as he had dreamed his Spanish brother.

The topic of the island and its relationship with the utopian genre, a literary output that was influenced by the Spanish exploration and conquest of the New World, these things highlight Cervantes's influence on Shakespeare. And those same concerns that appear in *The Tempest* and in *Don Quixote*, namely the criticism of affected erudition, a strong interest in the theory of education and the ability to convey autobiographical allusions, these further suggest such an influence.

Notes to Chapter 21

1. Quotations from *Don Quixote* are taken from Miguel de Cervantes Saavedra, *Don Quixote of La Mancha*, trans. by Walter Starkie (New York: New American Library, 1964).
2. References to *The Tempest* are made to act, scene and lines.
3. Not only does *The Tempest* provide many allusions to the New World, but we have references to the chronicles of the explorations and travels to the New World. Among many, let us fix our attention on two: the storm that inspired the title of the play, and the name of one of the characters, Caliban — a play on the word 'Cannibal'. Both storms and cannibals appear as the dominant features to be observed and feared in the new land in the leading publications, the *Libretto*, the *Paesi* and the *De Orbe Novo*, and several editions and translations of the same, down through the sixteenth century.
4. Joseph Quincy Adams, *A Life of William Shakespeare* (Boston and New York: Houghton Mifflin Company, 1925), p. 419.
5. Marcel Bataillon in his *Erasmo y España* (Mexico: Fondo de Cultura Económica, 1966), pp. 777–801, analyses the topic of Erasmus' influence on Cervantes. He begins his study by saying: 'La huella del erasmismo en las letras españolas se perdería de modo bastante miserable entre las recopilaciones de apotegmas o las misceláneas cuyo éxito persiste a comienzos del siglo XVII si esta época no hubiera visto surgir las grandes obras de Cervantes, que señorean la brillante producción de los ingenios de la época de Felipe III, que fundan verdaderamente la novela moderna y que, al mismo tiempo, están bañados por el espíritu del Renacimiento como por los rayos de un sol poniente' [The significance of Erasmus's influence on Spanish literature would have been regrettably lost among the collections of apothegms and the miscellaneas, still popular at the beginning of the seventeenth century, had it not been for the fact that this same period saw the rise of the great works of Cervantes, prominent among the brilliant output of the authors of Philip III's kingdom, the true founder of the modern novel and, at the same time, influenced by the spirit of the Renaissance, like by the rays of a sunset].
6. *The decades of the New World or West India, conteyning the navigations and conquests of the Spanyards,*

with the particular description of the most ryche and large landes and islands lately found in the west ocean parteyning to the inheritance of the kings of Spayne. In the wich the diligent reader may not only consyder what commodities may herby chance to the whole christian world in tyme to come, but also learn many secreates touchynge the land, the sea and the starres, very necessarie to knowe to all such as shal attempt any navigations or otherwise have delite to behold the strange and wonnderffull woorkes of God and Nature. Written in the latine tounge by Peter Martyr of Angleria, and translated in to englyshe by Richarde Eden. Londini in aedibus Guilhelmi Powell, anno 1555; Theodore de Bry, *Narratio regionum Indicarum per Hispanos quosdam deuastatrum verissima: prius quidem per Episc. Barth. Casaum, natione hispanum hispanice conscripta, et anno 1551. Hispali, hispanice. Annon vero hoc 1598. Latine excusa*, Frankfurt, 1598.

7. W. H. Auden, in *Lectures on Shakespeare*, ed. by Arthur Kirsch (Princeton, NJ: Princeton University Press, 2000), p. 300, states that in *The Tempest* one of the major issues is 'the nature of education'.

8. See Thomas More, *Utopia*, The Complete Works of St. Thomas More, ed. by Edward Surtz, SJ, and J. H. Hexter (New Haven, CT: Yale University Press, 1965), pp. 20–25.

9. See the Rita Guerlac, 'Introduction', in *Juan Luis Vives. Against the Pseudodialecticians. A Humanist Attack on Medieval Logic* (London: D. Reidel Publishing Company, 1977), p. 30.

10. Northrop Frye, *Northrop Frye on Shakespeare*, ed. by Robert Sandler (New Haven and London: Yale University Press, 1986), p. 171.

11. S. Schoenbaum, *Shakespeare's Lives* (Oxford: Clarendon Press, 1970), p. 63.

12. J. L. Borges, *El hacedor*, in *Obra poética* (Buenos Aires: Emecé, 1964), p. 45.

CHAPTER 22

Quixotic Idealism Triumphant:
Persiles and Sigismunda in Britain

Clark Colahan

Cervantes's last work, a romance entitled *Los trabajos de Persiles y Sigismunda: historia septentrional*, is as long as either of the halves of *Don Quixote* and almost certainly would have been longer had his imminent death not obliged him to wrap up the complicated plot as expeditiously as possible. It was written concurrently with *Don Quixote* Part II, and represented the author's hopes for a critical success comparable to the popular acclaim he had won with Part I. In this attempt he achieved posthumous success, as the *Persiles*, promptly published in 1617, was both highly regarded and frequently published throughout the seventeenth century and well into the eighteenth. The first anonymous English version, *The Travels of Persiles and Sigismunda: A Northern History*, by an anonymous translator, was based on a French translation, not the original Spanish, and came out in 1619.[1] Though the work's reception has doubtless been boosted by the popularity of *Don Quixote*, it has nonetheless generated in English four translations (one each century), a Jacobean comedy, a neo-Jacobean drama, and the title of a major twentieth-century novel.

The title-page description of the eighteenth-century translation,[2] also anonymous, stresses the entertainment value of what today is viewed as the work's complex mix of themes, characters, settings and parody of literary theory: *Persiles and Sigismunda: A Celebrated Novel intermixed with a great Variety of Delightful Histories and Entertaining Adventures*. Though based on Cervantes's own text, on occasion it embellishes to bring out the drama of the situations. The nineteenth-century translator, who in 1853 signs her preface LDS (Louisa Dorothea Stanley), is more critical. Calling the work *The Wanderings of Persiles and Sigismunda: A Northern Story*, she describes it (citing Sismondi) as 'the offspring of a rich, but at the same time of a wandering imagination, which confines itself within no bounds of the possible or the probable, and which is not sufficiently founded on reality'.[3] However, a Romantic perspective triumphs shortly thereafter: 'In spite of the absurdities [... there is] a good deal of imagination as well as beauty [...] I need not apologize further for making them [i.e., readers of English] acquainted with these wondrously beautiful and almost angelic pilgrims'.[4] Stanley's Victorian sensibilities surface in her practice (related to the attitude that we will see in some critics of the work's primary English adaptation, *The Custom of the Country*) of omitting phrases, and indeed two or three pages at a time, when she considers the subject matter sexually indelicate. In 1989, at a time when the genre of romance was receiving renewed critical appreciation vis-à-vis the novel and the work was beginning to recapture the interest of specialists on Cervantes, the University of California Press published a standard, annotated translation entitled *The Trials of Persiles and Sigismunda: A Northern Story*, by Celia Weller and Clark Colahan.

John Fletcher and Philip Massinger seized on the 1619 translation and together wrote a play for the King's Men entitled *The Custom of the Country* (1620). At that time James I was looking for a Spanish bride for the crown prince, who took the initiative to go off himself incognito to Madrid with Buckingham to see what attractive possibilities they could find. As a result, Spanish settings, especially when placed in stories adapted from Spanish authors, drew good theatre crowds, a situation of which Fletcher was keenly aware and several times contributed to.

The play was hugely popular in the seventeenth century, twice performed at court, and brought back to the stage several times. In 1628 alone, it took in more box office than *Othello*, *Richard II*, and *The Alchemist* together.[5] Cervantes's work, modelled on Heliodorus's Byzantine romance but combined with sensational chivalric elements that the author of *Don Quixote* knew well, translated culturally into a high-adventure, low-life comedy.[6] Of course in such a far-flung story it was necessary, as was pointed out forty years ago by Alejandro Ramírez and then studied in detail by Darby, to put it all into manageable bounds by selecting out only a few memorable characters who would bring out the theme.[7] This need for simplification and focus explains why the shorter, individual tales from Cervantes's *Novelas ejemplares* generated several Jacobean plays but the *Persiles* only this one.

Neither Persiles nor Sigismunda fitted the requirements for memorable characters, very probably because they are too self-possessed to fit well into a rowdy comedy and because covering the major *peripetiae* involved in either of their dramatic arcs would have resulted in a very long text. Instead the playwrights chose two women as suitable to their theme, which is essentially the same as Cervantes's — violent, barbaric lust versus disciplined, civilized love. One is Hipólita, the elegant Roman courtesan under the thumb of the dangerous pimp, Pirro, who between them first attempt to seduce and then later murder Persiles. The other is Guiomar, the forgiving mother of the irascible Portuguese nobleman, killed by the rash Ortel Banedre in an alley fight that he did not provoke.

This theme, and the play's frequent introduction of sexual activity, has evoked strong and varied reactions. Among recent commentators, Darby has particularly stressed that it 'is unabashedly a play about sex [...] driven by sexual energy'.[8] In contrast, Ramírez emphasizes that Fletcher and Massinger are basically defending a moral position, focusing on the leading couple's search for a pure love.[9] Eastop's formulation is similar, and it recalls the *trabajos*, 'the struggles' or 'trials' of the two protagonists in Cervantes's romance: 'The central plot is timeless in its depiction of innocent love beset on all sides by the base desires of those corrupted by lust'.[10] Prager sees a general manumission of figurative slavery to lust, especially in the case of the large number of licentious secondary characters, as the culmination toward which the whole play moves.[11]

The happy ending is, in keeping with play's comic tone, even more thorough-going than in the romance, where several characters, upon failing the sorts of trials that the main characters deal with successfully, pay with their lives. The English avatar of Don Duarte, for example, makes a miraculous recovery from his wounds and his arrogance.[12] His mother, a purely maternal figure in the romance, is granted a second marriage. And even though Count Clodio — not Cervantes's slanderer but an Italian count who concentrates into one self-indulgent tyrant all of Ladislao's disgusting male relatives, eager to join in the defloration of the bride — begins by claiming his wedding night privilege under the 'custom of the country', he reforms at the end and endorses monogamy.

This controlling obsession of lust is exemplified several times in the form of socially sanctioned physical enslavement, most likely suggested to the playwrights by the brutal would-be world conquerors on the Barbarian Island and the pirates that are so prominent in the first two books of the *Persiles*. The most notorious example in the play is the compulsory service by the protagonist's randy brother in a male brothel. There the ladies of Lisbon exhaust him totally, curing him of his fascination with rutting. Hence comes the appropriateness of his name, Rutilio, which in the *Persiles* (even though the play on the name's sound, in English, is obviously absent) is also attached to a lustful young Italian, who (while not Persiles's brother) learns to overcome the same vice.

The deft plotting with which the several story lines are woven together has been often noted, but the playwrights also use concerted imagery, related closely to Cervantes's, to unify the material.[13] Immediately in the play's opening scene the same motifs of savagery typical of the *Persiles* — cannibalism, lust, animalism, and barbaric religion — appear in the imagery used to flesh out the description of the custom and its enforcer, Count Clodio. Later, in a lighter mood, but with the same references to beasts, dogs, horses and hell, there is a narration of the hardships of life in 'the male stews'.

On the side of civilized restraint, the female protagonist is, like Sigismunda, clearly linked to the Virgin Mary, while the renunciation of revenge (and of Count Clodio's violent intentions) in favour of forgiveness is expressed in both works by changing black mourning clothes into bright, joyful marriage dress. Ruperta's sudden abandonment of her macabre and perpetual funeral for her husband when the light from a lamp reveals to her the beauty of her intended victim is paralleled, in the play, by Guiomar's sudden metamorphosis from revenger to bride.

To return to the question of the polarized reactions to the play, the factor that most shapes the critical response seems to be not so much the extent of the reader's openness to frank portrayal of sexual desire in general, but how he or she feels about the way that material is managed in relation to women's dignity and/or freedom. Seventeenth-century British men and women were seemingly far from being offended, and Cervantes, who differs more in his presentation than the subjects he opens up, has not been censured.

How would Cervantes's episodes have played to those of delicate sensibilities if the playwrights had included such shocking situations as those of Taurisa (handed over by Prince Arnaldo to pirates, who let her die of disease while fighting to the death over possession of her moribund body), or of the former English royal mistress Rosamunda (who with equine imagery advocates sex before marriage and later chooses death in preference to getting so old that a younger man no longer finds her attractive)? Both cases are of course too grim for the full-blown optimism that triumphs in the stage version. But Fletcher and Massinger's decision to keep all of Hipólita — her character, arc, and name, bearing in mind that she represents both a prominent case of feminine freedom and the final recovery of dignity through moral reform — shows that they, like Cervantes, wanted to illustrate the attractions of both lust and amorous self-discipline, while at the same time balancing out the parallel case of Rutilio with a strong female character.

With an insistence on uniform exemplarity typical of the Enlightenment, both Pepys and Dryden resorted to superlatives of condemnation. The former exclaimed that it was, 'of all the plays I did see, the worst, having neither plot, language, nor anything in the earth that is acceptable'.[14] Recently Diana de Armas Wilson has waxed eloquent in the same vein, concluding on feminist grounds that the play is unacceptable due to its 'virulent masculinism' and excoriating 'the meretricious manner in which Fletcher wrenches a narrative of rape into a comedy of errors'. She calls on readers to speculate with her as to whether the Cervantine model has been itself 'disfigured by the indecency of Fletcher's imitation'.[15]

In sharp contrast, Mary Bjork, in her 2005 thesis that also shows concerns about women's issues, extols the liberated, flawed women characters.[16] Eastop commends the exploration of 'women's voracious sexual appetites' as a source of comic fun on stage and praises the whole work as 'a wonderfully lively, moving, funny play which contains so much within it that could have been written today'.[17] Such positive views, though not always coloured primarily by women's issues, have been around for longer than one is often led to believe, as Wallis has documented.[18]

Darby, who focuses on the female lead, Zenocia, characterizes her as deprived of 'the autonomy and initiative of her Cervantine model in that she prefers to resist legalized rape with bow and arrow and with the help of two supportive men, instead of unaided and carrying a lance. In the romance, the female character does not have such men available. Darby sees Jacobean misogyny as the root of this change.'[19] Additional evidence bearing on this question is that in the relevant scene the play-wrights explicitly compare Zenocia to Diana, showing her aiming a drawn bow at her attacker, and ready to die rather than submit.[20] In both *Don Quixote* and the *Persiles* the punishment of Acteon for watching her bathe naked is referred to. Similarly, the first chapter of the *Persiles* dwells on the very real threat to the protagonist's life represented by an arrow on a drawn bow. In short, though, Zenocia could be interpreted as a little more demure than Transila in defending her sexual autonomy, and if one takes that view then she matches Sigismunda, her most important counterpart as leading lady of the whole romance. Still, even from that perspective, she does not break with the larger pattern (so intriguing to some readers and offensive to others) of women whose will is as strong as that of men, including Hipólita (who dominates Arnaldo) and the Ladies of Lisbon (who use Rutilio).

In the twentieth century, the American expatriate novelist Edith Wharton entitled one of her longest and most ambitious narratives *The Custom of the Country*

(1913). The novel details the abuses of the marriage market among the wealthy, where young women are sold to the highest bidder. For this reason she was attracted to the play's depiction of sexual enslavement and understood the word 'custom' as a reference to the money with which a rich man could buy a young woman's maidenhead. In Fletcher and Massinger's feudalization of the tribal defloration practised on Cervantes's Hibernia, we are told that 'the Governor of the country may claim the bride's maiden head, / Or ransom it for money at his pleasure'.[21] One is reminded of the use in the romance of primitive chunks of gold to buy women, as beautiful as possible, on whom the inhabitants of the Barbarian Island attempt to sire the future conqueror of the world.

Nicholas Wright's neo-Jacobean drama, also entitled *The Custom of the Country*,

> takes the same themes of social oppression as expressed through sexuality, sets them in colonial Africa, and makes a statement on the evils of European imperialism. Wright was familiar with both the *Persiles* and the homonymous play, and while the latter was the principal inspiration, there are prominent mythic elements present that are highly visible in the romance. The first performance was in London by the Royal Shakespeare Company in 1983, with a successful run of forty-nine performances and strong reviews. In *The Observer* the play was described as 'a brave attempt [...] to fashion a romantic comedy, with African political overtones, on the Jacobean model',[22] while James Fenton of the *Sunday Times* called it 'an essay in the modern Jacobean style, brilliantly achieved'.[23]

Cervantes imagines, with quixotic idealism, the flight of a couple in love from a barbaric society at the fringe of Christian Europe to the centre of the Catholic world, in Rome. There, though human nature is as predatory as anywhere else, centuries of Christian teaching have created a society that, on average, protects and encourages the spiritual growth of the individual better than on the Barbarian Island. Following this geographical journey in reverse, but retaining the idea of social improvement, Wright's play tells the story of a couple, a Shona woman and an Englishman, escaping from the degenerate heritage of the Portuguese, English and Dutch, to arrive at last at a region whose culture, as the ending dares to hope, will in the future be a mixture of the best of Africa and Europe. They are fleeing the custom of the country incarnated in an African Chief, Count Antonio de Rosario, whose vices, like his name, are primarily the result of imported European traditions, just as at the gates of Rome the Duke of Nemours and Arnaldo fight almost to the death (as though they were barbarians in the benighted north) for possession of the most material aspect of Sigismunda, her portrait.

In the intricate interweaving of the subplots, Wright brings together the stories of three strong female characters, and Fenton writes that 'the play belongs to three extraordinary women'.[24] In a letter to Celia Weller and myself on 23 March 1985, he confirmed the importance of this observation: 'It seemed clear to me that [... the playwrights] had set up a trilogy of three different men's ideas of women, one a love-goddess, one a mother and one a virgin. I built this idea up a lot through reading Frances Yates on the subject — her notes on Botticelli, etc'.

The love goddess, comparable to Cervantes's Hipólita, is Daisy Bone, a brothel-keeper in Johannesburg, who falls in love with Paul, an innocent missionary and the equivalent of Persiles. The mother figure, referring back to the noblewoman Guiomar, is Henrietta Van Es, the owner of the Nooitgedache goldfields. She hides Roger, Paul's brother, in her bed to protect him from detection after he has killed her son in self-defence, just as happens with Ortel Banedre in the romance. Later she contemplates revenge, but with her son's revival, she chooses marriage to Roger instead, just as in the Jacobean model. Significantly it is Tendai, using native herbs and African healing practices, who saves Roger. Her foil in this context is the evil European Dr. Jameson, whose corruption renders him unable to heal. At the root of the episode are the two Cervantine witches, Cenotia and Julia, whose evil spells are nearly fatal and function as a sign for the psychological state of the characters.

The third woman, the virginal Tendai, is like Sigismunda in that she and her new husband offer us the author's parting hope for social enlightenment. Just as Tendai and Paul seek to establish a more peaceful and egalitarian society in war-torn and ethnically divided southern Africa by uniting their cultural inheritances, so too Sigismunda, after studying with theologians in Rome, returns home to join with her husband not only to unite their two island kingdoms in peace, after interminable wars begun by his brother, but to bring the true light of Christian civilization to new generations in a region that has been scourged by not only barbarism but the dangerous errors of Protestantism.

Both the play and the romance, even more than the Jacobean theatrical model, reach not only a triumph of true love for the protagonists but also brother- and sisterhood for their fascinatingly exotic but suffering peoples. National groups take on the simplified, symbolic nature traditionally found in myth and romance, just as the settings themselves assume positive or negative connotations. The contrasts between good and evil are sharp and illustrate a struggle to found a better society, in the African case a struggle projected back into an archetypal time of beginnings. Finally, both works reject violence and affirm traditional moral values of love and restraint in response to the deadly problems of customs so often spawned in hearts of darkness.

In sum, although eclipsed as a romance over the last two centuries by the paramount place of *Don Quixote* within the history of the novel, *Persiles and Sigismunda* has lived up to Cervantes's high hopes for it as one of the best works of fiction written in Spanish, as its reception in Britain shows. The far-reaching ethical concerns and startling surprises woven into the title-couple's spiritual and physical pilgrimage have attracted well-known writers in English and generated worthy adaptations. Though Cervantes's irony is certainly not absent from his final work, its offspring in Albion can testify to the assertion that its protagonist stands out as the culmination of the author's deep-seated idealism, as the hero who succeeds in the noble quest that his flawed alter ego, Don Quixote, was never intended to achieve.

Notes to Chapter 22

1. See Trudi L. Darby, 'Resistance to Rape in *Persiles y Sigismunda* and *The Custom of the Country*', *Modern Language Review*, 90 (1995), 273–84 (p. 273).
2. It was printed in London in 1741 for three booksellers, Ward, Chandler and Wood.
3. See L. D. Stanley, 'Preface by the Translator', in Miguel de Cervantes Saavedra, *The Wanderings of Persiles and Sigismunda: A Northern Story* (London: Cundall, 1854), pp. vii–xii (p. viii).
4. See Stanley, 'Preface by the Translator', pp. ix, xii.
5. See Carolyn Prager, 'The Problem of Slavery in *The Custom of the Country*', *SEL*, 28 (1988), 301–17 (p. 301).
6. See Nick de Somogyi, 'Editor's Introduction', in *The Custom of the Country / John Fletcher and Philip Massinger*, ed. by Nick de Somogyi (New York: Globe Education and Theatre Arts Books/ Routledge, 1999), pp. vii–viii (p. vii).
7. See Alejandro Ramírez, 'Cervantes y Fletcher: El *Persiles* y *The Custom of the Country*', in *Homenaje a Sherman H. Eoff*, ed. by José Schraibman (Madrid: Castalia, 1970), pp. 203–20 (p. 218); and Darby, 'Resistance to Rape', pp. 277–78. For the contrast with the *Exemplary Novels* see Trudi Darby, 'Cervantes in England: The Influence of Golden-Age Prose Fiction on Jacobean Drama, c.1615–1625', *Bulletin of Hispanic Studies*, 79 (1997), 425–41 (p. 433).
8. See Darby, 'Resistance to Rape', p. 279.
9. See Ramírez, 'Cervantes y Fletcher', p. 219.
10. See Jenny Eastop, 'A Note from the Co-ordinator', in Nick de Somogyi (ed.), *The Custom of the Country*, p. v.
11. See Prager, 'The Problem of Slavery in *The Custom of the Country*', p. 219.
12. See Darby, 'Resistance to Rape', p. 279.
13. See Celia E. Weller and Clark A. Colahan, 'Cervantine Imagery and Sex-Role Reversal in Fletcher and Massinger's *The Custom of the Country*', *Cervantes*, 5 (1985), 27–43 (pp. 29–36).
14. Cited by Somogyi, p. viii.
15. See Diana de Armas Wilson, 'Contesting the Custom of the Country: Cervantes and Fletcher', in *From Dante to García Márquez*, ed. by Gene H. Bell-Villada, Antonio Giménez and George Pistorius (Williamstown, MA; Williams College, 1987), pp. 60–75 (pp. 62, 61).
16. See Mary Lucille Dudy Bjork, *Golden Age Spanish prose and Jacobean drama (Miguel de Cervantes Saavedra, Salas Barbadillo, John Fletcher)* (University of California at Santa Barbara, 780126/38), *DAI*, 66, no. 09A (2005), p. 3308. The chapter on *The Custom of the Country* is entitled 'Revisiting the *Custom of the Country*, Fletcher, Massinger, and Cervantes', pp. 102–37, and the same passage cited here is found on p. xi. Subsequent references to Bjork's work are to the complete thesis.
17. See Eastop, 'A Note from the Co-ordinator', p. v.
18. For a sampling of eighteenth- and nineteenth-century criticism, see Lawrence B. Wallis, *Fletcher, Beaumont and Company, Entertainers to the Jacobean Gentry* (New York: King's Crown Press, 1947), pp. 21–22, 83, 118, 175.
19. See Darby, 'Resistance to Rape', p. 283.
20. Bjork (pp. 114–15) presents historical evidence for the prestige of bow and arrow as a weapon of war in seventeenth-century England, though she does not mention the reference to Diana the huntress.
21. Cited in Prager, 'The Problem of Slavery in *The Custom of the Country*', p. 311.
22. See the 'Briefing' column, *The Observer*, 30 October 1983, p. 30.
23. James Fenton, 'The Long March to Conformity', *The Sunday Times*, 23 October 1983, p. 39. Except for reviews written in 1983, the only study of the work is by Clark Colahan and Celia Weller, 'The Persistence of Cervantine Romance in Nicholas Wright's *The Custom of the Country*', *Cervantes*, 10 (1990), 69–77.
24. See Fenton, 'The Long March to Conformity', p. 39.

CHAPTER 23

William Rowley:
A Case Study in Influence

Trudi L. Darby

He was 'beloved of those Great Men *Shakespear, Fletcher,* and *Johnson*', wrote Gerard Langbaine of William Rowley in 1691,[1] and it is Rowley's many associations with the dramatists of the Jacobean era that earn him a place in a study of the influence of Cervantes on English literature. William Rowley himself had a hand in several plays with a Spanish theme, one of them based on two of the *Novelas ejemplares*; and he was enmeshed in a network of writers, patrons and publishers that helped to spread knowledge of the works of Cervantes through the London of King James VI and I. This chapter seeks to place him in his social network,[2] and to illustrate how the influence of Cervantes may have reached him.

Nothing is known of William Rowley until he began writing plays, in collaboration with several other playwrights, for Queen Anne's Men in the early years of King James's reign.[3] For the rest of his life — he died early in 1626 — his most common way of writing would be as a co-writer: the majority of his plays were written in partnership.[4] 'In a word,' noted the eighteenth-century scholar David Erskine Baker, 'he was a very great benefactor to the English stage' before mentioning 'his aid lent to Middleton, Day, Heywood, Webster, &c.'[5] One of his networks, then, was of fellow-dramatists, writing for the London audience and hoping to please the paying public. By 1610, however, Rowley was a member of another network, when he became a founder-member of the playing company patronized by Prince Charles, known as the Duke of York's Men until 1612, and then as Prince Charles's Men. For its first five years, until 1614, the company toured the provinces as well as playing regularly at court in winter seasons; later it played in various London theatres including the Red Bull at Newington, the Curtain in Shoreditch and, briefly, in 1619–20, at the Phoenix in Drury Lane.[6]

Rowley was clearly an important member of this company. When the Prince's Men played at court, it was William Rowley who collected their earnings; when Prince Charles wanted to contact his players at their theatre in Shoreditch in February 1620, it was to Rowley that he sent his messenger;[7] when Prince Charles's Men and Lady Elizabeth's Men were in trouble in March 1615 for playing during Lent, Rowley was one of those who made the companies' joint representations to the Privy Council.[8] For the last two and a half years of his life, from mid-

1623 onwards, Rowley was a member of the King's Men and was one of those who received a grant of cloth in May 1625 for King James's funeral.[9] It would be an exaggeration to call him a courtier, but he was known at court. When, in 1620, George Purslowe printed *The World Tossed at Tennis* of which Rowley was a co-author, he described the playwright on the title page as a Gentleman, as he did when he printed Rowley's *A New Wonder, A Woman Never Vexed* in 1632, some six years after the author's death. Rowley's network thus went up the social ladder, as well as horizontally to his colleagues. The significance here is that by about 1615 James's court was becoming increasingly interested in whether or not Prince Charles would marry the Infanta María and by the time Parliament met in 1621, the 'Spanish Match' was something of a fixation.[10] Rowley was well placed to be aware of what interested the court audience as well as London playgoers more generally.

The impact on Rowley's work of this interest in Spanish matters is first seen at a time when he had been working with Prince Charles's Men for almost a decade, in 1619. This was the year in which Rowley wrote his first play on a Spanish theme: *All's Lost by Lust*. The play seems to have been regarded as a serious contribution to literature, for when it was published (some seven years after Rowley's death, in 1633) the argument of the play was set out at the beginning, as was sometimes done for editions of classical works. The major plot concerns Roderigo, last Visigothic king of Spain, who relies on his general Julianus to defend him against an invasion by the Moors led by Mulymumen. Roderigo rapes Julianus's daughter, Jacinta, and Julianus, in revenge, defects to Mulymumen. Roderigo, in despair, breaks a taboo by opening a set of forbidden doors in his castle before fleeing the country, thus letting the Moors into Spain. Once he has won the kingdom, Mulymumen blinds Julianus and tricks him into killing Jacinta, before killing the general himself. The subplot is a variant on the eternal triangle: '*Antonio* marries *Margaretta,* faire, but low in fortunes, and comming to these warres, fals in love with *Dionysia,* daughter to *Alonzo,* but the women come to tragicall ends, and *Antonio* for upbraiding *Iulianus* with selling his King and Country to the Moore, is by *Iulianus* slaine'.[11] This quarto edition also prefaces the text proper with a Prologue — again, suggesting that this play was given a relatively high status by whoever prepared the text for publication. The title page states that the play had been acted by the Lady Elizabeth's Servants (the acting company of which Elizabeth, King James's daughter and Queen of Bohemia was patron), 'And now lately by her Majesties Servants, with great applause, at the *Phoenix* in *Drury Lane*'. This type of title page puff is relatively common and it is impossible to know exactly how successful the play had actually been on the stage; however, it is worth noting that at the time of its publication the play was still in repertory, now being performed by the company patronized by another queen, Charles I's wife, Henrietta Maria. Further, the play was still sufficiently familiar in 1705 for it to have been adapted by Mary Pix as *The Conquest of Spain, a tragedy.* The play was edited twice in two years at the start of the twentieth century, by two scholars working independently of each other.[12] However, it has never been mainstream repertoire, although the play was successfully given a semi-staged reading on 29 February 2004 by the Education Centre at Shakespeare's Globe, in London.

This play is unique among Rowley's works for being a tragedy: his earlier plays had been comedies or histories, and he seems to have preferred to set his plays in England, if not in London itself. Until this point, Rowley was a very local playwright: for example, his sole-authored play of 1617, *A Shoemaker, A Gentleman*, was about Roman Britain, the persecution of local saints and two heroes, Crispin and Crispianus, who would become the patron saints of shoemakers. Although set historically more than a thousand years earlier, the world of the London Livery Companies is never far away. *A Fair Quarrel*, also from 1617 and co-written with Thomas Middleton, was about contemporary London and was notorious for including among the characters one of the celebrities of the time, Moll Cutpurse. Some time between 1623 and 1625 Rowley would write another history play, *A New Wonder, A Woman Never Vexed*, set this time in medieval London but again with strong resonances for the Livery Companies and, around 1624, two plays set in London in the present day: *A Cure for a Cuckold*, with John Webster, which takes place in Blackwall, and *The Late Murder of the Son upon the Mother; or, Keep the Widow Waking*, with Thomas Dekker and John Ford. This latter play does not survive, but was the cause of a suit to the Star Chamber from which it is clear that the action took place in Whitechapel.[13] In 1621 Rowley had collaborated with Dekker and Ford on *The Witch of Edmonton*, another contemporary play set close to London. As an actor, Rowley seems to have made a speciality of playing rotund characters: in 1620 he would play Plumporridge in *The Inner Temple Masque*, and in 1624 the Fat Bishop in *A Game at Chess*, both characters who are depicted in title-page engravings. Author analysis of the plays to which he is known to have contributed demonstrates that Rowley would usually write the comic subplot. Before he wrote *All's Lost by Lust*, Rowley's work would have been characterized as comedy, generally with a London setting and usually including a genial, stout Clown whom Rowley would play himself.

No English source has ever been identified for *All's Lost by Lust* although the story has its roots in accounts of King Roderigo, who reigned from 711 to 714. There was no obvious work in English from which Rowley could have taken the Roderigo plot; rather, to judge by the sources for *A Shoemaker, A Gentleman* (1617) and *A New Wonder, A Woman Never Vexed* (1623–25), Rowley's reading at this time was in English chronicles and histories such as Holinshed's *Chronicles* and Stowe's *Survey of London*, and Roman historians such as Strabo;[14] yet the tale of the last of the Visigothic kings who opened the forbidden doors and let in the Moors is commonplace in Spanish folklore.[15] So how did Rowley know of it? There is no evidence that Rowley read this story through the intermediary of another language, although he could have read a Latin chronicle account. But in a consideration of an analogous case — George Pettie's source material in Italian — Jason Lawrence has recently contested the notion that English writers worked solely from translations. He argues that language-learning techniques of the time made great use of parallel texts in the target and the native language, and that writers may well have worked from an original text in a relatively unfamiliar language even if a translation into English or another, more familiar, language (such as French), was to hand.[16] He also suggests, again in relation to translations from Italian, that, 'certain renderings from Italian were made by translators who could not actually *speak* the language of the original texts.'[17] In 1609 Rowley had published a prose pamphlet, *A Search for Money*, which is larded with enough Latinisms and classical allusions to demonstrate that he had had at least the standard grammar school education and would have been proficient in Latin — sufficient, perhaps, to enable him to pick his way through a Spanish text, particularly a narrative one, without necessarily understanding all the nuances of language or being able to hold a conversation. In the case of *All's Lost by Lust*, then, I would argue that we should keep an open mind about whether or not Rowley read a Spanish version of the main plot, heard it from a Spanish-speaker or read it in another language. In his 1908 edition, Edgar Morris pointed out that the plot about Antonio's being loved by two women has some similarities with *Las dos doncellas,* one of Cervantes's *novelas ejemplares* and in which two women fall in love with a man named Antonio.[18] However, the protagonist's name and the triangular relationship are the only points of similarity; indeed, Cervantes's story has a happy ending and the correspondence between the two texts is not sufficiently distinctive to be able to say that Rowley had read Cervantes at this stage. Rather, the significance of the play is that it marks a noticeable change in the trajectory of Rowley's career, varying his subject matter to locations beyond London and introducing a new, more sombre tone. By 1619, Rowley had felt the influence of the contemporary interest in Spain.

From about 1616 onwards Rowley had formed a particularly fruitful partnership with Thomas Middleton, the playwright for Lady Elizabeth's Men. Middleton also regularly wrote 'Triumphs', or pageants, for the annual inauguration of the new Lord Mayor, and his offering in 1617 included a speech in Spanish;[19] so he certainly was familiar with the language. His first plays with Rowley, such as *A Fair Quarrel*, had been comedies; in 1620, they would write a more satirical vehicle for the Prince's Men, *The World Tossed at Tennis*, printed in that same year by George Purslowe, as we have seen. It was in 1622, however, that their masterpiece was licensed for performance: *The Changeling*, played by Lady Elizabeth's Men at the Cockpit in Drury Lane.

The Changeling drew upon a description of a real-life murder in Alicante. The source was a book by John Reynolds demonstrating that 'murder will out': *The Triumph of God's Revenge against the Crying and Execrable Sin of Premeditated Murder* (1621). A second source was a translation by Leonard Digges of a work by Céspedes y Meneses published in English as *Gerardo the Unfortunate Spaniard*. Digges's book was printed in 1622 by George Purslowe and sold by Edward Blount: we shall come across these two men again but at this point we should note that Blount was a leading member of the consortium that at this time was engaged in putting together the Shakespeare First Folio, which would be published in 1623. Middleton was responsible for most of the main, tragic, plot of *The Changeling* and Rowley for the first scene, the last scene and a subplot set in a mad-house which, in as much as no one is killed, can be described as comic. The subplot in particular remained in repertory until the 1660s.[20] The action concerns the moral degeneration of Beatrice-Joanna, daughter of the governor of the castle of Alicante, who procures the murder of an unwanted fiancé by her father's follower, De Flores, under whose influence she subsequently falls, and the parallel trials of the wife of the madhouse keeper, who keeps her wits about her, resists attempts to seduce her and remains faithful to her foolish husband. For our present purposes, however, a significant aspect of the production of this work is the very fact that it relies in part on a translation, and that that translation was made by Leonard Digges. Digges's book was printed no more than two months before *The Changeling* was licensed, which suggests that at least one of the playwrights read it eagerly and may have already known the Spanish text — the timescale between the two dates is very short. As we shall see, Digges is a link into another network: the translators who were in the process of making Cervantes's works available to an English-speaking readership. He also contributed a commendatory verse to the First Folio.

A year after *The Changeling*, in 1623, Lady Elizabeth's Men staged a thoroughly Cervantine play: *The Spanish Gipsy*. The main plot of this play is taken from *La fuerza de la sangre* [*The Power of Blood*] and the subplot derives from *La gitanilla* [*The Little Gipsy Girl*] — the only example in the period of two of the *Novelas ejemplares* being brought into use for the same English play. *The Power of Blood* tells of a respectable young woman who is brutally raped and bears a child by her attacker, but seven years later marries him with no reproach. In *The Little Gipsy Girl* aristocratic young men become entangled with a band of gipsies, especially a girl who is famous for her wit, her voice and her virtue, and who turns out to be the daughter of a nobleman, abducted as a baby. The playwrights ingeniously intertwine the two plots by making the father of the rapist in *The Power of Blood* the brother of the mother of the gipsies in *The Little Gipsy Girl*. The seven-year timescale in the *novela* is reduced in the English play to a few days and the focus of attention shifts from the woman who has been raped, and how she achieves justice, to the rapist and how he is affected by remorse. Some of the changes, such as the loss of a female character in the play and the condensed time frame, are attributable to the exigencies of theatrical playing conditions. Others, such as the emphasis on the rapist's conscience rather than on redemption through blood, reflect the influence of Protestant theology on the way that the playwrights manipulated the plot.[21]

While ascribed on the title page to Middleton and Rowley, authorship studies have suggested, on stylistic grounds, that John Ford was involved in writing *The Spanish Gipsy*, and possibly also Thomas Dekker.[22] By 1623 Rowley had working relationships with Middleton (with whom he had recently completed *The Changeling*) and with Dekker and Ford, with whom he had collaborated on *The Witch of Edmonton* in 1621 and with whom he would shortly start on *The Late Murder of the Son upon the Mother* (produced the following year). More salient, however, is the point that whoever wrote the play was very familiar with the *Novelas ejemplares* of Cervantes, at a time when they were not available in English. The first, partial, translation (by James Mabbe) would not be published until 1640 and would include *La fuerza de la sangre* (as *The Power of Blood*) but not *La gitanilla*.[23] Neither Dekker nor Ford is otherwise associated with Cervantine material, or even Spanish material in general (although Dekker did write one play with a Spanish setting, *Match Me in London*, 1611). Rowley, however, was already familiar with Spanish material, and we know that Middleton could write Spanish because, as noted above, his 1617 *Triumph* for the City of London included a Spanish speech. So it seems a fair assumption that the plot material was introduced by Middleton or Rowley, or both, rather than Dekker or Ford. We thus have a progression from 1619, when Rowley first wrote a play from a Spanish source, to 1622 when he and Middleton used an English story set in Spain and an English translation of a Spanish source, to *The Spanish Gipsy*, in 1623, which is undoubtedly a dramatization of Cervantine material. The introduction to Cervantes may have come from Middleton, or it may have come from one of those great men of whom Langbaine said Rowley was beloved: John Fletcher, Shakespeare's successor as playwright to the King's Men.

When Rowley joined the King's Men in 1623 he and Fletcher immediately collaborated on a new play, *The Maid in the Mill*, licensed for performance on 29 August 1623. This was at the time that Prince Charles was in Madrid, wooing the Spanish Infanta; concern about the Spanish Match was at its peak and, predictably enough, *The Maid in the Mill* is set in Spain. Fletcher already had a deep interest in Cervantes and had written *The Custom of the Country*, based on Cervantes's *Los trabajos de Persiles y Sigismunda*, only two or three years earlier. He had already been an 'early adopter' of Cervantine material, writing *Cardenio* with Shakespeare in 1613, a play based on an inset narrative from *Don Quixote*. His last play, in 1625, would be *The Fair Maid of the Inn*, based on Cervantes's *La ilustre fregona*. Fletcher died in 1625 and Rowley shortly afterwards, in the first weeks of 1626 (Middleton survived only until 1627); whether or not they would have continued to collaborate on plays for the King's Men, and what use they might have made of the Cervantine canon, can only be a matter of speculation.

As we have noted, some names have been recurring in the story of William Rowley's interest in Spain, among them Leonard Digges and Edward Blount. This brings us back to the concept of Rowley's social networks, and the groups with which he interacted.[24] During the Jacobean period Blount handled the sale of eight translations from the Spanish, the majority in the period from 1620–23 and including both parts of Thomas Shelton's translation of *Don Quijote*, in 1612 and 1620 and *The Rogue*, James Mabbe's translation of *Guzmán de Alfarache*, in 1622 and 1623. As we have seen, *Gerardo the Unfortunate Spaniard*, sold by Blount and printed by Purslowe (1622) was known to Middleton and Rowley. Blount was the centre of a rich network of contacts among London's Spanish-speakers. As a publisher he dealt with the printers who were setting the translations and thus had a link back to the translators: through George Eld, for example, to James Mabbe who, like Digges, contributed commendatory material to the First Folio, and through Richard Field not only to Shakespeare (Field and Shakespeare were friends from Stratford-upon-Avon and Field had become a successful printer in London with a particular interest in foreign languages),[25] but also to Anthony Munday, a prolific writer and translator of, among other things, *Amadís de Gaule*. A connection to Edward Blount would take Rowley into an intellectually stimulating milieu, and bring him once again into the orbit of the court, for the First Folio was dedicated to the two Herbert brothers, Earls of Montogomery and of Pembroke and cousins of the Master of the Revels Henry Herbert. By contrast, George Purslowe's usual printing work was prose: publishing William Rowley's plays *The World Tossed at*

Tennis in 1620 and *A New Wonder, A Woman Never Vexed* in 1632 was unusual for him and perhaps indicate a personal connection with the dramatist.

But to return to Edward Blount: once Rowley had come into contact with him, how did that extend his social network among Spanish-speakers? The eight translations that Blount handled represented seven translators and compilers: Francis Meres for *The Sinner's Guide*, Thomas Shelton for the two parts of *Don Quixote*, John Wadsworth for *Grammar Spanish and English*, John Minsheu and Richard Percyval jointly for the *Dictionary in Spanish and English*, James Mabbe for the two parts of *The Rogue*, including a reprint of the first part, and Leonard Digges for *Gerardo the Unfortunate Spaniard*. We have already noted that Purslowe may have had his own connections with the King's Men. Edward Blount is thus a node in a network of connections that takes us from Spanish translations to the Jacobean stage. Purslowe also acted sometimes as a bookseller as well as a printer and sold the two editions of Anthony Munday's translation of *Amadís de Gaule*, Parts III and IV, that came out in 1618 with dedications to Philip Herbert the Earl of Montgomery: and so we can see the network extending back again to include the court circle, with whom Rowley was already familiar through leading the Prince's Men. (Anthony Munday himself had been a playwright and still lived in Cripplegate,[26] near to the theatre district of Shoreditch; Rowley, who was buried in the neighbouring parish of St James Clerkenwell, must have lived close by.) Other works dedicated to either the Earl of Montgomery or his wife, the Countess Susan, were *The Treasury of Modern Times* and *Archaeorautos*, both published by William Jaggard (another leading member of the First Folio consortium) in 1619; and both Herbert brothers, as well as being dedicatees of the First Folio, received the dedication to Digges's *Gerardo*.

We can look now at another node in another network. Matthew Lownes sold nine editions of Spanish translations or grammar books during King James's reign: five editions of *Janua Linguarum*, a language-learning textbook which be brought out for the first time in 1615, *The History of All the Roman Emperors*, *The Imperial History*, *The Travails of Persiles and Sigismunda* and Minsheu and Percyval's *Dictionary in Spanish and English*. In one sense Lownes's social network is slightly less rich than Blount's because his brother Humphrey printed six of these editions and so he was interacting with fewer printers; the others with whom he placed Spanish translations were Francis Kingston, Richard Field and John Haviland. Haviland also printed the Minsheu and Percyval dictionary for Edward Blount as well as for William Aspley, yet another of the First Folio consortium, all in 1623. Of the other books, *The Travails of Persiles and Sigismunda* of 1619 is an anonymous translation of a novel by Cervantes. The dedication was signed by M. L. — Matthew Lownes himself — and was addressed to Philip Baron Stanhope, brother-in-law of the Earl of Huntingdon who had himself been a patron of John Fletcher and was a cousin of Fletcher's first collaborator, Francis Beaumont.[27]

We can thus see that, through his relationships with the playing companies, with playwrights, with members of the court and with the London bookselling trade, William Rowley was networked into a group of people who were interested in Spanish culture. Rowley himself was persuaded to venture out of his usual territory, based firmly on material relating to London, and into the Spanish world as interest in the Spanish Match at court and in London became more pronounced. From 1619 onwards there is evidence that he was increasingly in contact with those who knew Cervantes's works, and by 1623 was familiar with at least two of the *Novelas ejemplares*. Rowley's value as a case study, then, is to demonstrate the rising influence of Cervantes's works and how it affected the work of a writer whose feet were planted very firmly in London.

Notes to Chapter 23

1. Gerard Langbaine, *An account of the English dramatic poets. Or, some observations and remarks on the lives and writings, of all those that have published either comedies, tragedies, tragi-comedies, pastorals, masques, interludes, farces, or operas in the English tongue* (Oxford: L[eonard]. L[ichfield] for George West, and Henry Clements, 1691), pp. 428–29.
2. This chapter draws, in a very elementary fashion, on the technique of Social Network Analysis developed by management scientists as a tool for studying organization behaviour. At its simplest, the technique examines the roles of each member of a social network and the number of connections they generate, to analyse which roles have the richest networks.
3. *The Travels of the Three English Brothers*, with John Day and George Wilkins, 1607; *Fortune by Land and Sea*, with Thomas Heywood, c.1609.
4. For a succinct account of the Rowley canon, see David Gunby, 'Rowley, William', in *Oxford Dictionary of National Biography* (Oxford: Oxford University Press, 2004), online edition <http://www.oxforddnb.com/view/article/24227> [accessed 24 May 2007].
5. David Erskine Baker, *Biographica Dramatica; or, A Companion to the Playhouse*, 2 vols (London: Rivingtons and others, 1782), I, 375.
6. See Gerald Eades Bentley, *The Jacobean and Caroline Stage*, 7 vols (Oxford: Clarendon Press, 1941–68), I, 198; Andrew Gurr, *The Shakespearian Playing Companies* (Oxford: Clarendon Press, 1996), pp. 401–12.
7. Bentley, *The Jacobean and Caroline Stage*, VI, 134.
8. Bentley, *The Jacobean and Caroline Stage*, I, 137 n. 3, and I, 176.
9. Bentley, *The Jacobean and Caroline Stage*, I, 18 n. 8, and I, 209.
10. For discussions of the significance and context of the Spanish Match, see Glyn Redworth, *The Prince and the Infanta: The Cultural Politics of the Spanish Match* (New Haven and London: Yale University Press, 2003), and *The Spanish Match: Prince Charles's Journey to Madrid, 1623*, ed. by Alexander Samson (Aldershot: Ashgate, 2006).
11. William Rowley, *All's Lost by Lust* (London: Thomas Harper, 1633), pp. 2–3.
12. *The Spanish Gipsie; All's Lost by Lust, by Thomas Middleton and William Rowley*, ed. by E. C. Morris (Boston: Heath and Co., 1908); *William Rowley his All's Lost by Lust and A Shoemaker A Gentleman*, ed. by C. W. Stork (Philadelphia: Publications of the University of Pennsylvania, 1910).
13. C. J. Sisson, *Lost Plays of Shakespeare's Age* (Cambridge: Cambridge University Press, 1936) pp. 80–124.
14. *A Shoemaker, A Gentleman*, ed. by Trudi L. Darby (London: Nick Hern Books in association with Globe Education, 2002), pp. 1–2; *A Critical, Old-Spelling Edition of 'A New Wonder, A Woman Never Vexed'*, ed. by Trudi L. Darby (New York and London: Garland Publishing, 1998), pp. 28–33.
15. The argument, as set out in the 1633 quarto of the play, concentrates on the sensational, sex-and-violence features of the plot and omits the scene in which Roderigo opens the doors in his castle, which suggests that it was compiled by the publisher rather than being part of Rowley's original text.
16. Jason Lawrence, *'Who the devil taught thee so much Italian?' Italian Language Learning and Literary Imitation in Early Modern England* (Manchester and New York: Manchester University Press, 2005), p. 44.
17. Lawrence, *'Who the devil taught thee so much Italian?'*, p. 44.

18. Morris, *The Spanish Gipsie; All's Lost by Lust*, p. 138.

19. Thomas Middleton, *The Triumphs of Honor and Industry* (London: Nicholas Okes, 1617), B2–B2^{v}.

20. Thomas Middleton and William Rowley, *The Changeling*, ed. by N. W. Bawcutt (Manchester: Manchester University Press, 1958), pp. xxxi–xxxv, xxvii–xxviii.

21. For a detailed analysis of this play, see B. W. Ife and Trudi L. Darby, 'Remorse, Retribution and Redemption in *La fuerza de la sangre*: Spanish and English Perspectives', in *A Companion to Cervantes's Novelas Ejemplares*, ed. by Stephen Boyd (Woodbridge: Tamesis, 2005), pp. 172–90.

22. The new Oxford edition of Thomas Middleton includes *The Spanish Gipsy* and attributes it to Middleton, Rowley, Dekker and Ford (*Thomas Middleton: The Collected Works*, ed. by Gary Taylor and John Lavagnino (Oxford: Oxford University Press, 2007), pp. 433–37, 1723. I am grateful to Dr Lavagnino for showing me these pages in proof.

23. *Exemplary Novels in Six Books. The two damsels. The Lady Cornelia. The liberal lover. The force of blood. The Spanish lady. The jealous husband. Full of various accidents both delightful and profitable. By Miguel de Cervantes Saavedra; one of the prime wits of Spain, for his rare fancies and witty inventions. Turned into English by Don Diego Puede-Ser*, trans. By James Mabbe (London: Laurence Blaicklocke, 1640). 'Puede ser', meaning 'may be', is Mabbe's pun on his own name.

24. The information that follows is drawn from the 'Early Modern Spanish–English Translations Database 1500–1640', compiled by Alan Paterson and Alexander Samson and hosted by the Early Modern Spain website at King's College London <http://www.ems.kcl.ac.uk/content/proj/anglo/tldb/index.html> [accessed August 2007].

25. See, e.g., Stephen Greenblatt, *Will in the World: How Shakespeare Became Shakespeare* (London: Jonathan Cape, 2004), pp. 193–94.

26. Tracey Hill, *Anthony Munday and Civic Culture: Theatre, History and Power in Early Modern London, 1580–1633* (Manchester: Manchester University Press, 2004), p. 31.

27. Gordon MacMullan, *The Politics of Unease in the Plays of John Fletcher* (Amherst: University of Massachusetts Press, 1994) pp. 14–15.

CERVANTES IN BRITAIN:
A BIBLIOGRAPHY

Jane Neville

This bibliography is intended to be comprehensive. It includes papers published in conference proceedings regardless of their quality. Chapters published in multiple-author volumes are omitted. This includes the books edited by Fernández-Morera et al, Martínez Torrón et al, Luis-Martínez et al, and Barrio Marco et al. Generally speaking, this bibliography includes studies which focus on one aspect of Cervantes's influence on, and reception in, Britain.

ACCARDO, P., 'The Puppet Show of Memory: Chesterton, Calderón and Cervantes', *The Chesterton Review*, 18 (1992), 395–404.

ACOSTA, SANTIAGO, 'El influjo del *Quijote* en *Joseph Andrews*', *Revista Canaria de Estudios Ingleses*, 11 (1985), 69–80.

ALLEN, JOHN J., '*Traduttori Traditori*: *Don Quixote* in English', *Crítica Hispánica*, 1. 2 (1979), 1–13.

ALVAR, CARLOS (ed.), *Gran Enciclopedia Cervantina* (Madrid: Castalia, 2005–07).

ANTÓN-PACHECO, LUISA, *Sátira y parodia en el Quijote y Joseph Andrews* (Madrid: Universidad Complutense, 1989).

ARDILA, J. A. G., 'Cervantes y la *quixotic fiction*: la parodia de géneros', *Anales Cervantinos*, 34 (1998), 145–68.

——'Cervantes y la *quixotic fiction*: el hibridismo genérico', *Cervantes*, 21. 2 (2001), 5–26.

——'Cervantes y la *quixotic fiction*: sucesión episódica y otros recursos narrativos', *Cervantes*, 21. 1 (2001), 43–65.

——'La influencia de la narrativa del Siglo de Oro en la novela británica del XVIII', *Revista de Literatura*, 63. 126 (2001), 401–23.

——'Intertextualidad general y restringida en el *Don Quixote* de Smollett', *Anuario de Estudios Filológicos*, 25 (2002), 137–51.

——'La teoría cervantina de la novela en *Roderick Random*', *Bulletin of Spanish Studies*, 79 (2002), 543–61.

——'Sancho Panza en Inglaterra: *Sancho at Court* de Ayres y *Barataria* de Pilon', *Bulletin of Hispanic Studies*, 82. 5 (2005), 551–69.

——'Traducción y recepción del *Quijote* en Gran Bretaña, 1612–1774', *Anales Cervantinos*, 37 (2005), 253–65.

——*Cervantes en Inglaterra: el Quijote en los albores de la novela británica*, preface by Jean Canavaggio (Liverpool: Liverpool University Press, 2006).

——'Thomas D'Urfey y la recepción del *Quijote* en el siglo XVII inglés', *Hispanic Research Journal* (forthcoming).

ARGELLI, ANALISA, 'De Cervantes y Butler: análisis de una transposición', *Estudios Ingleses de la Universidad Complutense*, 7 (1999), 265–78.

——'Cervantes y Butler en la cultura inglesa del seiscientos', *Symposium*, 53 (1999), 123–35.

——'Don Quijote y sus andanzas por las tierras de John Bull', *RILCE*, 17. 1 (2001), 1–16.

——'Don Quixote's Adventures in England, from Pre-Restoration to Romanticism', *Rivista di Letterature Moderne e Comparate*, 55. 2 (2002), 13–33.

——'*La Señora Cornelia*: viaggio di andata e ritorno da un ipotesto cervantino ad un hipertexto teatrale nell'Inghilterra del Seicento', in *Le mappe nascoste di Cervantes*, ed. by Carlos Romero Muñoz (Tremiso: Santi Quaranta, 2004), pp. 159–91.

——'Una "Novela ejemplar" al teatro: hacia un estudio de las adaptaciones teatrales inglesas de Cervantes', *Hispanófila*, 123 (2001), 53–68, also published in *Estudios Ingleses de la Universidad Complutense*, 9 (2001), 237–52.

Armas Cárdenas, J. de, *Cervantes en la literatura inglesa* (Madrid: Renacimiento, 1916).

Avalle-Arce, Juan Bautista, 'Quijotes y quijotismos del inglés', *Ojáncano*, 2 (1989), 58–66.

——'Shakespeare y Cervantes?', *Letras de Deusto*, 28 (1998), 217–21.

Ayala, Francisco, 'Los dos amigos', *Revista de Occidente*, 10 (1965), 287–306.

Bahlsen, Leopold, 'Spanische Quellen der dramatischen Litteratur, besonders Englands zu Shakespeares Zeit', *Zeitschrift für vergleichende Litteraturgeschichte*, 6 (1893), 151–59.

Ballesteros, Isolina, 'La presencia del *Quijote* de Cervantes en *Joseph Andrews* de Fielding', *Anales Cervantinos*, 27 (1989), 215–24.

Bannet, Eve Tavor, 'Quixotes, Imitations, and Transatlantic Genres', *Eighteenth Century Studies*, 40 (2007), 553–69.

Barrio Marco, José Manuel and María José Crespo Allué (eds.), *La huella del Cervantes y del Quijote en la cultura anglosajona* (Valladolid: Universidad de Valladolid, 2007).

Battestin, Martin, 'Introduction', in Miguel de Cervantes, *The History and Adventures of the Renowned Don Quixote*, trans. by Tobias Smollett (Athens, GA: University of Georgia Press, 2003).

——'The Authorship of Smollett's Don Quixote', *Studies in Bibliography*, 50 (1997), 295–312.

Bawcutt, N. W., '*Don Quixote*, Part I, and *The Duchess of Malfi*', *Modern Language Review*, 66 (1971), 488–91.

Becker, Gustav, 'Die erste englische Don Quijotiade', *Archiv für das Studium der neueren Sprachen und Literaturen*, 123 (1909), 298–304.

——*Die Aufnahme des Don Quijote in die englische Litteratur (1605–c.1770)* (Berlin: Mayer & Müller, 1906).

Bond, Warwick, 'On Six Plays in Beaumont and Fletcher, 1679', *The Review of English Studies*, 11 (1935), 257–75.

Booth, Wayne, 'The Self-Conscious Narrator in Comic Fiction before *Tristram Shandy*', *PMLA*, 76 (1952), 163–85.

Boynton, Mary Fuertes, 'An Oxford Don Quixote', *Hispania*, 407 (1964), 738–50.

Bradford Jr., Gamaliel, '*The History of Cardenio* by Mr. Fletcher and Shakespeare', *Modern Language Notes*, 15 (1910), 51–56.

Britton, R. K., 'Don Quixote's Fourth Sally: Cervantes and the Eighteenth-Century Novel', *New Comparison*, 15 (1993), 21–32.

Brooks, Douglas, 'The Interpolated Tales in *Joseph Andrews* Again', *Modern Philology*, 45 (1968), 208–13.

Buck, Gerhard, 'Written in Imitation of the Manner of Cervantes', *Germanische-Romanische Monatsschrift*, 24 (1941), 53–61.

Burton, A. P., 'Cervantes the Man Seen Through English Eyes in the Seventeenth and Eighteenth Centuries', *Bulletin of Hispanic Studies*, 45 (1968), 1–15.

Byron, Kirsten Anne, 'Romance and Narrative Games of Illusion and Reality: Parody in *El ingenioso hidalgo Don Quijote de La Mancha* y *Northanger Abbey*', unpublished master's thesis, University of Alberta, 1994.

Caminero, Juventino, '*Joseph Andrews* y *Don Quijote de la Mancha*: dos castos varones', *Letras de Deusto*, 9 (1979), 95–129.

CANAVAGGIO, JEAN, '*Monseñor Don Quijote*, de Graham Greene, o el penúltimo avatar del quijotismo', in *Actas del coloquio cervantino, Würzburg 1983*, ed. by Theodor Berchem and Hugo Laintenberger (Münster: Aschendorffsche Verlagsbuchhandlung, 1987), pp. 1–10.

—— *Don Quichotte du livre au mythe. Quatre siécles d'errance* (Paris: Fayard, 2005).

—— 'Don Quijote pasa el Pirineo: algunos hitos de una primera recepción', in *Cervantes y el Quijote en la música. Estudios sobre la recepción de un mito*, ed. by Begoña Lolo (Alcalá : Centro de Estudios Cervantinos, 2007), pp. 21–38.

CARRASCOSA, PABLO Y ELISA DOMÍNGUEZ DE PAZ, 'Swift, lector de Cervantes', in *Actas del primer coloquio internacional de la Asociación de Cervantistas, Alcalá de Henares 29/30 nov.–1/2 dic. 1988* (Barcelona: Anthropos, 1990), pp. 377–91.

CASADO VEGAS, ALICIA 'Don Quijote en Lilliput', in *Actas de la Asociación de Cervantistas*, ed. by Giuseppe Grilli (Naples: Instituto Universitario Orientale, 1995), pp. 831–37.

CASTELLS, ISABEL, '*Monseñor Don Quijote*, de Graham Greene, o la crucifixión del texto cervantino según el Evangelio de Unamuno', in *Desviaciones lúdicas en la crítica cervantina: Primer convivio internacional de "Locos Amenos"*, ed. by Antonio Bernat Vistarini and José María Casasayas (Salamanca: Ediciones Universidad de Salamanca, 2000), pp. 173–88.

CHOI, JAE-SUCK, *Greene and Unamuno: Two Pilgrims to La Mancha* (New York: Peter Lang, 1990).

CLARK, SANDRA, 'Cervantes' "The Curious Impertinent" in Some Jacobean Plays', *Bulletin of Hispanic Studies*, 79 (2002), 477–89.

COATES, J., 'The Restoration of the Past and the War of Values: The Image of D. Quixote in Chesterton's Work', *The Chesterton Review*, 6 (1980), 280–304.

CORDASCO, FRANCESCO, 'Smollett and the Translation of *Don Quixote*: Important Unpublished Letters', *Notes & Queries*, 193 (1948), 363–64.

COX, R. MERRITT, *The Rev. John Bowle: The Genesis of Cervantean Criticism* (Chapel Hill: University of North Carolina Press, 1971).

CRO, STELIO, 'Structure and Symbol in Cervantes, Shakespeare, and Pirandello', *Studies in Language and Literature*, 6 (1994), 63–64.

—— 'The Play within the Play: Pirandello, Cervantes, and Shakespeare', *Romance Languages Annual*, 6 (1994), 230–37.

CUNCHILLOS, CARMELO, 'La primera traducción inglesa del *Quijote* de Thomas Shelton (1612–1620)', *Cuadernos de Investigación Filológica*, 9 (1983), 63–89.

—— 'Traducciones inglesas del *Quijote*: la traducción de Phillips (1687)', *Miscelánea*, 6 (1984), 3–44.

—— 'Traducciones inglesas del *Quijote* (1612–1800)', in *De clásicos y traducciones. Clásicos españoles en versiones inglesas: los siglos XVI y XVII*, ed. by Julio César Santoyo and Isabel Verdaguer (Barcelona: PPU, 1987), pp. 89–113.

CUNNINGHAM, ROBERT N., *Peter Anthony Motteux* (Oxford: Blackwell, 1933).

DARBY, TRUDI L., 'Cervantes in England: the Influence of Golden-Age Prose Fiction on Jacobean Drama, *c.*1615–1625', *Bulletin of Hispanic Studies*, 74 (1997), 425–41.

—— 'Resistance to Rape in *Persiles and Sigismunda* and *The Custom of the Country*', *Modern Language Review*, 90 (1995), 273–84.

DE BRUYN, FRANS, 'Edmund Burke the Political Quixote: Romance, Chivalry, and the Political Imagination', *Eighteenth-Century Fiction*, 16 (2004), 695–733.

DESMOND, JOHN F., 'The Heart of (the) Matter: The Mystery of the Real in *Monsignor Quixote*', *Religion and Literature*, 22. 1 (1990), 59–77.

DRISKELL, LEON L., 'Interpolated Tales in *Joseph Andrews* and *Don Quixote*: The Dramatic Method', *South Atlantic Bulletin*, 33 (1968), 5–8.

DUFFIELD, ALEXANDER, 'Of this Translation and Others', in Miguel de Cervantes, *The Ingenious Knight, Don Quixote de la Mancha*, trans. by A. J. Duffield (London: C. Kegan-Paul, 1881).

DUNN, PETER N., 'Don Quixote through the Looking Glass', *Cervantes*, 12. 1 (1992), 5–17.

EASSON, ARGUS, 'Don Pickwick: Dickens and the Transformation of Cervantes', in *Rereading Victorian Fiction*, ed. by Alice Jenkins, Juliet John and John Sutherland (New York: Macmillan, 2000), pp. 173–88.

ENTWISTLE, WILLIAM, 'Un Quijote inglés', in *Miguel de Cervantes Saavedra. Homenaje de Ínsula en el cuarto centenario de su nacimiento* (Madrid: Ínsula, 1947), pp. 79–85.

ERICKSON, ROBERT A., "Tis Tris-Something: Fatherhood and Naming in *Don Quixote* and *Tristram Shandy*', in *Laurence Sterne: Riddles and Mysteries*, ed. by Valerie Grosvenor Myer (Totowa, NJ: Barnes & Noble, 1984), pp. 39–56.

FERNÁNDEZ-MORERA, DARIO and MICHAEL HANKE (eds.), *Cervantes in the English-Speaking World. New Essays* (Barcelona and Kassel: Edition Reichenberger, 2005).

FITZMAURICE-KELLY, JAMES, 'Cervantes in England', *Proceedings of the British Academy*, 3 (1905–06), 11–30.

—— 'Introduction', Miguel de Cervantes, *The History of Don Quixote of the Mancha* (London: David Nutt, 1896), pp. xlvi–li.

—— *The Relations between Spanish and English Literatures* (Liverpool: Liverpool University Press, 1910).

FREEHAFER, JOHN, '*Cardenio*, by Shakespeare and Fletcher', *PMLA*, 84 (1969), 501–13.

FRIEDMAN, EDWARD H., 'Voices Within: Robin Chapman's *The Duchess' Diary* and the Intertextual Conundrum of Don Quixote', *Romance Language Annual*, 2 (1990), 400–05.

GALE, STEVEN, 'The Relationship between Beaumont's *The Knight of the Burning Pestle* and Cervantes' *Don Quixote*', *Anales Cervantinos*, 11 (1972), 87–96.

GALE, S. H., 'Cervantes' Influence on Dickens, with Comparative Emphasis on *Don Quixote* and *Pickwick Papers*', *Anales Cervantinos*, 12 (1973), 135–56.

GARDINER, ELLEN, 'Writing Men Reading in Charlotte Lennox's *The Female Quixote*', *Studies in the Novel*, 28 (1996), 1–11.

GARRETT, ERIN, 'Recycling Zoraida: The Muslim Heroine in Mary Shelley's *Frankenstein*', *Cervantes*, 20. 1 (2000), 133–56.

GASTON, PATRICIA S., 'The Waverley Series and Don Quixote: Manuscripts Found and Lost', *Cervantes*, 11. 1 (1991), 45–59.

GERHARD, SANDRA, *Don Quixote and the Shelton Translation* (Madrid and Potomac: José Porrúa, 1982).

GERLI, MICHAEL, '"Pray, landlord, bring me those books?": Notes on Cervantes, Walter Scott, and the Social Legitimacy of the Novel in Early Nineteenth-Century England', in *'Corónente tus hazañas': Studies in Honor of John Jay Allen*, ed. by Michael J. McGrath (Newark, DE: Juan de la Cuesta, 2005), pp. 231–42.

GILLESPIE, DIANE F., '"The Rain in Spain": Woolf, Cervantes, Andalusia, and The Waves', in *Virginia Woolf Out of Bounds*, ed. by Jessica Berman and Jane Goldman (New York: Pace University Press, 2001), pp. 271–79.

GILMAN, STEPHEN, 'On Henry Fielding's Reception of Don Quijote', in *Medieval and Renaissance Studies in Honour of Robert B. Tate*, ed. by Ian Michael and Richard A. Cardwell (Oxford: Dolphin, 1986), pp. 27–38.

GNUTZMANN, RITA, '*Don Quixote in England* de Henry Fielding con relación al *Don Quijote* de Cervantes', *Anales Cervantinos*, 22 (1984), 77–101.

GOLDBERG, HOMER, 'The Interpolated Stories in *Joseph Andrews* or "The History of the World in General" Satirically Revised', *Modern Philology*, 53 (1963), 295–310.

GORDON, SCOTT PAUL, *The Practice of Quixotism: Postmodern Theory and Eighteenth-Century Women's Writing* (Basingstoke: Palgrave Macmillan, 2006).

GOULIPIAN, ARMAND, '*Monsignor Quixote*, autoportrait du dernier Graham Greene', in *Don Quixote au XXe siècle. Réceptions d'une figure mythique dans la littérature et les arts*, ed. by Danielle Perrot (Clermont-Ferrand: Presses Universitaires Blaise Pascal, 2003), pp. 469–75.

GRANT, R. PATRICIA, 'Cervantes' *El casamiento engañoso* and Fletcher's *Rule a Wife and Have a Wife*', *Hispanic Review*, 12 (1944), 330–38.

GREENE, LEE J., 'Fielding Gypsy Episode and Sancho Panza's Governorship', *South Atlantic Bulletin*, 34 (1974), 117–21.

GRIERSON, HERBERT, *Don Quixote. Some Wartime Reflections on its Character and Influence* (London: English Association Pamphlet, 1921).

GUERRA DE GLOSS, TERESA, 'The Humour in Cervantes and Swift', *Revista Canaria de Estudios Ingleses*, 16 (1988), 213–24.

HAMMOND, BREAN, 'Mid-Century Quixotism and the Defence of the Novel', *Eighteenth-Century Fiction*, 10. 3 (1998), 247–68.

HAYES, JULIE C., 'Tobias Smollett and the Translations of the *Quijote*', *Huntington Library Quarterly*, 67. 4 (2001), 651–68.

HENRÍQUEZ, SANTIAGO, 'Algunos paralelismos argumentales entre *Don Quijote de la Mancha* y *Monsignior Quixote*', *Revista Canaria de Estudios Ingleses*, 17 (1988), 237–44.

HENRY, PATRICK, 'Cervantes, Unamuno, and Gram. Greene's *Monsignor Don Quixote*', *Comparative Literature Studies*, 23 (1986), 12–25.

HINZ, JOHN, 'Alice Meets the Don', *South Atlantic Quarterly*, 52 (1953), 253–66.

HOBBS, EDNA EARLE, 'Spanish Influence on the Plays of Beaumont and Fletcher', unpublished doctoral dissertation, Florida State University, 1963.

HORST, ROBERT TER, 'Cervantes and the Paternity of the English Novel', in *Cultural Authority in Golden Age Spain*, ed. by M. S. Brownlee and H. U. Gumbrecht (Baltimore: Johns Hopkins University Press, 1995), pp. 165–77

——'The Spanish Etymology of the English Novel', *Indiana Journal of Hispanic Studies*, 5 (1994), 291–307.

HOWARTH, W. D., 'Cervantes and Fletcher: A Theme with Variations', *Modern Language Review*, 56 (1961), 563–66.

HURD, ROBERT, 'Canonical Coercion: A Reception History and Generic Analysis of Lennox's *The Female Quixote*', unpublished master's thesis, East Carolina University, 1995.

JONES, JOSEPH R., 'Two Notes on Sterne: Spanish Sources. The Hinde Tradition', *Revue de Littérature Comparée*, 46 (1972), 437–44.

KAUVAR, ELAINE M., 'Jane Austen and *The Female Quixote*', *Studies in the Novel*, 2 (1970), 211–21.

KNAPP, LEWIS and LILLIAN DE LA TORRE, 'Forged Smollett Setter', *Modern Language Quarterly*, 14 (1953), 228.

KNOWLES, EDWIN B., 'The Vogue of Don Quixote in England, 1605–1660', unpublished doctoral dissertation, New York University, 1938.

——'Don Quixote through English Eyes', *Hispania*, 23. 2 (1940), 103–15.

——'The First and Second Editions of Shelton's *Don Quixote* Part I: A Collation and Dating', *Hispanic Review*, 9 (1941), 254–65.

——'Allusions to Don Quixote before 1660', *Philological Quarterly*, 20 (1941), 573–86.

——*Four Articles on Don Quixote in England* (New York: New York University Press, 1941).

——'Some Textual Peculiarities of the First English Don Quixote', *Papers of the Bibliographical Society of America*, 37 (1943), 226–38.

——'Thomas Shelton, Translator of Don Quixote', *Studies in the Renaissance*, 5 (1958), 160–75.

——'Cervantes and English Literature', in *Cervantes Across the Centuries*, ed. by Á. Flores and M. J. Benardete (New York: Gordian Press, 1969), pp. 277–303.

KOEPPEL, EMIL, 'Don Quixote, Sancho Panza und Dulcinea in der englischen Litteratur bis zur Restauration (1660)', *Archiv für das Studium der neueren Sprachen und Literraturen*, 101 (1898), 87–98.

——*Quellen-Studien zu den Dramen Ben Jonsons, John Marstons und Beaumonts und Fletchers* (Erlangen and Leipzig: Deichertsche Verlag, 1985).

——*Quellen-Studien zu den Dramen George Chapmans, Philip Massingers und John Fords* (Strasbourg: Karl J. Trüber, 1897).

LAMB, JONATHAN, 'The Comic Sublime and Sterne's Fiction', *English Literary History*, 48 (1981), 110–43.

LEVIN, HARRY, 'The Quixotic Principle: Cervantes and Other Novelists', *Harvard English Studies*, 1 (1970), 45–66.

LINSALATA, CARMINE ROCCO, *Smollett's Hoax: Don Quixote in English* (Stanford: Stanford University Press, 1956).

LO RÉ, A. G., 'Las primeras ediciones inglesas del Don Quixote, 1612–1620', in *Actas del Segundo Coloquio Internacional de la Asociación de Cervantistas* (Alcalí: Anthropos, 1989), 541–50.

——*Essays on the Periphery of the Quixote* (Newark, DE: Juan de la Cuesta, 1991).

LONG, PAMELA H., 'Fagin and Monipodio: The Source of *Oliver Twist* in Cervantes's *Rinconete and Cortadillo*', *The Dickensian*, 90 (1994), 117–24.

LUIS-MARTÍNEZ, ZENÓN and LUIS GÓMEZ CANSECO (eds.), *Entre Cervantes y Shakespeare: sendas del Renacimiento / Between Shakespeare and Cervantes: Trails Along the Renaissance* (Newark, DE: Juan de la Cuesta, 2006).

LUTTIKHUIZEN, FRANCES, 'Traducciones inglesas de las *Novelas Ejemplares*', in *De clásicos y traducciones: versiones inglesas de clásicos españoles (s. XVI–XVII)*, ed. by Julio César Santoyo and Isabel Verdaguer (Barcelona: PPU, 1987), pp. 147–64.

MANCING, HOWARD, *The Cervantes Encyclopedia* (Westport and London: Greenwood Press, 2004).

——'The Quixotic Novel in British and American Literature'. *CIEFL Bulletin*, New Series, 15–16 (2005/06), 1–18.

MARTÍNEZ TORRÓN, DIEGO and BERND DIETZ (eds.), *Cervantes en el ámbito anglosajón* (Madrid: Sial, 2005).

MARTÍNEZ TORRÓN, DIEGO, 'John Bowle y el cervantismo español', in *Cervantes y su mundo III*, ed. by Robert Lauer and Kurt Reichenberger (Kassel: Reichenberger, 2005), pp. 419–504.

MAXWELL, BALDWIN, *Studies in Beaumont, Fletcher, and Massinger* (Chapel Hill: University of North Carolina Press, 1939).

McDONALD, W. U. JR., 'Scott's Conception of Don Quixote', *Midwest Review*, 1 (1959), 37–42.

MEDRANO, ISABEL, *Integración de épica y comedia en la narrativa de Fielding y Cervantes* (Madrid: Editorial Universidad Complutense, 1988).

——'CHARLOTTE LENNOX Y EL *Quijote*: el romance como subversión', in *Estudios de Filología Inglesa: Homenje al Dr. Pedro Jesús Marcos Pérez*, ed. by F. Rodríguez González (Alicante: Universidad de Alicante, 1990), pp. 275–84.

MILLS, CHESTER ST. H., 'Eliot's Spanish Connection: Casaubon, the Avatar of Quixote', *George Eliot–George Henry Lewes Studies*, 26/27 (1994), 1–6.

MORÓN ARROYO, CIRIACO, 'Fielding: *Tom Jones*', in *Para entender el Quijote* (Madrid: Rialp, 2005), pp. 276–91.

MOSKAL, JEAN, 'To Speak in Ranchean Phrase', in *Mary Shelley and her Times*, ed. by Betty Bennett and Stuart Curran (Baltimore: Johns Hopkins University Press, 2000), pp. 23–28.

MOTOOKA, WENDY, *The Age of Reasons: Quixotism, Sentimentalism, and Political Economy in Eighteenth-Century Britain* (London: Routledge, 1998).

MÜLLENBROCK, HEINZ-JOACHIM, 'Don Quijote and Eighteenth-Century English Literature', in *Intercultural Encounters: Studies in English Literature*, ed. by Heinz Antor and Kevin L. Cope (Heidelberg: Winter, 1999), pp. 197–209.

NEWMAN, MICHAEL T., 'Variations on a Theme: *Don Quixote* in Eighteenth-century English Literature', unpublished doctoral dissertation, Georgia State University, 1996.

NIEHUS, EDWARD L., 'Quixotic Figures in the Novels of Sterne', *Essays in Literature*, 12 (1985), 41–60.

NOWICKI, WOJCIECH, '"La locura literaria" en los *Quijotes* ingleses del siglo XVIII. Algunas observaciones de un proyecto', *Catalina de Aragón-Regina Angliae*, 2 (1995), 93–107.

PABÓN, TOMÁS, 'Cardenio en Cervantes, Shakespeare and Fletcher', in *Actas del II Congreso Internacional de la Asociación de Cervantistas*, ed. by G. Grilli (Naples: Instituto Universitario Orientale, 1996), pp. 369–76.

PARDO GARCÍA, PEDRO JAVIER, 'La tradición cervantina en la novela inglesa del siglo XVII', doctoral dissertation, Universidad de Salamanca, 1995. Published in diskettes in the Víctor Series of Doctoral Theses by Ediciones Universidad de Salamanca, 1997.

——'La otra cara de Cervantes en la novela inglesa del siglo XVIII: *Tom Jones* y *Humphry Clinker*', in *Actas del II Congreso Internacional de la Asociación de Cervantistas*, ed. by Giuseppe Grillo (Naples: Instituto Universitario Orientale, 1995), pp. 839–54.

——'La novela como juego. La paradoja metaficcional en Cervantes, Fielding y Sterne', in *Actas del X Simposio de la Sociedad Española de Literatura General y Comparada* (Santiago: Universidad de Santiago de Compostela, 1996), pp. 203–17.

——'Formas de imitación del *Quijote* en la novela inglesa del siglo XVIII: *Joseph Andrews* y *Tristram Shandy*', *Anales Cervantinos*, 33 (1995–97), 133–64.

——'Parody, Satire and Quixotism in Beaumont's *The Knight of the Burning Pestle*', *Sederi*, 10 (1999), 141–52.

——'Cervantes, Sterne, Diderot: Les paradoxes du roman, les roman des paradoxes', *Exemplaria. Revista de Literatura Comparada*, 3 (1999), 51–92.

——'El quijote femenino como variante del mito quijotesco', in *Actas del V Congreso Internacional de la Asociación de Cervantistas*, ed. by Alicia Villar Lecumberri (Lisbon: Fundação Calouste Gulbenkian, 2004), pp. 1627–44.

——'El *Quijote* y la novela inglesa: de Laurence Sterne a James Joyce', in *La ficción novelesca en los siglos de oro y la literatura europea*, ed. by Ricardo Senabre and María Cruz Buitrago Gómez (Madrid: Secretaría General Técnica. Centro de Publicaciones, 2005), pp. 57–71.

PARKER, ALEXANDER A., 'Fielding and the Structure of *Don Quixote*', *Bulletin of Hispanic Studies*, 33 (1959), 1–16.

PARTZSCH, HENRIETTE, 'El *Quijote* en el mundo', in *La imagen del Quijote en el mundo*, ed. by José Manuel Lucía Megías (Madrid: Lunwerg y Centro de Estudios Cervantinos, 2004), pp. 115–27.

PAULSON, RONALD, *Don Quixote in England: The Aesthetics of Laughter* (Baltimore: The Johns Hopkins University Press, 1998).

PAWL, AMY, 'Femenine Transformations of the Quixote in Eighteenth-Century England: Lennox's *Female Quixote* and Her Sisters', in *Echoes and Inscriptions: Comparative Approaches to Early Modern Spanish Literatures*, ed. by Barbara A. Simerka and Christopher B. Weimer (Lewisburg, PA: Bucknell University Press, 2000), pp. 142–59.

PAZ GAGO, JOSÉ MARÍA, 'La noble lectora: Las lecturas caballerescas de la duquesa', *Edad de Oro*, 26 (2007), 175–83.

PEERS, E. ALLISON, 'Cervantes in England', *Bulletin of Spanish Studies*, 25 (1947), 226–38.

PEERY, WILLIAM, '*The Curious Impertinent* in *Amends for Ladies*', *Hispanic Review*, 14 (1946), 344–53.

PENNER, ALLEN R., 'Fielding's Adaptation of Cervantes' Knight and Squire. The Character of Joseph', *Revue de Littérature Comparée*, 51 (1967), 508–14.

PÉREZ FIRMAT, GUSTAVO, 'Don Quixote in *Heart of Darkness*: Two Notes', *Comparative Literature Studies*, 12. 4 (1975), 374–83.

PONS, ÉMILE, 'Fielding, Swift et Cervantes. De *Don Quichotte in England* à *Joseph Andrews*', *Studia Neophilologica*, 15 (1942/43), 305–33.

POTAU, MERCEDES, 'Notes on Parallels between *The Pickwick Papers* and *Don Quixote*', *Dickens Quarterly*, 10. 2 (1993), 105–10.

PYM, ANTHONY, 2005. 'The Translator as Author: Two Quixotes', *Translation and Literature*, 14. 1 (2005), 71–81.

RAMÍREZ, ALEJANDRO, 'Cervantes y Fletcher: El *Persiles* y *The Custom of the Country*', in *Homenaje a Sherman H. Eoff* (Madrid: Castalia, 1970), pp. 203–20.

RANDALL, DALE B. J., *The Golden Tapestry: A Critical Survey of Non-Chilvaric Spanish Fiction in English Translation (1543–1657)* (Durham, NC: Duke University Press, 1963).

RANDALL, DALE B. J. and JACKSON C. BOSWELL, *Cervantes in Seventeenth-Century England: The Tapestry Turned* (Oxford: Oxford University Press, forthcoming 2009).

REED, WALTER, *An Exemplary History of the Novel: The Quixotic versus the Picaresque* (Chicago: Chicago University Press, 1981).

RILEY, E. C., 'Whatever Happened to Heroes?: Don Quixote and Some Major European Novels of the Twentieth Century', in *Cervantes and the Modernists: The Question of Influence*, ed. by Edwin Williamson (London: Tamesis, 1994), pp. 73–84.

RODDEN, J., 'Orwell as Quixote: Analogy, Anecdote, and Repute', *College Literature*, 16. 2 (1989), 129–47.

ROMERO CAMBRA, JAVIER, 'Massinger and Carranza: A Note on Fencing and Point of Honour in Sixteenth- and Seventeenth-Century Drama', *Notes and Queries*, 54 (2007), pp. 392–93.

ROSENBACH, ABRAHAM S. WOLF, '*The Curious-Impertinent* in English Dramatic Literature Before Shelton's Translation of Don Quixote', *Modern Language Notes*, 17 (1902), 357–67.

ROTELLA, PILAR V., 'Smollett's *Sir Launcelot Greaves* as Cervantine Romance: An Honorable Failure', *Letras Hispanas*, 1 (1994), 52–65.

——'Cervantes y Smollett: una relectura de *The Expedition of Humphry Clinker*', in *Actas del IV Congreso Internacional de la Asociación de Cervantistas, Lepanto, 1 / 5 de octubre de 2000*, ed. by Antonio Pablo Bernat Vistarini, 2 vols (Palma: Universidad de las Islas Baleares, 2001), II, 1267–74.

ROUND, NICHOLAS, 'What Made Mabbe So Good?', *Bulletin of Hispanic Studies* (Glasgow), 78. 1 (2001), 145–66.

RUSSELL, P. E., 'English Seventeenth-Century Interpretations of Spanish Literature', *Atalante*, 1 (1953), 65–77.

——'A Stuart Hispanist: James Mabbe', *Bulletin of Hispanic Studies*, 30 (1953), 75–84.

RUTHERFORD, JOHN, 'The Translator as Artisan and as Artist: *Don Quixote* into English', *Insights into Translation*, 1 (1998), 67–80.

SÁNCHEZ IMIZCOZ, RUTH, 'La influencia de *Don Quijote* en *El caballero del pistadero ardiente*', *Cervantes*, 15 (1995), 75–83.

SANTAMARÍA, JOSÉ MIGUEL, 'Captain John Stevens', *Livius*, 1 (1992), 211–19.

SANTISTEBAN, FRANCISCO, 'Las alusiones cervantinas en *Tristram Shandy*', in *Homenaje a Esteban Pujals* (Oviedo: Universidad de Oviedo and AEDEAN, 1981).

SARMIENTO, EDWARD, 'Wordsworth and Don Quixote', *Bulletin of Hispanic Studies*, 38 (1961), 113–19.

SCHEVILL, RUDOLPH, 'On the Influence of Spanish Literature upon English in the Early 17th Century', *Romanische Forschungen*, 20 (1907), 604–34.

SCHMIDT, RACHEL, *Critical Images: The Canonization of Don Quixote Through Illustrated Editions of the Eighteenth Century* (London: McGill–Queen's University Press, 1998).

SCOTT, GARDNER D., 'Some Borrowings in Sterne from Rabelais and Cervantes', *English Language Notes*, 3 (1965), 111–18.

SILES ARTÉS, JOSÉ, 'La influencia de *Don Quijote* en *Hudibras*', *Filología Moderna*, 5 (1965), 185–92.

SINGLETON, MARK, 'Cervantes, John Locke, and Dr Johnson', *Studia Hispanica in Honorem Rafael Lapesa*, ed. by E. Bustos, J. Guillón, and A. Castro (Madrid: Gredos, 1972), 531–47.

SMALL, MIRIAM ROSSITER, 'The Female Quixote and Other Quixotic Imitations of the Eighteenth Century', in Charlotte Ramsey Lennox: An Eighteenth-century Lady of Letters (New Haven, CT: Yale University Press, 1935), pp. 64–117.

STARKIE, WALTER, 'Miguel de Cervantes and the English Novel', Essays by Diverse Hands, 34 (1966), 159–79.

STAVES, SUSAN, 'Don Quixote in Eighteenth-century England', Comparative Literature, 24 (1972), 193–215.

TERRAZAS, MELANIA, 'El tratamiento de la falsa pareja en la obra de Miguel de Cervantes Don Quijote de la Mancha y su huella en la literatura modernista británica', in La literatura en la literatura. Actas del XIV Simposio de la Sociedad Española de Literatura General y Comparada, ed. by M. Leon (Alcalí: Centro de Estudios Cervantinos, 2004).

TODD, F. M., 'Webster and Cervantes', Modern Language Review, 51 (1956), 321–23.

UNDERHILL, JOHN, Spanish Literature in the England of the Tudors (New York: Macmillan, 1899).

UNGERER, GUSTAV, 'The Earl of Southampton's Donation to the Bodleian in 1605 and its Spanish Books', Bodleian Library Record, 16 (1997), 17–41.

——'Recovering Unrecorded Quixote Allusions in Ephemeral Publications of the Late 1650s', Bodleian Library Record, 17 (2000), 65–69.

VÁZQUEZ DE PRADA, MARÍA TERESA, 'El Quijote y Oliver Twist', ES, 21 (1998), 129–43.

VEGA RODRÍGUEZ, PILAR, 'El regreso de Don Quijote de Chesterton. Tradición y Utopía', Anales Cervantinos, 37 (2005), 239–51.

WANN, LOUISE, 'The Oriental in Elizabethan Drama', Modern Philology, 12 (1914/15), 423–47.

WEHRS, DONALD R., 'Sterne, Cervantes, Montaigne: Fideistic Skepticism and the Rhetoric of Desire', in Tristram Shandy, ed. by Melvyn New (London: Macmillan, 1992), pp. 133–54.

WEINFIELD, HENRY, '"Knowledge Not Purchase by the Loss of Power": Wordsworth's Meditation on Books and Death in Book 5 of The Prelude', Texas Studies in Literature and Languages, 42. 3 (2001), 334–64.

WELLER, CELIA E. and CLARK A. COLAHAN, 'Cervantine Imagery and Sex-Role Reversal in Fletcher and Massinger's The Custom of the Country', Cervantes, 5. 1 (1985), 27–43.

WELSH, ALEXANDER, 'Waverley, Pickwick and Don Quixote', Nineteenth-Century Fiction, 22 (1967), 19–30.

——Reflections on the Hero as Quixote (Princeton, NJ: Princeton University Press, 1981).

——'The Influence of Cervantes', in The Cambridge Companion to Cervantes, ed. by Anthony J. Cascardi (Cambridge: Cambridge University Press, 2002), pp. 80–99.

WILSON, DIANA DE ARMAS, 'Contesting the Custom of the Country: Cervantes and Fletcher', in From Dante to García Márquez, ed. by Gene H. Bell-Villada, Antonio Giménez and George Pistorius (Williamstown, MA; Williams College, 1987), pp. 60–75.

——'Of Piracy and Plackets: Cervantes' La señora Cornelia and Fletcher's The Chances', in Cervantes for the 21st Century/Cervantes para el siglo XXI: Studies in Honor of Edward Dudley, ed. by. Francisco La Rubia Prado (Newark, DE: Juan de la Cuesta, 2000), pp. 49–60.

——'The Novel as "Moletta": Cervantes and Defoe', in Cervantes, the Novel and the New World (Oxford: Oxford University Press, 2000), pp. 60–77.

WILSON, EDWARD M., 'Cervantes and English Literature of the Seventeenth Century', Bulletin Hispanique, 50 (1948), 45–52.

WOOD, SARAH F., 'An "Inconsistent Discourse": Don Quixote in British Letters', in Quixotic Fictions of the USA, 1792–1815 (Oxford: Oxford University Press, 2005), pp. 1–36.

YAMADA, YUMIKO, Ben Jonson and Cervantes: Tilting against Chivalric Romance (Tokyo: Maruzen, 2000).

ZIOLKOWSKI, E., The Sanctification of Don Quixote: From Hidalgo to Priest (University Park: Pennsylvania State University Press, 1991).

INDEX

Philosophical Quixote; or, Memories of David Wilkins 12, 157

Pícara Justina 2

picaresque 2-3, 7, 11, 20, 23, 25 n. 5, 25 n. 8, 63, 87, 105, 117, 134, 137, 151, 153, 157, 159, 161 n. 1, 184, 190, 199, 212, 225, 228, 229

Pilon, Frederick:
Barataria, or Sancho Turn'd Governor 10

Pope, Alexander 38, 67, 88, 97, 101, 125

Pope, Walter 58, 86-87

Priestly, J. B. 22

Proust, Marcel 112

Purbeck, Jane:
William Thornborough, the Benevolent Quixote 12, 157

Purcell, Henry 34

Putnam, Samuel Whitehall 58, 59, 64, 92-93

Quevedo, Francisco de:
Buscón 2, 225

Quixotic principle 40

Rabelais 68, 69, 96, 112

Radcliffe, Ann 15, 105, 173

Raffel, Burton 60 n. 1

Raleigh, Walter 23

Randolph, Thomas:
The Conceited Peddler Hey for Honesty 3

Rapin, René 55

Reeve, Clara:
The Progress of Romance 11

Richardson, Samuel 2, 14, 19, 24, 99-101, 104, 125-27, 129, 130, 131, 145, 149, 156

Richter, Jean Paul 44

Ríos, Vicente de los 185

Rojas, Fernando de:
Celestina 4, 5, 19, 23, 58, 59, 134, 136, 230

Romantic irony 45

Roscoe, Thomas 58, 90, 191, 192

Rosset, François 5, 66

Rowe, Nicholas:
The Fair Penitent 10

Rowley, Thomas:
The Spanish Gipsy 5, 212, 218, 253-54

Rowson, Susanna 18-19

Rushdie, Salman:
The Moor's Last Sigh 111

Ruskin, John 18, 21, 32

Saint-Martin, Filleau de 55, 64

San Pedro, Diego de:
Cárcel de Amor 4

satire 7, 9, 11, 12, 13, 15, 17, 19, 32, 35, 36, 39, 40, 49, 56, 65, 71, 76, 87, 100, 114, 124, 125, 131, 154-60, 162, 170, 172, 192, 194, 213

Scarron, Paul 64

Schelegel, August Wilhelm 44, 45

Schelegel, Friedrich 44

Schelling, Friedrich 23, 44

Scott, Walter 16, 19, 48, 99, 105-06, 114 n. 11, 124

Scudéry, Madelaine de 12

Shakespeare, William 2, 4, 5-6, 11, 23, 36, 37, 41, 43, 47, 97, 157, 187, 208, 212, 213, 215, 223, 234,-40, 246, 250, 252, 254

Shelley, Mary:
Frankenstein 20, 106, 114 n. 17, 182-85
Life of Cervantes 20, 185-88
Lodore 20, 106, 184

Shelton, John 4, 5, 9, 54-55, 57, 61-65, 66, 67, 68, 69, 72, 76, 97, 213, 214, 254, 255

Sherwood, Mary Martha 89-90

Shirley, James:
Honoria and Mammon 4

Sismondi, J. C. L. Simonde de 43-44, 46, 242

Smirke, Mary 89

Smith, Charlotte:
The Old Manor House 12
The Young Philosopher 12

Smith, Robinson 60 n. 2

Smollet, Tobias:
Humphry Clinker 14, 151, 160-61
'The Life of Cervantes' 14, 17, 42
Peregrine Pickle 155-56
Roderick Random 14, 151, 153-55
Sir Launcelot Greaves 3, 12, 100, 101, 151, 156-60
Translation of *Don Quixote* 14, 18, 56, 57, 69-72, 152-53

Sotherne, Thomas:
The Disappointment 6

Southampton, Earl of 4, 6, 212

Spark, Muriel 22, 112

Spiritual Quixote; or, the Entertaining History of Don Ignatius Loyola, founder of the Order of Jesuits 12

Stanley, Louisa Dorothea 59, 242-43

Steele, Richard 11, 39

Steinarr, Stein 23, 31 n. 116

Steiner, George 72

Stephey, William:
The Spanish Schoole-Master 4

Stevens, John 55, 66-67, 68, 69, 70, 72

Stuart, Mrs. Matthew 19

Swift, Jonathan 9, 40, 45, 63, 68, 96-97, 101, 125

Tacio, Aquiles 120

Tarrataria, or Don Quixote the Second 12, 157

Teague O'Dively; or, the Irish Rogue 2

Temple, William 38, 96

Tenney, Tabitha Gilman:
Female Quixotism 13, 105, 166

Thackeray, William Makepeace:
The Newcomers 20
Vanity Fair 20

The Amicable Quixote; or, The Enthusiasm of Friendship 12, 13, 157

Theobald, Lewis 97